Love Hina

By

Ken Akamatsu

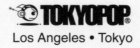

Los Angeles • Tokyo

Translator – Nan Rymer
English Adaptation – Adam Arnold
Retouch and Lettering – Max Porter
Graphic Designer – Anna Kernbaum

Editor – Luis Reyes
Production Manager – Joaquin Reyes
Art Director – Matthew Alford
Brand Manager – Kenneth Lee
VP Production – Ron Klamert
Publisher – Stuart Levy

Email: editor@TOKYOPOP.com
Come visit us online at www.TOKYOPOP.com

A 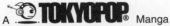 Manga

TOKYOPOP® is an imprint of Mixx Entertainment, Inc.
5900 Wilshire Blvd. Ste 2000, Los Angeles, CA 90036

ISBN: 1-59182-014-6

First TOKYOPOP® printing: June 2002

10 9 8 7 6 5 4 3 2

Printed in the USA.

Love Hina

The Story Thus Far ...

Fifteen years ago, Keitaro Urashima made a promise with a girl (whose name he can't quite remember) that they would both go to Tokyo University together. Now at the age of twenty, he's finding it more and more difficult to keep that promise, much less actually find that girl again.

He has already failed the entrance exam for Tokyo University twice, and has decided to have another go at it, thus spending another year stigmatized as a ronin. He's also inherited from his globetrotting grandmother the Hinata House, a quiet residential dorm where he can work as the landlord and prepare for his upcoming exams in peace... if it isn't for that fact that Hinata House is actually a girls' dormitory with a clientele none too pleased that their new, live-in landlord is a man — or as close to a man as poor Keitaro can be. The lanky loser incessantly (and accidentally) crashes their sessions in the hot springs, walks in on them changing... and pokes his nose pretty much everywhere it can get broken, if not by the hot-headed Naru, then by one of the other Hinata inmates — Kitsune, a mid-twenties alcoholic with a diesel libido; Motoko, a swordswoman who struggles with feminine issues; Shinobu, a pre-teen princess with a troubling crush on Keitaro; and Su, a foreign girl with a big appetite.

Studying hasn't been going well, and so Keitaro has solicited the help of Naru, who also just happens to be the number one student in their prep school. As they work closely together, Keitaro begins to suspect, and then becomes absolutely convinced, that Naru is that girl to whom he made that promise so many moons ago.

CONTENTS

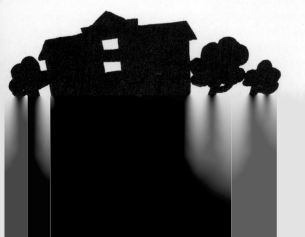

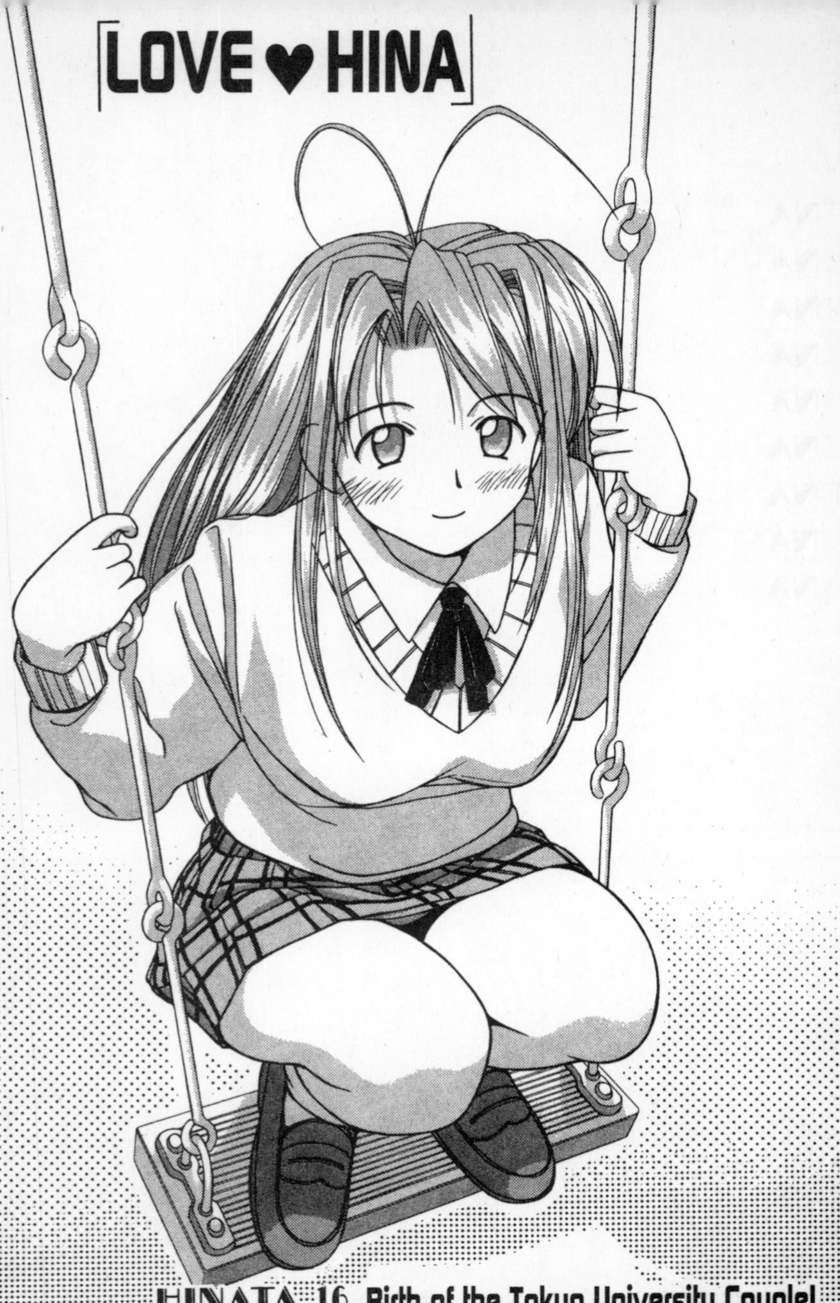
LOVE ♥ HINA

HINATA. 16 Birth of the Tokyo University Couple!

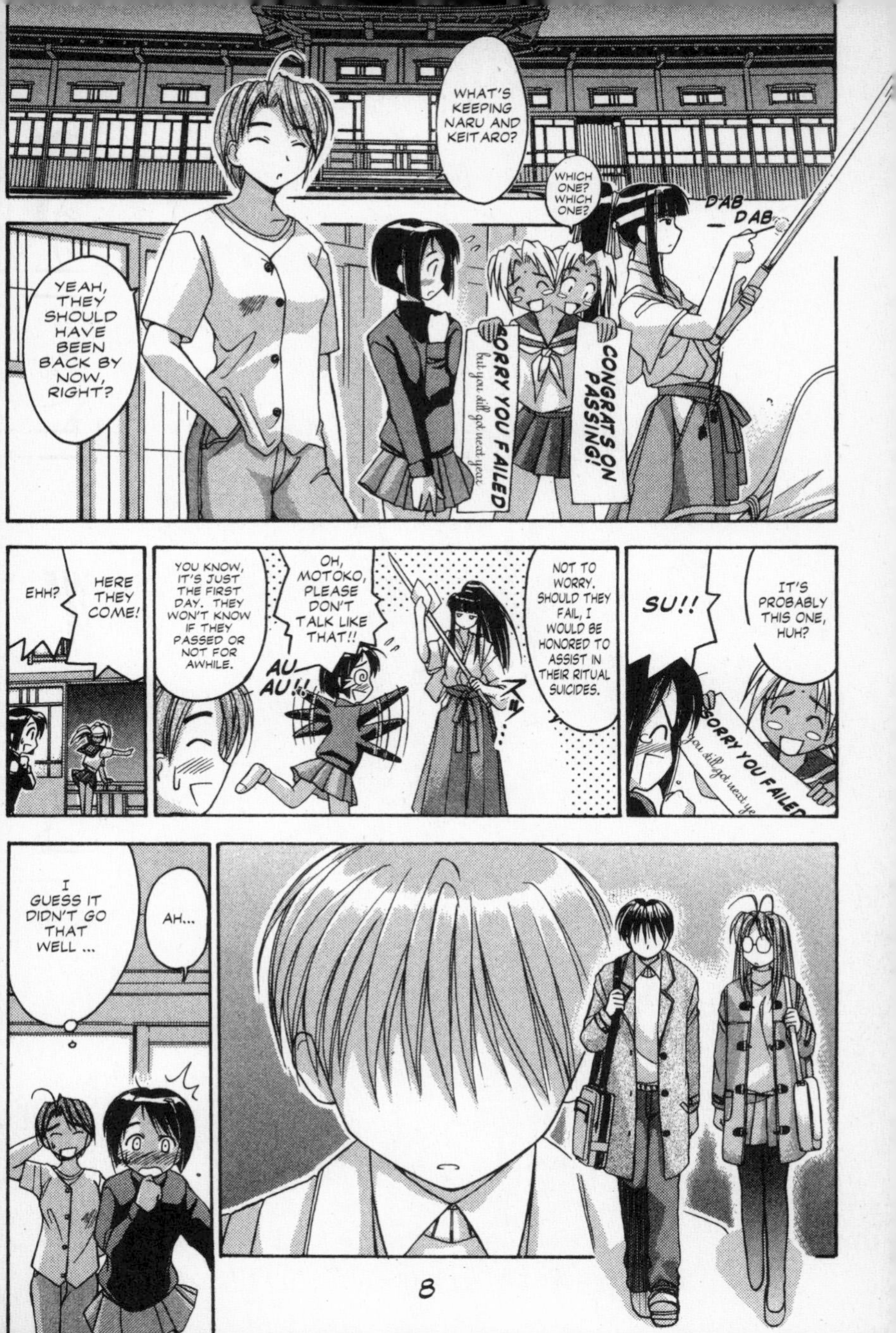
WHAT'S KEEPING NARU AND KEITARO?
WHICH ONE? WHICH ONE?
DAB DAB
CONGRATS ON PASSING!
SORRY YOU FAILED but you still got next year.
YEAH, THEY SHOULD HAVE BEEN BACK BY NOW, RIGHT?
IT'S PROBABLY THIS ONE, HUH?
SU!!
SORRY YOU FAILED you still got next ye
NOT TO WORRY. SHOULD THEY FAIL, I WOULD BE HONORED TO ASSIST IN THEIR RITUAL SUICIDES.
OH, MOTOKO, PLEASE DON'T TALK LIKE THAT!!
AU AU!!
YOU KNOW, IT'S JUST THE FIRST DAY. THEY WON'T KNOW IF THEY PASSED OR NOT FOR AWHILE.
HERE THEY COME!
EHH?
AH...
I GUESS IT DIDN'T GO THAT WELL ...

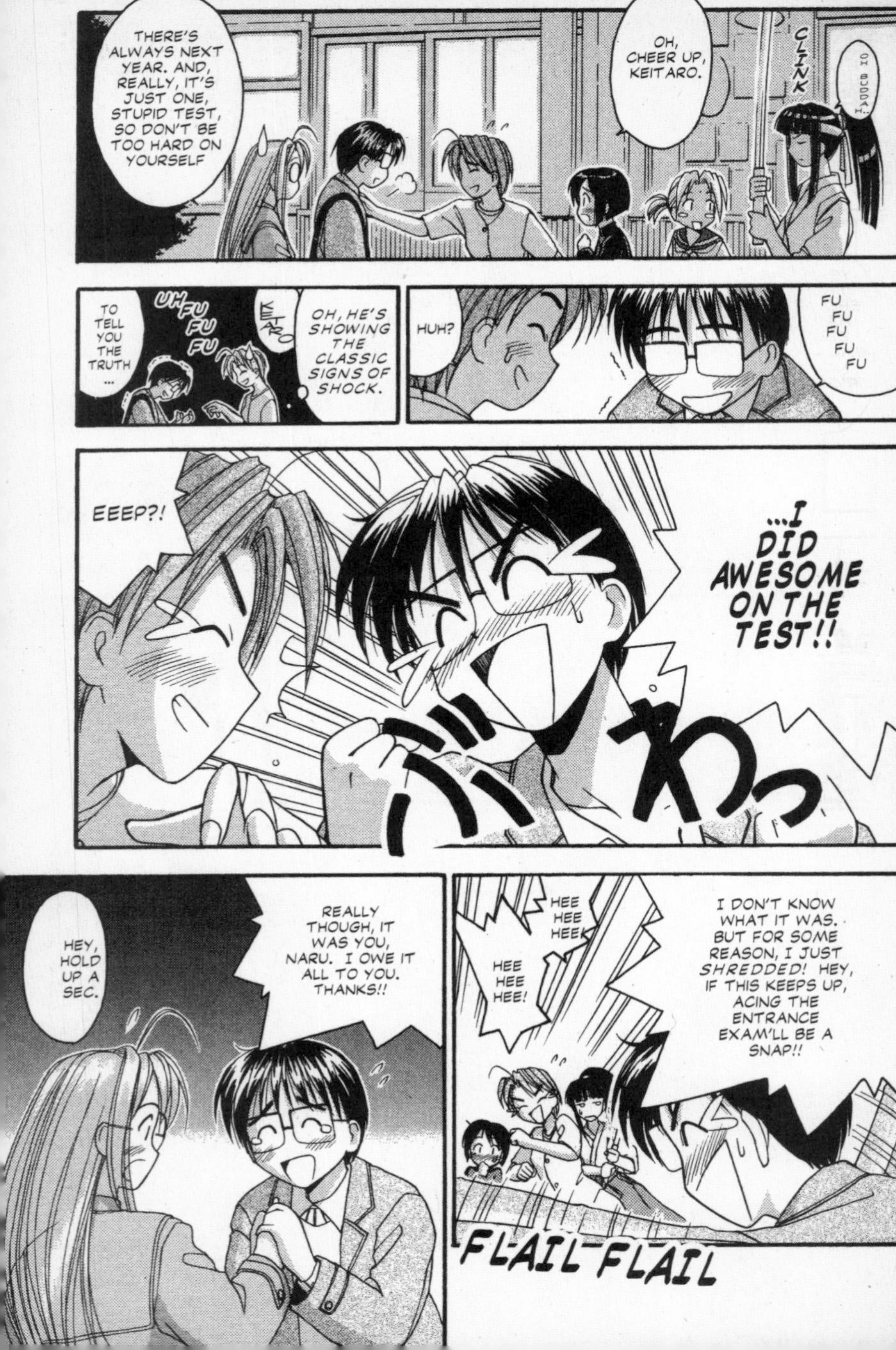
OH, CHEER UP, KEITARO.
THERE'S ALWAYS NEXT YEAR. AND, REALLY, IT'S JUST ONE, STUPID TEST, SO DON'T BE TOO HARD ON YOURSELF
CLINK
OH BUDDAH...
FU FU FU FU FU
HUH?
OH, HE'S SHOWING THE CLASSIC SIGNS OF SHOCK.
KEITARO
UH FU FU FU
TO TELL YOU THE TRUTH ...
...I DID AWESOME ON THE TEST!!
EEEP?!
ぶわっ
I DON'T KNOW WHAT IT WAS. BUT FOR SOME REASON, I JUST SHREDDED! HEY, IF THIS KEEPS UP, ACING THE ENTRANCE EXAM'LL BE A SNAP!!
HEE HEE HEE!
HEE HEE HEE!
FLAIL FLAIL
REALLY THOUGH, IT WAS YOU, NARU. I OWE IT ALL TO YOU. THANKS!!
HEY, HOLD UP A SEC.

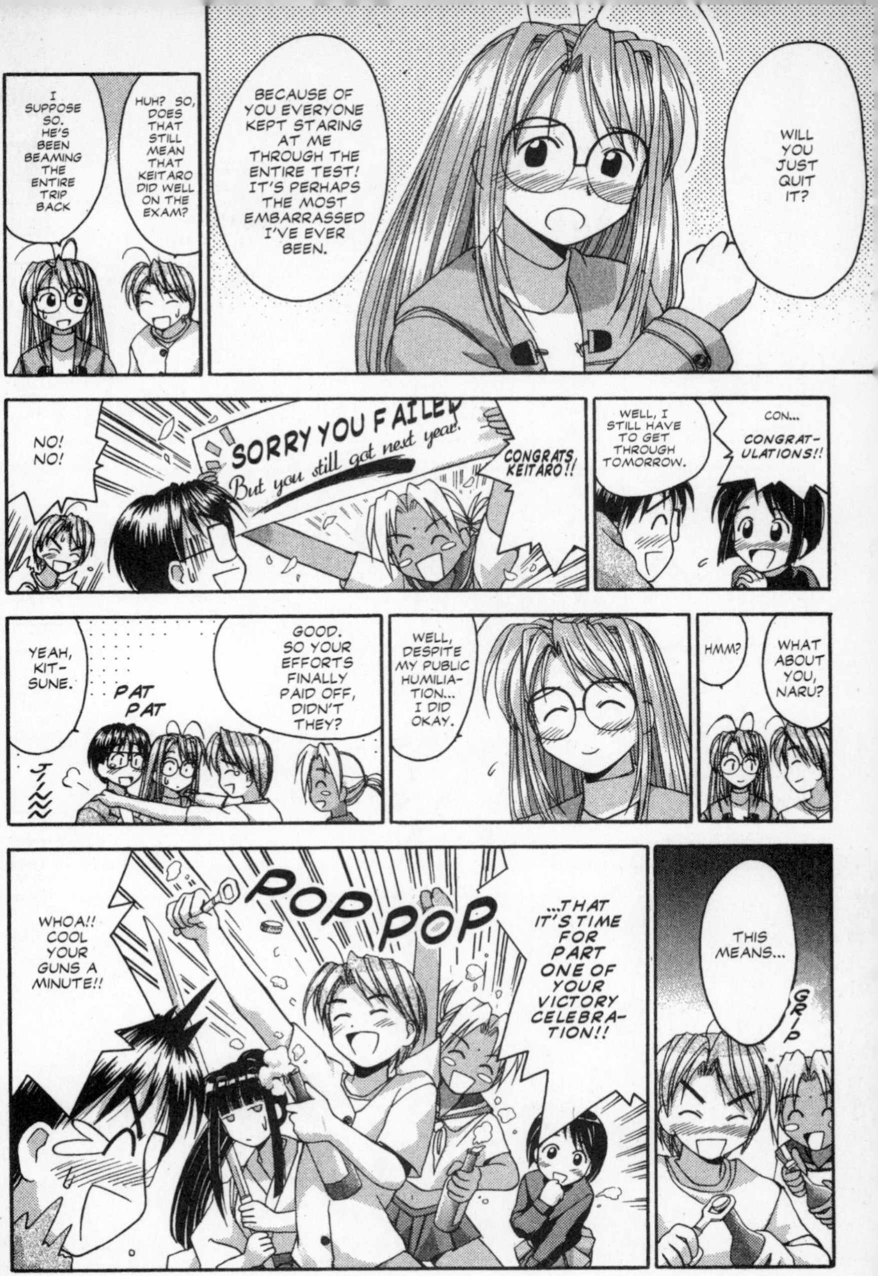
BECAUSE OF YOU EVERYONE KEPT STARING AT ME THROUGH THE ENTIRE TEST! IT'S PERHAPS THE MOST EMBARRASSED I'VE EVER BEEN.
WILL YOU JUST QUIT IT?
HUH? SO, DOES THAT STILL MEAN THAT KEITARO DID WELL ON THE EXAM?
I SUPPOSE SO. HE'S BEEN BEAMING THE ENTIRE TRIP BACK
CON... CONGRAT-ULATIONS!!
WELL, I STILL HAVE TO GET THROUGH TOMORROW.
CONGRATS KEITARO!!
SORRY YOU FAILED
But you still got next year.
NO! NO!
WHAT ABOUT YOU, NARU?
HMM?
WELL, DESPITE MY PUBLIC HUMILIA-TION... I DID OKAY.
GOOD. SO YOUR EFFORTS FINALLY PAID OFF, DIDN'T THEY?
YEAH, KIT-SUNE.
PAT PAT
THIS MEANS...
GRIP
...THAT IT'S TIME FOR PART ONE OF YOUR VICTORY CELEBRA-TION!!
POP POP
WHOA!! COOL YOUR GUNS A MINUTE!!

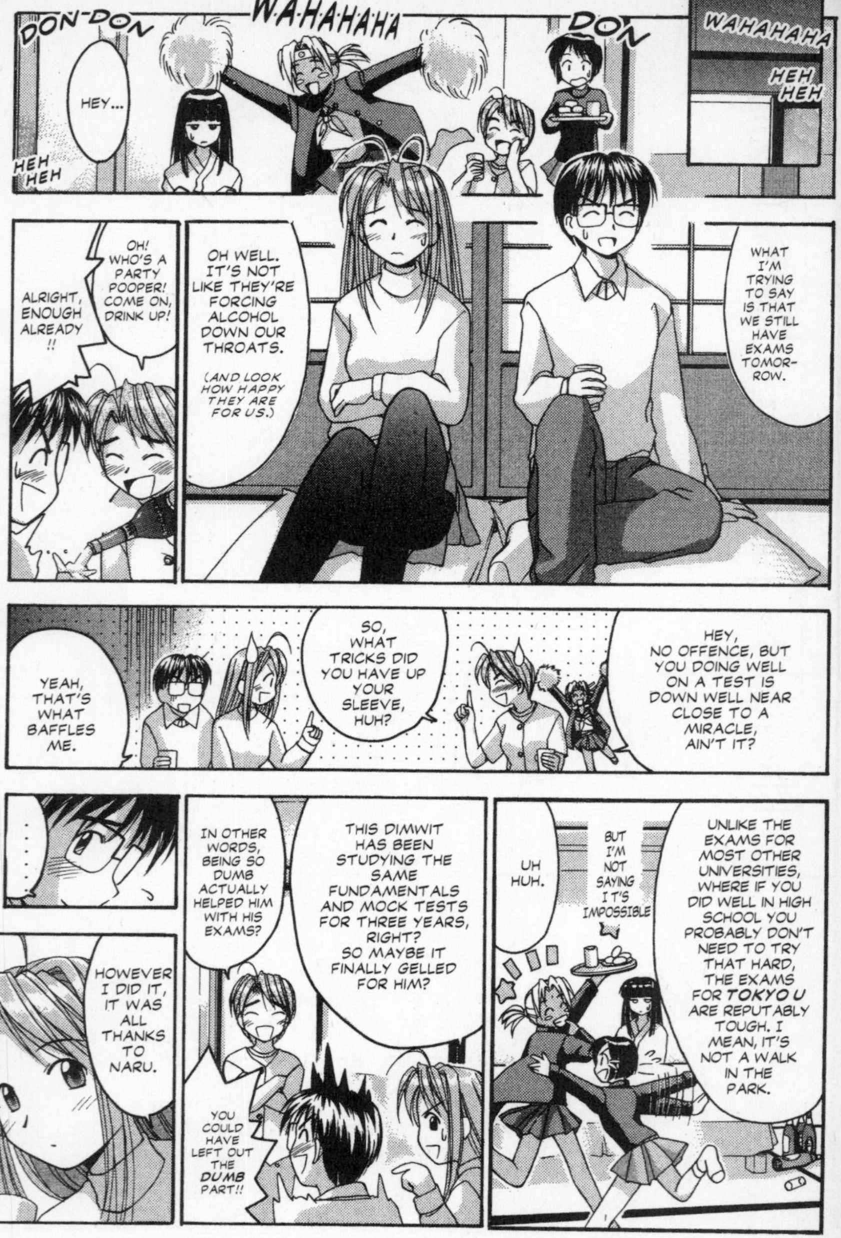
WAHAHAHA
HEH HEH
DON
W·A·H·A·H·A·H·A
HEY...
DON-DON
HEH HEH
WHAT I'M TRYING TO SAY IS THAT WE STILL HAVE EXAMS TOMORROW.
OH WELL. IT'S NOT LIKE THEY'RE FORCING ALCOHOL DOWN OUR THROATS.
(AND LOOK HOW HAPPY THEY ARE FOR US.)
OH! WHO'S A PARTY POOPER! COME ON, DRINK UP!
ALRIGHT, ENOUGH ALREADY!!
HEY, NO OFFENCE, BUT YOU DOING WELL ON A TEST IS DOWN WELL NEAR CLOSE TO A MIRACLE, AIN'T IT?
SO, WHAT TRICKS DID YOU HAVE UP YOUR SLEEVE, HUH?
YEAH, THAT'S WHAT BAFFLES ME.
UNLIKE THE EXAMS FOR MOST OTHER UNIVERSITIES, WHERE IF YOU DID WELL IN HIGH SCHOOL YOU PROBABLY DON'T NEED TO TRY THAT HARD, THE EXAMS FOR TOKYO U ARE REPUTABLY TOUGH. I MEAN, IT'S NOT A WALK IN THE PARK.
BUT I'M NOT SAYING IT'S IMPOSSIBLE
UH HUH.
THIS DIMWIT HAS BEEN STUDYING THE SAME FUNDAMENTALS AND MOCK TESTS FOR THREE YEARS, RIGHT? SO MAYBE IT FINALLY GELLED FOR HIM?
IN OTHER WORDS, BEING SO DUMB ACTUALLY HELPED HIM WITH HIS EXAMS?
YOU COULD HAVE LEFT OUT THE DUMB PART!!
......
HOWEVER I DID IT, IT WAS ALL THANKS TO NARU.
EH?

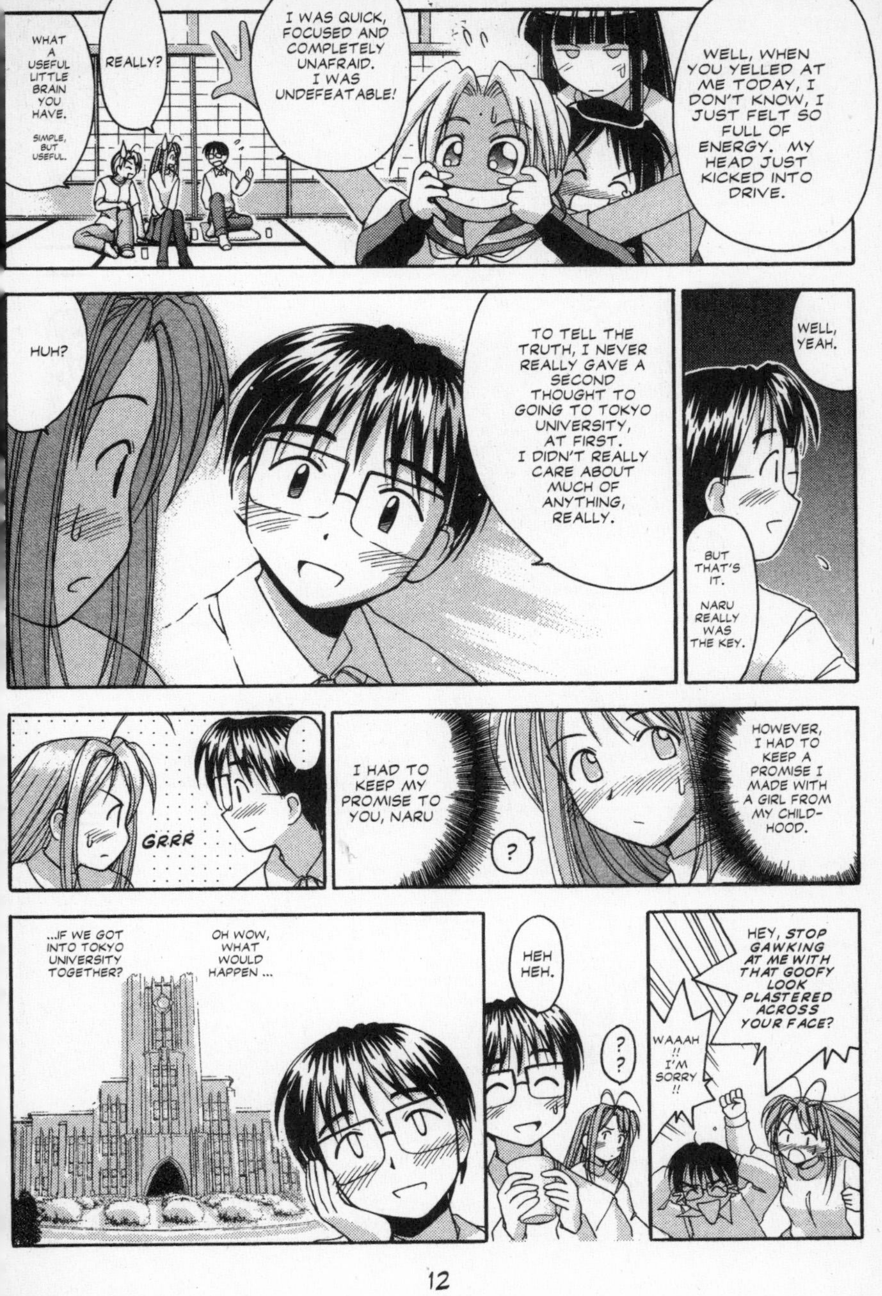
WELL, WHEN YOU YELLED AT ME TODAY, I DON'T KNOW, I JUST FELT SO FULL OF ENERGY. MY HEAD JUST KICKED INTO DRIVE.
I WAS QUICK, FOCUSED AND COMPLETELY UNAFRAID. I WAS UNDEFEATABLE!
REALLY?
WHAT A USEFUL LITTLE BRAIN YOU HAVE.
SIMPLE, BUT USEFUL.
WELL, YEAH.
BUT THAT'S IT.
NARU REALLY WAS THE KEY.
TO TELL THE TRUTH, I NEVER REALLY GAVE A SECOND THOUGHT TO GOING TO TOKYO UNIVERSITY, AT FIRST. I DIDN'T REALLY CARE ABOUT MUCH OF ANYTHING, REALLY.
HUH?
HOWEVER, I HAD TO KEEP A PROMISE I MADE WITH A GIRL FROM MY CHILD-HOOD.
I HAD TO KEEP MY PROMISE TO YOU, NARU
?
...
GRRR
HEY, STOP GAWKING AT ME WITH THAT GOOFY LOOK PLASTERED ACROSS YOUR FACE?
WAAAH!! I'M SORRY!!
HEH HEH.
??
OH WOW, WHAT WOULD HAPPEN ...
...IF WE GOT INTO TOKYO UNIVERSITY TOGETHER?

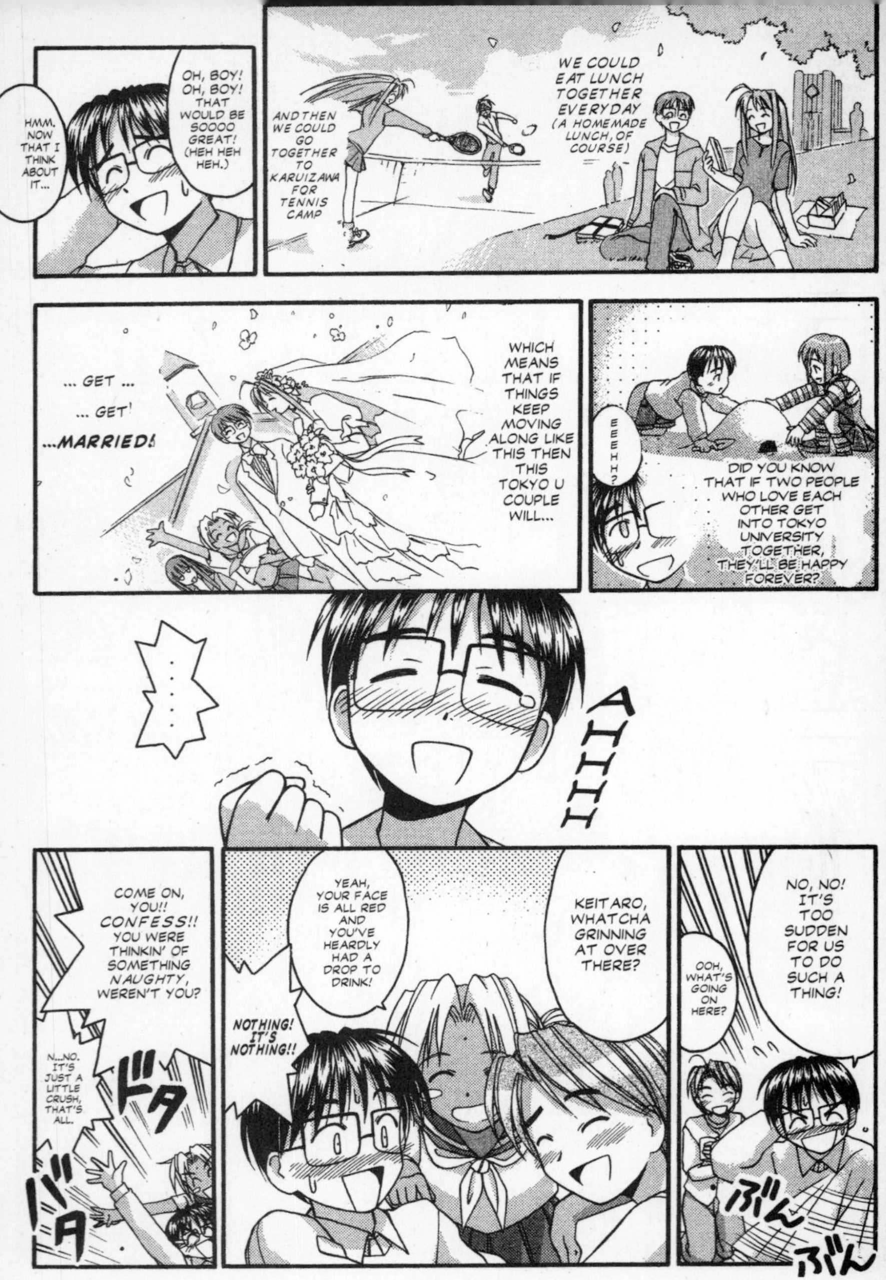
WE COULD EAT LUNCH TOGETHER EVERYDAY (A HOMEMADE LUNCH, OF COURSE)
AND THEN WE COULD GO TOGETHER TO KARUIZAWA FOR TENNIS CAMP
OH, BOY! OH, BOY! THAT WOULD BE SOOOO GREAT! (HEH HEH HEH.)
HMM. NOW THAT I THINK ABOUT IT...
DID YOU KNOW THAT IF TWO PEOPLE WHO LOVE EACH OTHER GET INTO TOKYO UNIVERSITY TOGETHER, THEY'LL BE HAPPY FOREVER?
EEEHH?
WHICH MEANS THAT IF THINGS KEEP MOVING ALONG LIKE THIS THEN THIS TOKYO U COUPLE WILL...
... GET ...
... GET
...MARRIED!
AHHHHH
......
NO, NO! IT'S TOO SUDDEN FOR US TO DO SUCH A THING!
OOH, WHAT'S GOING ON HERE?
ぶん
ぶん
KEITARO, WHATCHA GRINNING AT OVER THERE?
YEAH, YOUR FACE IS ALL RED AND YOU'VE HEARDLY HAD A DROP TO DRINK!
NOTHING! IT'S NOTHING!!
COME ON, YOU!! CONFESS!! YOU WERE THINKIN' OF SOMETHING NAUGHTY, WEREN'T YOU?
N...NO. IT'S JUST A LITTLE CRUSH, THAT'S ALL.
ドタ
バタ

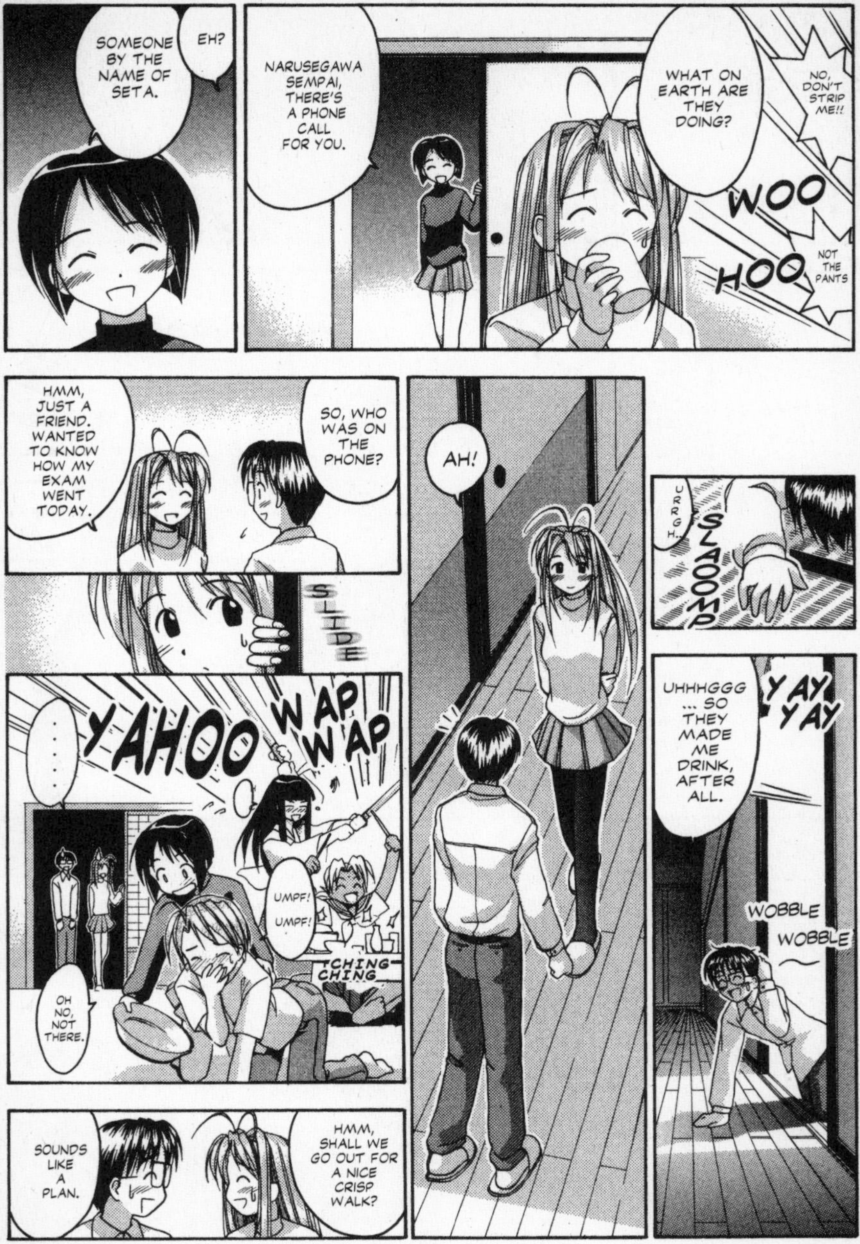
NO, DON'T STRIP ME!!
WHAT ON EARTH ARE THEY DOING?
WOO
HOO
NOT THE PANTS
NARUSEGAWA SEMPAI, THERE'S A PHONE CALL FOR YOU.
EH?
SOMEONE BY THE NAME OF SETA.
URRGH...
SLAOOMP
YAY YAY
UHHHGGG ... SO THEY MADE ME DRINK, AFTER ALL.
WOBBLE WOBBLE
AH!
SO, WHO WAS ON THE PHONE?
HMM, JUST A FRIEND. WANTED TO KNOW HOW MY EXAM WENT TODAY.
SLIDE
WAP WAP
YAHOO
. . . . .
UMPF!
UMPF!
CHING CHING
OH NO, NOT THERE.
HMM, SHALL WE GO OUT FOR A NICE CRISP WALK?
SOUNDS LIKE A PLAN.

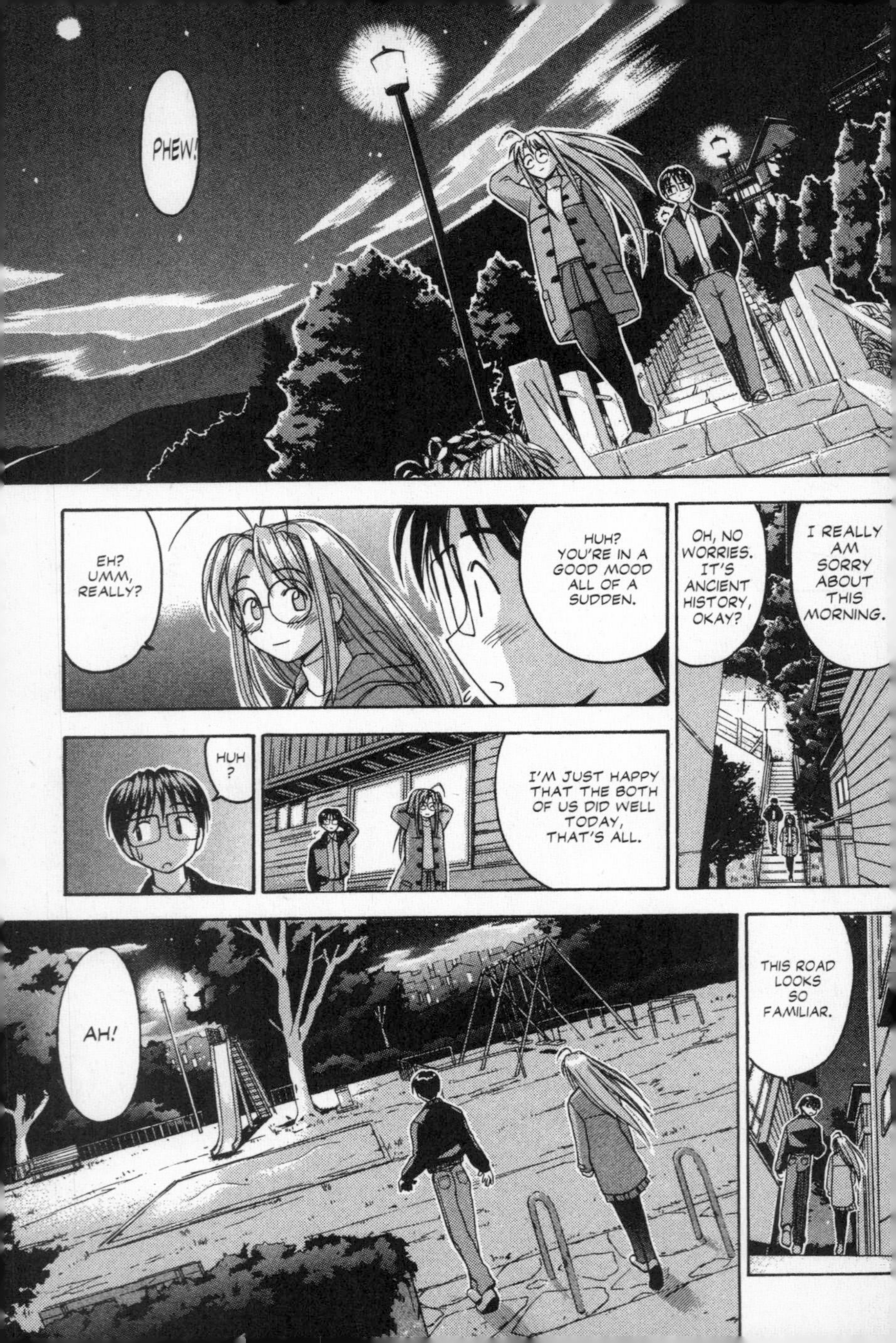
PHEW!
I REALLY AM SORRY ABOUT THIS MORNING.
OH, NO WORRIES. IT'S ANCIENT HISTORY, OKAY?
HUH? YOU'RE IN A GOOD MOOD ALL OF A SUDDEN.
EH? UMM, REALLY?
I'M JUST HAPPY THAT THE BOTH OF US DID WELL TODAY, THAT'S ALL.
HUH ?
THIS ROAD LOOKS SO FAMILIAR.
AH!

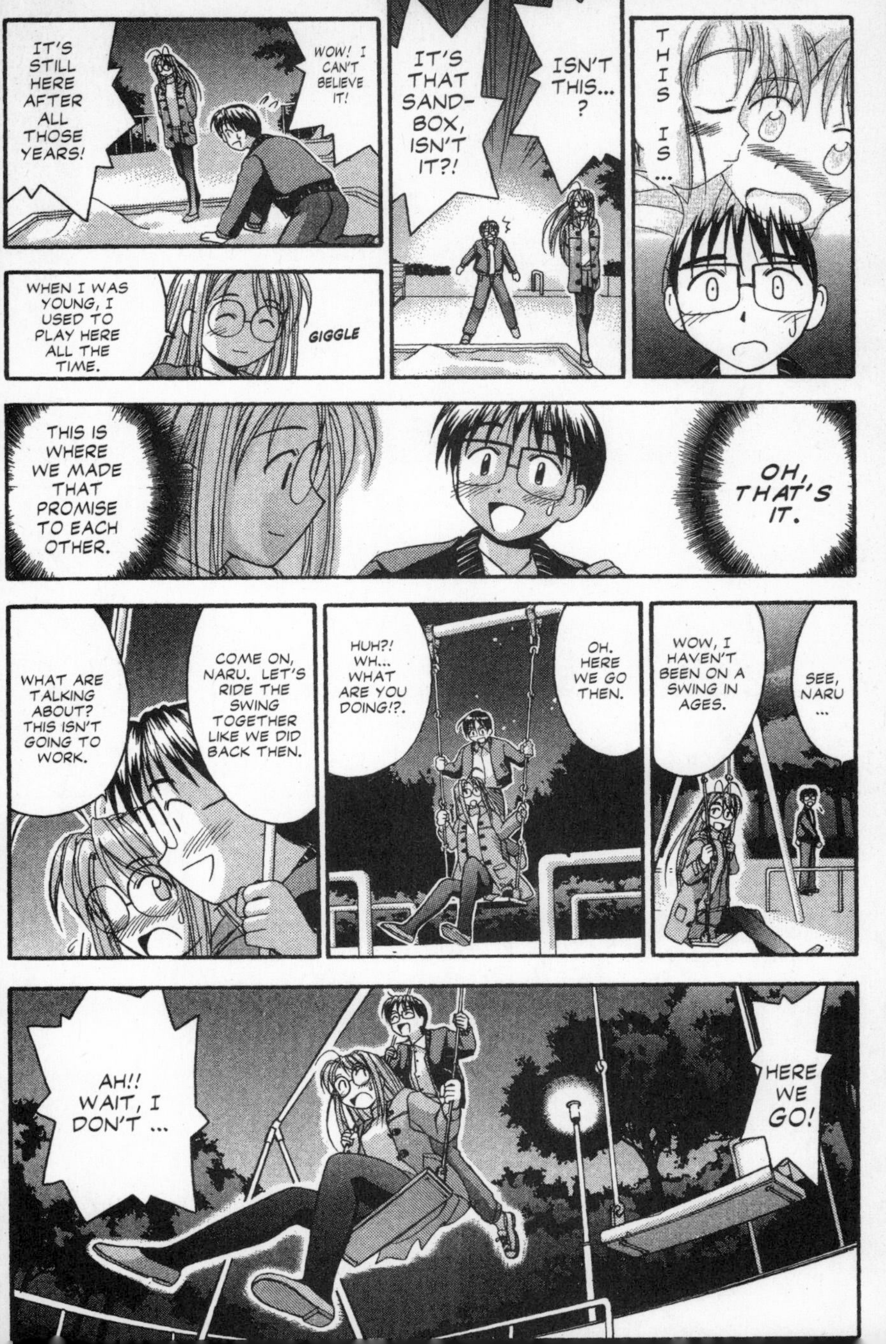
THIS IS ...
ISN'T THIS... ?
IT'S THAT SANDBOX, ISN'T IT?!
WOW! I CAN'T BELIEVE IT!
IT'S STILL HERE AFTER ALL THOSE YEARS!
GIGGLE
WHEN I WAS YOUNG, I USED TO PLAY HERE ALL THE TIME.
OH, THAT'S IT.
THIS IS WHERE WE MADE THAT PROMISE TO EACH OTHER.
SEE, NARU ...
WOW, I HAVEN'T BEEN ON A SWING IN AGES.
OH. HERE WE GO THEN.
HUH?! WH... WHAT ARE YOU DOING!?.
COME ON, NARU. LET'S RIDE THE SWING TOGETHER LIKE WE DID BACK THEN.
WHAT ARE TALKING ABOUT? THIS ISN'T GOING TO WORK.
HERE WE GO!
AH!! WAIT, I DON'T ...

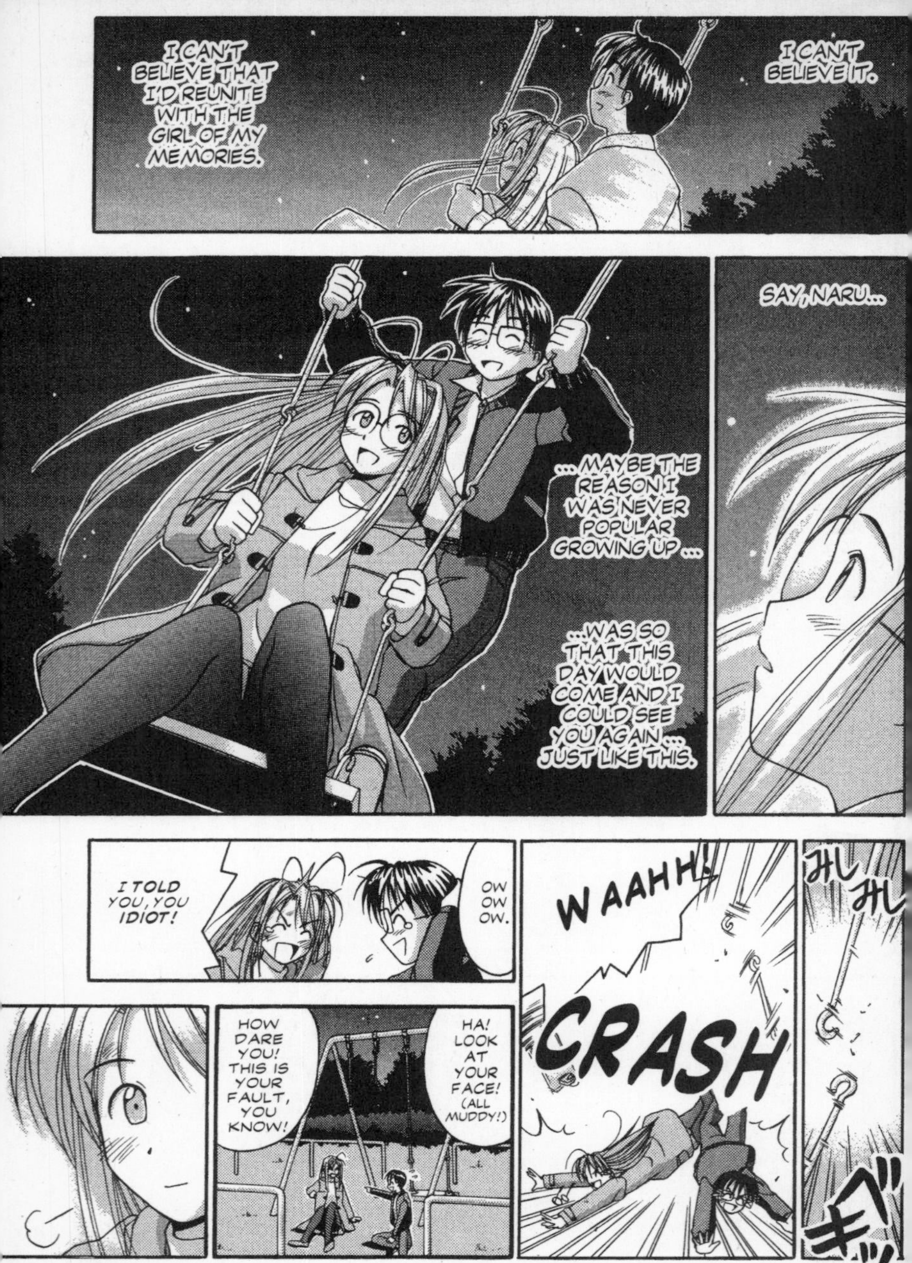
I CAN'T BELIEVE IT.
I CAN'T BELIEVE THAT I'D REUNITE WITH THE GIRL OF MY MEMORIES.
SAY, NARU...
...MAYBE THE REASON I WAS NEVER POPULAR GROWING UP...
...WAS SO THAT THIS DAY WOULD COME AND I COULD SEE YOU AGAIN... JUST LIKE THIS.
みしみし
ベキッ
WAAHH!
CRASH
OW OW OW.
I TOLD YOU, YOU IDIOT!
HA! LOOK AT YOUR FACE! (ALL MUDDY!)
HOW DARE YOU! THIS IS YOUR FAULT, YOU KNOW!

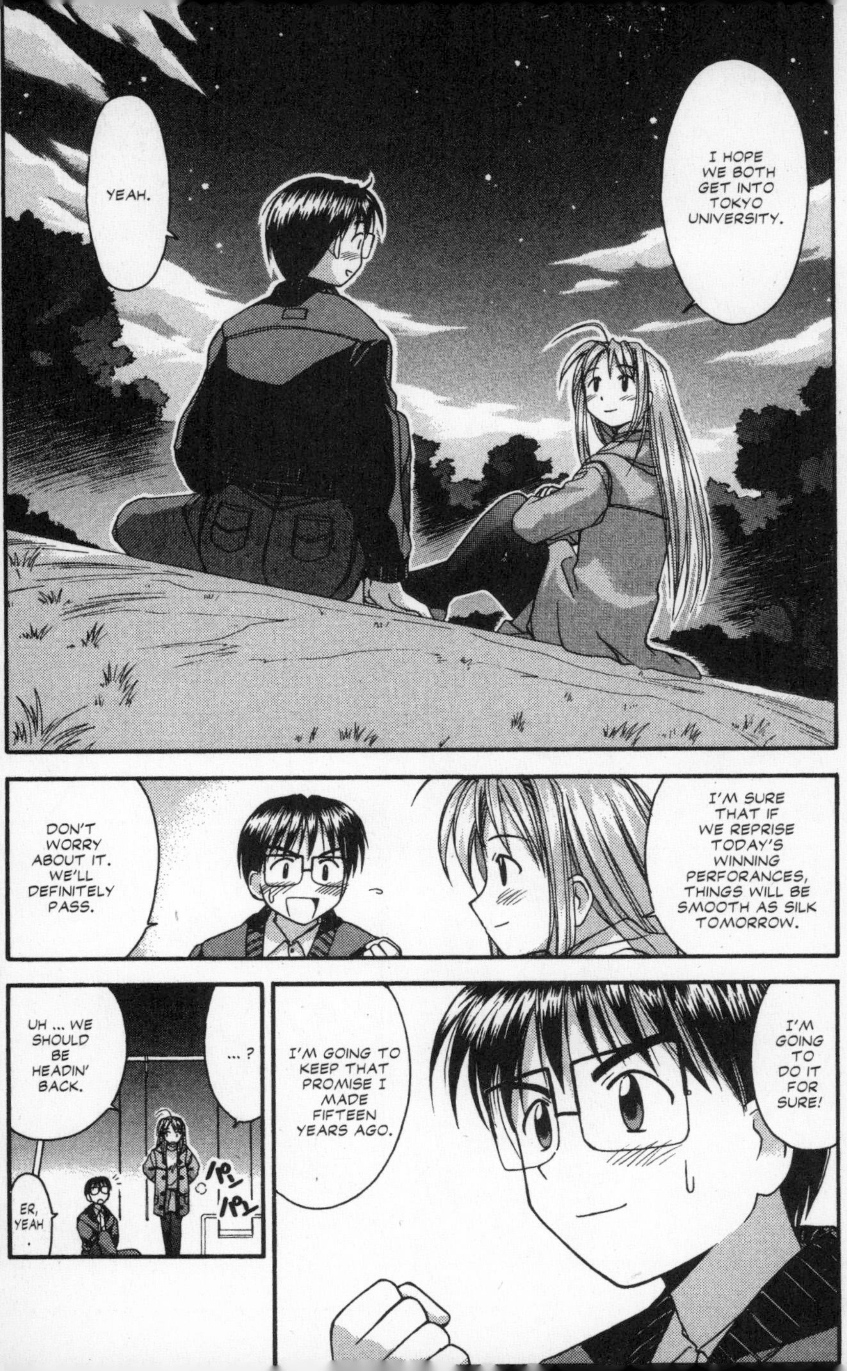
I HOPE WE BOTH GET INTO TOKYO UNIVERSITY.
YEAH.
I'M SURE THAT IF WE REPRISE TODAY'S WINNING PERFORANCES, THINGS WILL BE SMOOTH AS SILK TOMORROW.
DON'T WORRY ABOUT IT. WE'LL DEFINITELY PASS.
I'M GOING TO DO IT FOR SURE!
I'M GOING TO KEEP THAT PROMISE I MADE FIFTEEN YEARS AGO.
... ?
UH ... WE SHOULD BE HEADIN' BACK.
パン パン
ER, YEAH.

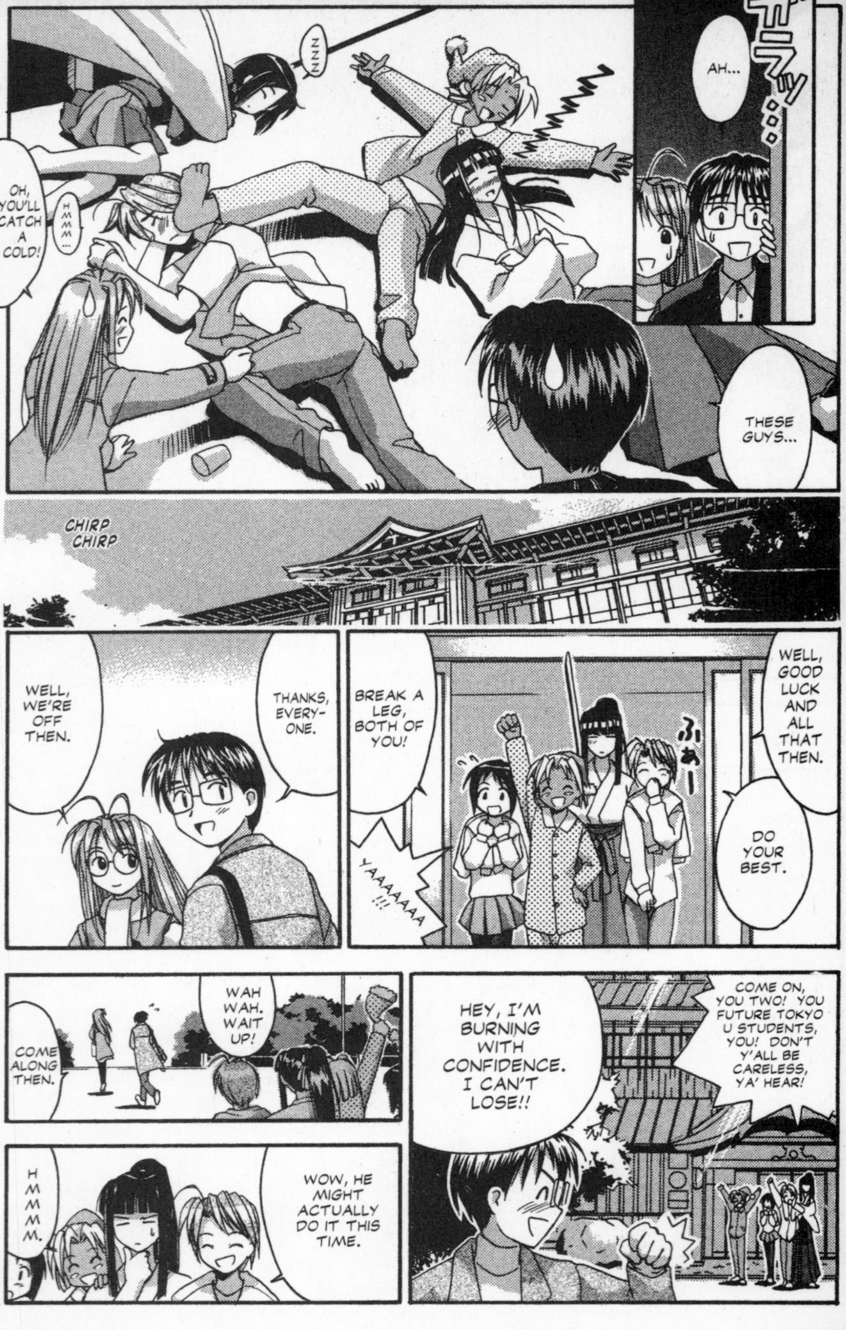
ガラッ
AH...
ZZZ
HMMM...
OH, YOU'LL CATCH A COLD!
THESE GUYS...
CHIRP CHIRP
WELL, GOOD LUCK AND ALL THAT THEN.
ふぁー
DO YOUR BEST.
BREAK A LEG, BOTH OF YOU!
YAAAAAAA!!!
THANKS, EVERY-ONE.
WELL, WE'RE OFF THEN.
COME ON, YOU TWO! YOU FUTURE TOKYO U STUDENTS, YOU! DON'T Y'ALL BE CARELESS, YA' HEAR!
HEY, I'M BURNING WITH CONFIDENCE. I CAN'T LOSE!!
WAH WAH. WAIT UP!
COME ALONG THEN.
WOW, HE MIGHT ACTUALLY DO IT THIS TIME.
HMMMM.

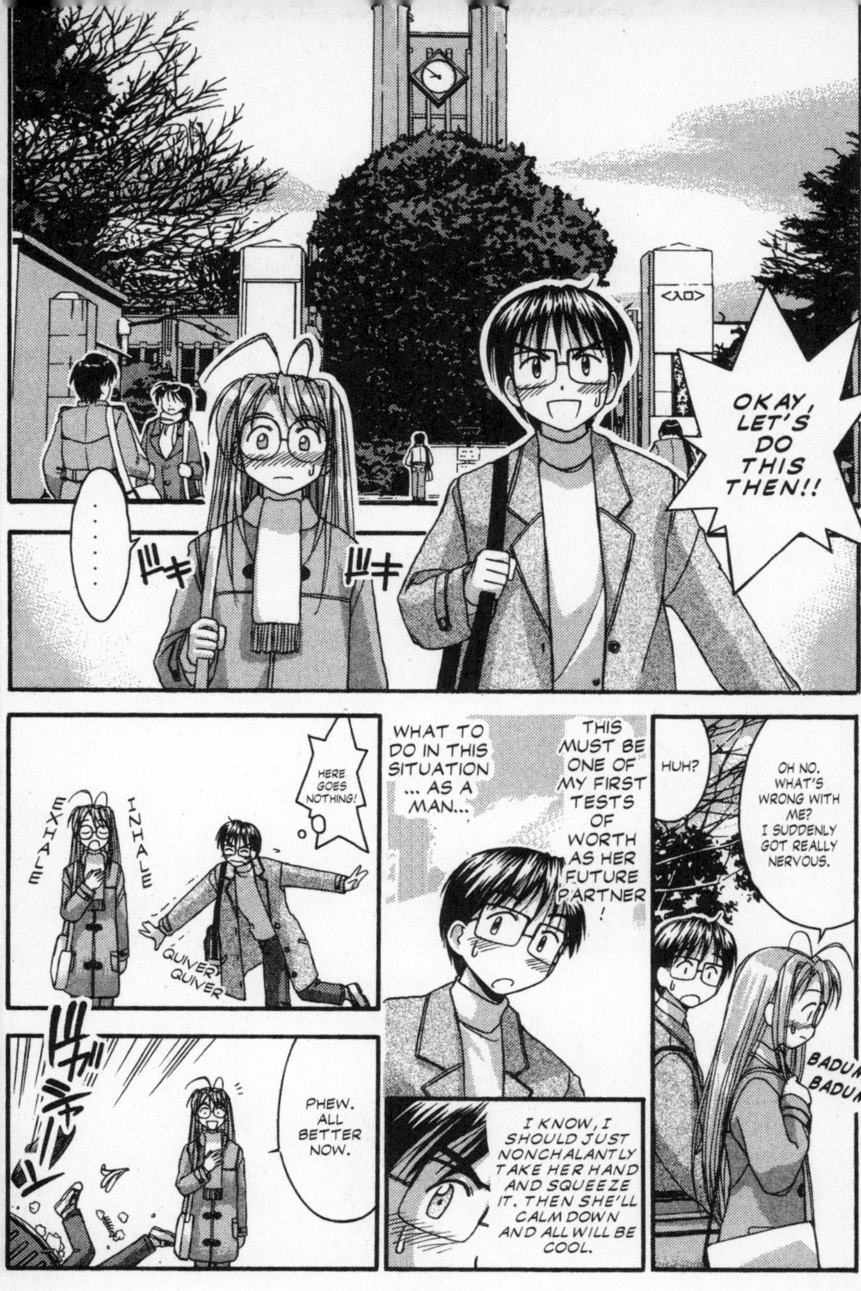

OKAY, LET'S DO THIS THEN!!
ドキ
ドキ
......
OH NO. WHAT'S WRONG WITH ME? I SUDDENLY GOT REALLY NERVOUS.
HUH?
BADUMP BADUMP
THIS MUST BE ONE OF MY FIRST TESTS OF WORTH AS HER FUTURE PARTNER!
WHAT TO DO IN THIS SITUATION ... AS A MAN...
I KNOW, I SHOULD JUST NONCHALANTLY TAKE HER HAND AND SQUEEZE IT. THEN SHE'LL CALM DOWN AND ALL WILL BE COOL.
HERE GOES NOTHING!
INHALE
EXHALE
QUIVER QUIVER
PHEW. ALL BETTER NOW.

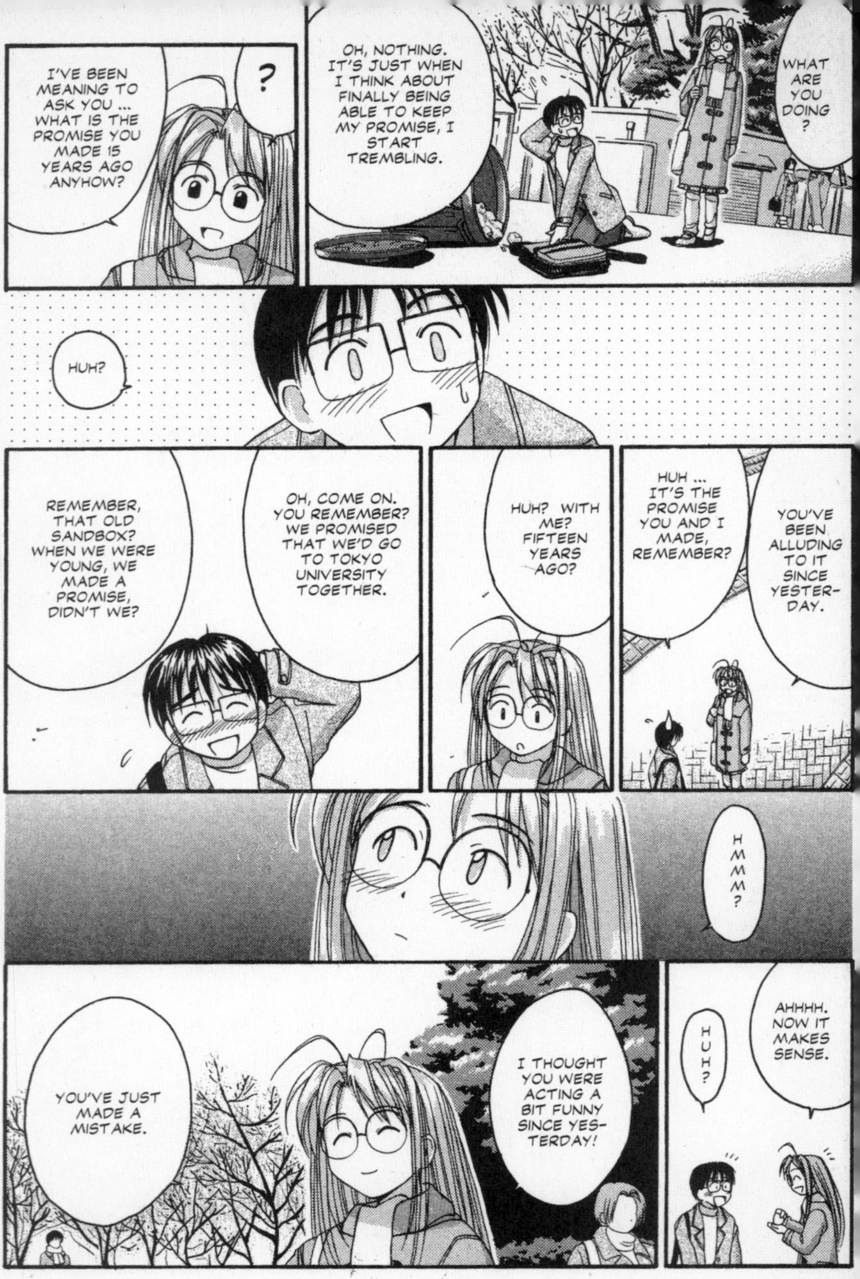
WHAT ARE YOU DOING?
OH, NOTHING. IT'S JUST WHEN I THINK ABOUT FINALLY BEING ABLE TO KEEP MY PROMISE, I START TREMBLING.
?
I'VE BEEN MEANING TO ASK YOU ... WHAT IS THE PROMISE YOU MADE 15 YEARS AGO ANYHOW?
HUH?
YOU'VE BEEN ALLUDING TO IT SINCE YESTER-DAY.
HUH ... IT'S THE PROMISE YOU AND I MADE, REMEMBER?
HUH? WITH ME? FIFTEEN YEARS AGO?
OH, COME ON. YOU REMEMBER? WE PROMISED THAT WE'D GO TO TOKYO UNIVERSITY TOGETHER.
REMEMBER, THAT OLD SANDBOX? WHEN WE WERE YOUNG, WE MADE A PROMISE, DIDN'T WE?
HMMM?
AHHHH. NOW IT MAKES SENSE.
HUH?
I THOUGHT YOU WERE ACTING A BIT FUNNY SINCE YES-TERDAY!
YOU'VE JUST MADE A MISTAKE.

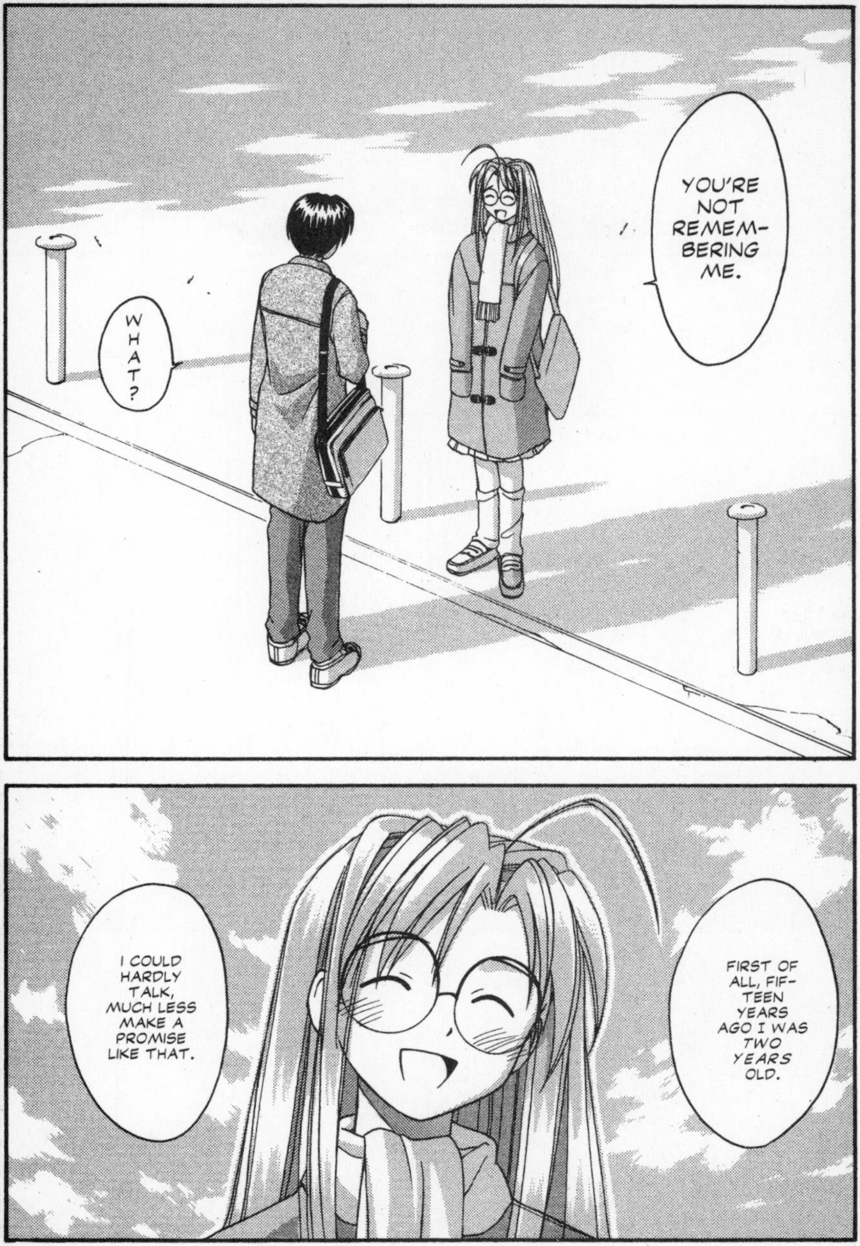
YOU'RE NOT REMEM-BERING ME.
WHAT?
FIRST OF ALL, FIF-TEEN YEARS AGO I WAS TWO YEARS OLD.
I COULD HARDLY TALK, MUCH LESS MAKE A PROMISE LIKE THAT.

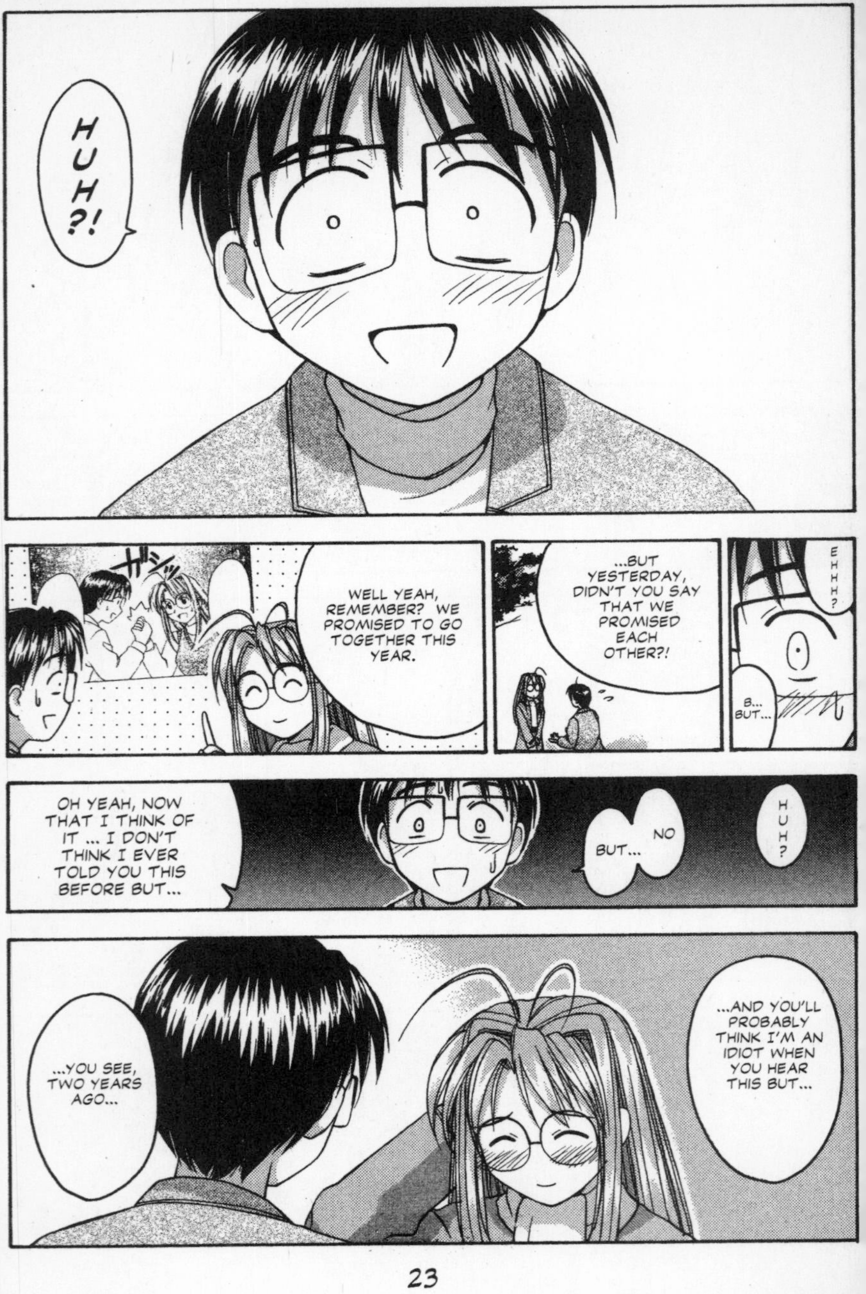
HUH?!
EHHH?
B... BUT...
...BUT YESTERDAY, DIDN'T YOU SAY THAT WE PROMISED EACH OTHER?!
WELL YEAH, REMEMBER? WE PROMISED TO GO TOGETHER THIS YEAR.
HUH?
NO BUT...
OH YEAH, NOW THAT I THINK OF IT ... I DON'T THINK I EVER TOLD YOU THIS BEFORE BUT...
...AND YOU'LL PROBABLY THINK I'M AN IDIOT WHEN YOU HEAR THIS BUT...
...YOU SEE, TWO YEARS AGO...

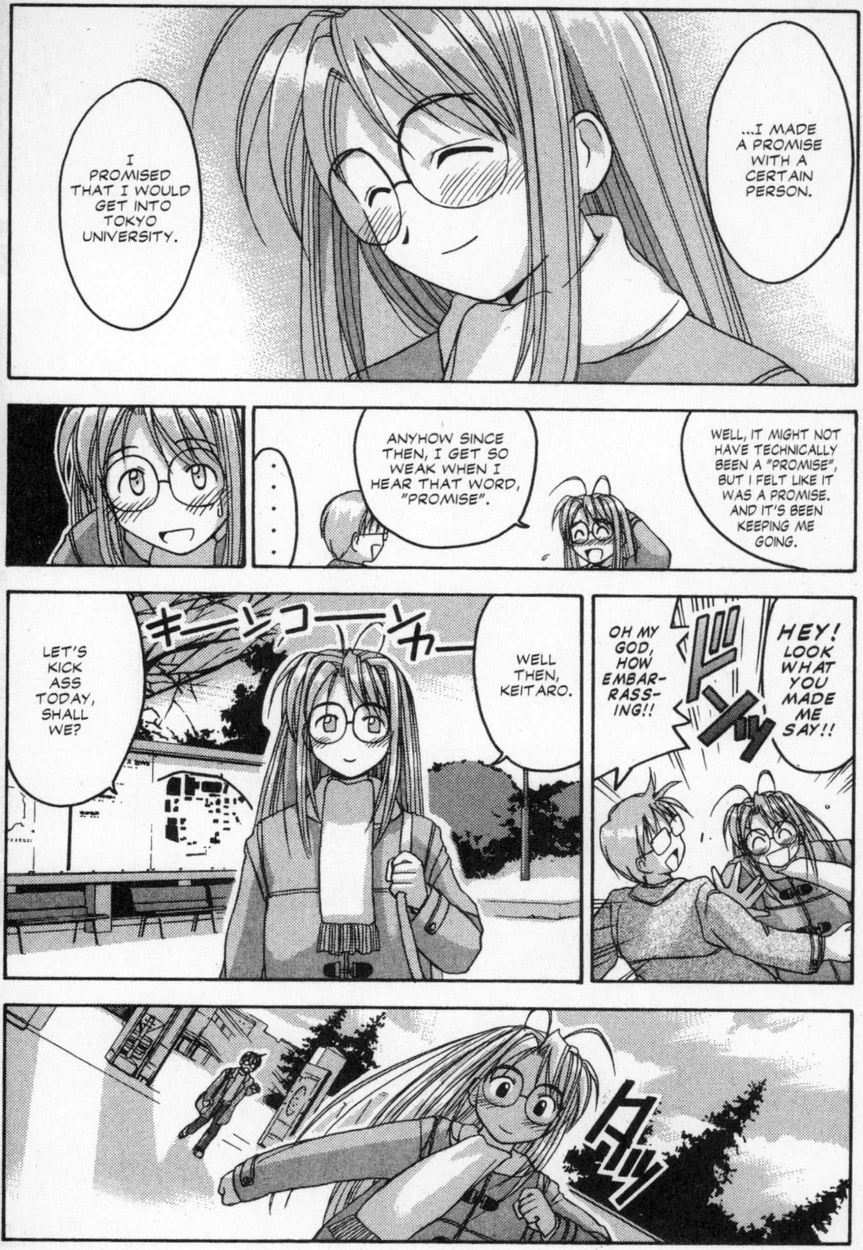
...I MADE A PROMISE WITH A CERTAIN PERSON.
I PROMISED THAT I WOULD GET INTO TOKYO UNIVERSITY.
WELL, IT MIGHT NOT HAVE TECHNICALLY BEEN A "PROMISE", BUT I FELT LIKE IT WAS A PROMISE. AND IT'S BEEN KEEPING ME GOING.
ANYHOW SINCE THEN, I GET SO WEAK WHEN I HEAR THAT WORD, "PROMISE".
......
HEY! LOOK WHAT YOU MADE ME SAY!!
ドンッ
OH MY GOD, HOW EMBARRASSING!!
WELL THEN, KEITARO.
キーンコーンカーン
LET'S KICK ASS TODAY, SHALL WE?

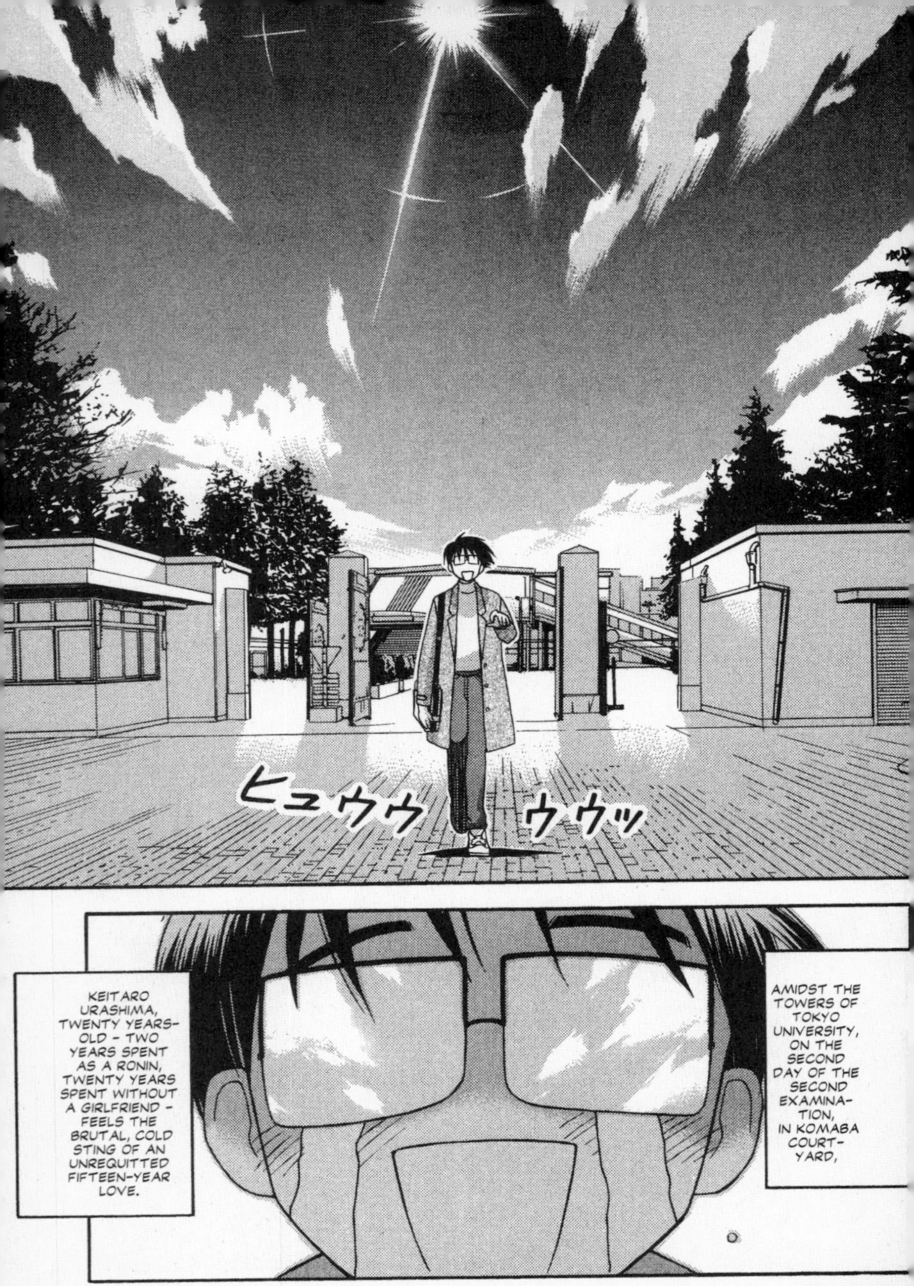
ヒュウウ ウウッ
AMIDST THE TOWERS OF TOKYO UNIVERSITY, ON THE SECOND DAY OF THE SECOND EXAMINATION, IN KOMABA COURTYARD,
KEITARO URASHIMA, TWENTY YEARS-OLD - TWO YEARS SPENT AS A RONIN, TWENTY YEARS SPENT WITHOUT A GIRLFRIEND - FEELS THE BRUTAL, COLD STING OF AN UNREQUITTED FIFTEEN-YEAR LOVE.

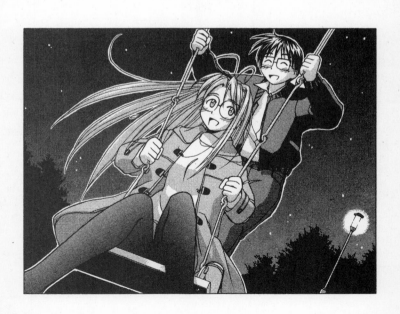

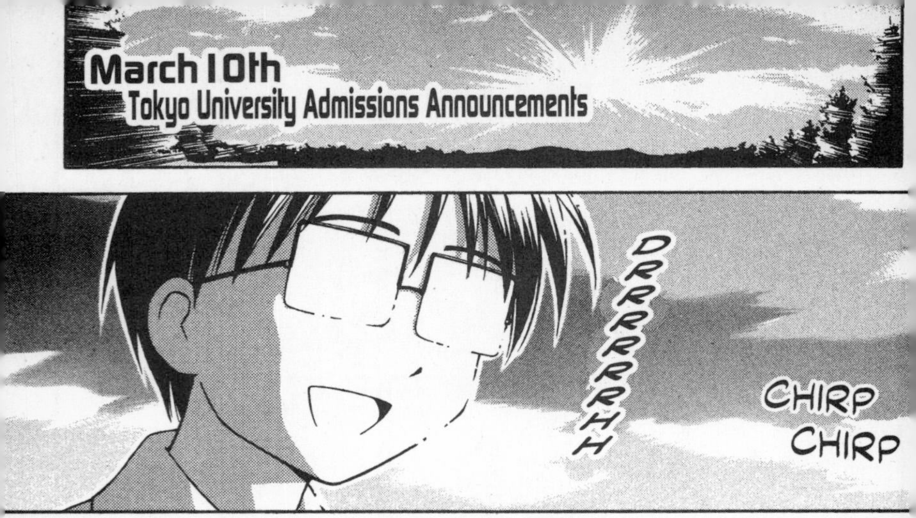
March 10th
Tokyo University Admissions Announcements
CHIRP CHIRP
DRRRRRRRHH

LOVE ♥ HINA

HINATA..17 Congratulations on Getting Into Tokyo U!

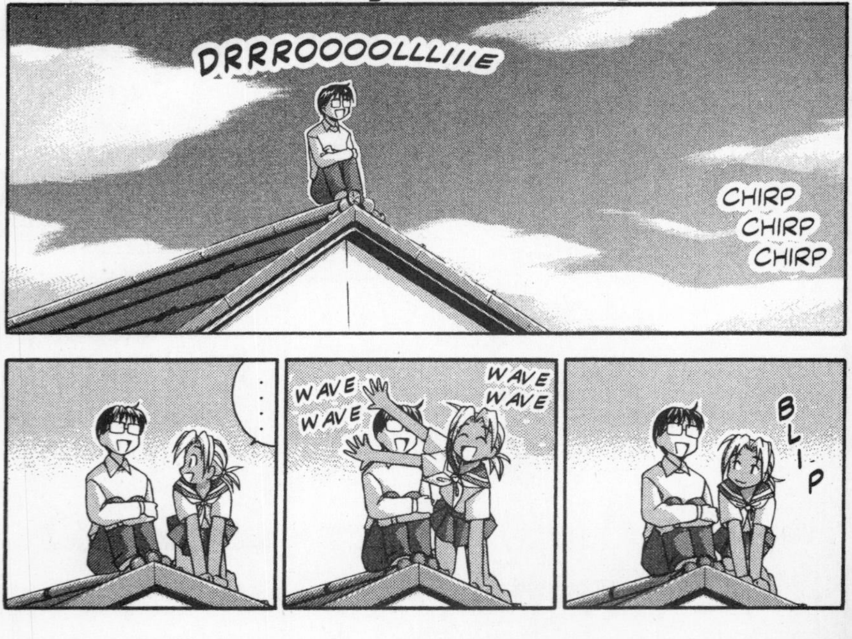
DRRROOOOOLLLIIIE
CHIRP CHIRP CHIRP
BLIP
WAVE WAVE
WAVE WAVE
...

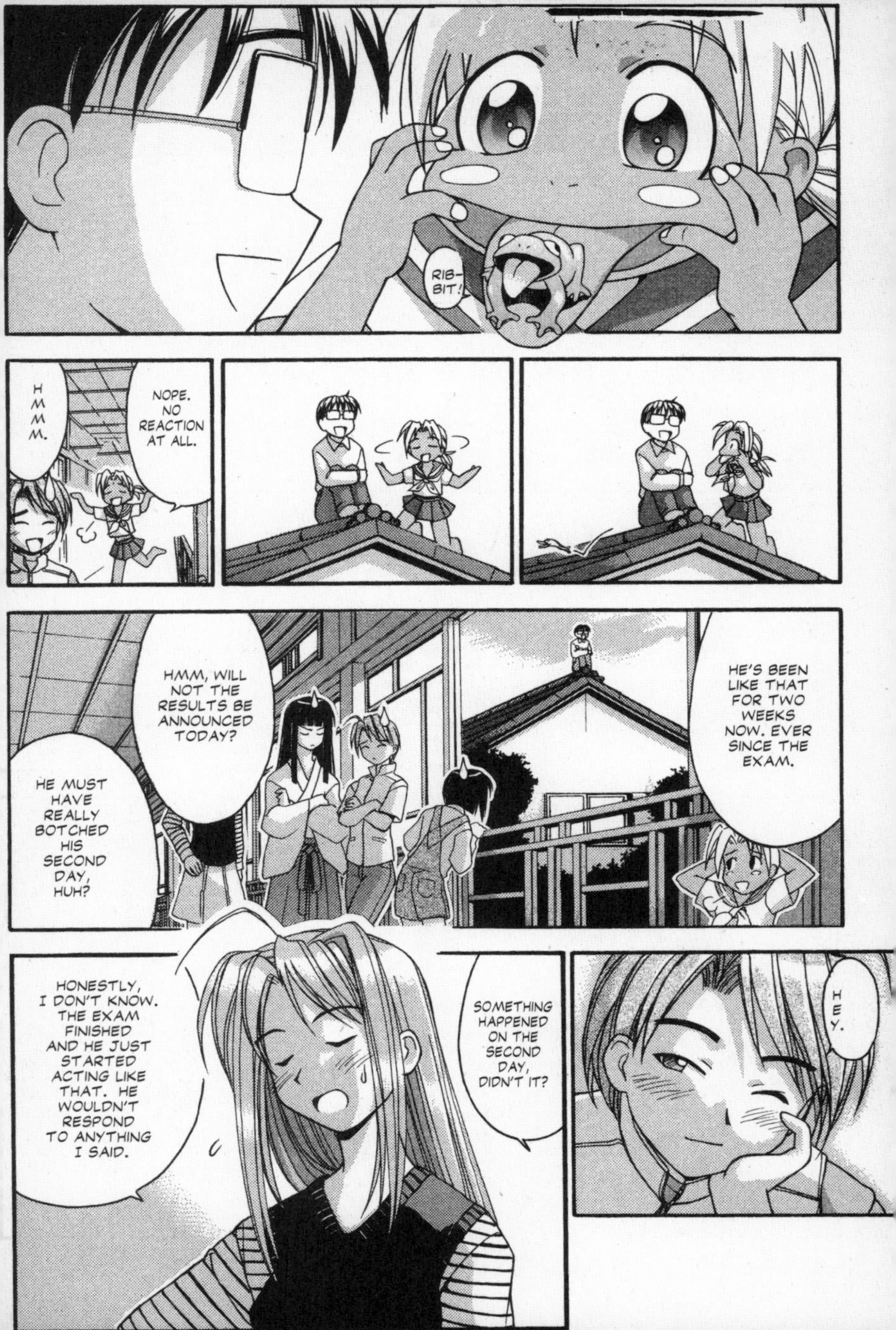
RIB-BIT!
NOPE. NO REACTION AT ALL.
HMMM.
HE'S BEEN LIKE THAT FOR TWO WEEKS NOW. EVER SINCE THE EXAM.
HMM, WILL NOT THE RESULTS BE ANNOUNCED TODAY?
HE MUST HAVE REALLY BOTCHED HIS SECOND DAY, HUH?
HEY.
SOMETHING HAPPENED ON THE SECOND DAY, DIDN'T IT?
HONESTLY, I DON'T KNOW. THE EXAM FINISHED AND HE JUST STARTED ACTING LIKE THAT. HE WOULDN'T RESPOND TO ANYTHING I SAID.

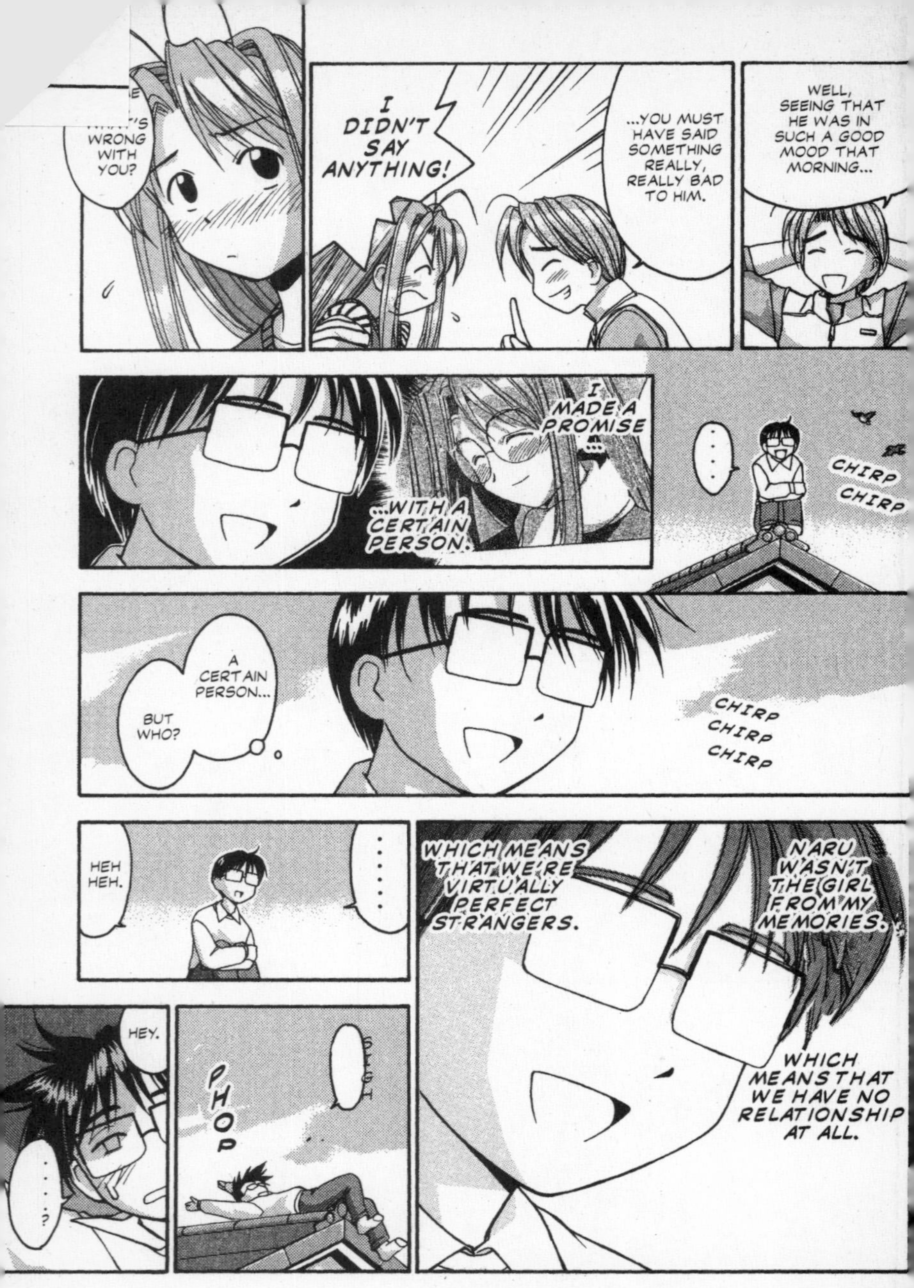
WELL, SEEING THAT HE WAS IN SUCH A GOOD MOOD THAT MORNING...
...YOU MUST HAVE SAID SOMETHING REALLY, REALLY BAD TO HIM.
I DIDN'T SAY ANYTHING!
WRONG WITH YOU?
...
CHIRP
CHIRP
I MADE A PROMISE...
...WITH A CERTAIN PERSON.
CHIRP
CHIRP
CHIRP
A CERTAIN PERSON...
BUT WHO?
NARU WASN'T THE GIRL FROM MY MEMORIES.
WHICH MEANS THAT WE'RE VIRTUALLY PERFECT STRANGERS.
WHICH MEANS THAT WE HAVE NO RELATIONSHIP AT ALL.
......
HEH HEH.
SIGH
PHOP
HEY.
...?

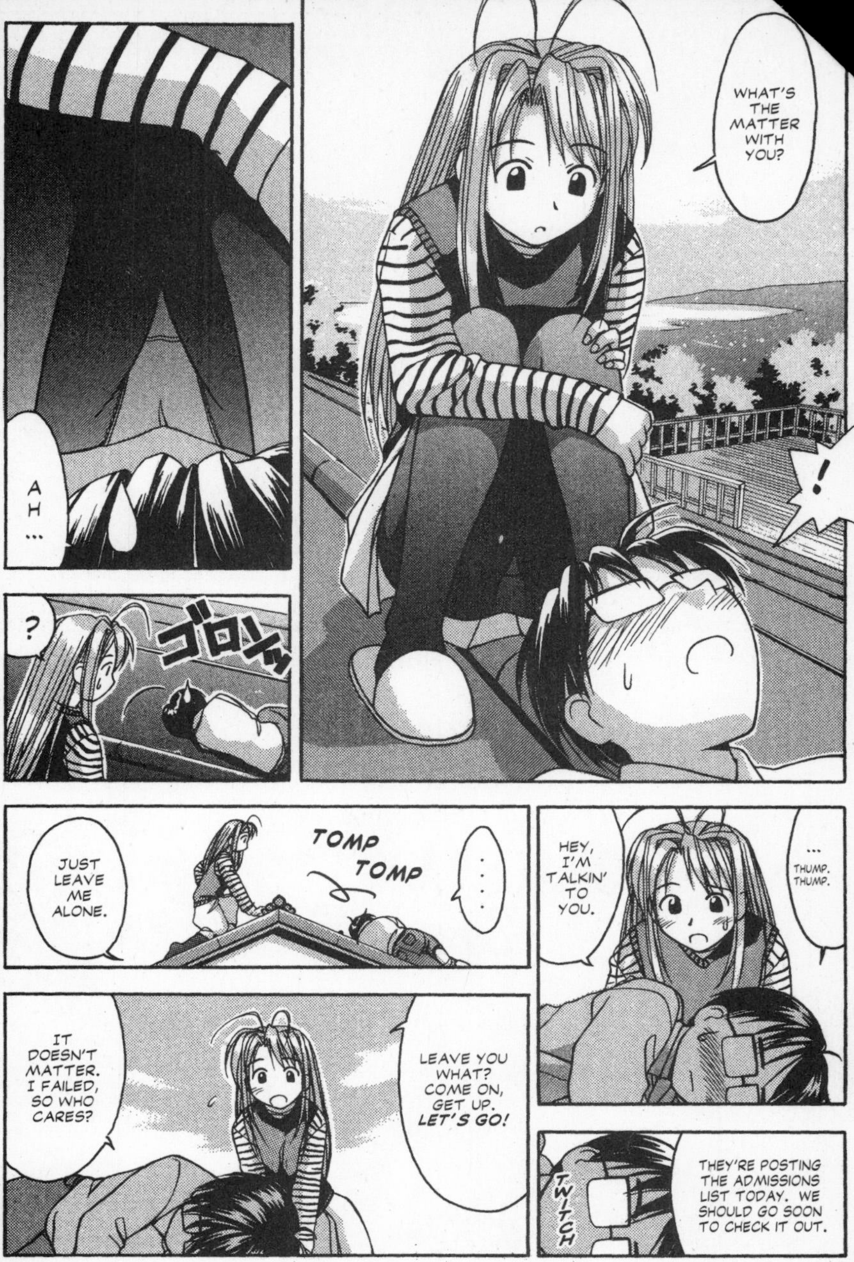
WHAT'S THE MATTER WITH YOU?
!
AH ...
?
ゴロン
HEY, I'M TALKIN' TO YOU.
... THUMP. THUMP.
....
TOMP TOMP
JUST LEAVE ME ALONE.
LEAVE YOU WHAT? COME ON, GET UP. LET'S GO!
IT DOESN'T MATTER. I FAILED, SO WHO CARES?
THEY'RE POSTING THE ADMISSIONS LIST TODAY. WE SHOULD GO SOON TO CHECK IT OUT.
TWITCH

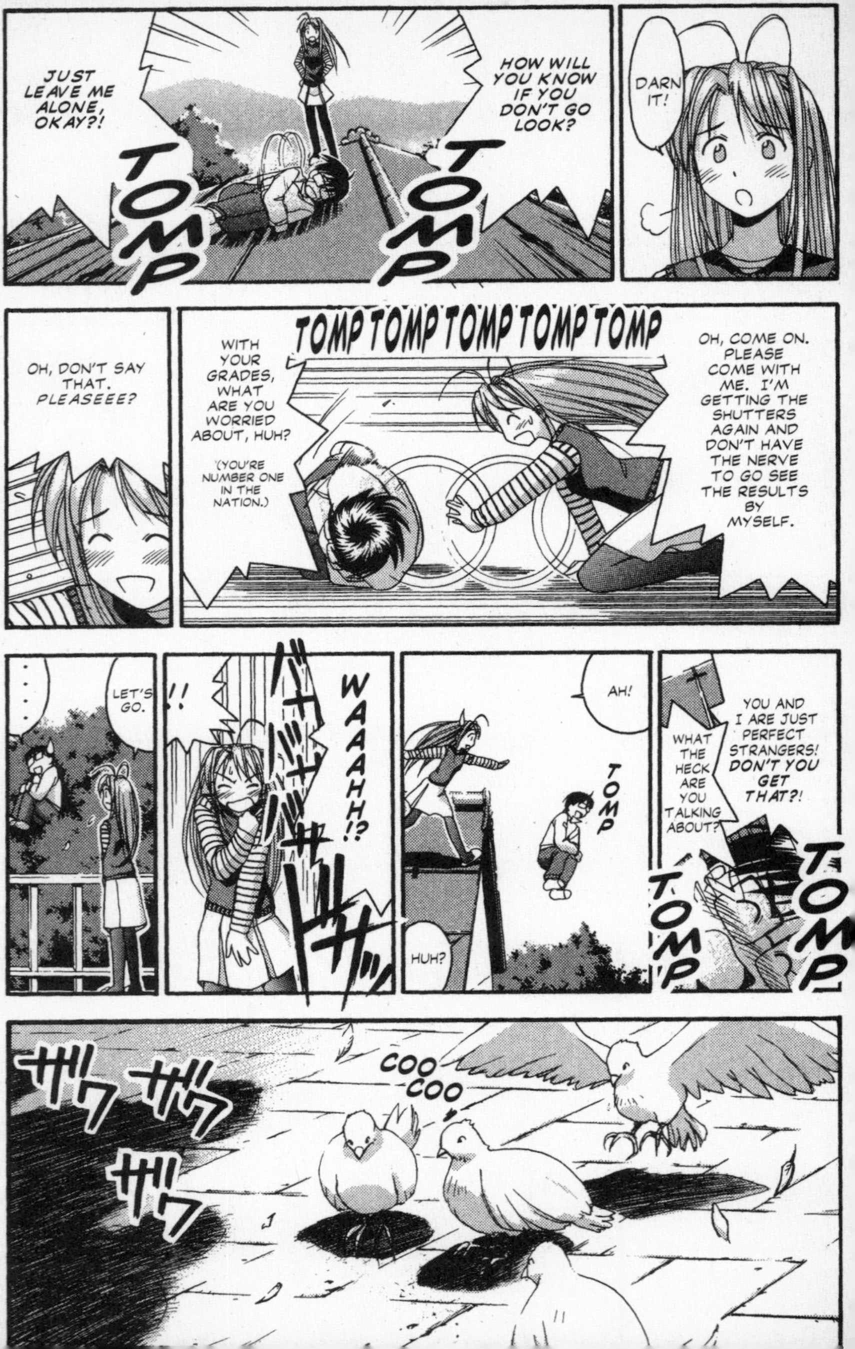
DARN IT!
HOW WILL YOU KNOW IF YOU DON'T GO LOOK?
TOMP
TOMP
JUST LEAVE ME ALONE, OKAY?!
TOMP TOMP TOMP TOMP TOMP
OH, COME ON. PLEASE COME WITH ME. I'M GETTING THE SHUTTERS AGAIN AND DON'T HAVE THE NERVE TO GO SEE THE RESULTS BY MYSELF.
WITH YOUR GRADES, WHAT ARE YOU WORRIED ABOUT, HUH?
(YOU'RE NUMBER ONE IN THE NATION.)
OH, DON'T SAY THAT. PLEASEEE?
YOU AND I ARE JUST PERFECT STRANGERS! DON'T YOU GET THAT?!
WHAT THE HECK ARE YOU TALKING ABOUT?
TOMP
TOMP
AH!
TOMP
HUH?
WAAAAHH!?
LET'S GO.
!!
. . . . .
COO COO
ザワ ザワ
ザワ

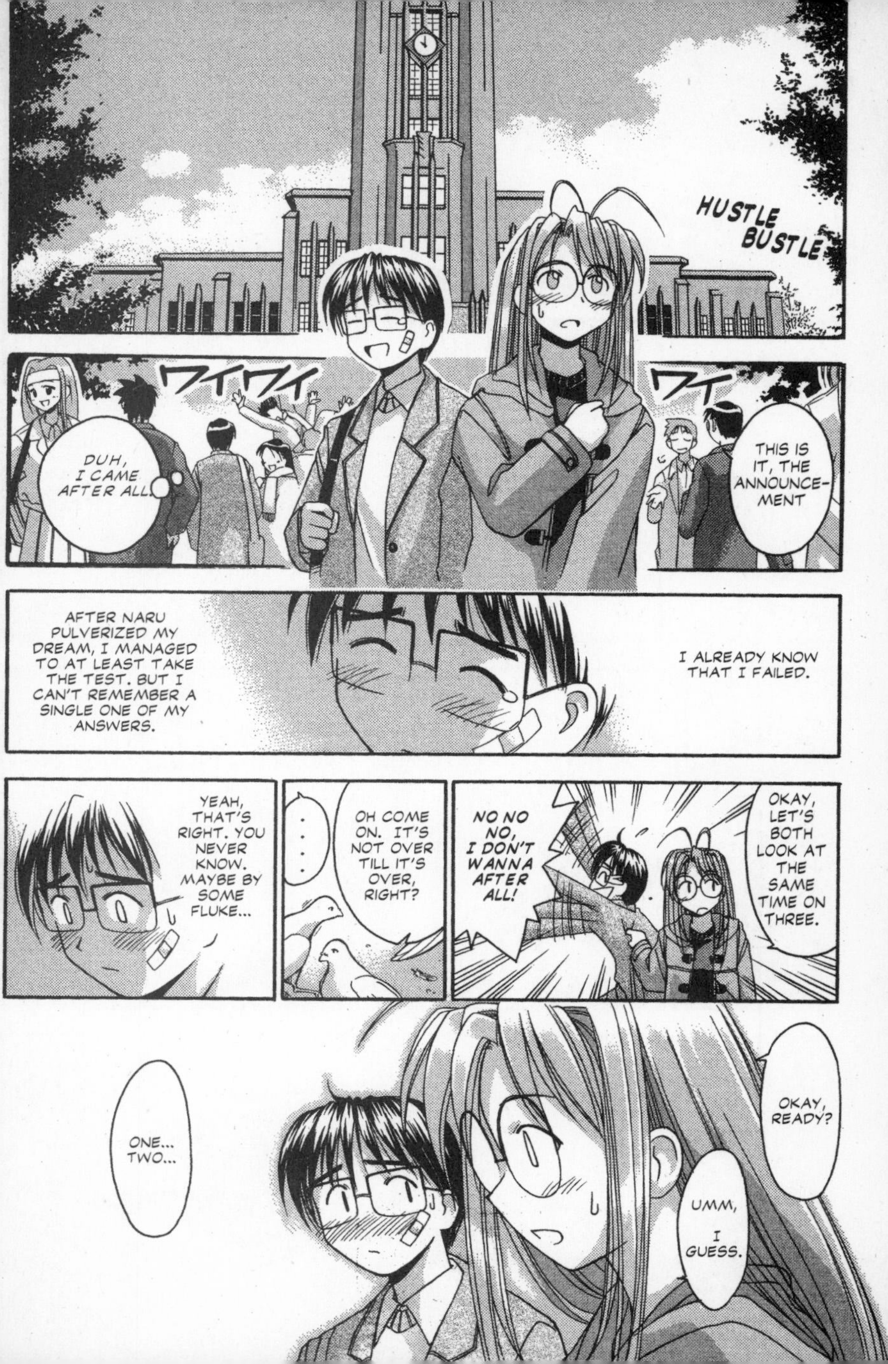
HUSTLE BUSTLE
ワイ
THIS IS IT, THE ANNOUNCEMENT
ワイワイ
DUH, I CAME AFTER ALL.
AFTER NARU PULVERIZED MY DREAM, I MANAGED TO AT LEAST TAKE THE TEST. BUT I CAN'T REMEMBER A SINGLE ONE OF MY ANSWERS.
I ALREADY KNOW THAT I FAILED.
OKAY, LET'S BOTH LOOK AT THE SAME TIME ON THREE.
NO NO NO, I DON'T WANNA AFTER ALL!
OH COME ON. IT'S NOT OVER TILL IT'S OVER, RIGHT?
......
YEAH, THAT'S RIGHT. YOU NEVER KNOW. MAYBE BY SOME FLUKE...
OKAY, READY?
UMM, I GUESS.
ONE... TWO...

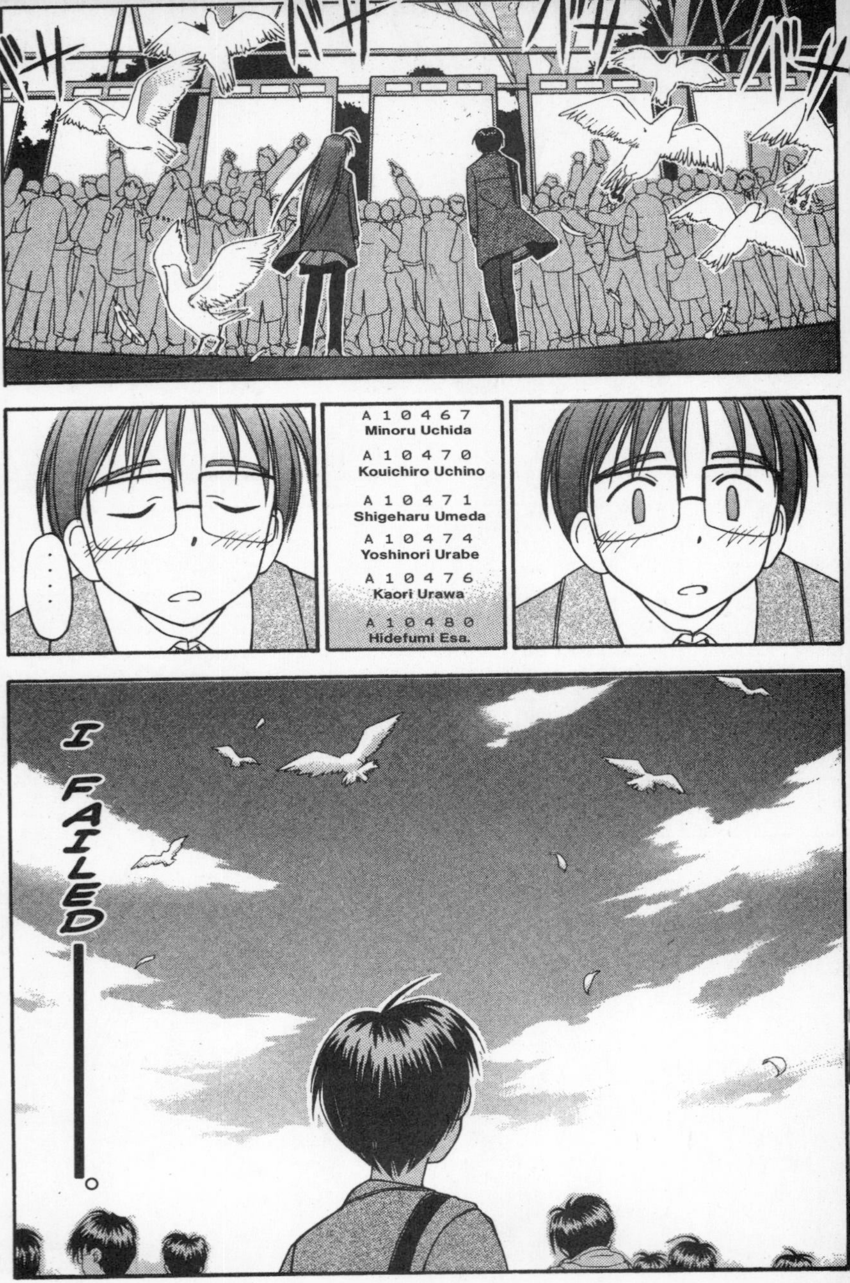
バサ
バサ
バサ
A 1 0 4 6 7
Minoru Uchida
A 1 0 4 7 0
Kouichiro Uchino
A 1 0 4 7 1
Shigeharu Umeda
A 1 0 4 7 4
Yoshinori Urabe
A 1 0 4 7 6
Kaori Urawa
A 1 0 4 8 0
Hidefumi Esa.
....
I FAILED—.

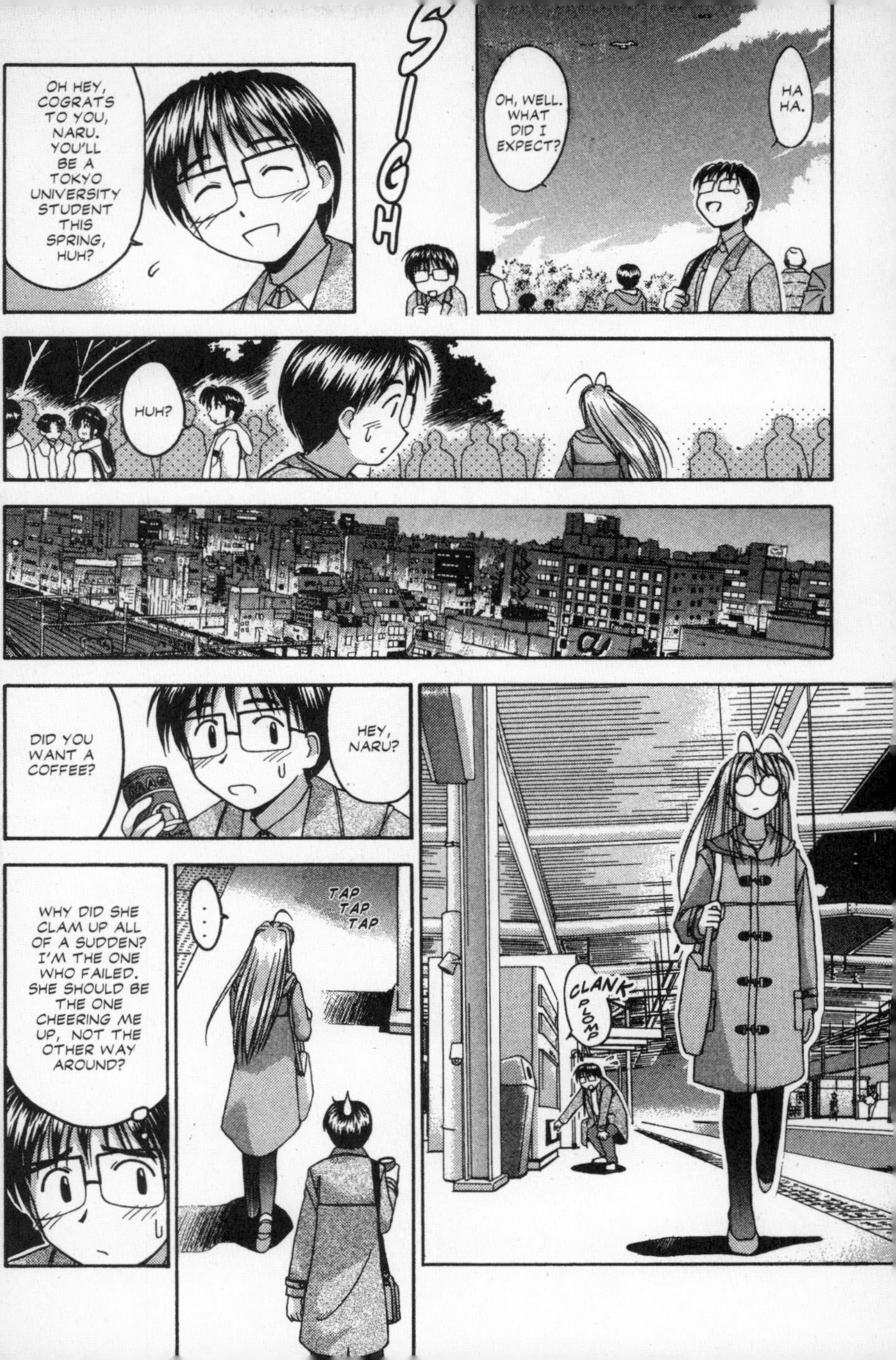
HA HA.
OH, WELL. WHAT DID I EXPECT?
SIGH
OH HEY, COGRATS TO YOU, NARU. YOU'LL BE A TOKYO UNIVERSITY STUDENT THIS SPRING, HUH?
HUH?
CLANK
PLOMP
HEY, NARU?
DID YOU WANT A COFFEE?
TAP TAP TAP
...
WHY DID SHE CLAM UP ALL OF A SUDDEN? I'M THE ONE WHO FAILED. SHE SHOULD BE THE ONE CHEERING ME UP, NOT THE OTHER WAY AROUND?

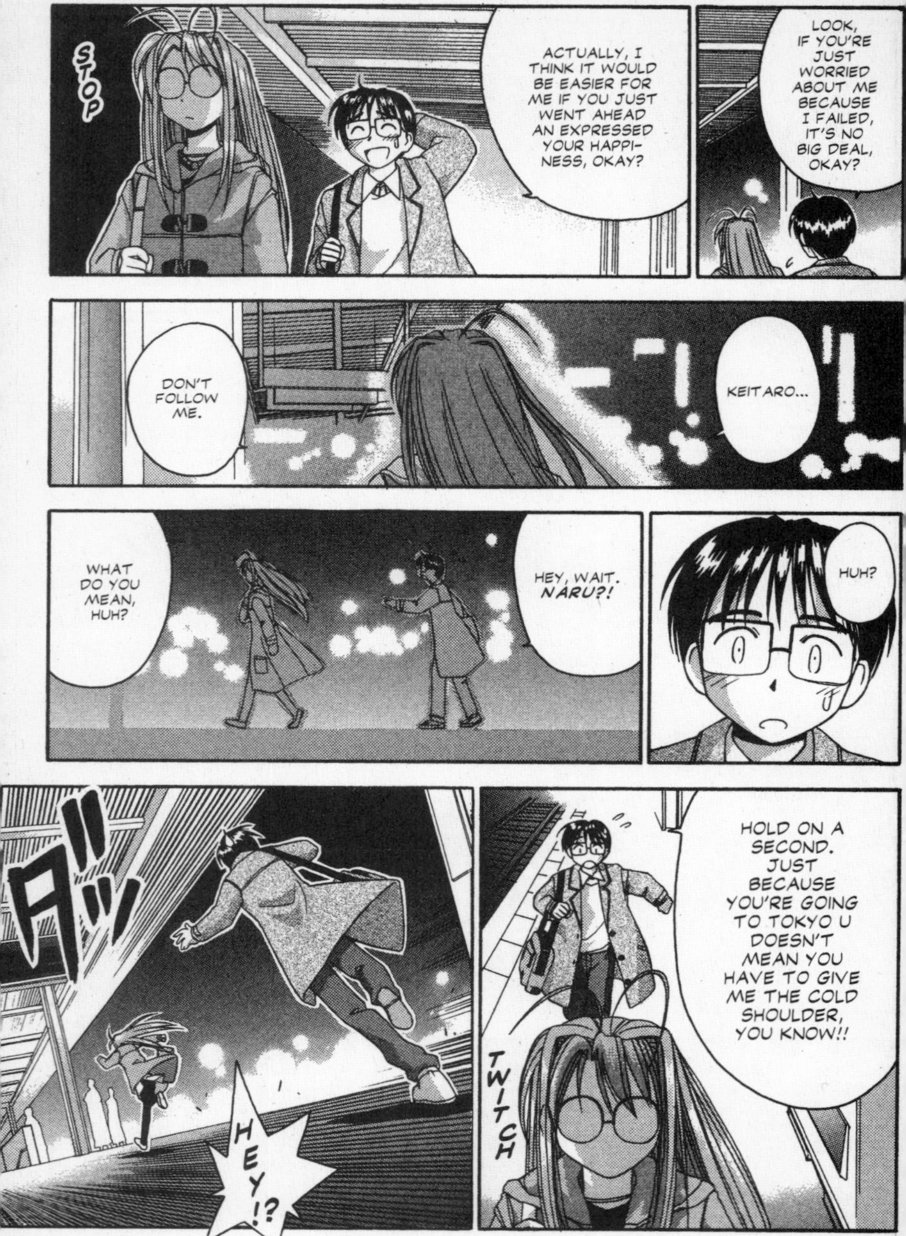
LOOK, IF YOU'RE JUST WORRIED ABOUT ME BECAUSE I FAILED, IT'S NO BIG DEAL, OKAY?
ACTUALLY, I THINK IT WOULD BE EASIER FOR ME IF YOU JUST WENT AHEAD AN EXPRESSED YOUR HAPPI- NESS, OKAY?
STOP
KEITARO...
DON'T FOLLOW ME.
HUH?
HEY, WAIT. NARU?!
WHAT DO YOU MEAN, HUH?
HOLD ON A SECOND. JUST BECAUSE YOU'RE GOING TO TOKYO U DOESN'T MEAN YOU HAVE TO GIVE ME THE COLD SHOULDER, YOU KNOW!!
TWITCH
ダッ
HEY!?

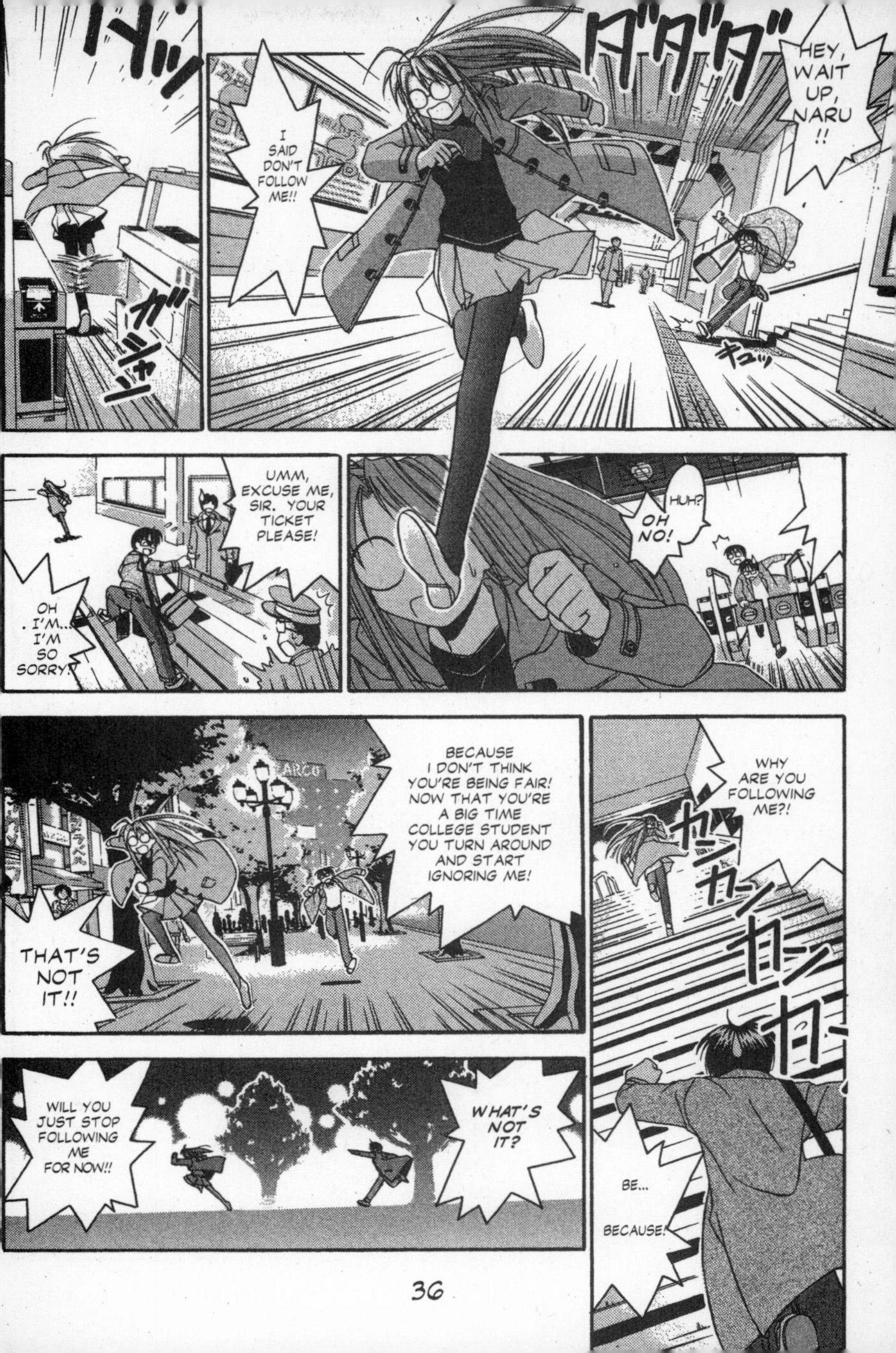
ダダダ
HEY, WAIT UP, NARU!!
I SAID DON'T FOLLOW ME!!
キュッ
ドッ
ガシャン
HUH?
OH NO!
UMM, EXCUSE ME, SIR. YOUR TICKET PLEASE!
OH. I'M... I'M SO SORRY!
WHY ARE YOU FOLLOWING ME?!
BE...
BECAUSE!
BECAUSE I DON'T THINK YOU'RE BEING FAIR! NOW THAT YOU'RE A BIG TIME COLLEGE STUDENT YOU TURN AROUND AND START IGNORING ME!
THAT'S NOT IT!!
WHAT'S NOT IT?
WILL YOU JUST STOP FOLLOWING ME FOR NOW!!

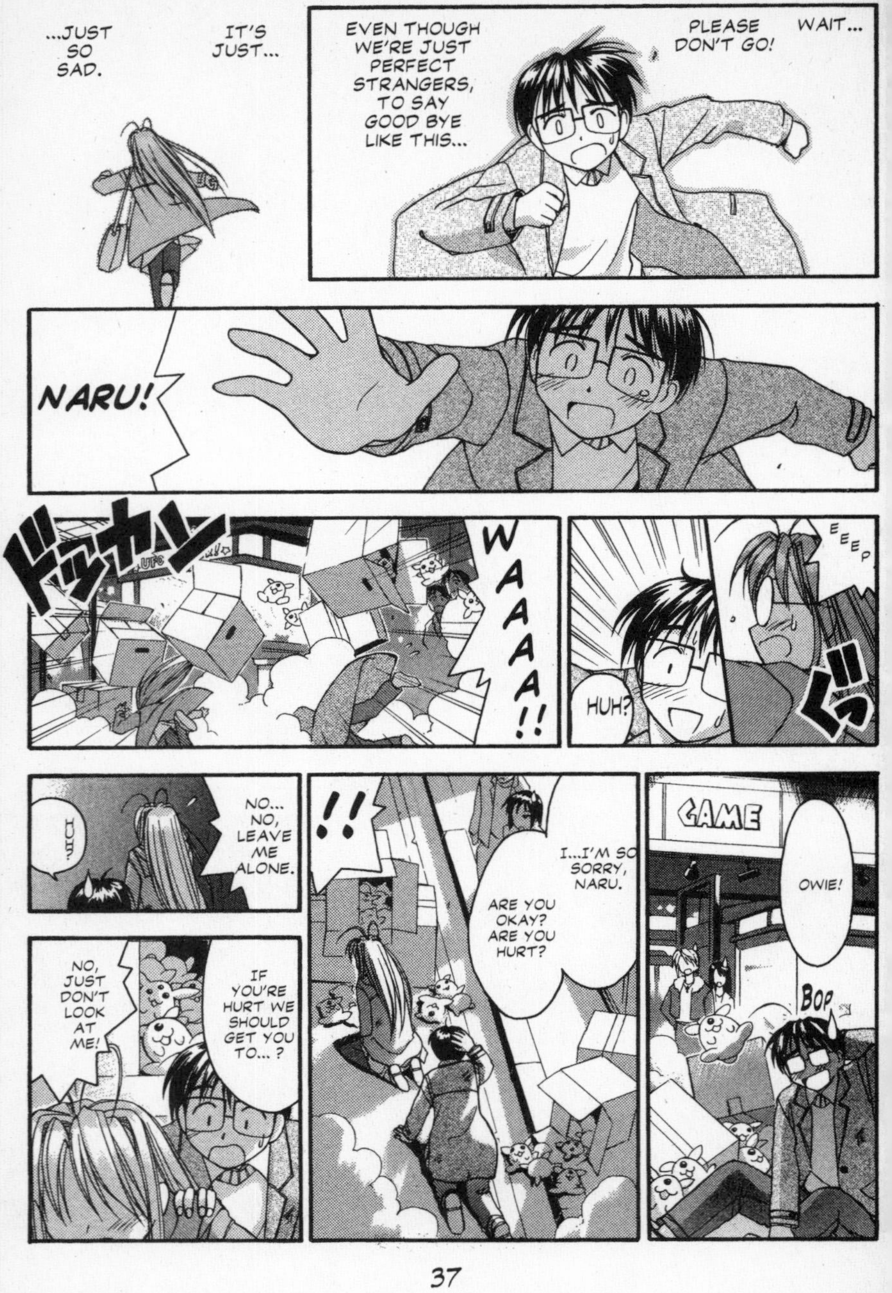
WAIT...
PLEASE DON'T GO!
EVEN THOUGH WE'RE JUST PERFECT STRANGERS, TO SAY GOOD BYE LIKE THIS...
IT'S JUST...
...JUST SO SAD.
NARU!
EEEP
HUH?
ぐっ
WAAAAA!!
ドッカン
OWIE!
BOP
I...I'M SO SORRY, NARU.
ARE YOU OKAY? ARE YOU HURT?
!!
NO... NO, LEAVE ME ALONE.
HUH?
IF YOU'RE HURT WE SHOULD GET YOU TO... ?
NO, JUST DON'T LOOK AT ME!

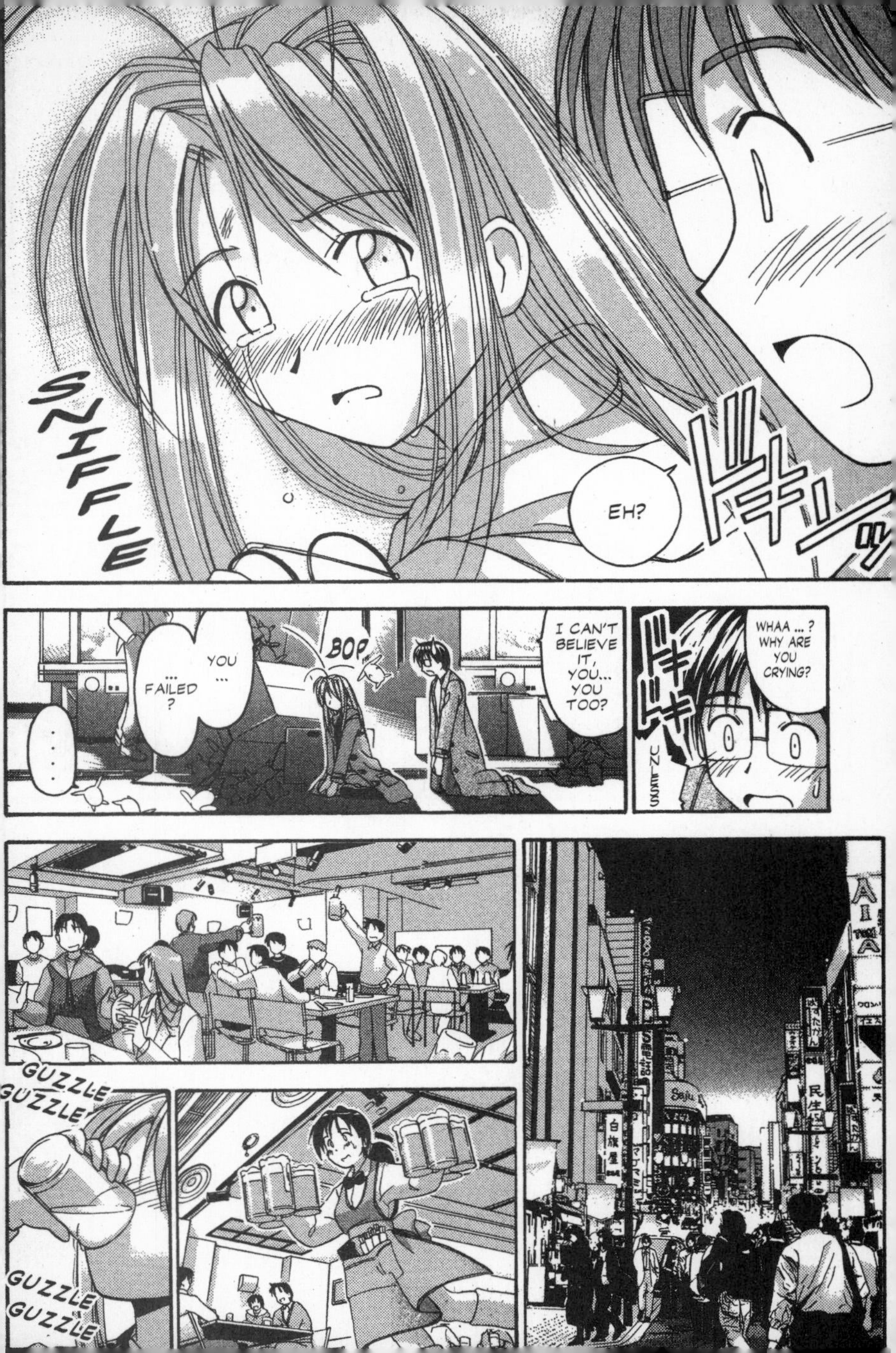
SNIFFLE
EH?
ドキーッ
WHAA ...? WHY ARE YOU CRYING?
ドキドキ
UNLESS
I CAN'T BELIEVE IT, YOU... YOU TOO?
BOP
YOU ... FAILED?
....
GUZZLE GUZZLE
GUZZLE GUZZLE

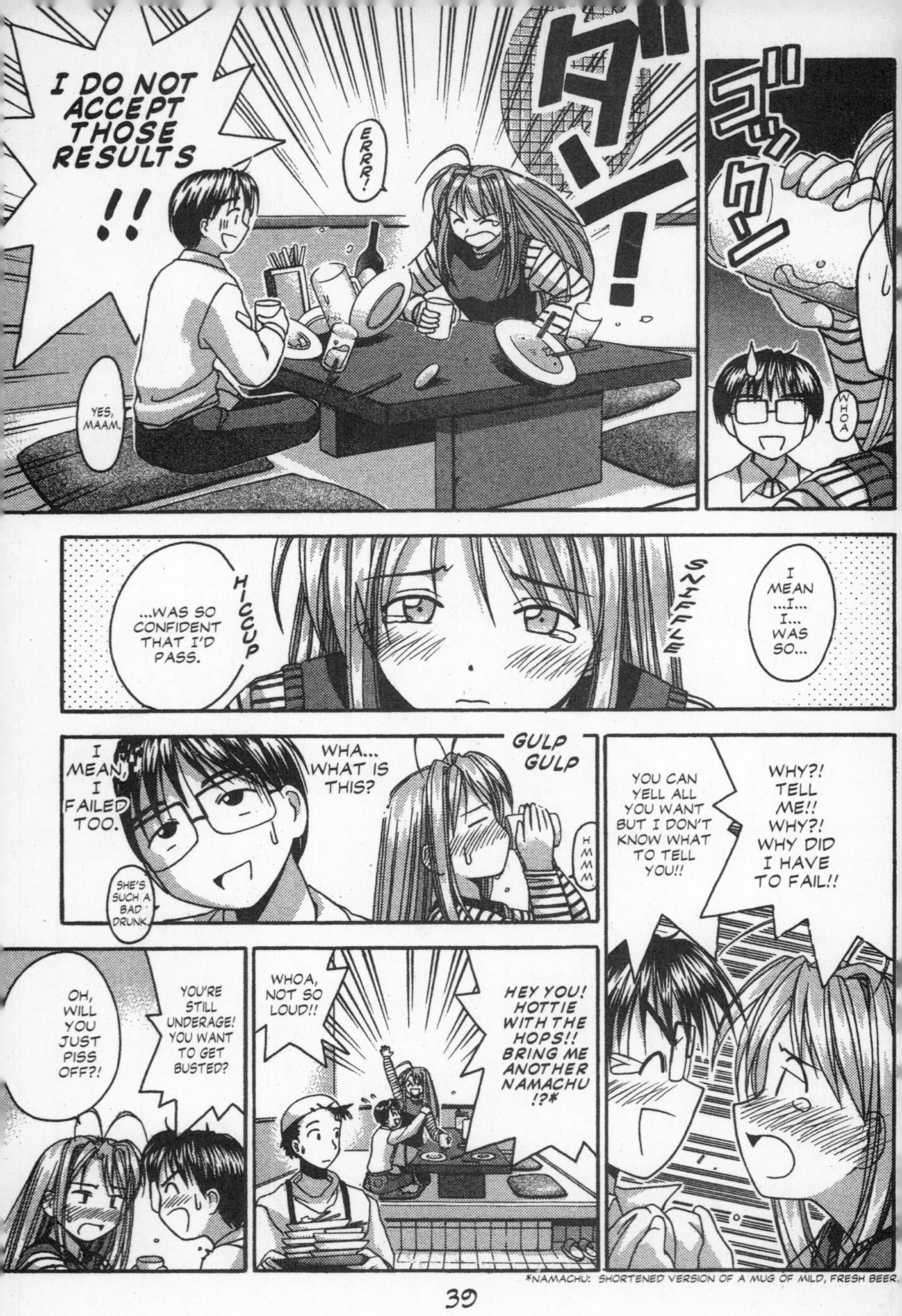
WHOA
ERRR!
I DO NOT ACCEPT THOSE RESULTS!!
YES, MAAM.
I MEAN ...I... I... WAS SO...
SNIFFLE
HICCUP
...WAS SO CONFIDENT THAT I'D PASS.
WHY?! TELL ME!! WHY?! WHY DID I HAVE TO FAIL!!
YOU CAN YELL ALL YOU WANT BUT I DON'T KNOW WHAT TO TELL YOU!!
GULP GULP
HMMM
WHA... WHAT IS THIS?
I MEAN, I FAILED TOO.
SHE'S SUCH A BAD DRUNK.
HEY YOU! HOTTIE WITH THE HOPS!! BRING ME ANOTHER NAMACHU!?*
WHOA, NOT SO LOUD!!
YOU'RE STILL UNDERAGE! YOU WANT TO GET BUSTED?
OH, WILL YOU JUST PISS OFF?!

*NAMACHU: SHORTENED VERSION OF A MUG OF MILD, FRESH BEER.

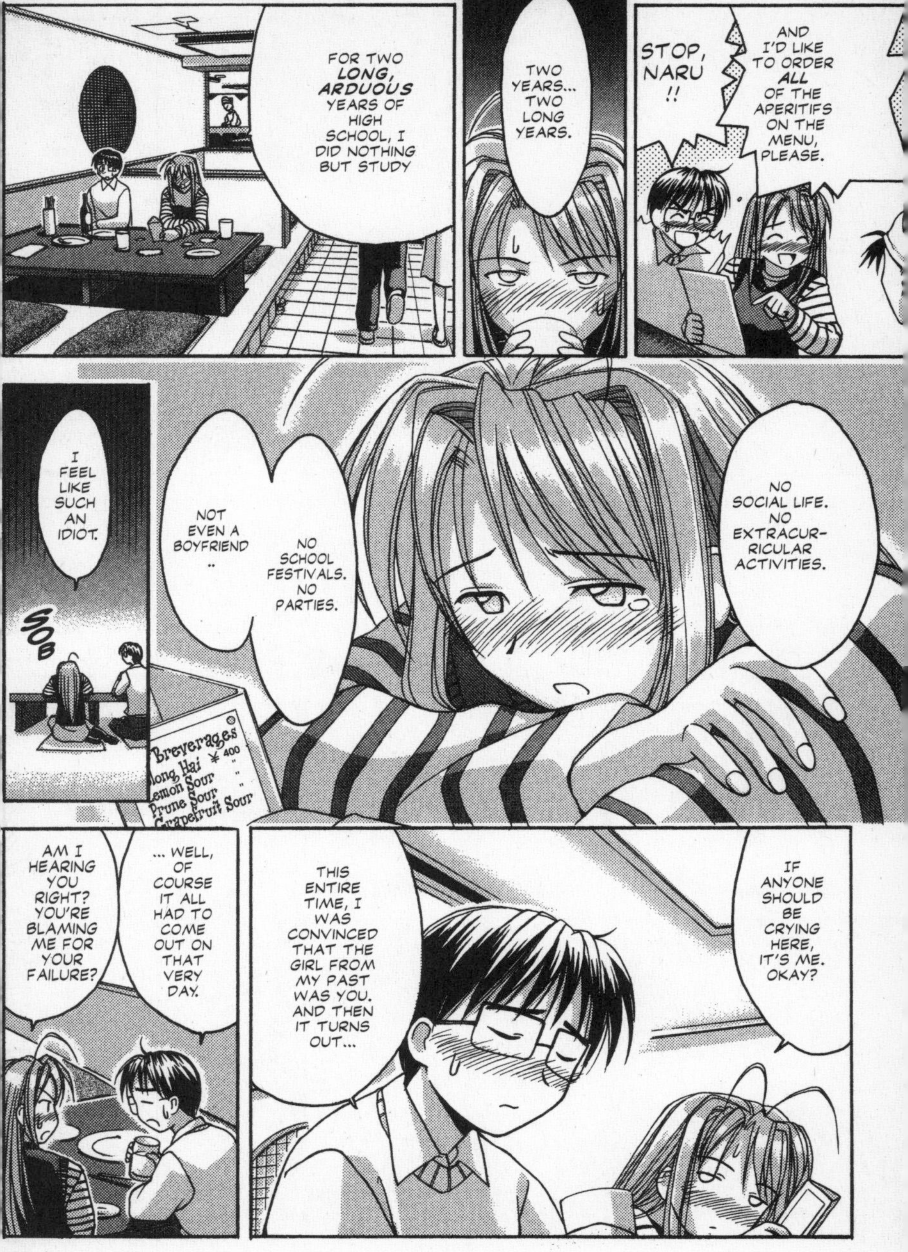
AND I'D LIKE TO ORDER ALL OF THE APERITIFS ON THE MENU, PLEASE.
STOP, NARU !!
TWO YEARS... TWO LONG YEARS.
FOR TWO LONG, ARDUOUS YEARS OF HIGH SCHOOL, I DID NOTHING BUT STUDY
NO SOCIAL LIFE. NO EXTRACURRICULAR ACTIVITIES.
NO SCHOOL FESTIVALS. NO PARTIES.
NOT EVEN A BOYFRIEND ..
Breverages ¥ 400
Prune Sour
Grapefruit Sour
I FEEL LIKE SUCH AN IDIOT.
SOB
IF ANYONE SHOULD BE CRYING HERE, IT'S ME. OKAY?
THIS ENTIRE TIME, I WAS CONVINCED THAT THE GIRL FROM MY PAST WAS YOU. AND THEN IT TURNS OUT...
... WELL, OF COURSE IT ALL HAD TO COME OUT ON THAT VERY DAY.
AM I HEARING YOU RIGHT? YOU'RE BLAMING ME FOR YOUR FAILURE?

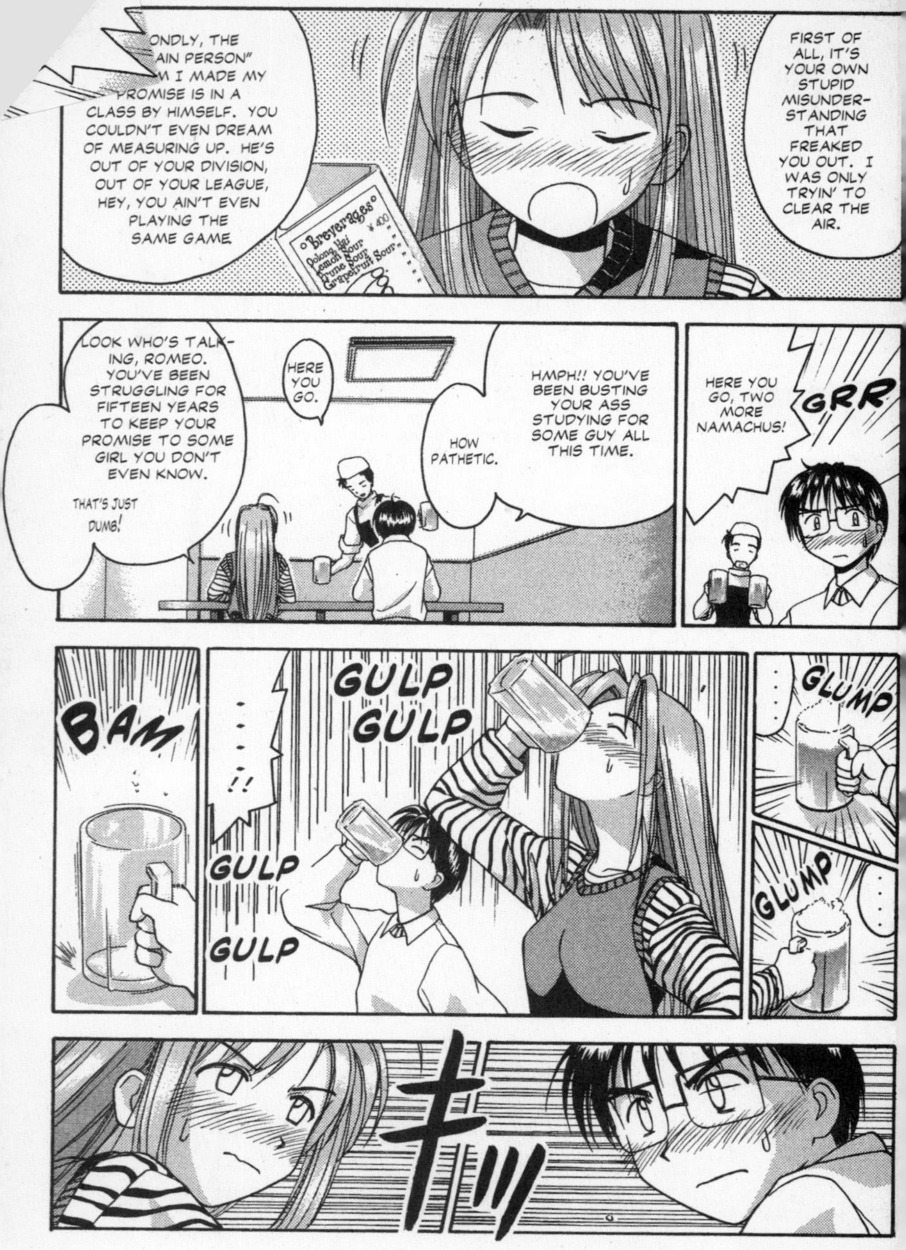
FIRST OF ALL, IT'S YOUR OWN STUPID MISUNDER-STANDING THAT FREAKED YOU OUT. I WAS ONLY TRYIN' TO CLEAR THE AIR.
Breverages ¥400 Oolong Hai Lemon Sour Prune Sour Grapefruit Sour
ONDLY, THE "AIN PERSON" M I MADE MY PROMISE IS IN A CLASS BY HIMSELF. YOU COULDN'T EVEN DREAM OF MEASURING UP. HE'S OUT OF YOUR DIVISION, OUT OF YOUR LEAGUE, HEY, YOU AIN'T EVEN PLAYING THE SAME GAME.
GRR
HERE YOU GO, TWO MORE NAMACHUS!
HMPH!! YOU'VE BEEN BUSTING YOUR ASS STUDYING FOR SOME GUY ALL THIS TIME.
HOW PATHETIC.
HERE YOU GO.
LOOK WHO'S TALKING, ROMEO. YOU'VE BEEN STRUGGLING FOR FIFTEEN YEARS TO KEEP YOUR PROMISE TO SOME GIRL YOU DON'T EVEN KNOW.
THAT'S JUST DUMB!
GLUMP
GLUMP
GULP GULP
......!!
GULP
GULP
BAM

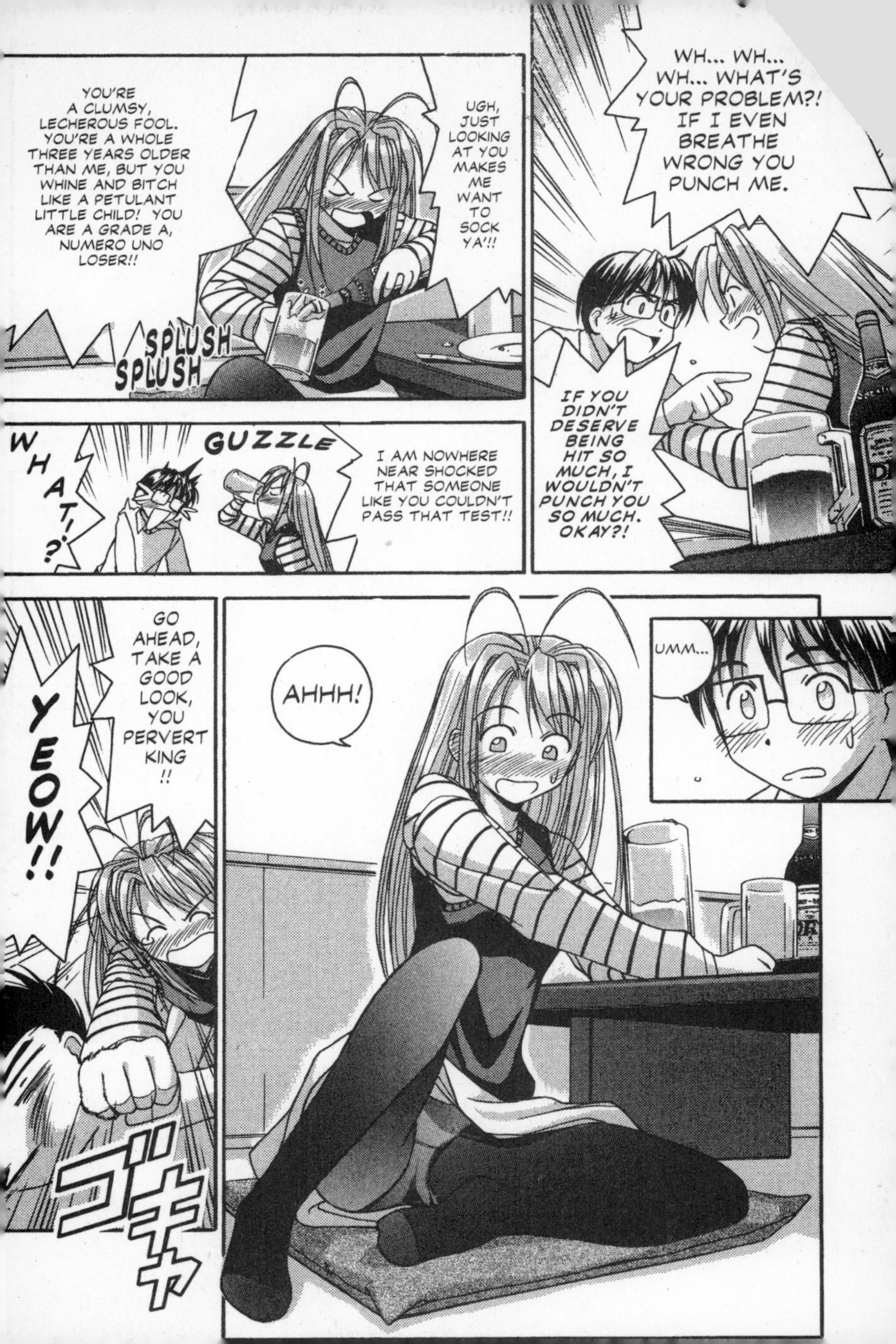
WH... WH... WH... WHAT'S YOUR PROBLEM?! IF I EVEN BREATHE WRONG YOU PUNCH ME.
IF YOU DIDN'T DESERVE BEING HIT SO MUCH, I WOULDN'T PUNCH YOU SO MUCH. OKAY?!
UGH, JUST LOOKING AT YOU MAKES ME WANT TO SOCK YA'!!
YOU'RE A CLUMSY, LECHEROUS FOOL. YOU'RE A WHOLE THREE YEARS OLDER THAN ME, BUT YOU WHINE AND BITCH LIKE A PETULANT LITTLE CHILD! YOU ARE A GRADE A, NUMERO UNO LOSER!!
SPLUSH SPLUSH
I AM NOWHERE NEAR SHOCKED THAT SOMEONE LIKE YOU COULDN'T PASS THAT TEST!!
GUZZLE
WHAT!?
UMM...
AHHH!
GO AHEAD, TAKE A GOOD LOOK, YOU PERVERT KING !!
YEOW!!
ゴキャ

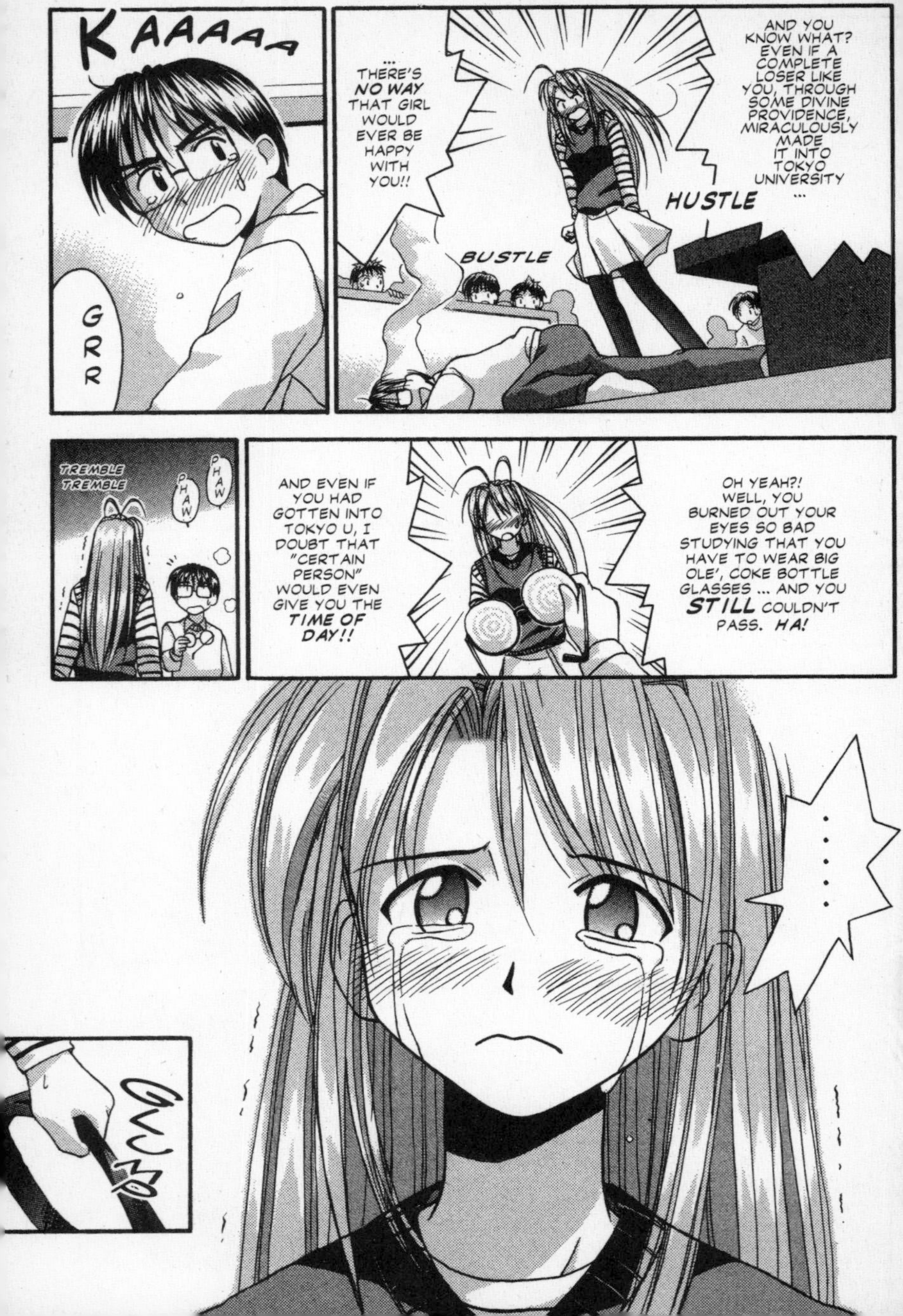
AND YOU KNOW WHAT? EVEN IF A COMPLETE LOSER LIKE YOU, THROUGH SOME DIVINE PROVIDENCE, MIRACULOUSLY MADE IT INTO TOKYO UNIVERSITY ...
... THERE'S NO WAY THAT GIRL WOULD EVER BE HAPPY WITH YOU!!
HUSTLE
BUSTLE
KAAAAA
GRR
OH YEAH?! WELL, YOU BURNED OUT YOUR EYES SO BAD STUDYING THAT YOU HAVE TO WEAR BIG OLE', COKE BOTTLE GLASSES ... AND YOU STILL COULDN'T PASS. HA!
AND EVEN IF YOU HAD GOTTEN INTO TOKYO U, I DOUBT THAT "CERTAIN PERSON" WOULD EVEN GIVE YOU THE TIME OF DAY!!
PHAW PHAW
TREMBLE TREMBLE
.....
GVUMP

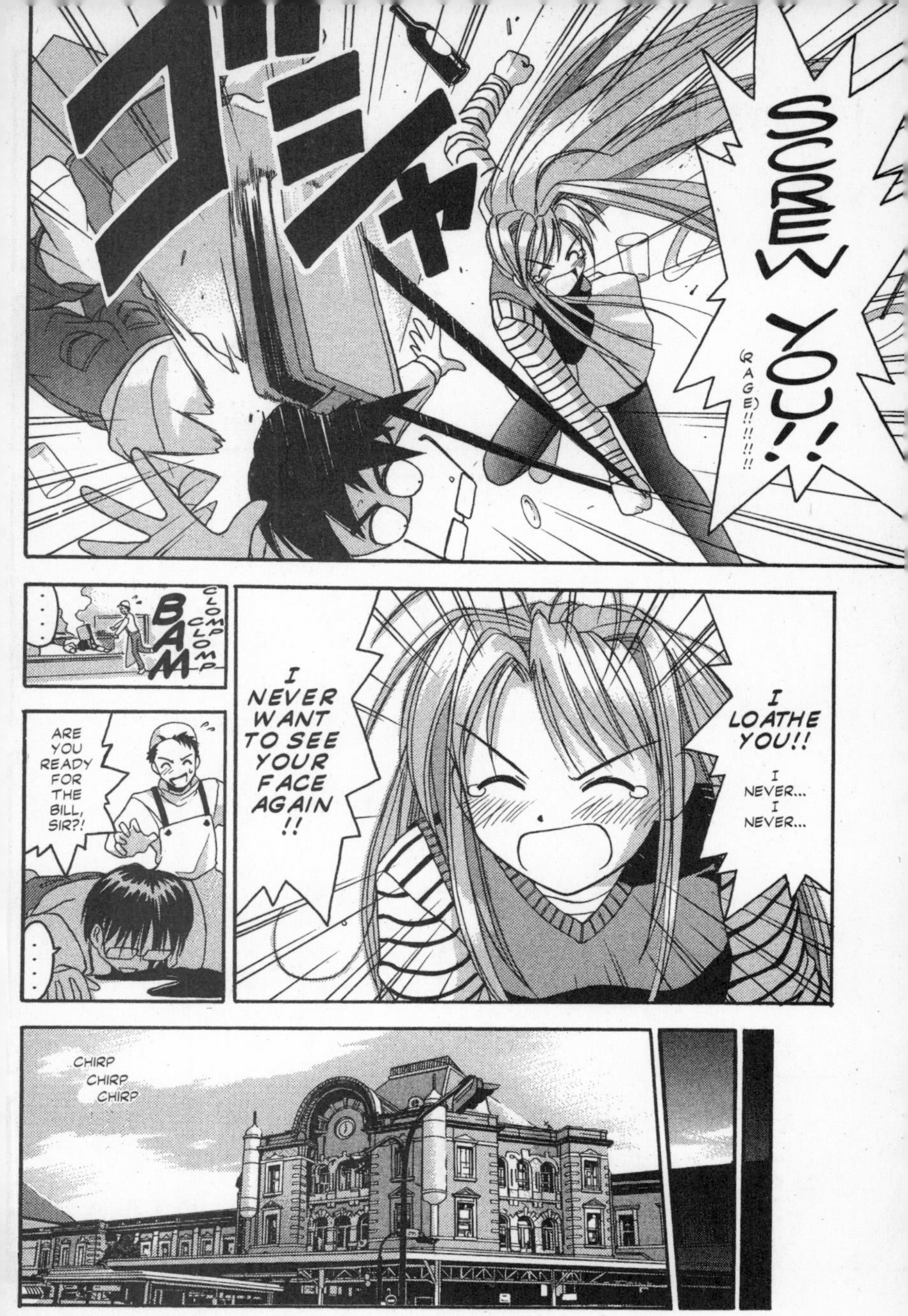
ゴシャ
SCREW YOU!!
(RAGE)!!!!!!
I LOATHE YOU!!
I NEVER... I NEVER...
I NEVER WANT TO SEE YOUR FACE AGAIN!!
...
BAM
CLOMP CLOMP
ARE YOU READY FOR THE BILL, SIR?!
...
CHIRP CHIRP CHIRP

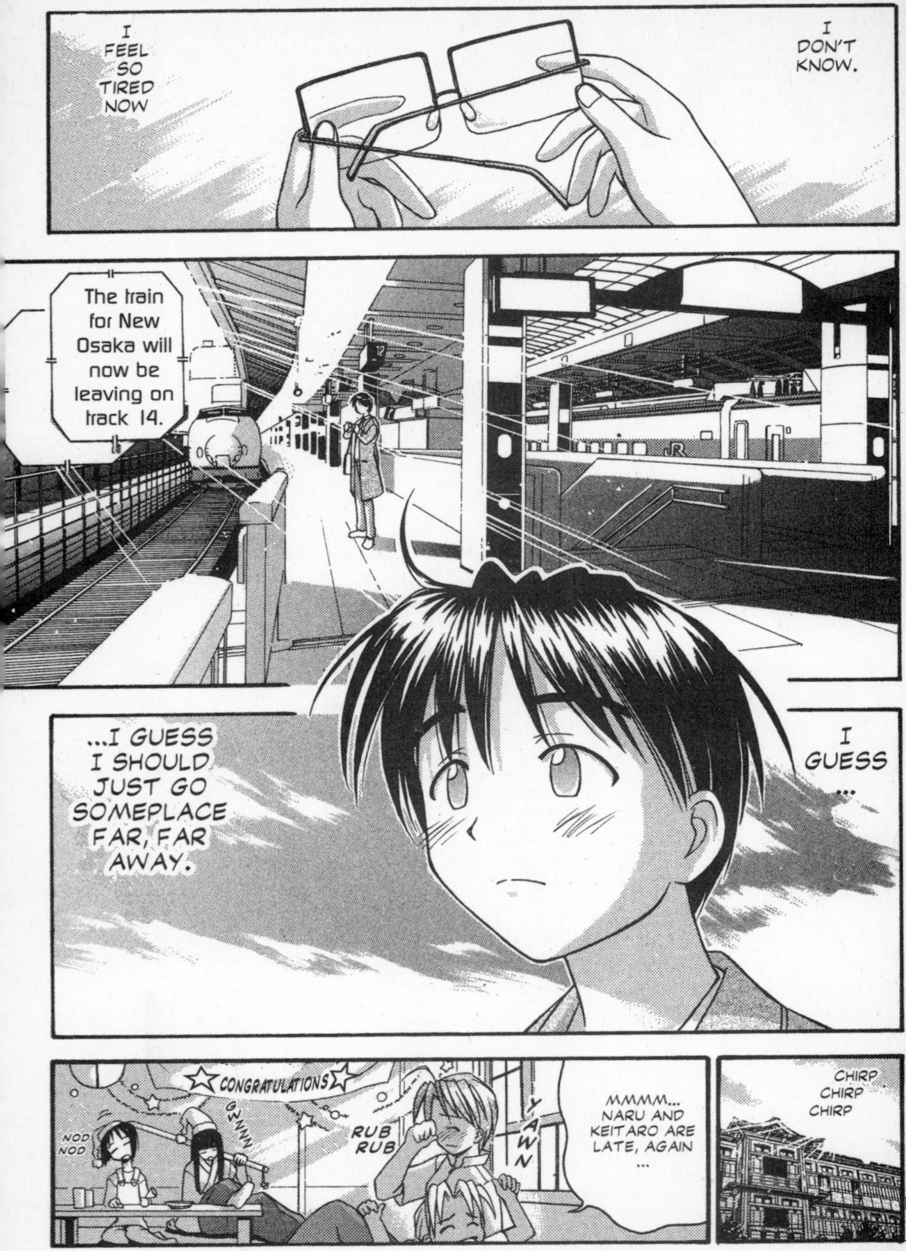
I DON'T KNOW.
I FEEL SO TIRED NOW
The train for New Osaka will now be leaving on track 14.
I GUESS ...
...I GUESS I SHOULD JUST GO SOMEPLACE FAR, FAR AWAY.
CHIRP CHIRP CHIRP
MMMM... NARU AND KEITARO ARE LATE, AGAIN ...
YAWN
RUB RUB
CONGRATULATIONS
GWNNN
NOD NOD

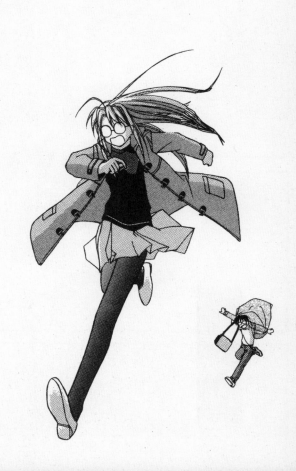

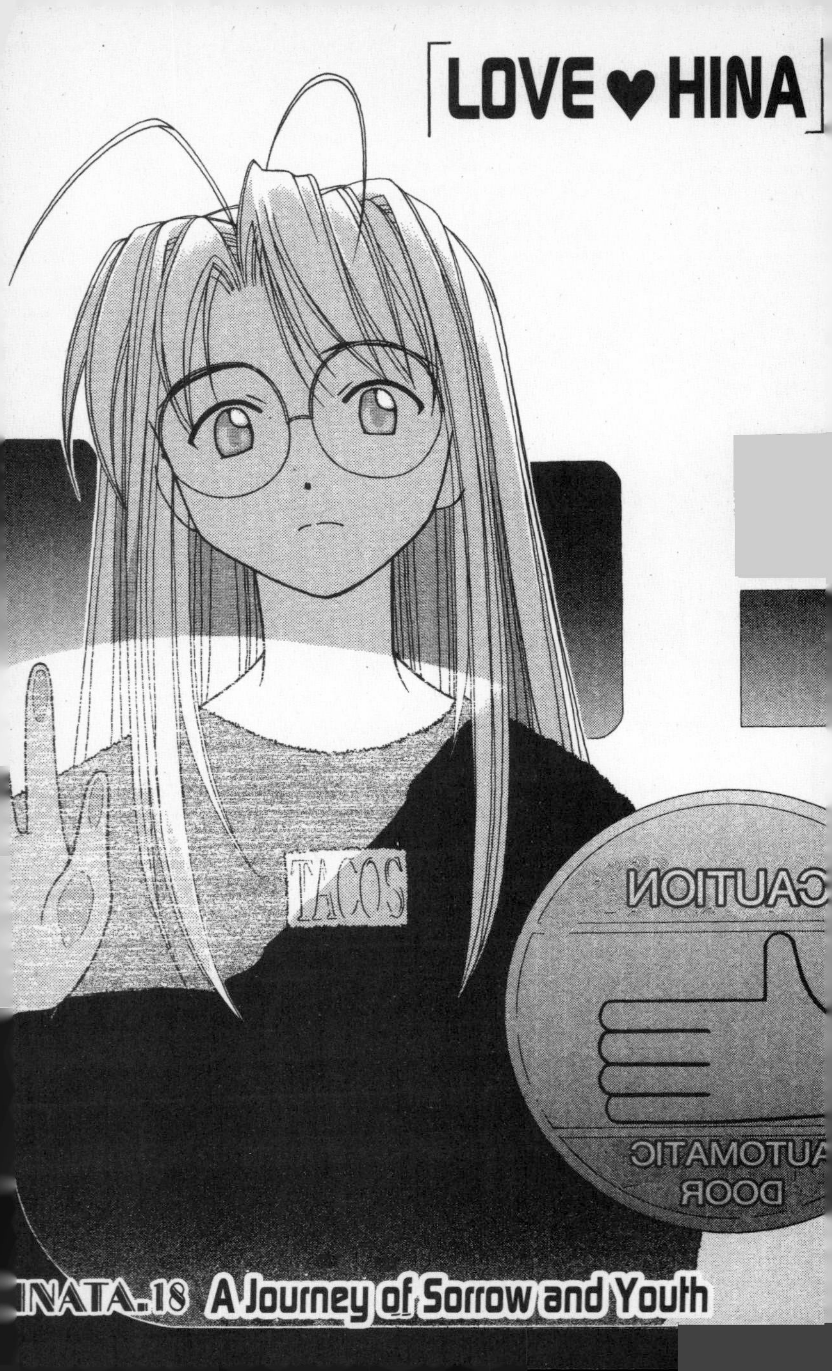
LOVE ♥ HINA
TACOS
CAUTION
AUTOMATIC DOOR
INATA.18 A Journey of Sorrow and Youth

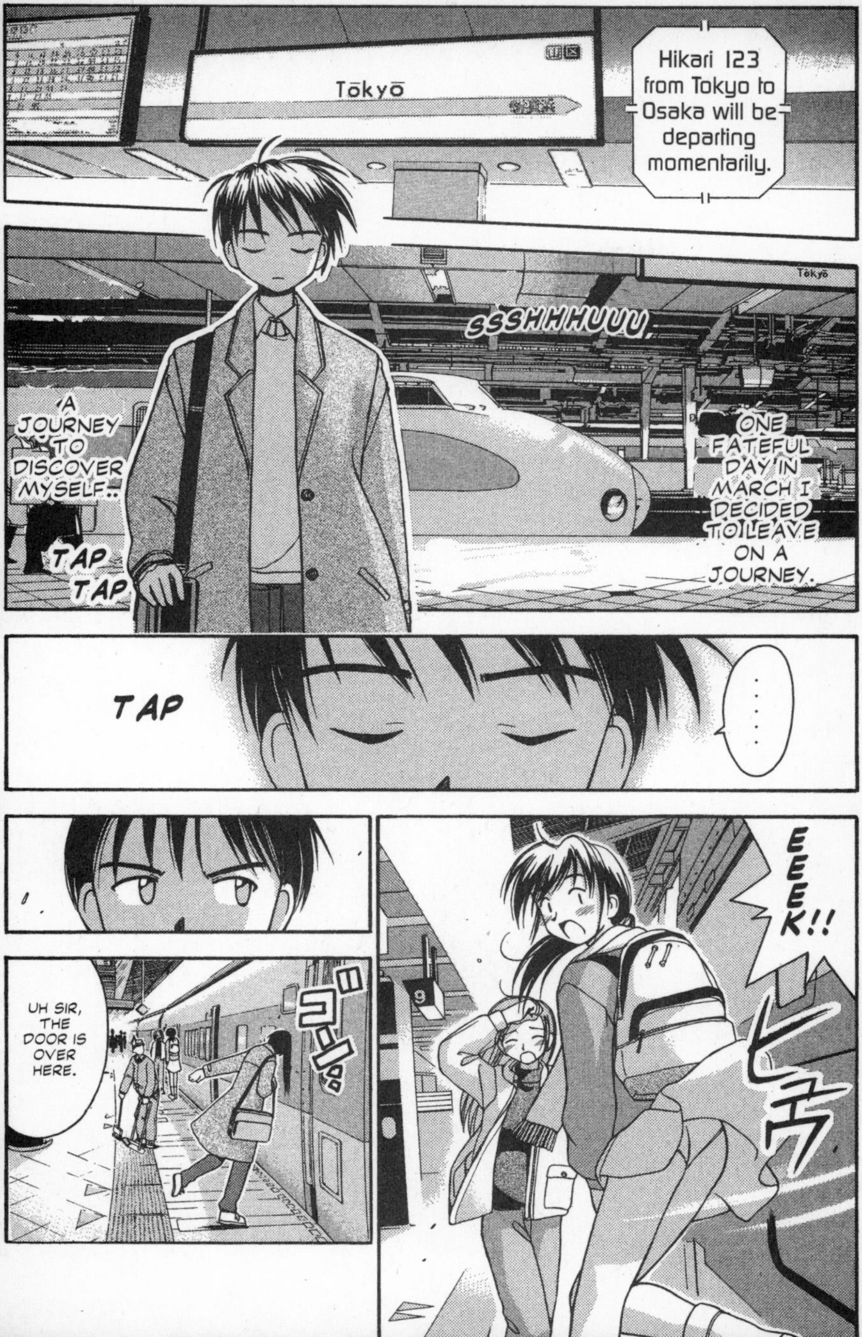
Tōkyo
Hikari 123 from Tokyo to Osaka will be departing momentarily.
Tōkyo
SSSHHHUUU
ONE FATEFUL DAY IN MARCH I DECIDED TO LEAVE ON A JOURNEY.
A JOURNEY TO DISCOVER MYSELF...
TAP TAP
......
TAP
EEEK!!
ヒュウ
!
UH SIR, THE DOOR IS OVER HERE.
ゴロ

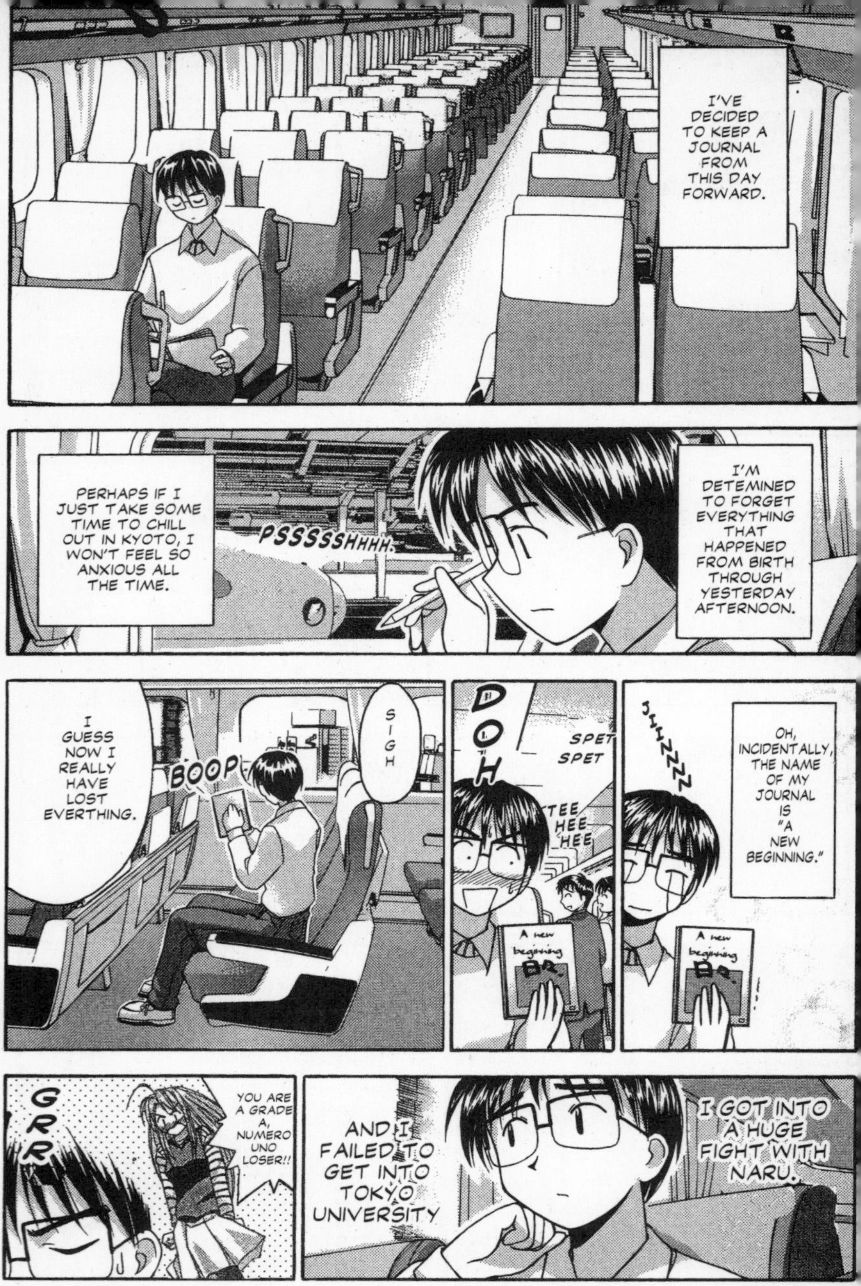
I'VE DECIDED TO KEEP A JOURNAL FROM THIS DAY FORWARD.
I'M DETEMINED TO FORGET EVERYTHING THAT HAPPENED FROM BIRTH THROUGH YESTERDAY AFTERNOON.
PSSSSSHHHH.
PERHAPS IF I JUST TAKE SOME TIME TO CHILL OUT IN KYOTO, I WON'T FEEL SO ANXIOUS ALL THE TIME.
OH, INCIDENTALLY, THE NAME OF MY JOURNAL IS "A NEW BEGINNING."
A new beginning
DOH
SPET SPET
TEE HEE HEE
A new beginning
SIGH
BOOP
I GUESS NOW I REALLY HAVE LOST EVERTHING.
I GOT INTO A HUGE FIGHT WITH NARU.
AND I FAILED TO GET INTO TOKYO UNIVERSITY
GRR
YOU ARE A GRADE A, NUMERO UNO LOSER!!

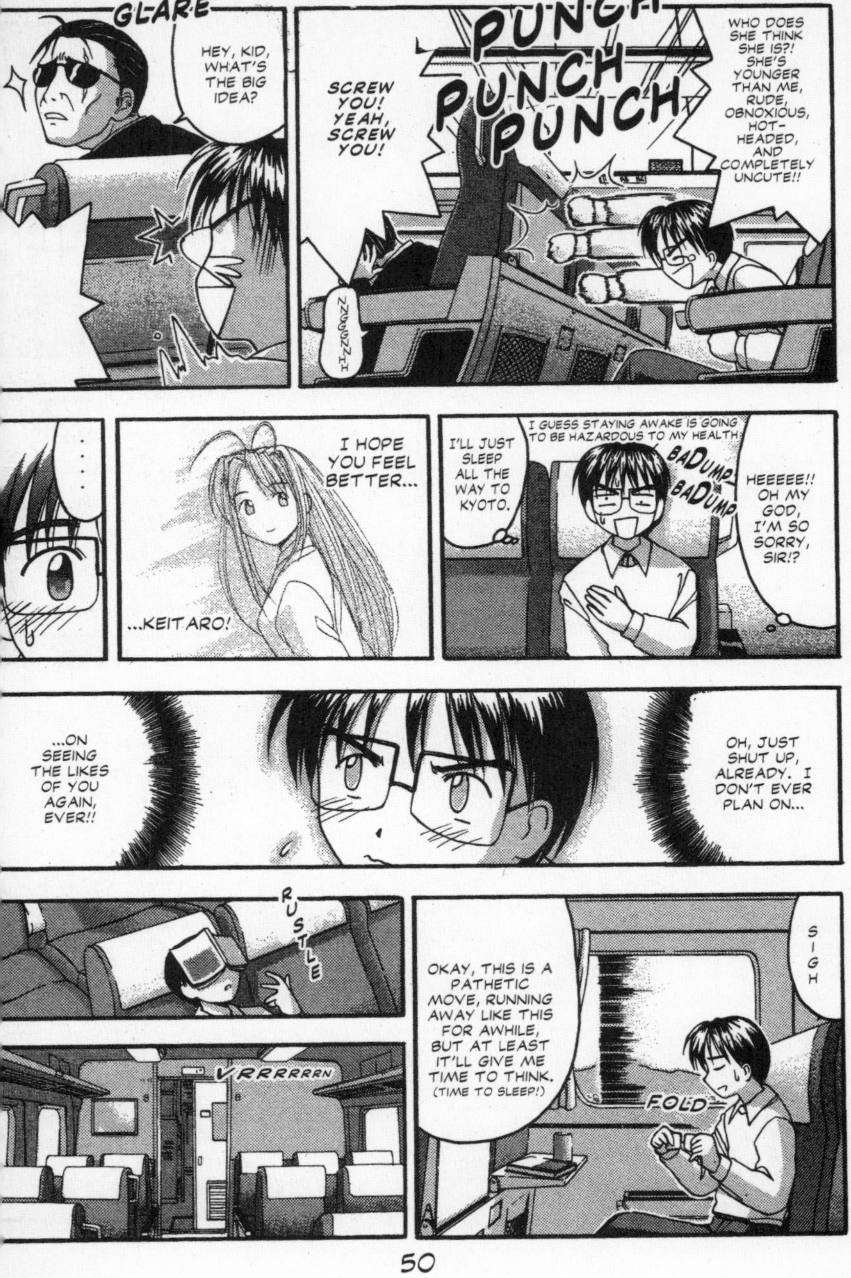
WHO DOES SHE THINK SHE IS?! SHE'S YOUNGER THAN ME, RUDE, OBNOXIOUS, HOT-HEADED, AND COMPLETELY UNCUTE!!
PUNCH PUNCH PUNCH
SCREW YOU! YEAH, SCREW YOU!
NNGGGNHH
GLARE
HEY, KID, WHAT'S THE BIG IDEA?
HEEEEE!! OH MY GOD, I'M SO SORRY, SIR!?
BADUMP BADUMP
I GUESS STAYING AWAKE IS GOING TO BE HAZARDOUS TO MY HEALTH
I'LL JUST SLEEP ALL THE WAY TO KYOTO.
I HOPE YOU FEEL BETTER...
...KEITARO!
....
OH, JUST SHUT UP, ALREADY. I DON'T EVER PLAN ON...
...ON SEEING THE LIKES OF YOU AGAIN, EVER!!
SIGH
OKAY, THIS IS A PATHETIC MOVE, RUNNING AWAY LIKE THIS FOR AWHILE, BUT AT LEAST IT'LL GIVE ME TIME TO THINK. (TIME TO SLEEP!)
FOLD
RUSTLE
VRRRRRRN

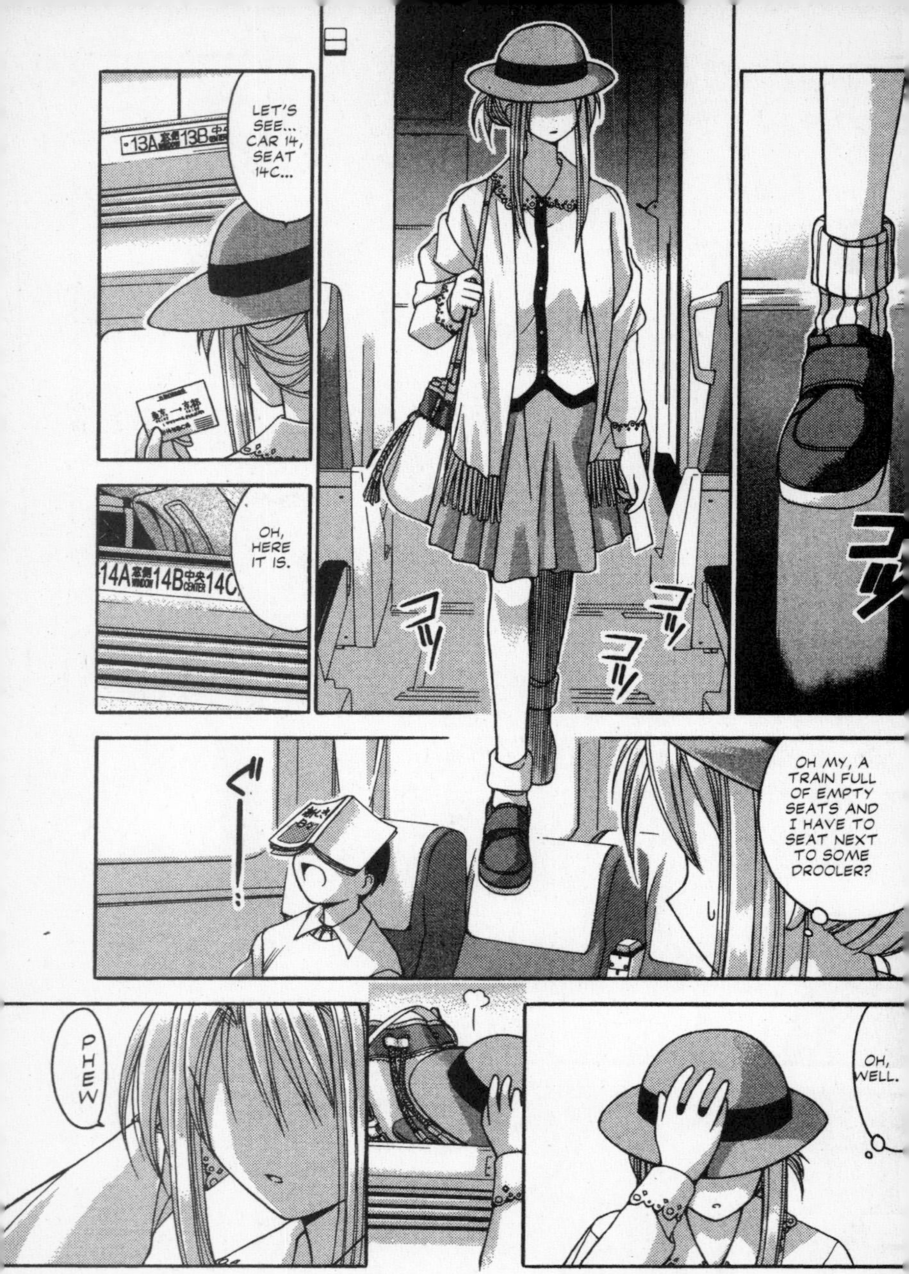

コッ
コツ
コツ
コツ
LET'S SEE... CAR 14, SEAT 14C...
OH, HERE IT IS.
OH MY, A TRAIN FULL OF EMPTY SEATS AND I HAVE TO SEAT NEXT TO SOME DROOLER?
ぐー!!
OH, WELL.
PHEW

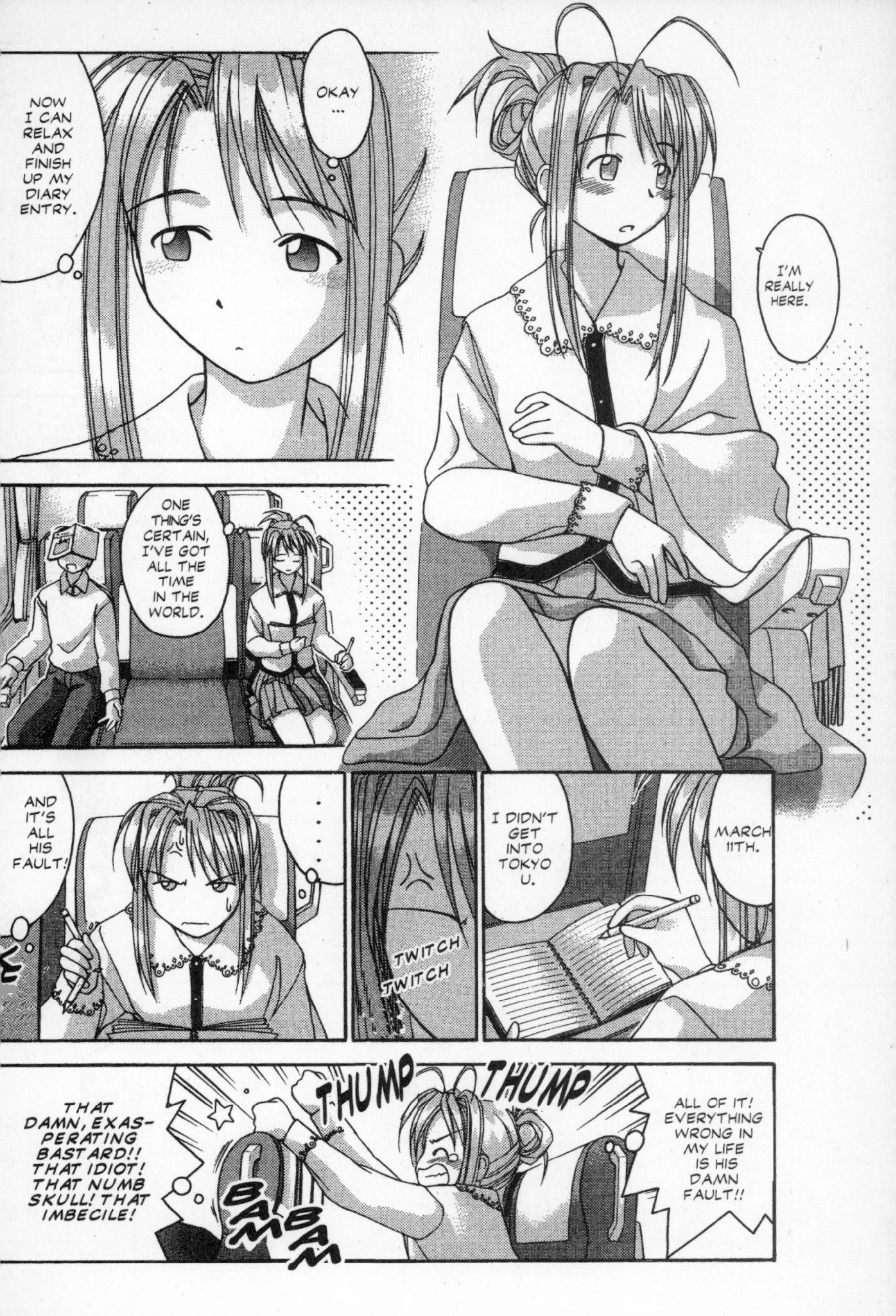
I'M REALLY HERE.
OKAY ...
NOW I CAN RELAX AND FINISH UP MY DIARY ENTRY.
ONE THING'S CERTAIN, I'VE GOT ALL THE TIME IN THE WORLD.
MARCH 11TH.
I DIDN'T GET INTO TOKYO U.
TWITCH TWITCH
. . . .
AND IT'S ALL HIS FAULT!
THUMP THUMP
ALL OF IT! EVERYTHING WRONG IN MY LIFE IS HIS DAMN FAULT!!
THAT DAMN, EXAS-PERATING BASTARD!! THAT IDIOT! THAT NUMB SKULL! THAT IMBECILE!
BAM BAM

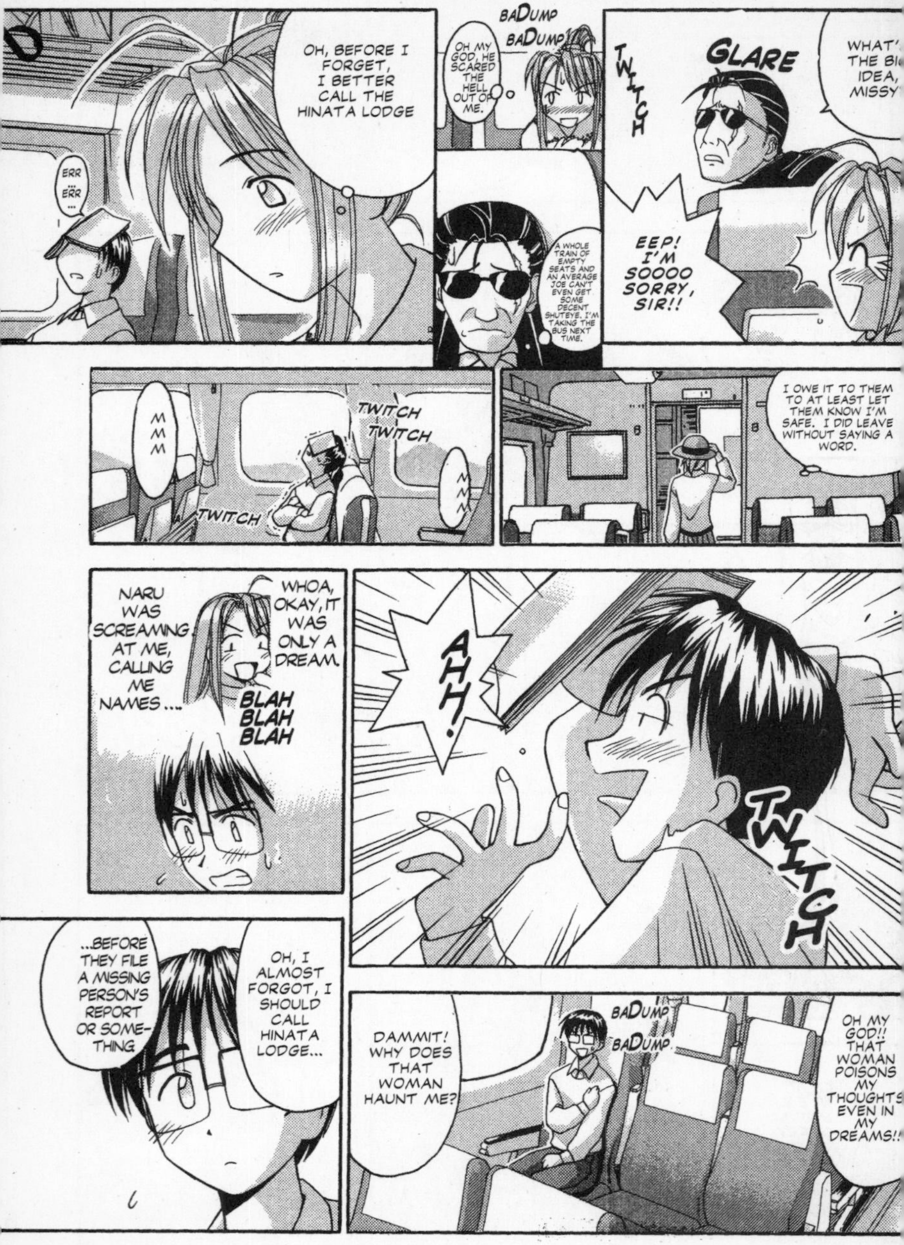
WHAT' THE BI IDEA, MISSY
GLARE
TWITCH
EEP! I'M SOOOO SORRY, SIR!!
BADUMP BADUMP
OH MY GOD, HE SCARED THE HELL OUT OF ME.
A WHOLE TRAIN OF EMPTY SEATS AND AN AVERAGE JOE CAN'T EVEN GET SOME DECENT SHUTEYE. I'M TAKING THE BUS NEXT TIME.
OH, BEFORE I FORGET, I BETTER CALL THE HINATA LODGE
ERR ... ERR ...
I OWE IT TO THEM TO AT LEAST LET THEM KNOW I'M SAFE. I DID LEAVE WITHOUT SAYING A WORD.
MMM
TWITCH TWITCH
MMM
TWITCH
AHH!
TWITCH
WHOA, OKAY, IT WAS ONLY A DREAM.
NARU WAS SCREAMING AT ME, CALLING ME NAMES....
BLAH BLAH BLAH
OH MY GOD!! THAT WOMAN POISONS MY THOUGHTS EVEN IN MY DREAMS!!
BADUMP BADUMP
DAMMIT! WHY DOES THAT WOMAN HAUNT ME?
OH, I ALMOST FORGOT, I SHOULD CALL HINATA LODGE...
...BEFORE THEY FILE A MISSING PERSON'S REPORT OR SOMETHING.

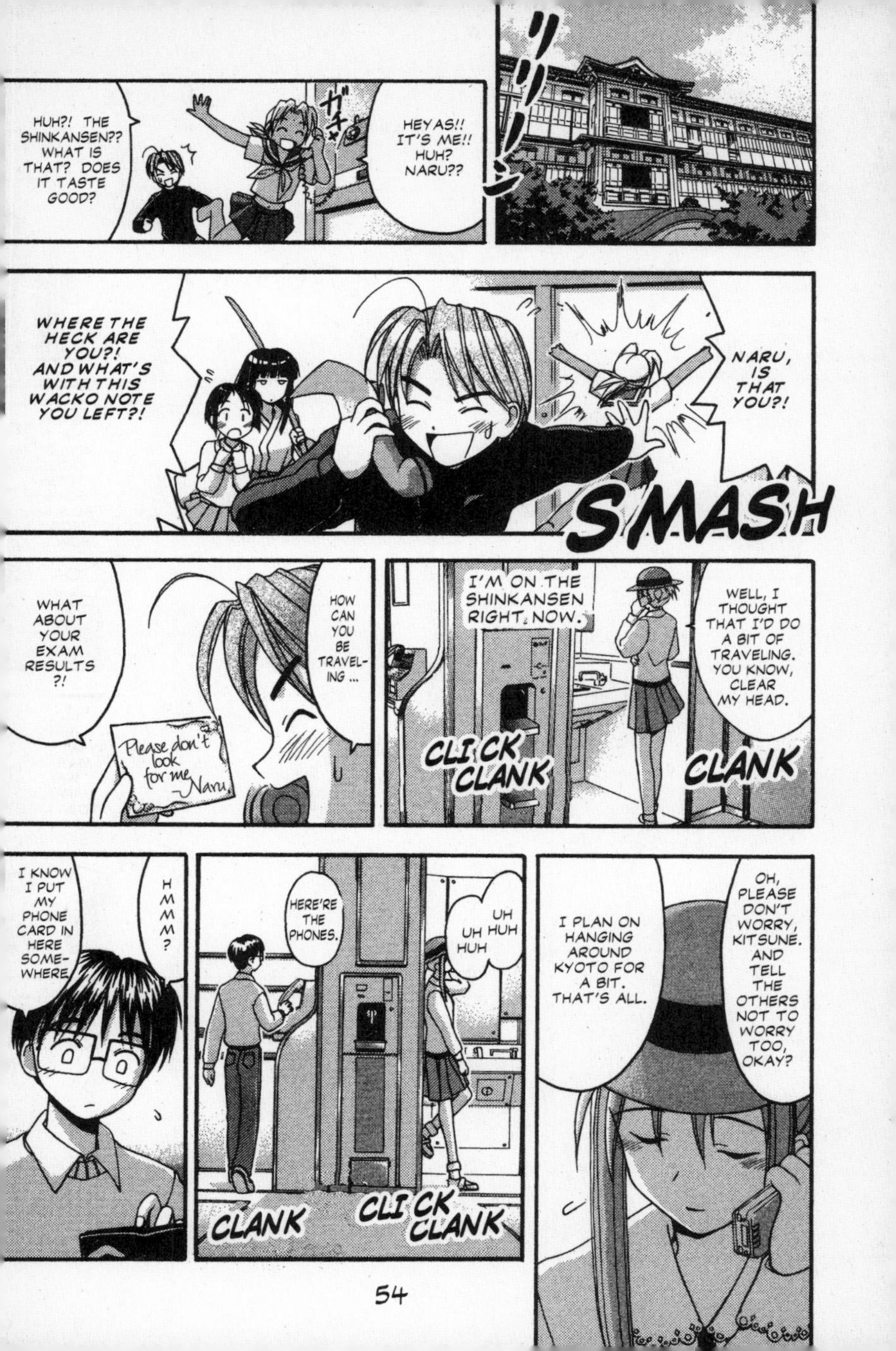

リリリーン
HEYAS!! IT'S ME!! HUH? NARU??
ガチャ
HUH?! THE SHINKANSEN?? WHAT IS THAT? DOES IT TASTE GOOD?
NARU, IS THAT YOU?!
WHERE THE HECK ARE YOU?! AND WHAT'S WITH THIS WACKO NOTE YOU LEFT?!
SMASH
WELL, I THOUGHT THAT I'D DO A BIT OF TRAVELING. YOU KNOW, CLEAR MY HEAD.
I'M ON THE SHINKANSEN RIGHT NOW.
CLANK
CLICK CLANK
HOW CAN YOU BE TRAVEL-ING ...
WHAT ABOUT YOUR EXAM RESULTS ?!
Please don't look for me ~Naru
OH, PLEASE DON'T WORRY, KITSUNE. AND TELL THE OTHERS NOT TO WORRY TOO, OKAY?
I PLAN ON HANGING AROUND KYOTO FOR A BIT. THAT'S ALL.
UH HUH UH HUH
HERE'RE THE PHONES.
CLICK CLANK
CLANK
HMMM?
I KNOW I PUT MY PHONE CARD IN HERE SOME-WHERE

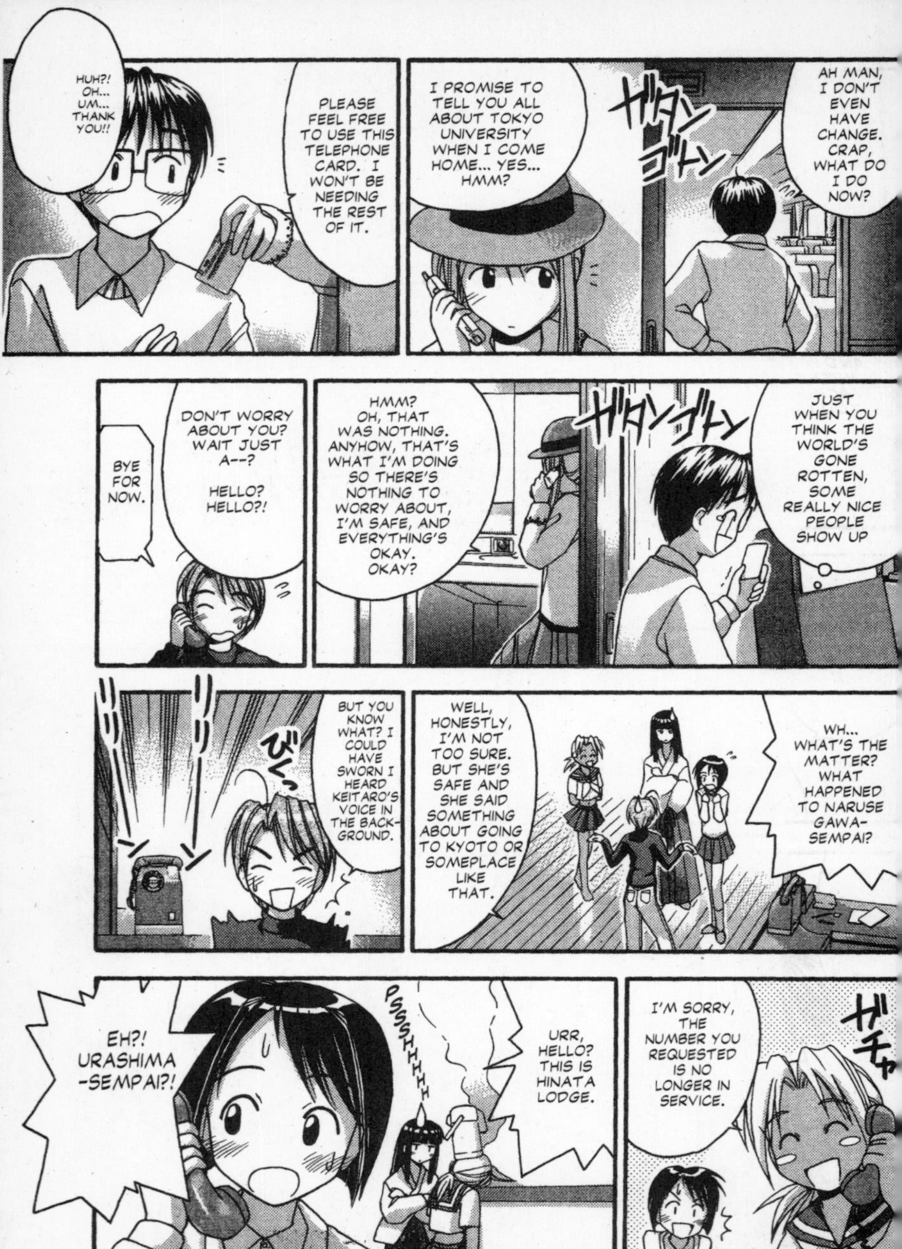
ガタン
ゴトン
AH MAN, I DON'T EVEN HAVE CHANGE. CRAP, WHAT DO I DO NOW?
I PROMISE TO TELL YOU ALL ABOUT TOKYO UNIVERSITY WHEN I COME HOME... YES... HMM?
PLEASE FEEL FREE TO USE THIS TELEPHONE CARD. I WON'T BE NEEDING THE REST OF IT.
HUH?! OH... UM... THANK YOU!!
ガタンゴトン
JUST WHEN YOU THINK THE WORLD'S GONE ROTTEN, SOME REALLY NICE PEOPLE SHOW UP
HMM? OH, THAT WAS NOTHING. ANYHOW, THAT'S WHAT I'M DOING SO THERE'S NOTHING TO WORRY ABOUT, I'M SAFE, AND EVERYTHING'S OKAY. OKAY?
DON'T WORRY ABOUT YOU? WAIT JUST A--? HELLO? HELLO?!
BYE FOR NOW.
WH... WHAT'S THE MATTER? WHAT HAPPENED TO NARUSE GAWA-SEMPAI?
WELL, HONESTLY, I'M NOT TOO SURE. BUT SHE'S SAFE AND SHE SAID SOMETHING ABOUT GOING TO KYOTO OR SOMEPLACE LIKE THAT.
BUT YOU KNOW WHAT? I COULD HAVE SWORN I HEARD KEITARO'S VOICE IN THE BACK-GROUND.
びくっ
ガチャ
I'M SORRY, THE NUMBER YOU REQUESTED IS NO LONGER IN SERVICE.
URR, HELLO? THIS IS HINATA LODGE.
PSSSHHHHH
EH?! URASHIMA -SEMPAI?!

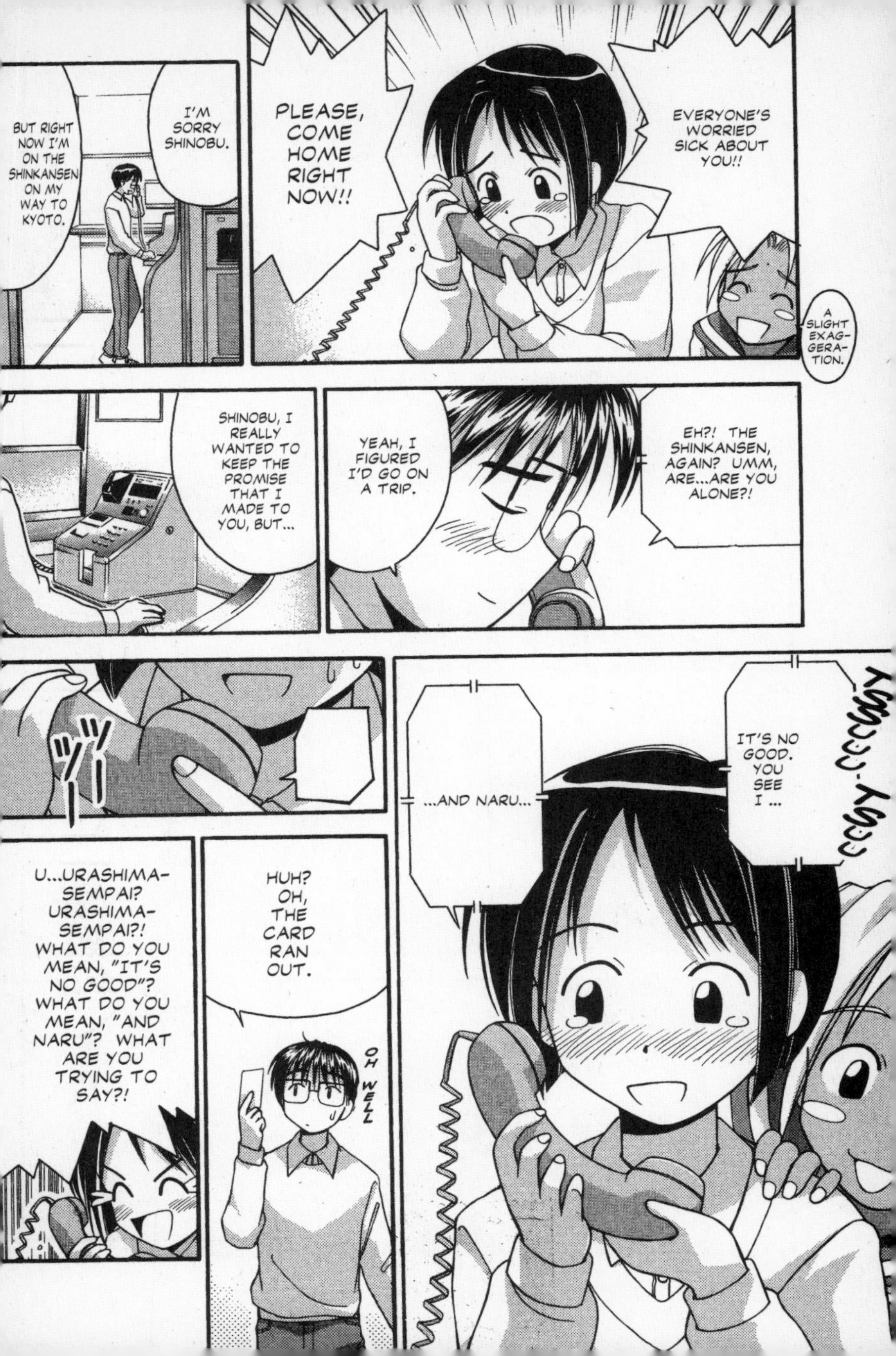
EVERYONE'S WORRIED SICK ABOUT YOU!!
PLEASE, COME HOME RIGHT NOW!!
A SLIGHT EXAGGERATION.
I'M SORRY SHINOBU.
BUT RIGHT NOW I'M ON THE SHINKANSEN ON MY WAY TO KYOTO.
EH?! THE SHINKANSEN, AGAIN? UMM, ARE...ARE YOU ALONE?!
YEAH, I FIGURED I'D GO ON A TRIP.
SHINOBU, I REALLY WANTED TO KEEP THE PROMISE THAT I MADE TO YOU, BUT...
IT'S NO GOOD. YOU SEE I ...
...AND NARU...
HUH? OH, THE CARD RAN OUT.
OH WELL
U...URASHIMA-SEMPAI? URASHIMA-SEMPAI?! WHAT DO YOU MEAN, "IT'S NO GOOD"? WHAT DO YOU MEAN, "AND NARU"? WHAT ARE YOU TRYING TO SAY?!

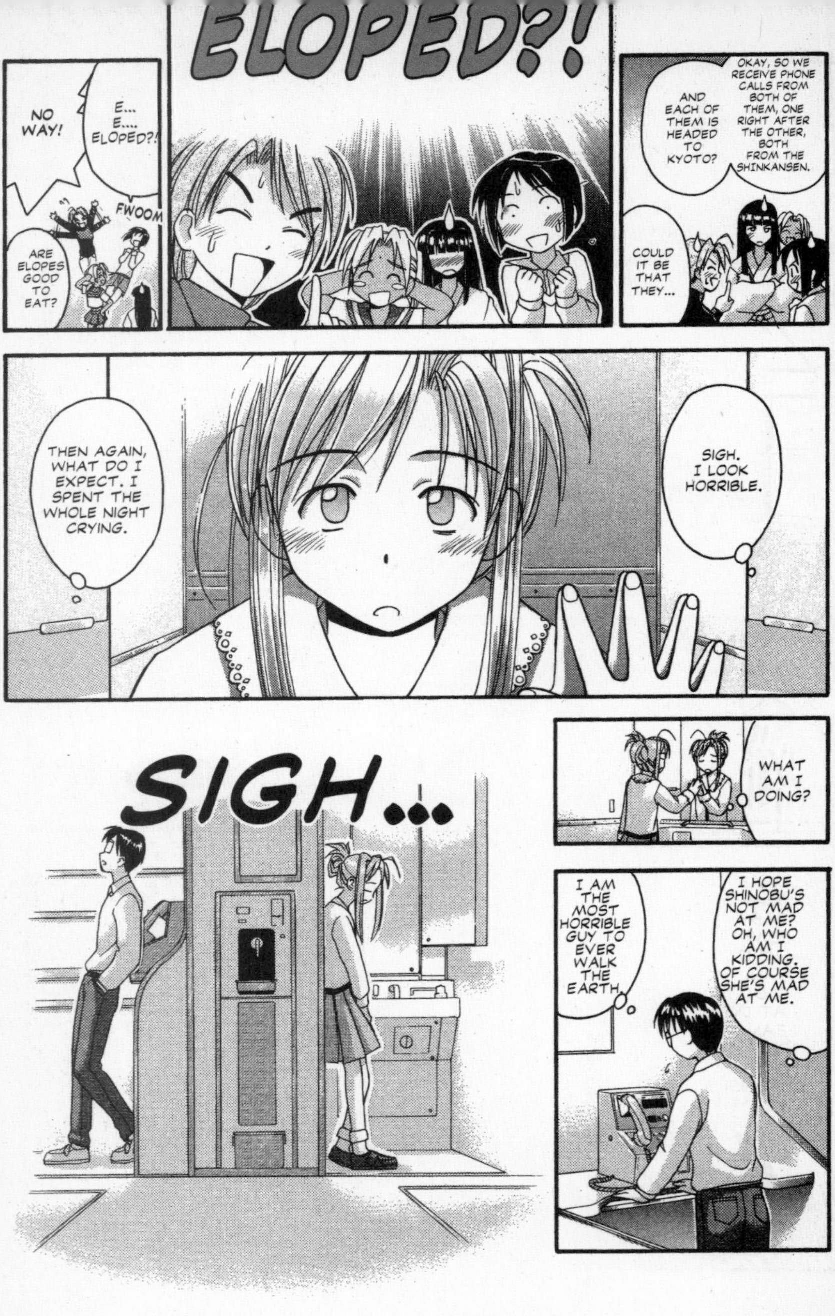
ELOPED?!
OKAY, SO WE RECEIVE PHONE CALLS FROM BOTH OF THEM, ONE RIGHT AFTER THE OTHER, BOTH FROM THE SHINKANSEN.
AND EACH OF THEM IS HEADED TO KYOTO?
COULD IT BE THAT THEY...
E... E.... ELOPED?!
NO WAY!
FWOOM
ARE ELOPES GOOD TO EAT?
SIGH. I LOOK HORRIBLE.
THEN AGAIN, WHAT DO I EXPECT. I SPENT THE WHOLE NIGHT CRYING.
WHAT AM I DOING?
I HOPE SHINOBU'S NOT MAD AT ME? OH, WHO AM I KIDDING. OF COURSE SHE'S MAD AT ME.
I AM THE MOST HORRIBLE GUY TO EVER WALK THE EARTH.
SIGH...

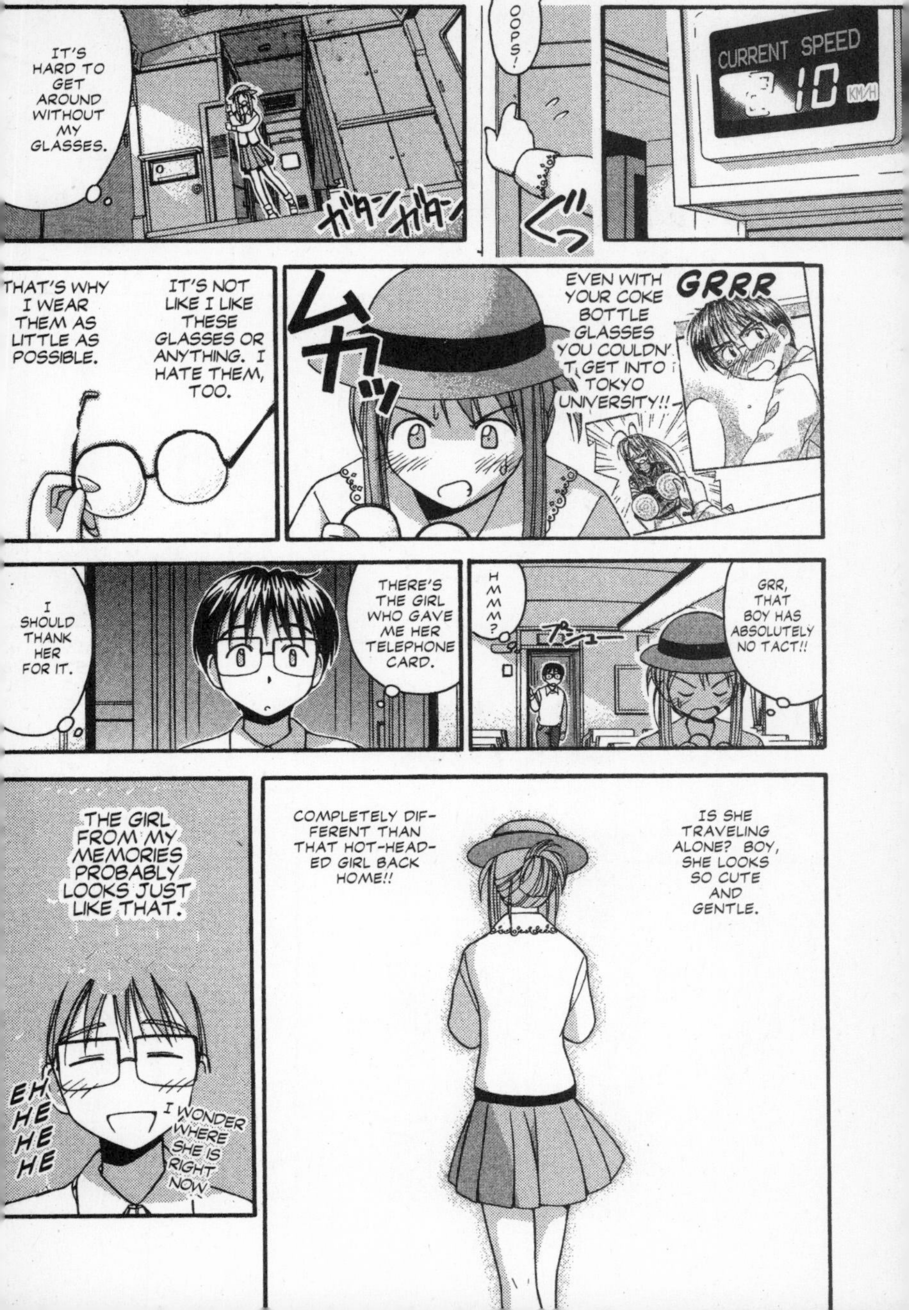
CURRENT SPEED
10 KM/H
OOPS!
ぐっ
IT'S HARD TO GET AROUND WITHOUT MY GLASSES.
ガタンガタン
GRRR
EVEN WITH YOUR COKE BOTTLE GLASSES YOU COULDN'T GET INTO TOKYO UNIVERSITY!!
ムカッ
IT'S NOT LIKE I LIKE THESE GLASSES OR ANYTHING. I HATE THEM, TOO.
THAT'S WHY I WEAR THEM AS LITTLE AS POSSIBLE.
GRR, THAT BOY HAS ABSOLUTELY NO TACT!!
プシュー
HMMM?
THERE'S THE GIRL WHO GAVE ME HER TELEPHONE CARD.
I SHOULD THANK HER FOR IT.
IS SHE TRAVELING ALONE? BOY, SHE LOOKS SO CUTE AND GENTLE.
COMPLETELY DIF-FERENT THAN THAT HOT-HEAD-ED GIRL BACK HOME!!
THE GIRL FROM MY MEMORIES PROBABLY LOOKS JUST LIKE THAT.
I WONDER WHERE SHE IS RIGHT NOW
EH HE HE HE

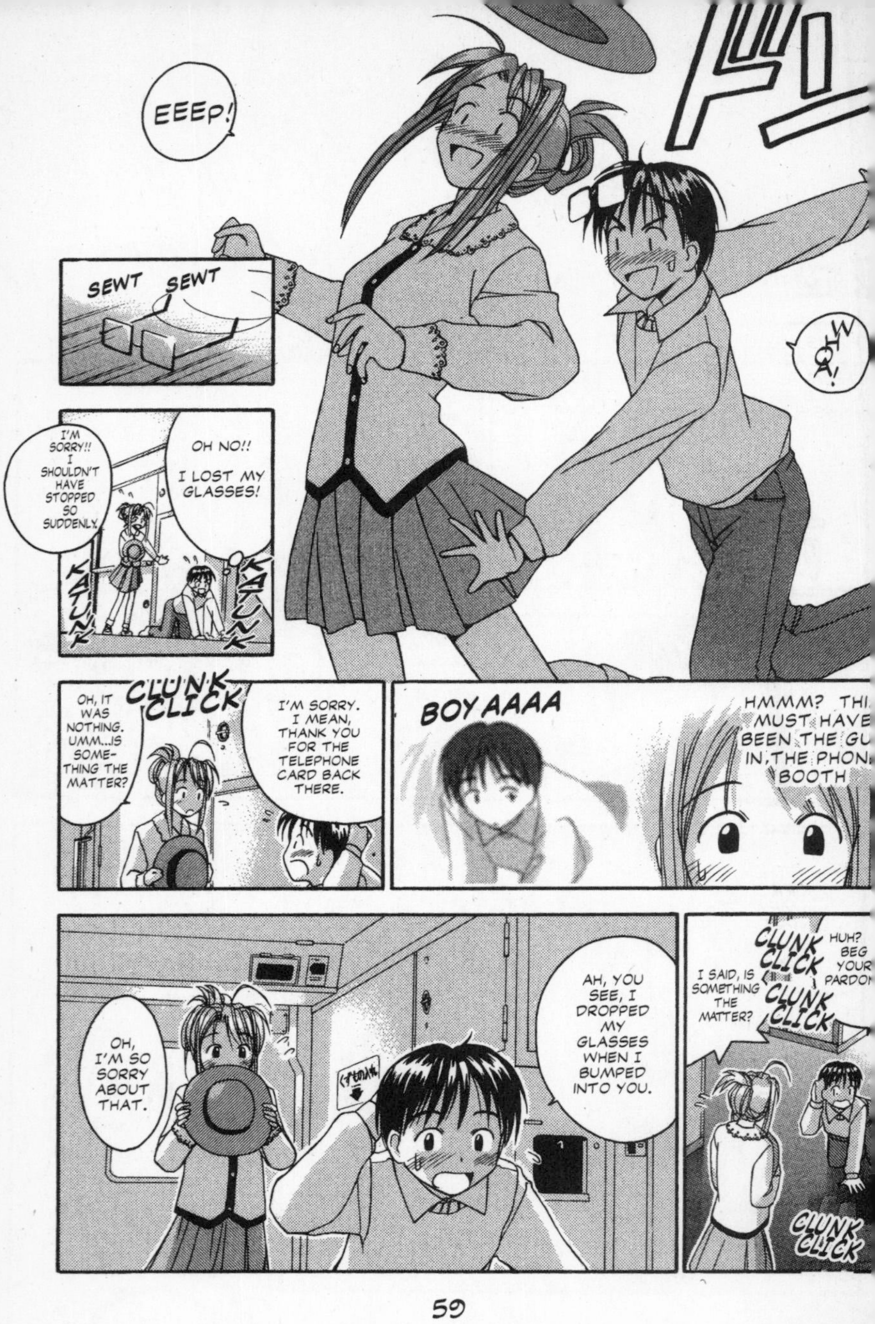
EEEP!
WHOA!
SEWT SEWT
OH NO!! I LOST MY GLASSES!
I'M SORRY!! I SHOULDN'T HAVE STOPPED SO SUDDENLY.
KATUNK
KATUNK
HMMM? THI MUST HAVE BEEN THE GU IN THE PHON BOOTH
BOYAAAA
I'M SORRY. I MEAN, THANK YOU FOR THE TELEPHONE CARD BACK THERE.
CLUNK CLICK
OH, IT WAS NOTHING. UMM...IS SOMETHING THE MATTER?
HUH? BEG YOUR PARDO
CLUNK CLICK
I SAID, IS SOMETHING THE MATTER?
CLUNK CLICK
CLUNK CLICK
AH, YOU SEE, I DROPPED MY GLASSES WHEN I BUMPED INTO YOU.
OH, I'M SO SORRY ABOUT THAT.

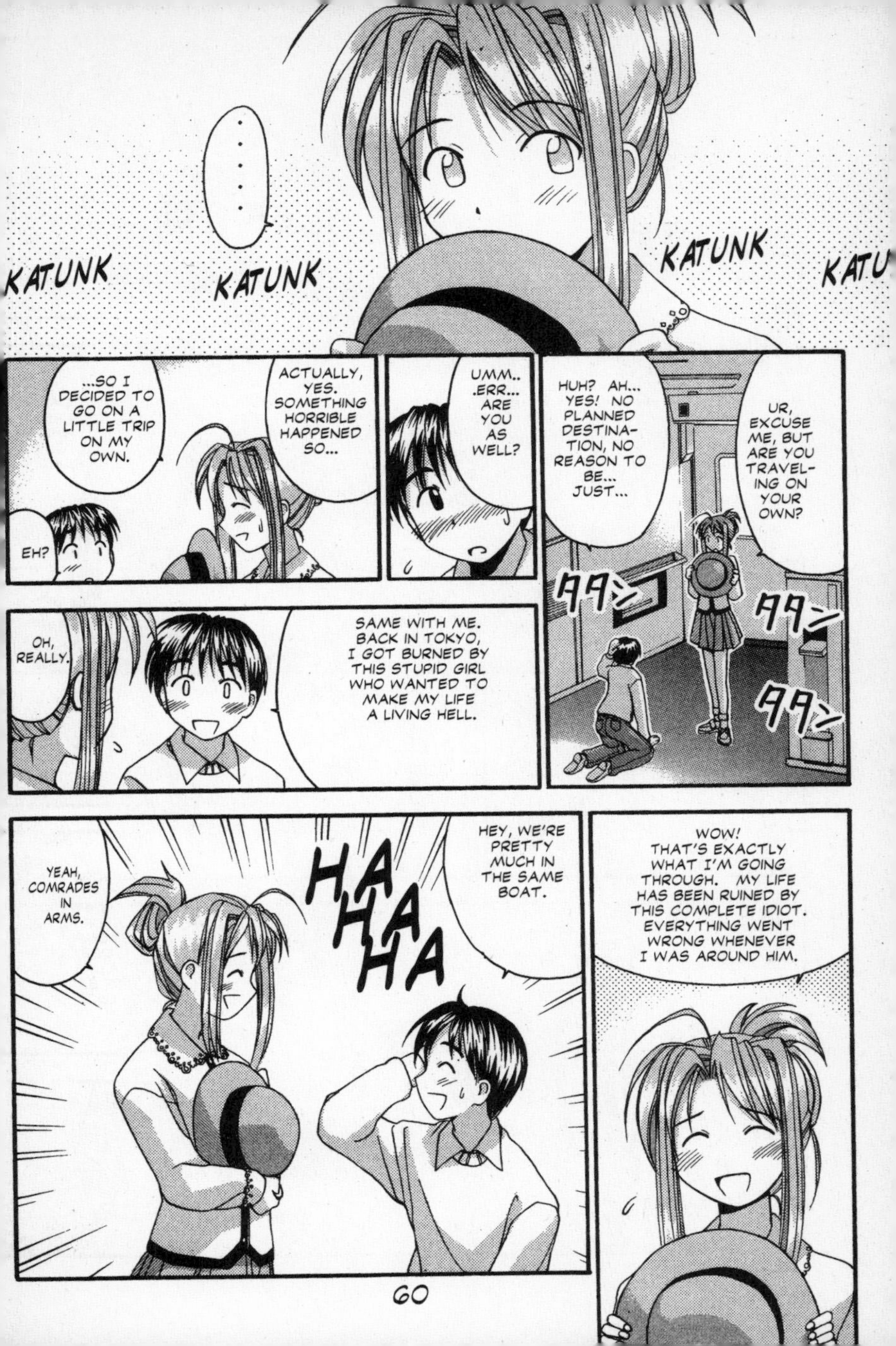
......
KATU
KATUNK
KATUNK
KATUNK
UR, EXCUSE ME, BUT ARE YOU TRAVEL-ING ON YOUR OWN?
HUH? AH... YES! NO PLANNED DESTINA-TION, NO REASON TO BE... JUST...
タタン
タタン
タタン
UMM.. .ERR... ARE YOU AS WELL?
ACTUALLY, YES. SOMETHING HORRIBLE HAPPENED SO...
...SO I DECIDED TO GO ON A LITTLE TRIP ON MY OWN.
EH?
SAME WITH ME. BACK IN TOKYO, I GOT BURNED BY THIS STUPID GIRL WHO WANTED TO MAKE MY LIFE A LIVING HELL.
OH, REALLY.
WOW! THAT'S EXACTLY WHAT I'M GOING THROUGH. MY LIFE HAS BEEN RUINED BY THIS COMPLETE IDIOT. EVERYTHING WENT WRONG WHENEVER I WAS AROUND HIM.
HEY, WE'RE PRETTY MUCH IN THE SAME BOAT.
HA HA HA HA
YEAH, COMRADES IN ARMS.

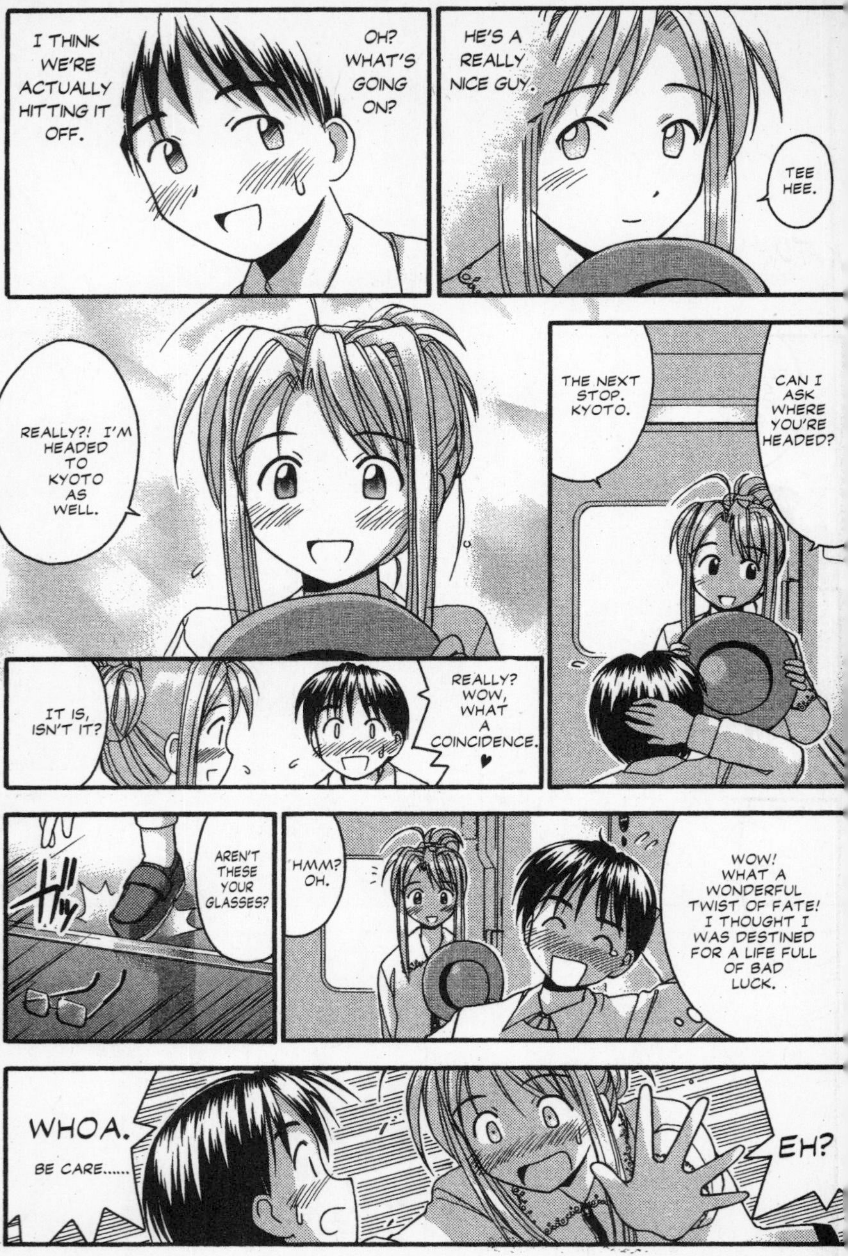
HE'S A REALLY NICE GUY.
TEE HEE.
OH? WHAT'S GOING ON?
I THINK WE'RE ACTUALLY HITTING IT OFF.
CAN I ASK WHERE YOU'RE HEADED?
THE NEXT STOP. KYOTO.
REALLY?! I'M HEADED TO KYOTO AS WELL.
REALLY? WOW, WHAT A COINCIDENCE. ♥
IT IS, ISN'T IT?
WOW! WHAT A WONDERFUL TWIST OF FATE! I THOUGHT I WAS DESTINED FOR A LIFE FULL OF BAD LUCK.
HMM? OH.
AREN'T THESE YOUR GLASSES?
EH?
WHOA.
BE CARE......

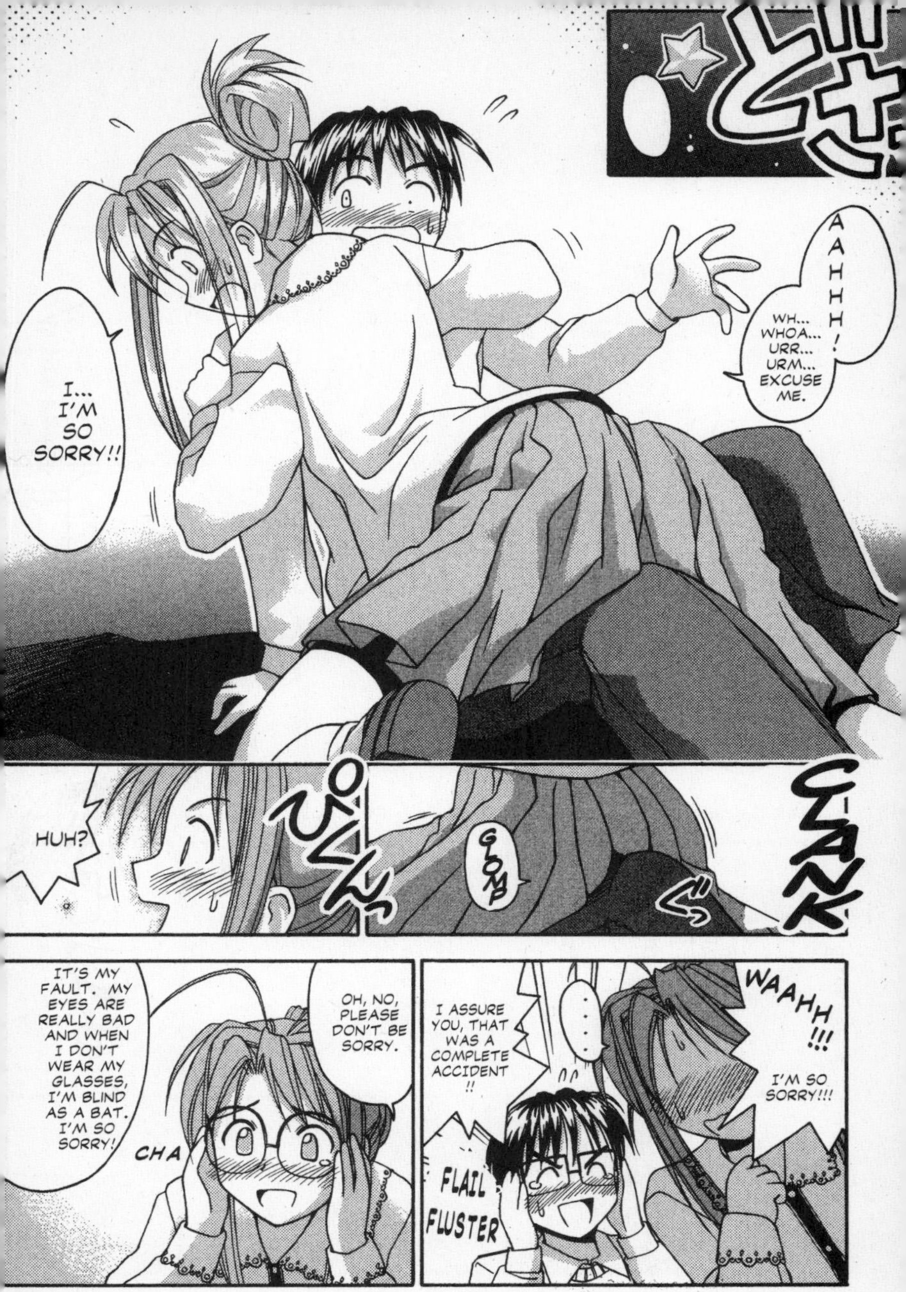
AAHHH!
WH... WHOA... URR... URM... EXCUSE ME.
I... I'M SO SORRY!!
CLANK
GLOMP
HUH?
WAAHH!!!
I'M SO SORRY!!!
...
I ASSURE YOU, THAT WAS A COMPLETE ACCIDENT!!
FLAIL FLUSTER
OH, NO, PLEASE DON'T BE SORRY.
IT'S MY FAULT. MY EYES ARE REALLY BAD AND WHEN I DON'T WEAR MY GLASSES, I'M BLIND AS A BAT. I'M SO SORRY!
CHA

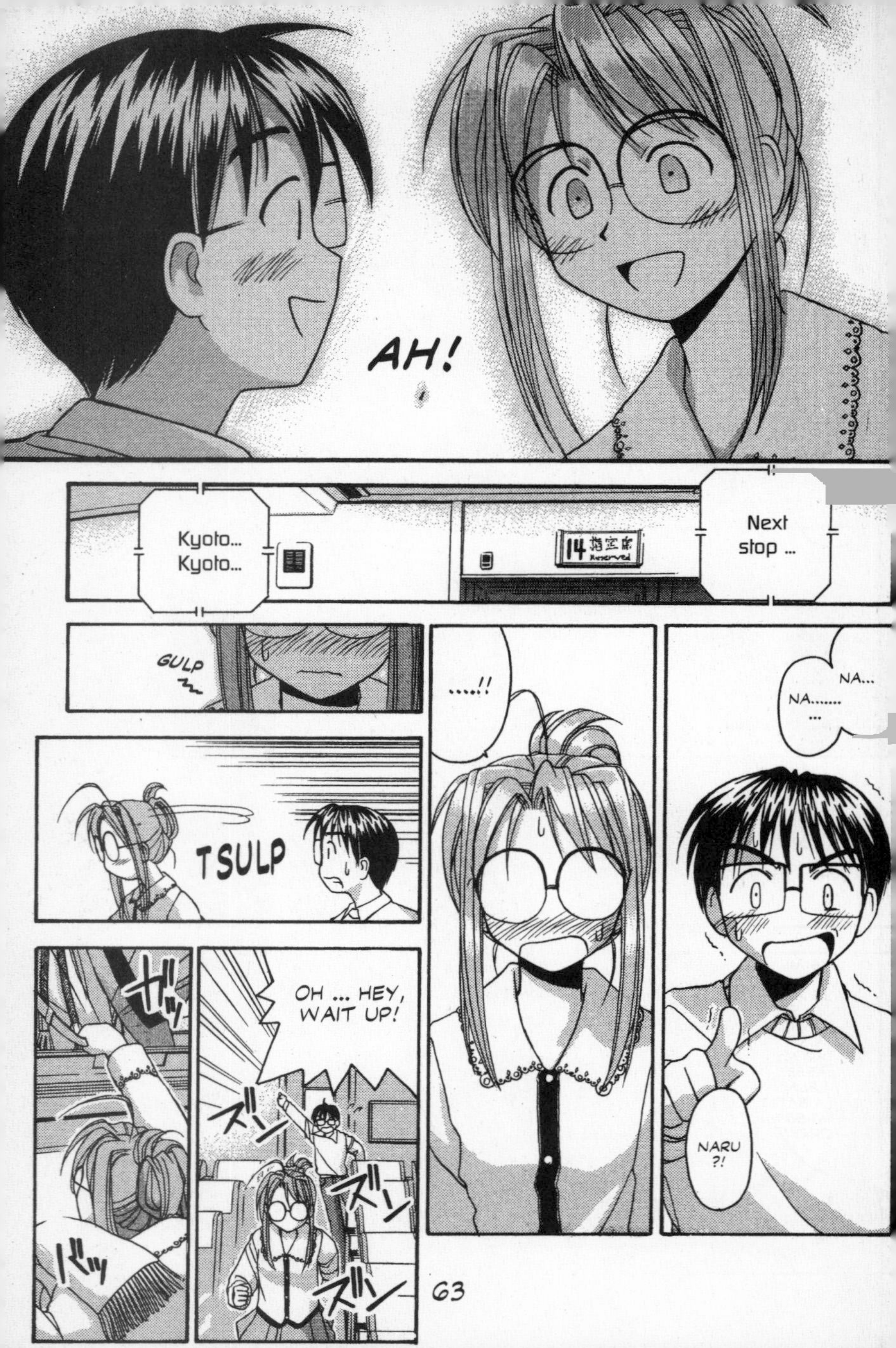
AH!
Next stop ...
Kyoto... Kyoto...
NA... NA....... ...
NARU ?!
.....!!
GULP
TSULP
OH ... HEY, WAIT UP!
ズン
ズン
ズン
ザッ
バッ

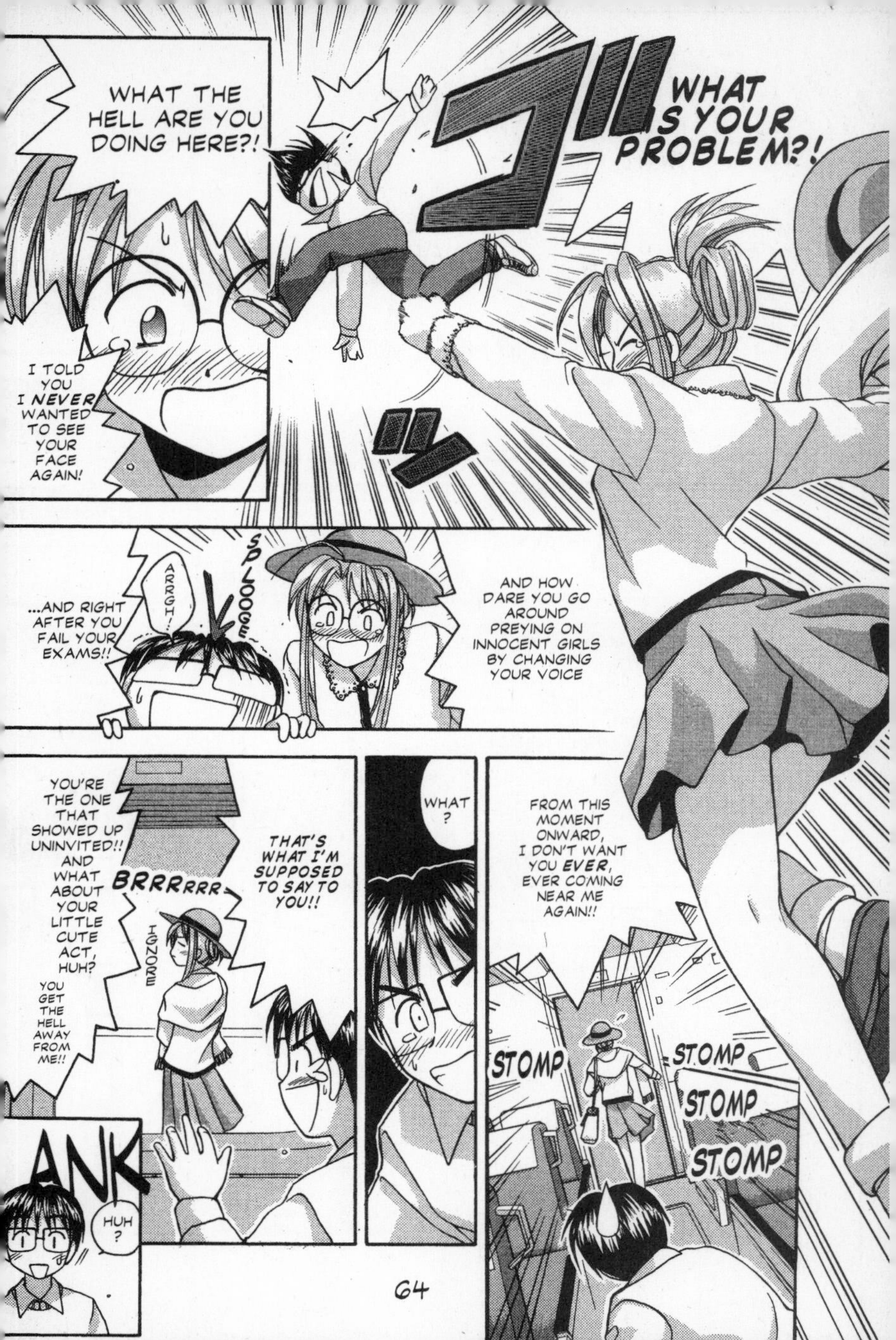
WHAT IS YOUR PROBLEM?!
WHAT THE HELL ARE YOU DOING HERE?!
I TOLD YOU I NEVER WANTED TO SEE YOUR FACE AGAIN!
AND HOW DARE YOU GO AROUND PREYING ON INNOCENT GIRLS BY CHANGING YOUR VOICE
SPLOOGE
ARRGH!!
...AND RIGHT AFTER YOU FAIL YOUR EXAMS!!
FROM THIS MOMENT ONWARD, I DON'T WANT YOU EVER, EVER COMING NEAR ME AGAIN!!
STOMP
STOMP
STOMP
STOMP
WHAT?
YOU'RE THE ONE THAT SHOWED UP UNINVITED!! AND WHAT ABOUT YOUR LITTLE CUTE ACT, HUH?
THAT'S WHAT I'M SUPPOSED TO SAY TO YOU!!
BRRRRRRR
IGNORE
YOU GET THE HELL AWAY FROM ME!!
ANK
HUH?

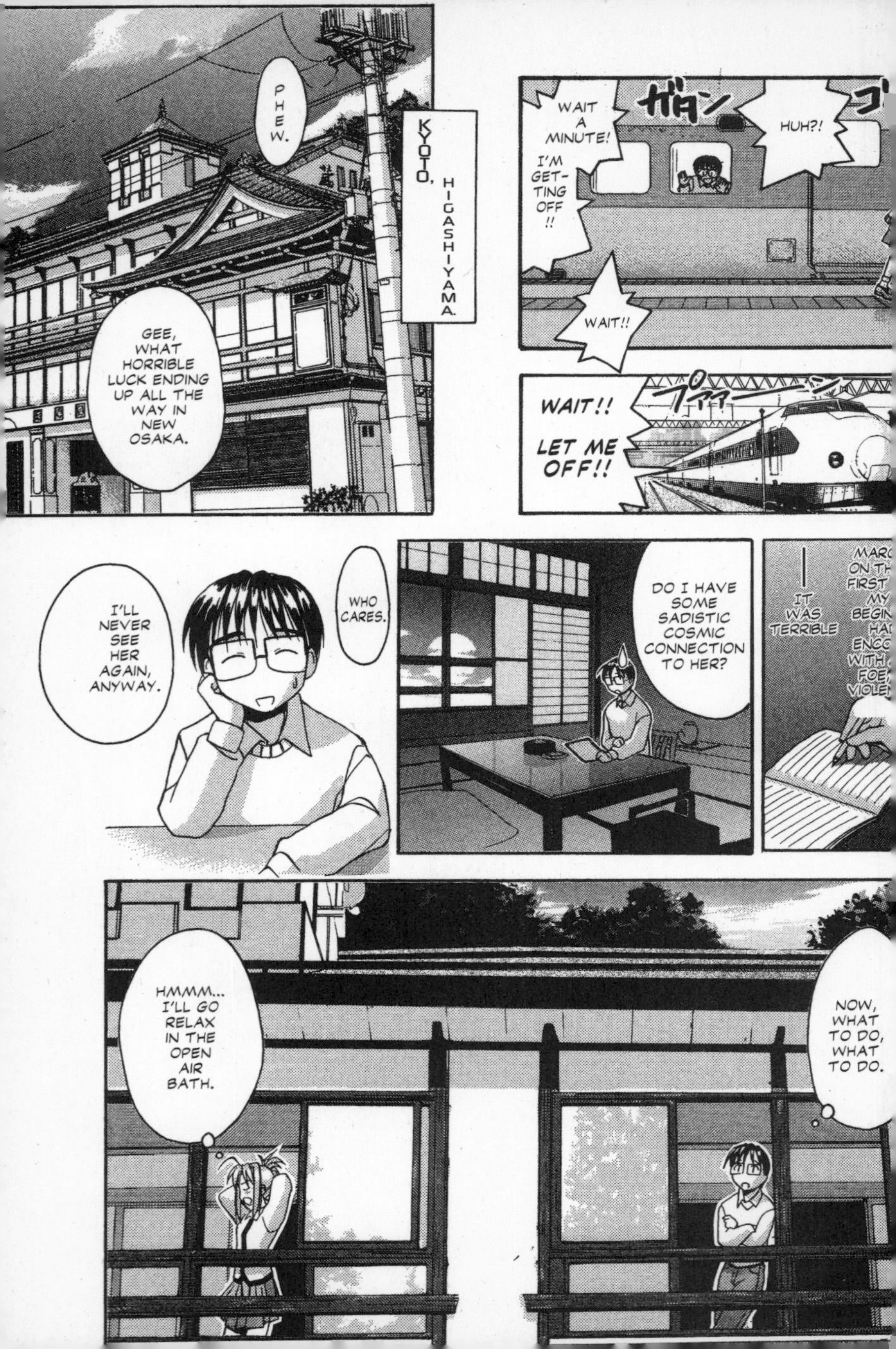
HUH?!
ガタン
WAIT A MINUTE!
I'M GETTING OFF!!
WAIT!!
WAIT!!
LET ME OFF!!
KYOTO, HIGASHIYAMA.
PHEW.
GEE, WHAT HORRIBLE LUCK ENDING UP ALL THE WAY IN NEW OSAKA.
IT WAS TERRIBLE
DO I HAVE SOME SADISTIC COSMIC CONNECTION TO HER?
WHO CARES.
I'LL NEVER SEE HER AGAIN, ANYWAY.
NOW, WHAT TO DO, WHAT TO DO.
HMMM... I'LL GO RELAX IN THE OPEN AIR BATH.

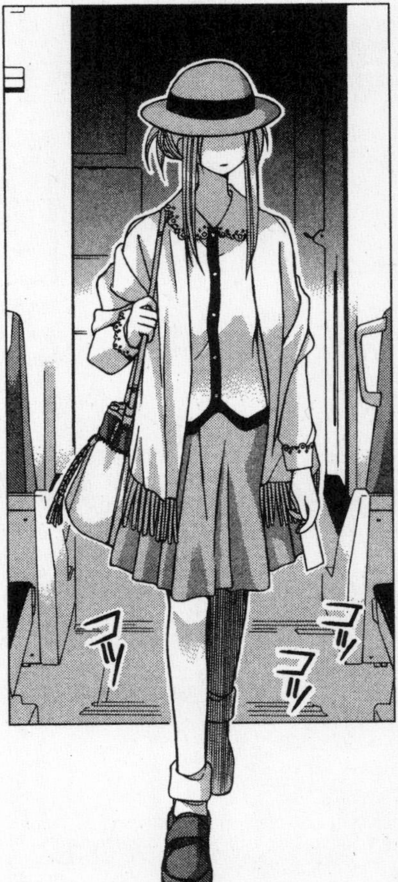
コツ
コツ
コツ

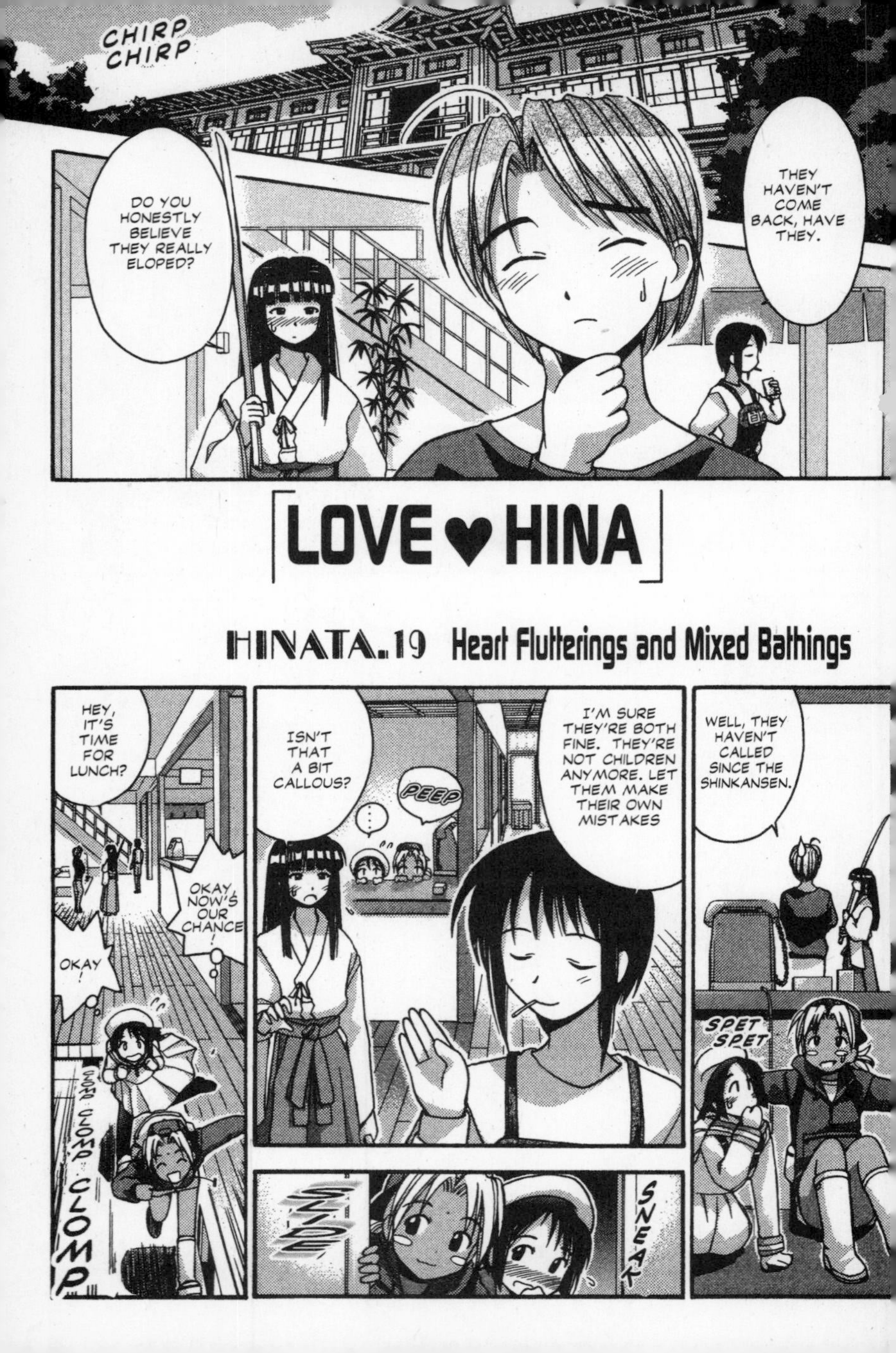
CHIRP CHIRP
THEY HAVEN'T COME BACK, HAVE THEY.
DO YOU HONESTLY BELIEVE THEY REALLY ELOPED?
LOVE♥HINA
HINATA.19 Heart Flutterings and Mixed Bathings
WELL, THEY HAVEN'T CALLED SINCE THE SHINKANSEN.
SPET SPET
I'M SURE THEY'RE BOTH FINE. THEY'RE NOT CHILDREN ANYMORE. LET THEM MAKE THEIR OWN MISTAKES
ISN'T THAT A BIT CALLOUS?
PEEP
...
SNEAK
SLIDE
HEY, IT'S TIME FOR LUNCH?
OKAY, NOW'S OUR CHANCE!
OKAY!
CLOMP CLOMP CLOMP CLOMP

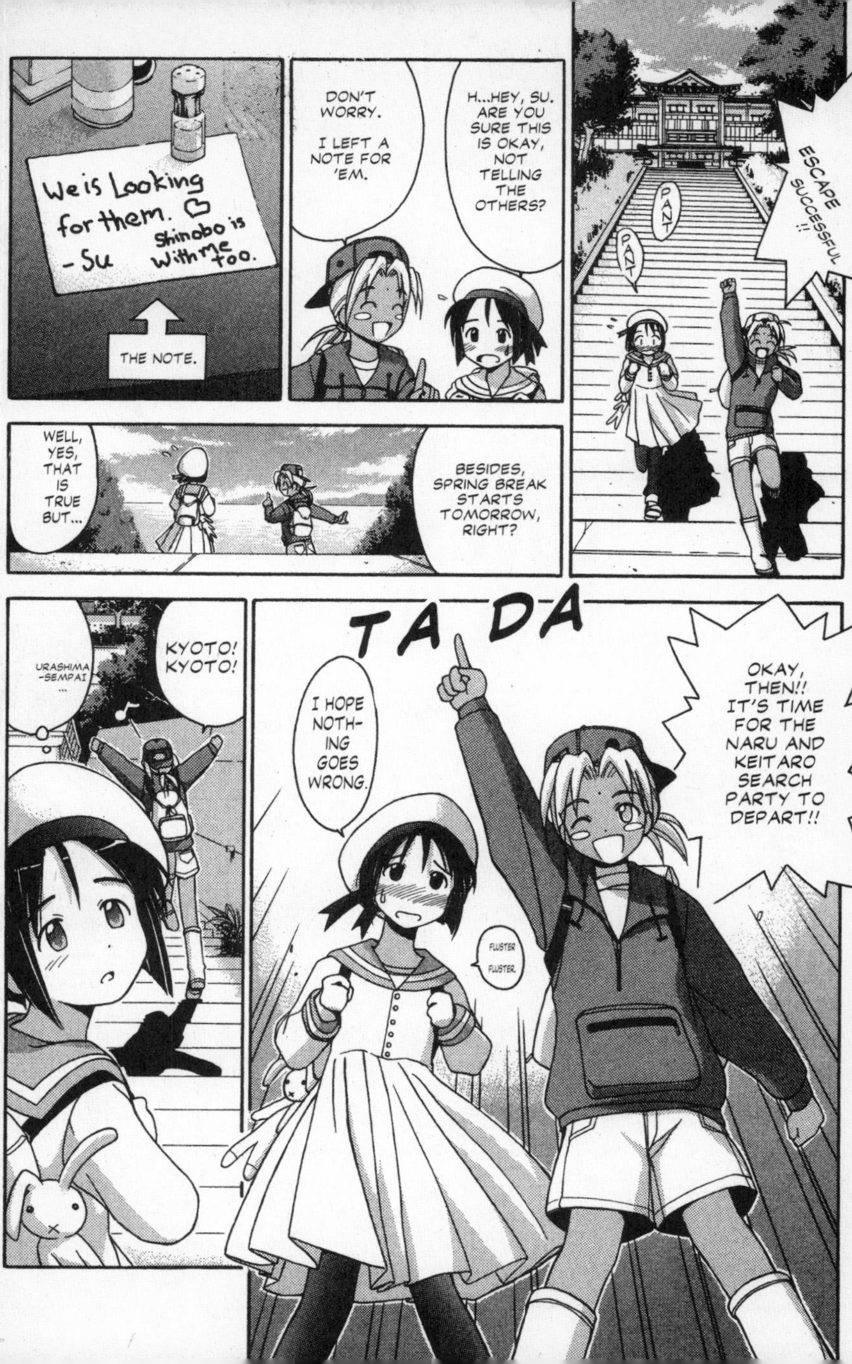
PANT
PANT
ESCAPE SUCCESSFUL!!
H...HEY, SU. ARE YOU SURE THIS IS OKAY, NOT TELLING THE OTHERS?
DON'T WORRY. I LEFT A NOTE FOR 'EM.
We is Looking for them. ♡ -Su
Shinobo is with me too.
THE NOTE.
BESIDES, SPRING BREAK STARTS TOMORROW, RIGHT?
WELL, YES, THAT IS TRUE BUT...
TA DA
OKAY, THEN!! IT'S TIME FOR THE NARU AND KEITARO SEARCH PARTY TO DEPART!!
I HOPE NOTHING GOES WRONG.
FLUSTER FLUSTER.
KYOTO! KYOTO!
URASHIMA-SEMPAI ...

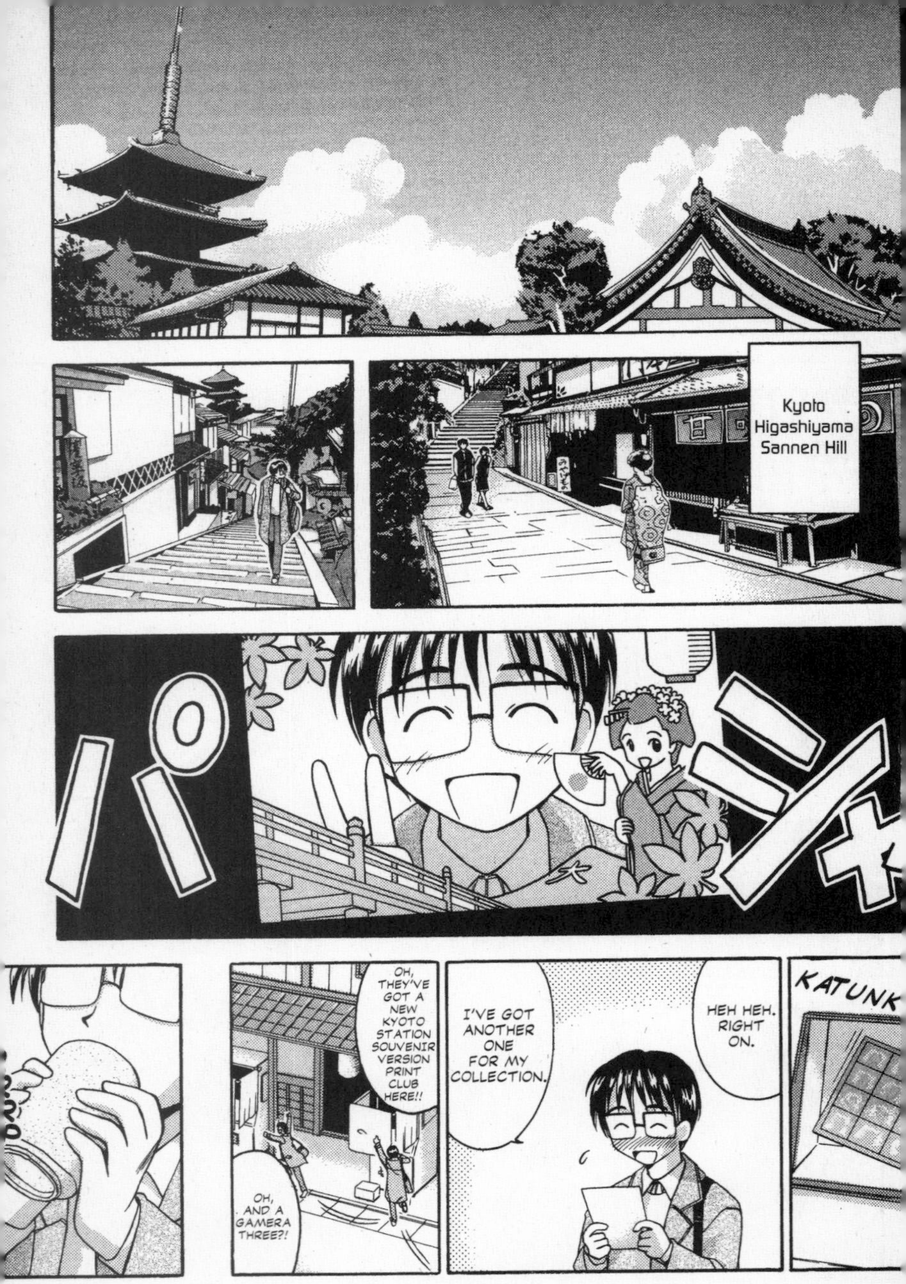
Kyoto Higashiyama Sannen Hill
KATUNK
HEH HEH. RIGHT ON.
I'VE GOT ANOTHER ONE FOR MY COLLECTION.
OH, THEY'VE GOT A NEW KYOTO STATION SOUVENIR VERSION PRINT CLUB HERE!!
OH, AND A GAMERA THREE?!

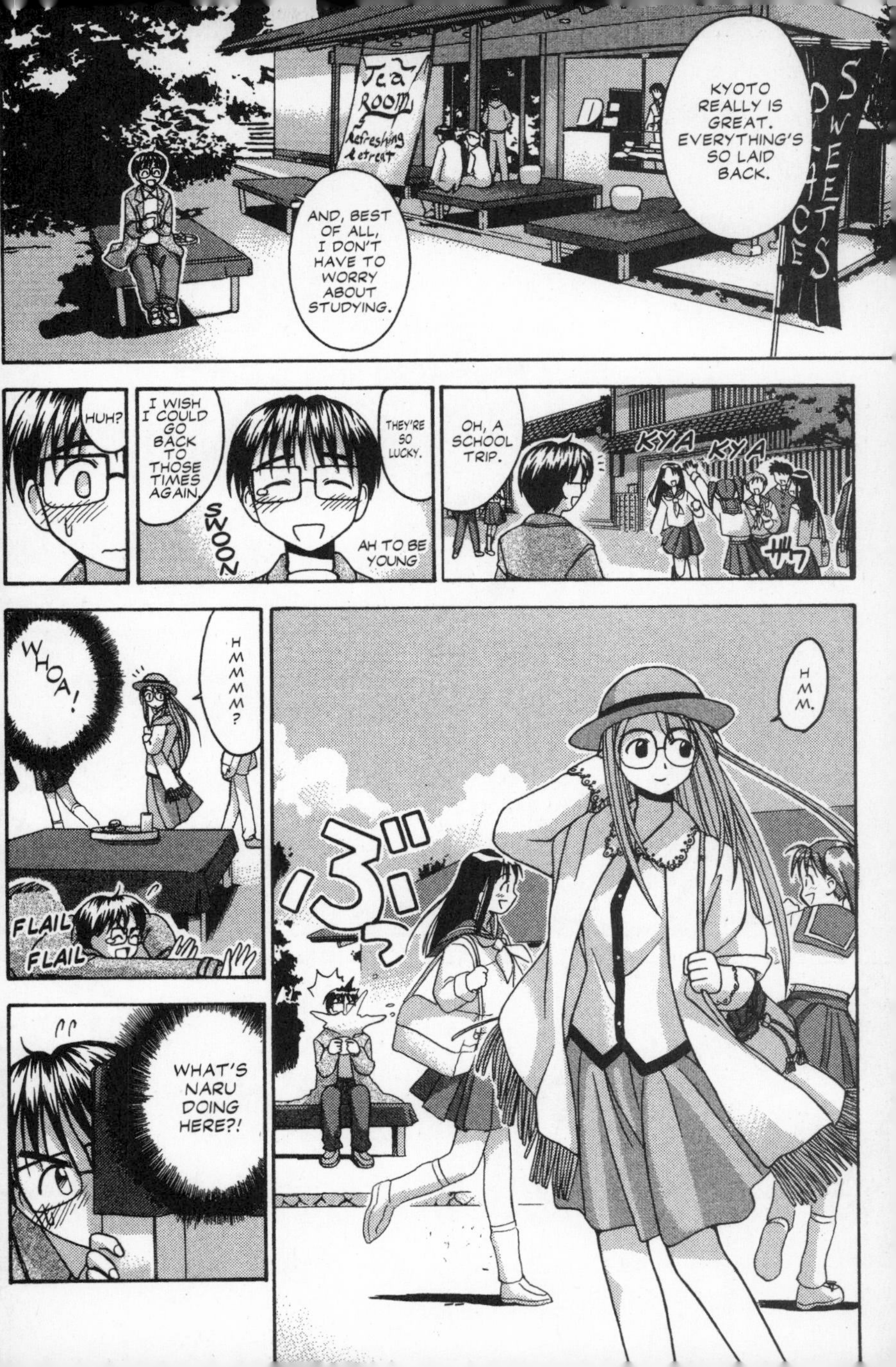

SWEETS
Tea Room
Refreshing retreat
KYOTO REALLY IS GREAT. EVERYTHING'S SO LAID BACK.
AND, BEST OF ALL, I DON'T HAVE TO WORRY ABOUT STUDYING.
OH, A SCHOOL TRIP.
KYA KYA
THEY'RE SO LUCKY.
I WISH I COULD GO BACK TO THOSE TIMES AGAIN.
SWOON
AH TO BE YOUNG
HUH?
HMM.
HMMMM?
WHOA!
FLAIL
FLAIL
WHAT'S NARU DOING HERE?!

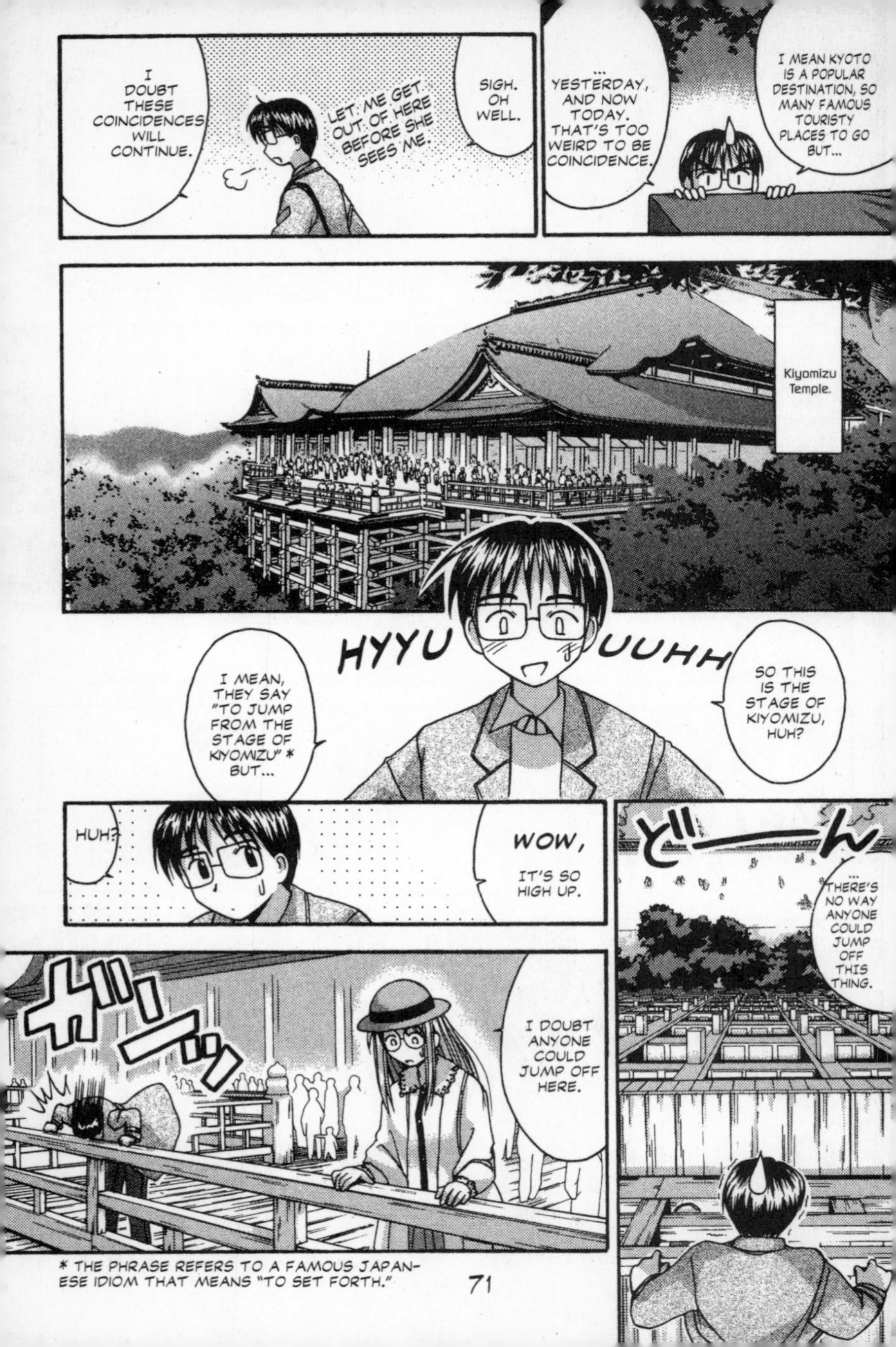
I MEAN KYOTO IS A POPULAR DESTINATION, SO MANY FAMOUS TOURISTY PLACES TO GO BUT...
... YESTERDAY, AND NOW TODAY. THAT'S TOO WEIRD TO BE COINCIDENCE.
SIGH. OH WELL.
LET ME GET OUT OF HERE BEFORE SHE SEES ME.
I DOUBT THESE COINCIDENCES WILL CONTINUE.
Kiyomizu Temple.
HYYU UUHH
SO THIS IS THE STAGE OF KIYOMIZU, HUH?
I MEAN, THEY SAY "TO JUMP FROM THE STAGE OF KIYOMIZU" * BUT...
どーん
... THERE'S NO WAY ANYONE COULD JUMP OFF THIS THING.
WOW,
IT'S SO HIGH UP.
HUH?
I DOUBT ANYONE COULD JUMP OFF HERE.

* THE PHRASE REFERS TO A FAMOUS JAPANESE IDIOM THAT MEANS "TO SET FORTH."

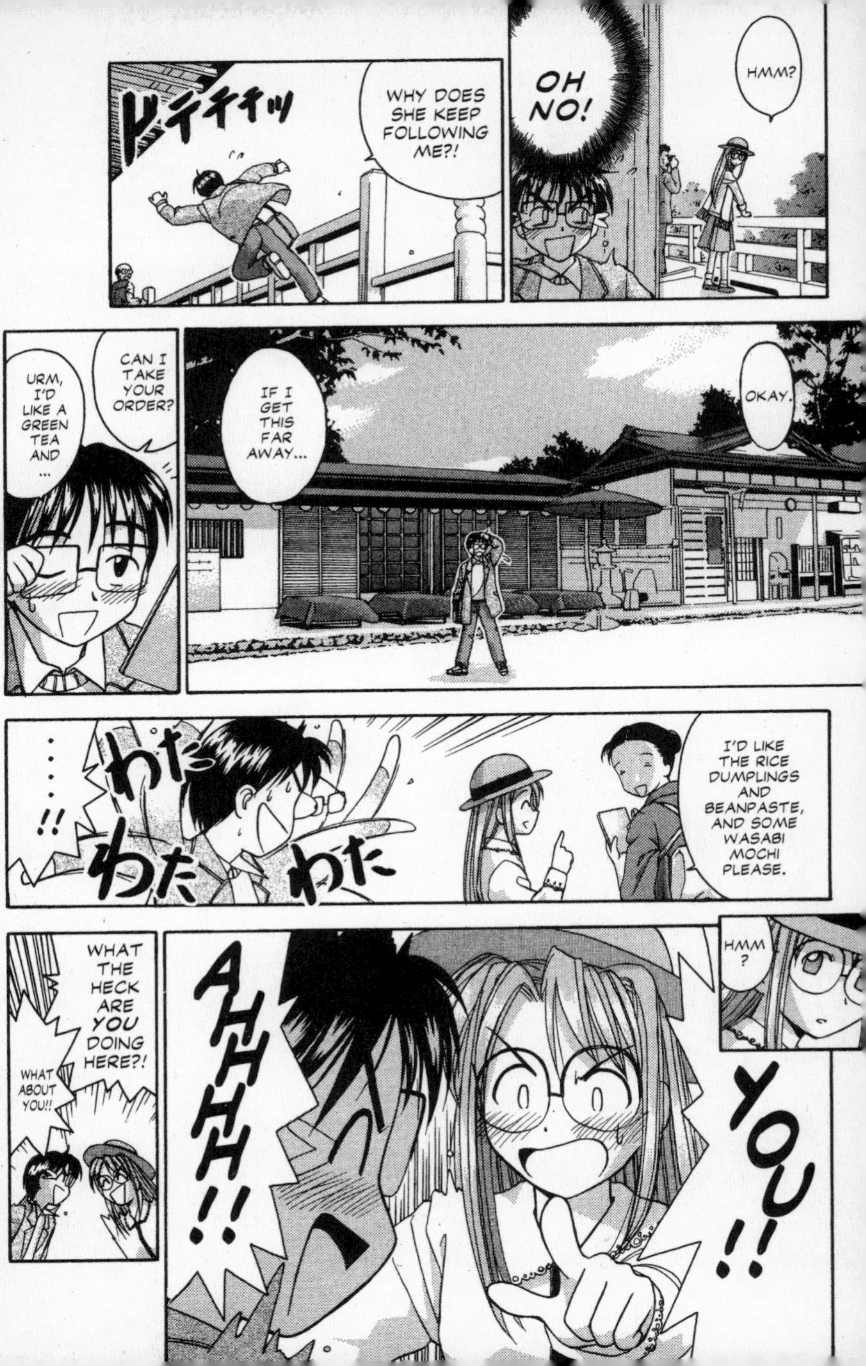
HMM?
OH NO!
WHY DOES SHE KEEP FOLLOWING ME?!
ドテチチッ
OKAY.
IF I GET THIS FAR AWAY...
CAN I TAKE YOUR ORDER?
URM, I'D LIKE A GREEN TEA AND ...
I'D LIKE THE RICE DUMPLINGS AND BEANPASTE, AND SOME WASABI MOCHI PLEASE.
わた
わた
わた
.....!!
HMM?
YOU!!
AHHHH!!
WHAT THE HECK ARE YOU DOING HERE?!
WHAT ABOUT YOU!!

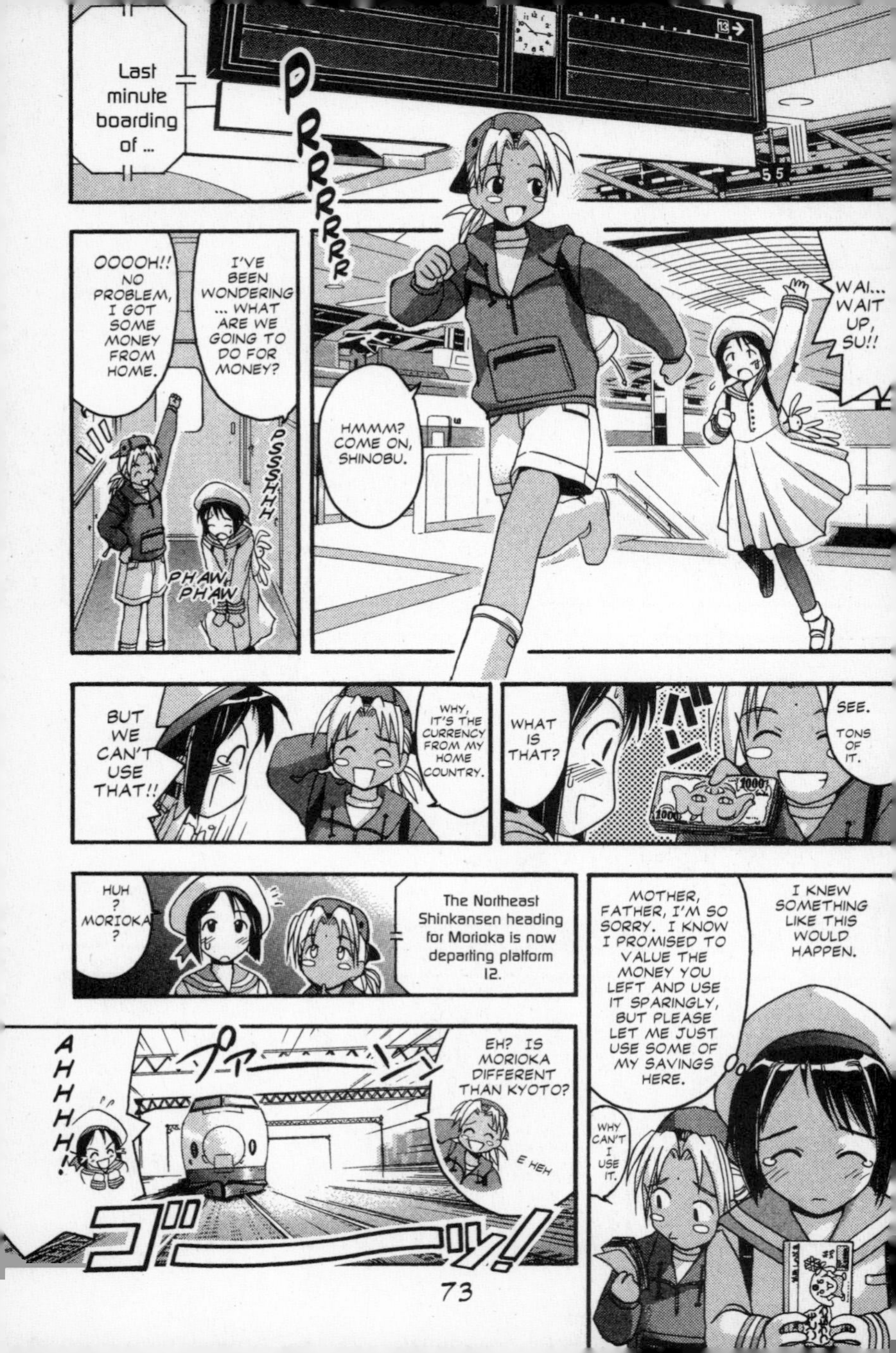
Last minute boarding of ...
PRRRRRRR
WAI... WAIT UP, SU!!
HMMM? COME ON, SHINOBU.
I'VE BEEN WONDERING ... WHAT ARE WE GOING TO DO FOR MONEY?
OOOOH!! NO PROBLEM, I GOT SOME MONEY FROM HOME.
PSSSHHH
PH'AW, PH'AW
SEE. TONS OF IT.
WHAT IS THAT?
WHY, IT'S THE CURRENCY FROM MY HOME COUNTRY.
BUT WE CAN'T USE THAT!!
I KNEW SOMETHING LIKE THIS WOULD HAPPEN.
MOTHER, FATHER, I'M SO SORRY. I KNOW I PROMISED TO VALUE THE MONEY YOU LEFT AND USE IT SPARINGLY, BUT PLEASE LET ME JUST USE SOME OF MY SAVINGS HERE.
WHY CAN'T I USE IT.
The Northeast Shinkansen heading for Morioka is now departing platform 12.
HUH? MORIOKA?
EH? IS MORIOKA DIFFERENT THAN KYOTO?
E HEH
AHHHHH!

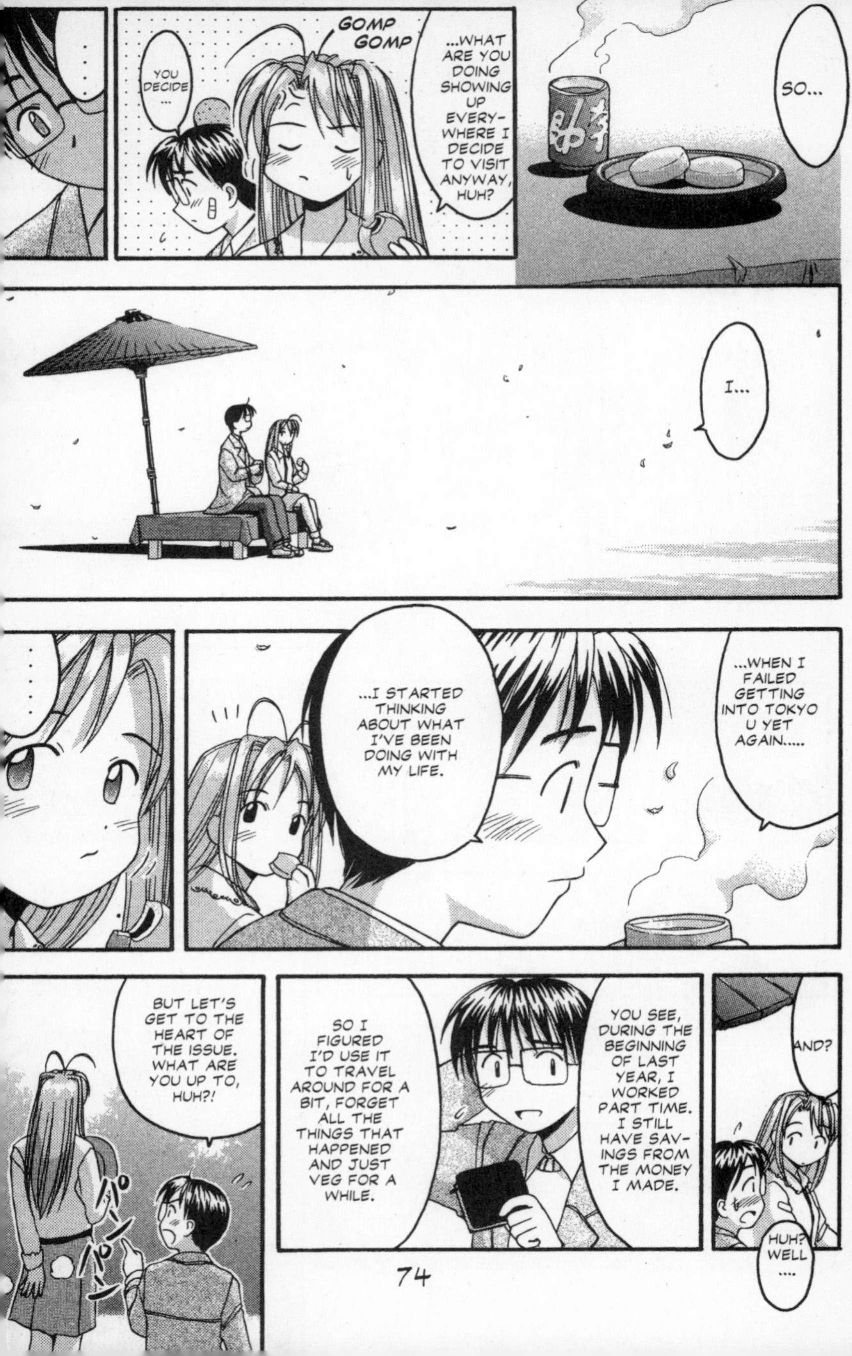
SO...
...WHAT ARE YOU DOING SHOWING UP EVERY-WHERE I DECIDE TO VISIT ANYWAY, HUH?
GOMP GOMP
YOU DECIDE ...
I...
...WHEN I FAILED GETTING INTO TOKYO U YET AGAIN.....
...I STARTED THINKING ABOUT WHAT I'VE BEEN DOING WITH MY LIFE.
AND?
HUH? WELL ....
YOU SEE, DURING THE BEGINNING OF LAST YEAR, I WORKED PART TIME. I STILL HAVE SAV-INGS FROM THE MONEY I MADE.
SO I FIGURED I'D USE IT TO TRAVEL AROUND FOR A BIT, FORGET ALL THE THINGS THAT HAPPENED AND JUST VEG FOR A WHILE.
BUT LET'S GET TO THE HEART OF THE ISSUE. WHAT ARE YOU UP TO, HUH?!

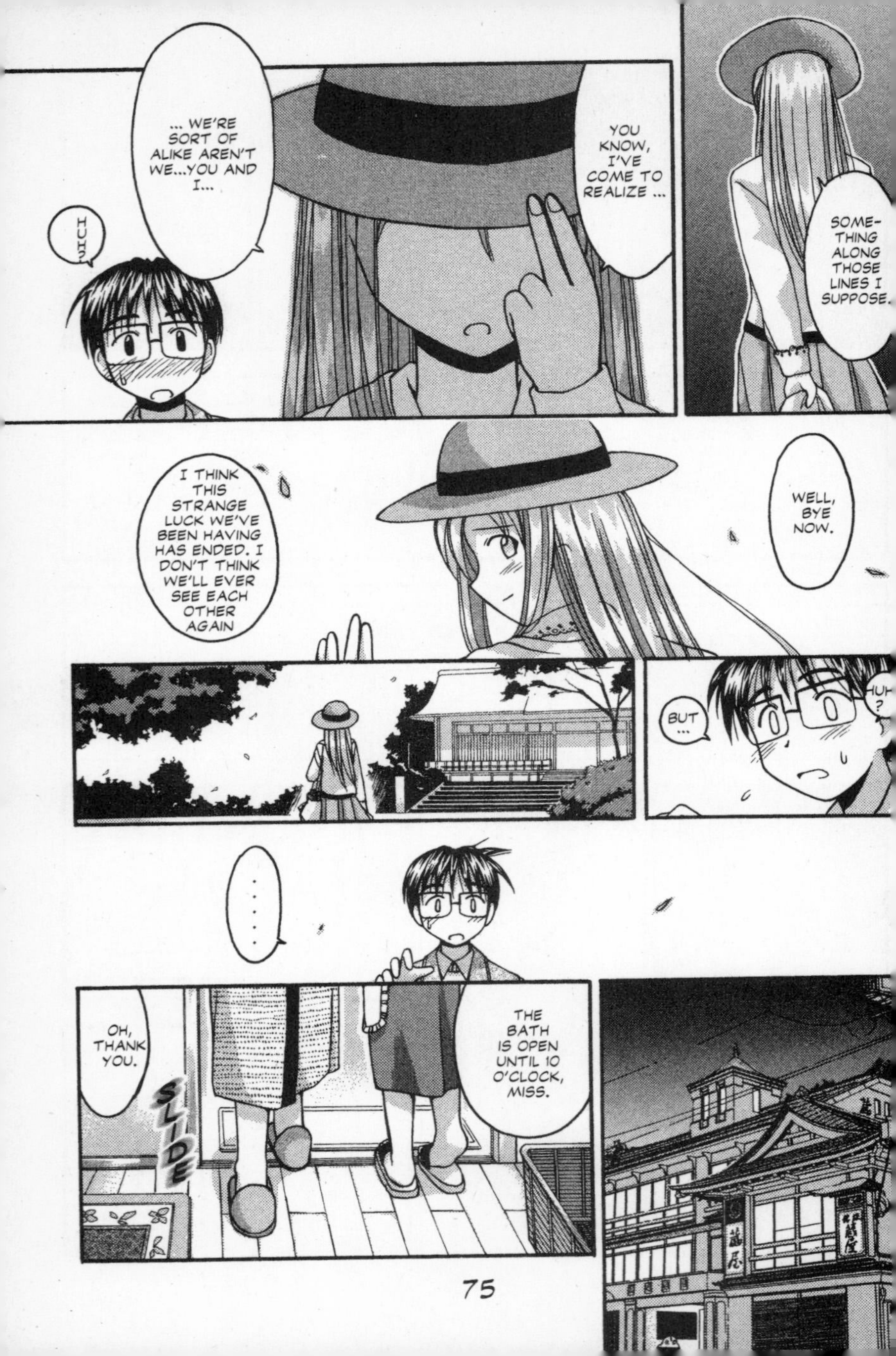
SOMETHING ALONG THOSE LINES I SUPPOSE.
YOU KNOW, I'VE COME TO REALIZE ...
... WE'RE SORT OF ALIKE AREN'T WE...YOU AND I...
HUH?
WELL, BYE NOW.
I THINK THIS STRANGE LUCK WE'VE BEEN HAVING HAS ENDED. I DON'T THINK WE'LL EVER SEE EACH OTHER AGAIN
HUH?
BUT ...
......
THE BATH IS OPEN UNTIL 10 O'CLOCK, MISS.
OH, THANK YOU.
SLIDE

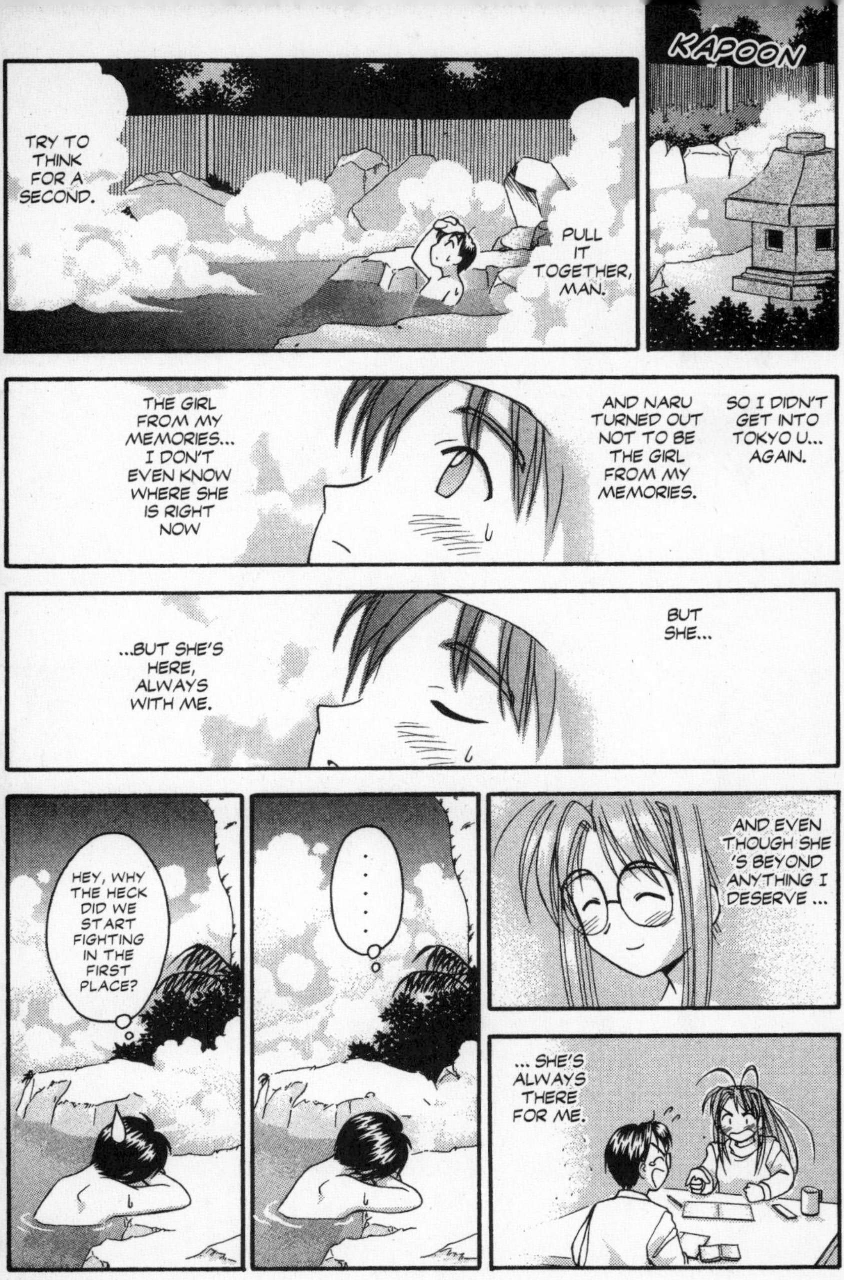
KAPOON
PULL IT TOGETHER, MAN.
TRY TO THINK FOR A SECOND.
SO I DIDN'T GET INTO TOKYO U... AGAIN.
AND NARU TURNED OUT NOT TO BE THE GIRL FROM MY MEMORIES.
THE GIRL FROM MY MEMORIES... I DON'T EVEN KNOW WHERE SHE IS RIGHT NOW
BUT SHE...
...BUT SHE'S HERE, ALWAYS WITH ME.
AND EVEN THOUGH SHE 'S BEYOND ANYTHING I DESERVE ...
... SHE'S ALWAYS THERE FOR ME.
. . . . . .
HEY, WHY THE HECK DID WE START FIGHTING IN THE FIRST PLACE?

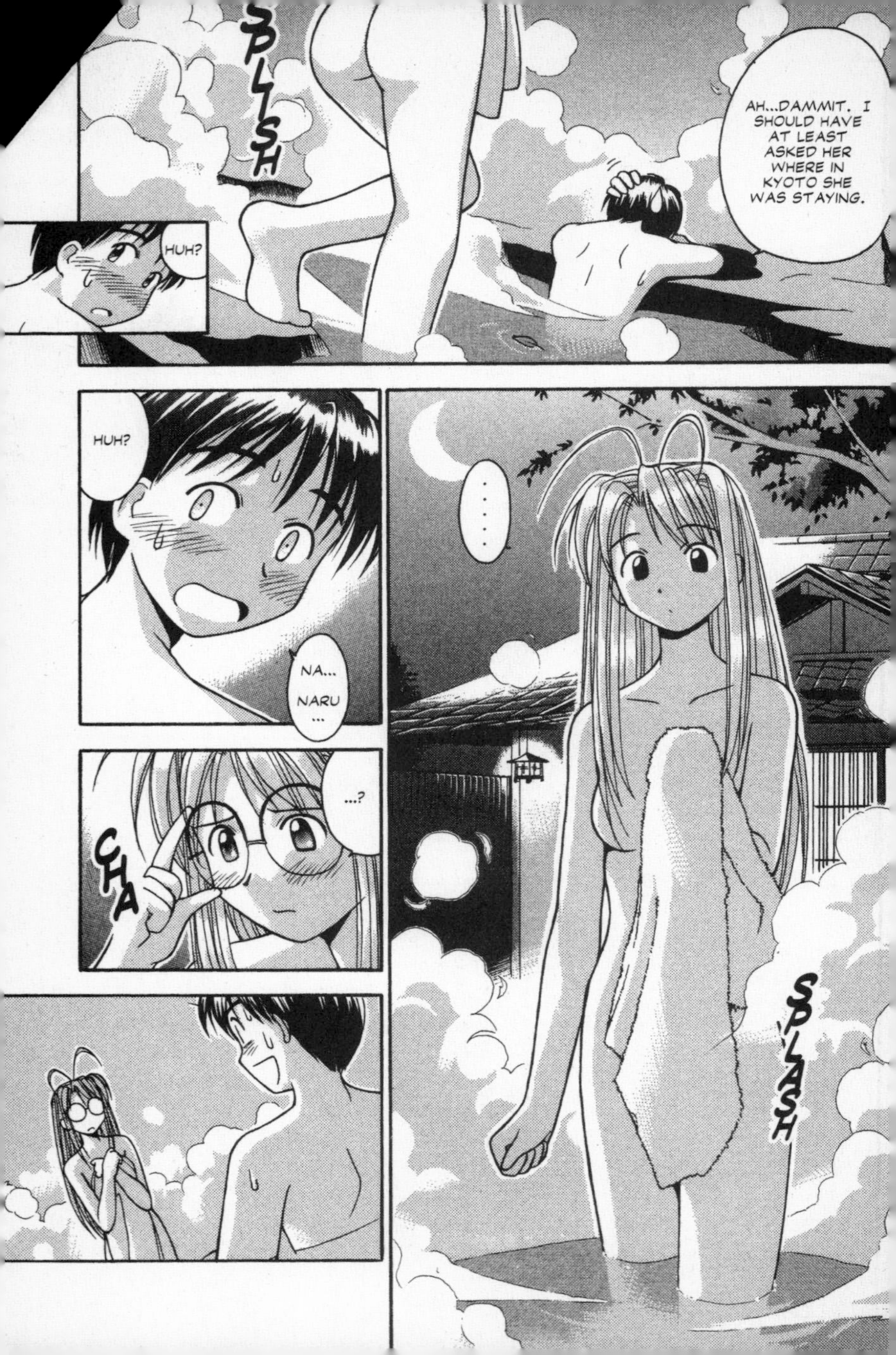

AH...DAMMIT. I SHOULD HAVE AT LEAST ASKED HER WHERE IN KYOTO SHE WAS STAYING.
SPLISH
HUH?
....
SPLASH
HUH?
NA... NARU ...
...?
CHA

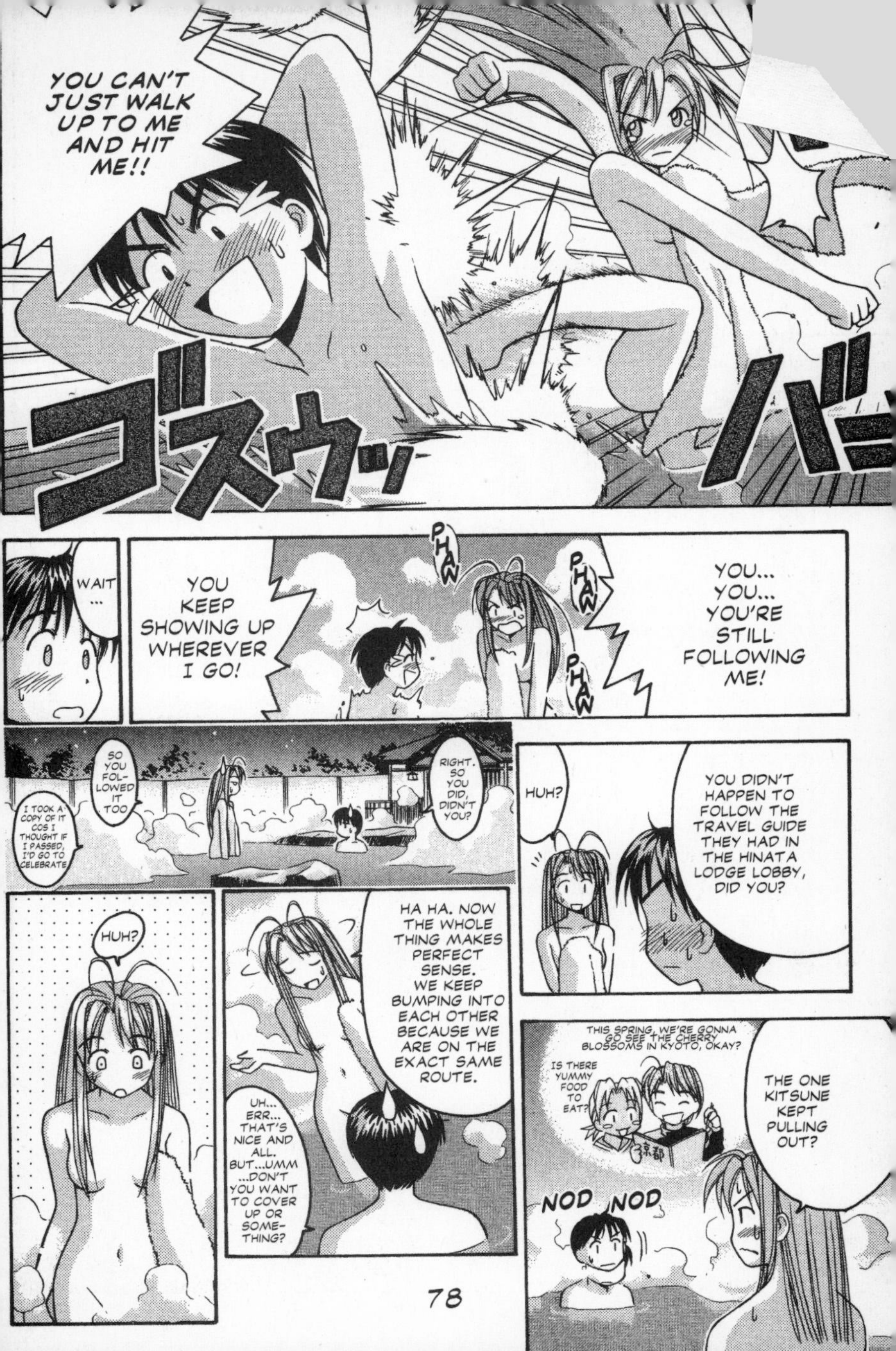
YOU CAN'T JUST WALK UP TO ME AND HIT ME!!
ゴスウッ
YOU... YOU... YOU'RE STILL FOLLOWING ME!
PHAW
PHAW
PHAW
YOU KEEP SHOWING UP WHEREVER I GO!
PHAW
WAIT ...
YOU DIDN'T HAPPEN TO FOLLOW THE TRAVEL GUIDE THEY HAD IN THE HINATA LODGE LOBBY, DID YOU?
HUH?
THE ONE KITSUNE KEPT PULLING OUT?
THIS SPRING, WE'RE GONNA GO SEE THE CHERRY BLOSSOMS IN KYOTO, OKAY?
IS THERE YUMMY FOOD TO EAT?
NOD NOD
RIGHT. SO YOU DID, DIDN'T YOU?
SO YOU FOLLOWED IT TOO
I TOOK A COPY OF IT COS I THOUGHT IF I PASSED, I'D GO TO CELEBRATE
HA HA. NOW THE WHOLE THING MAKES PERFECT SENSE. WE KEEP BUMPING INTO EACH OTHER BECAUSE WE ARE ON THE EXACT SAME ROUTE.
UH... ERR... THAT'S NICE AND ALL. BUT...UMM ...DON'T YOU WANT TO COVER UP OR SOME-THING?
HUH?

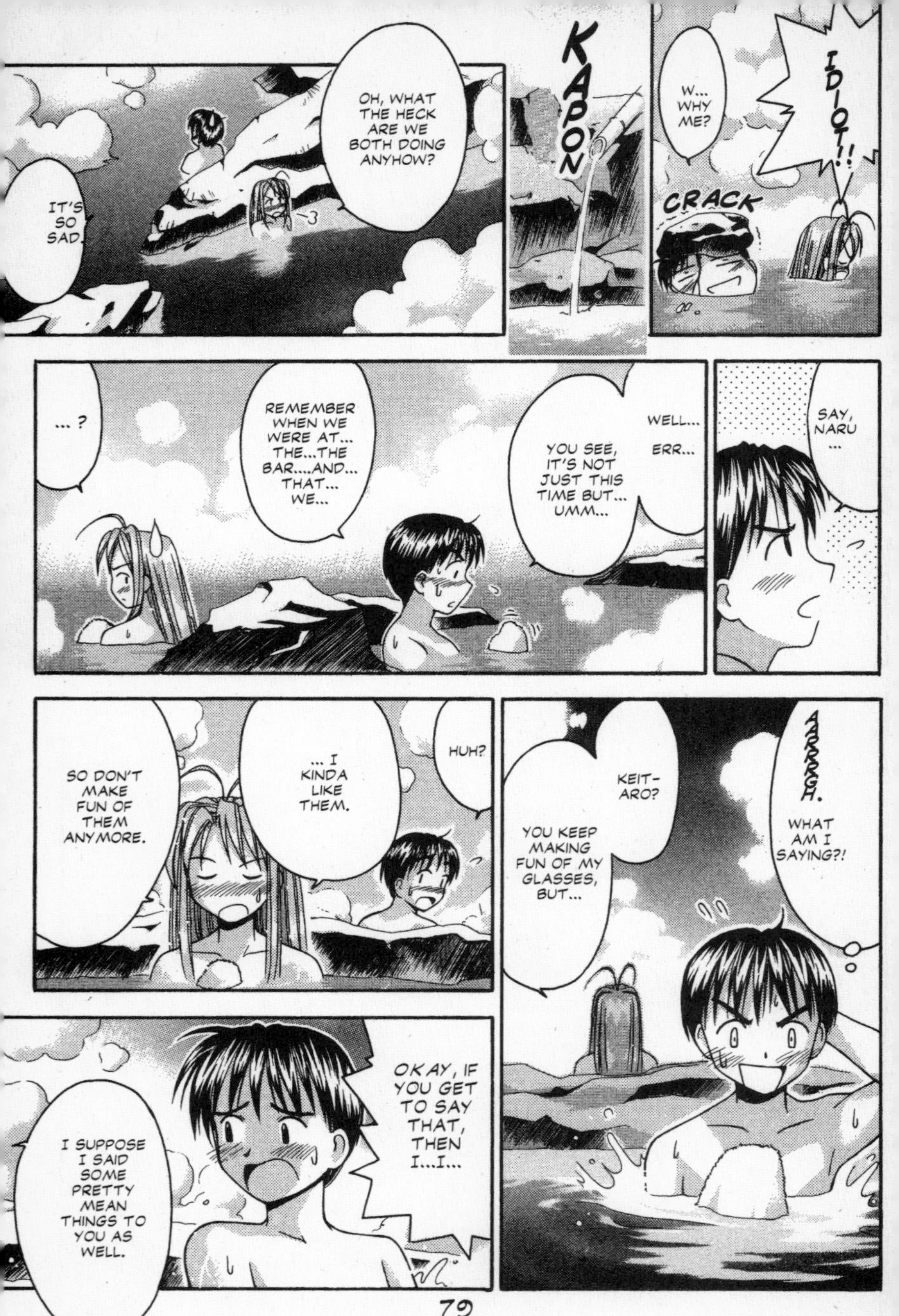
IDIOT!!
W... WHY ME?
CRACK
KAPON
OH, WHAT THE HECK ARE WE BOTH DOING ANYHOW?
IT'S SO SAD.
SAY, NARU...
WELL... ERR...
YOU SEE, IT'S NOT JUST THIS TIME BUT... UMM...
REMEMBER WHEN WE WERE AT... THE...THE BAR....AND... THAT... WE...
... ?
ARRRGH. WHAT AM I SAYING?!
KEIT-ARO?
YOU KEEP MAKING FUN OF MY GLASSES, BUT...
HUH?
... I KINDA LIKE THEM.
SO DON'T MAKE FUN OF THEM ANYMORE.
OKAY, IF YOU GET TO SAY THAT, THEN I...I...
I SUPPOSE I SAID SOME PRETTY MEAN THINGS TO YOU AS WELL.

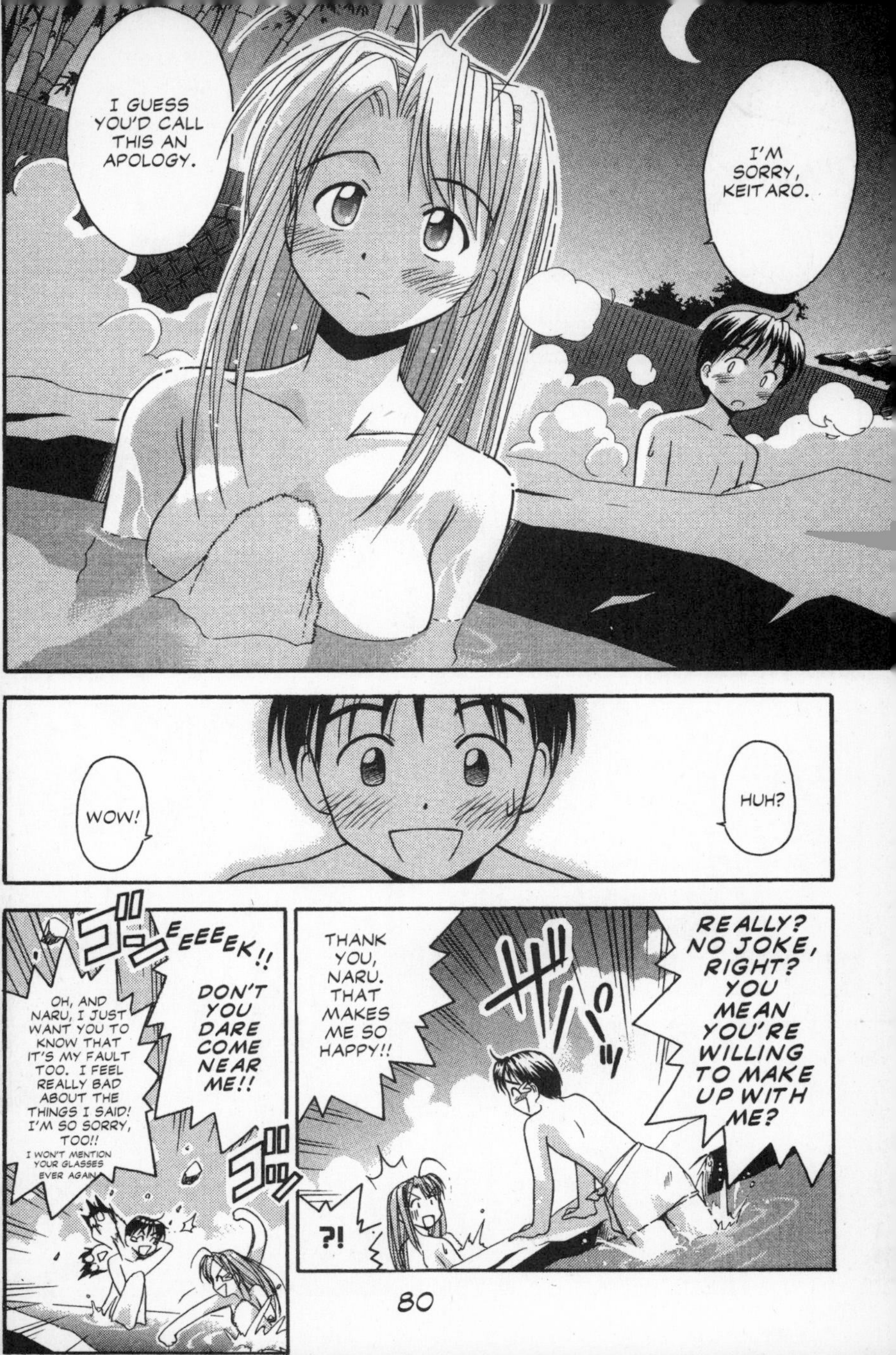
I'M SORRY, KEITARO.
I GUESS YOU'D CALL THIS AN APOLOGY.
HUH?
WOW!
REALLY? NO JOKE, RIGHT? YOU MEAN YOU'RE WILLING TO MAKE UP WITH ME?
THANK YOU, NARU. THAT MAKES ME SO HAPPY!!
?!
EEEEEK!!
DON'T YOU DARE COME NEAR ME!!
OH, AND NARU, I JUST WANT YOU TO KNOW THAT IT'S MY FAULT TOO. I FEEL REALLY BAD ABOUT THE THINGS I SAID! I'M SO SORRY, TOO!!
I WON'T MENTION YOUR GLASSES EVER AGAIN.

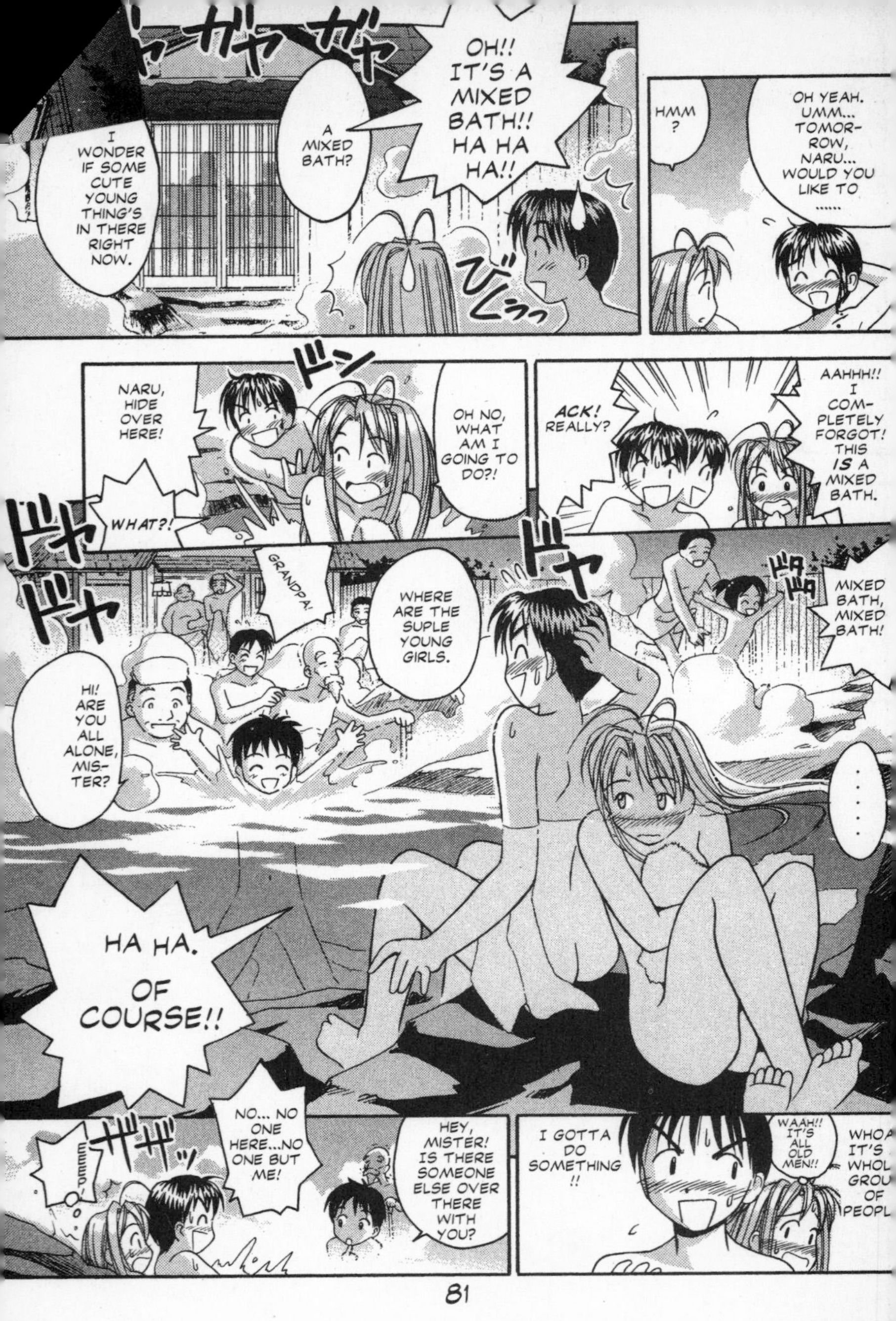
HMM ?
OH YEAH. UMM... TOMORROW, NARU... WOULD YOU LIKE TO ......
ガヤ ガヤ
OH!! IT'S A MIXED BATH!! HA HA HA!!
A MIXED BATH?
I WONDER IF SOME CUTE YOUNG THING'S IN THERE RIGHT NOW.
AAHHH!! I COMPLETELY FORGOT! THIS IS A MIXED BATH.
ACK! REALLY?
ドン
OH NO, WHAT AM I GOING TO DO?!
NARU, HIDE OVER HERE!
WHAT?!
ドヤ ドヤ
MIXED BATH, MIXED BATH!
. . . . . .
WHERE ARE THE SUPLE YOUNG GIRLS.
GRANDPA!
HI! ARE YOU ALL ALONE, MISTER?
HA HA. OF COURSE!!
WHOA IT'S WHOL GROU OF PEOPL
WAAH!! IT'S ALL OLD MEN!!
I GOTTA DO SOMETHING !!
HEY, MISTER! IS THERE SOMEONE ELSE OVER THERE WITH YOU?
NO... NO ONE HERE...NO ONE BUT ME!
EEEP!

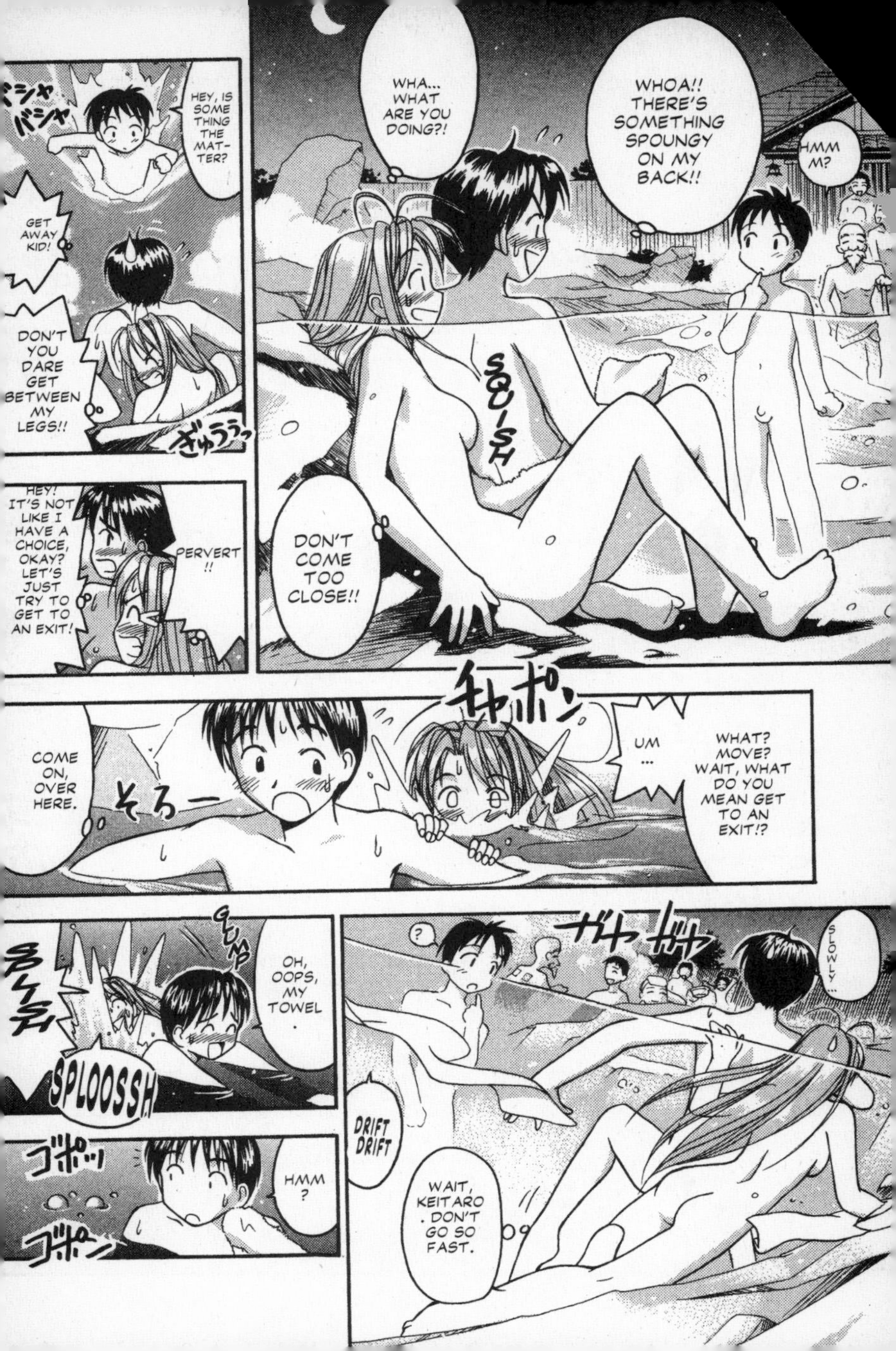
HMM M?
WHOA!! THERE'S SOMETHING SPOUNGY ON MY BACK!!
WHA... WHAT ARE YOU DOING?!
SQUISH
DON'T COME TOO CLOSE!!
バシャバシャ
HEY, IS SOME THING THE MAT-TER?
GET AWAY KID!
DON'T YOU DARE GET BETWEEN MY LEGS!!
ぎゅううっ
PERVERT !!
HEY! IT'S NOT LIKE I HAVE A CHOICE, OKAY? LET'S JUST TRY TO GET TO AN EXIT!
WHAT? MOVE? WAIT, WHAT DO YOU MEAN GET TO AN EXIT!?
UM ...
チャポン
そろー
COME ON, OVER HERE.
SLOWLY ...
ガヤガヤ
?
DRIFT DRIFT
WAIT, KEITARO. DON'T GO SO FAST.
OH, OOPS, MY TOWEL.
GLUMP
SPLASH
SPLOOSSH
ゴポッ
HMM ?
ゴポン

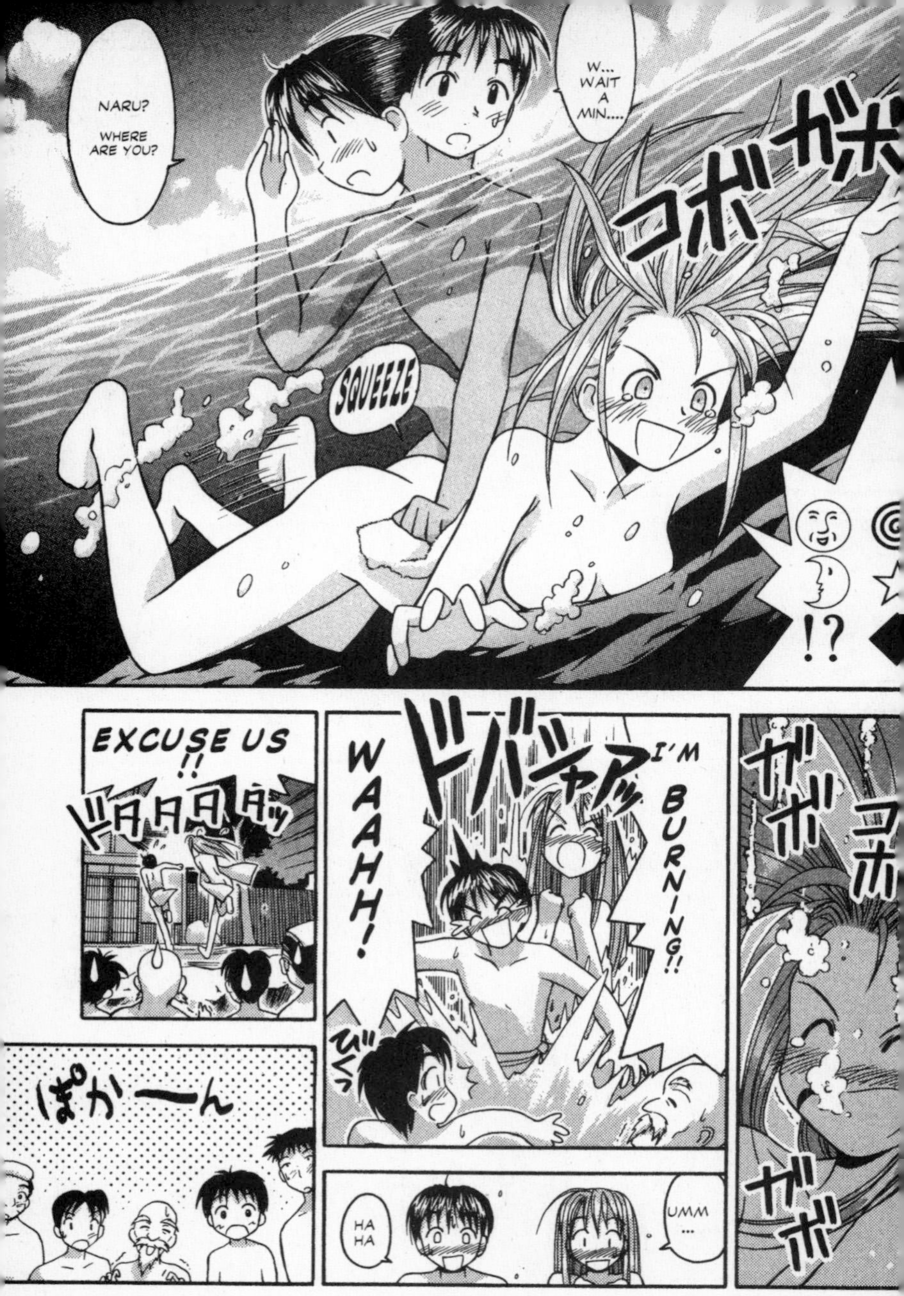

W... WAIT A MIN....
コボガボ
NARU? WHERE ARE YOU?
SQUEEZE
!?
ガボ
コボ
ガボ
ドバシャアッ
I'M BURNING!!
WAAHH!
びくっ
EXCUSE US!!
ドAAAAッ
UMM ...
HA HA
ぽかーん

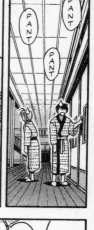

...!!

I'M SORRY!!

HOW COULD YOU DO SOMETHING LIKE THAT, YOU IDIOT!

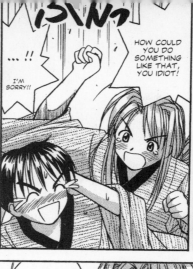

HUH?

THAT WAS SUCH A HORRIBLE EXPERINCE.

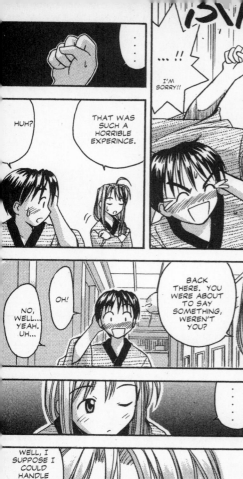

NO, WELL... YEAH. UH...

OH!

BACK THERE. YOU WERE ABOUT TO SAY SOMETHING, WEREN'T YOU?

HUH?

SO, WHAT WERE YOU SAYING?

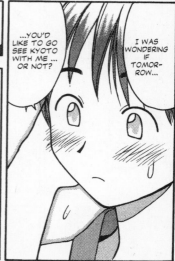

...YOU'D LIKE TO GO SEE KYOTO WITH ME ... OR NOT?

I WAS WONDERING IF TOMOR- ROW...

WELL, I SUPPOSE I COULD HANDLE THAT. IT'S NOT LIKE I HAVE ANYTHING BETTER TO DO.

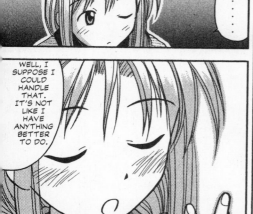

84

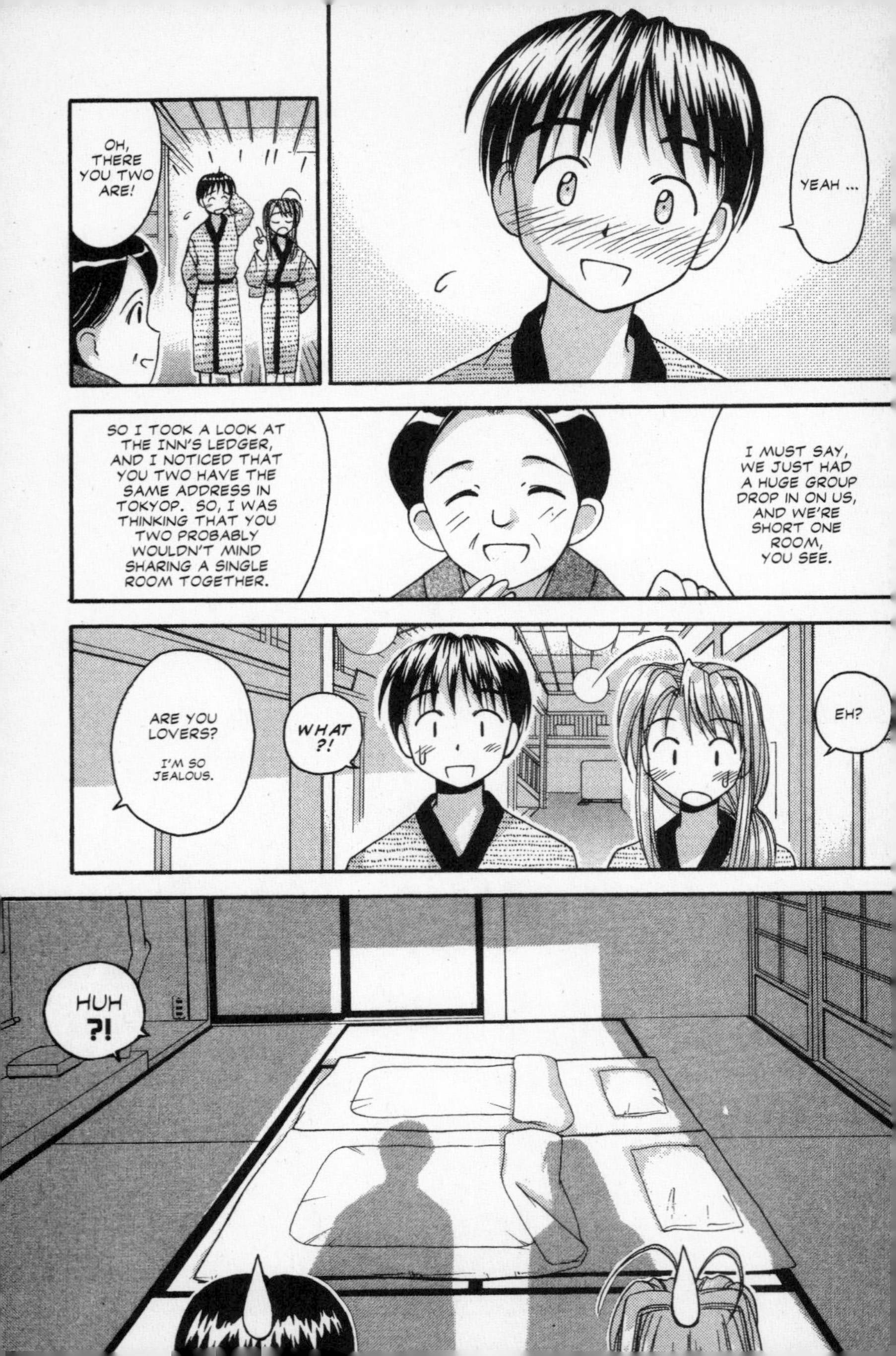
YEAH ...
OH, THERE YOU TWO ARE!
I MUST SAY, WE JUST HAD A HUGE GROUP DROP IN ON US, AND WE'RE SHORT ONE ROOM, YOU SEE.
SO I TOOK A LOOK AT THE INN'S LEDGER, AND I NOTICED THAT YOU TWO HAVE THE SAME ADDRESS IN TOKYOP. SO, I WAS THINKING THAT YOU TWO PROBABLY WOULDN'T MIND SHARING A SINGLE ROOM TOGETHER.
EH?
WHAT ?!
ARE YOU LOVERS?
I'M SO JEALOUS.
HUH ?!

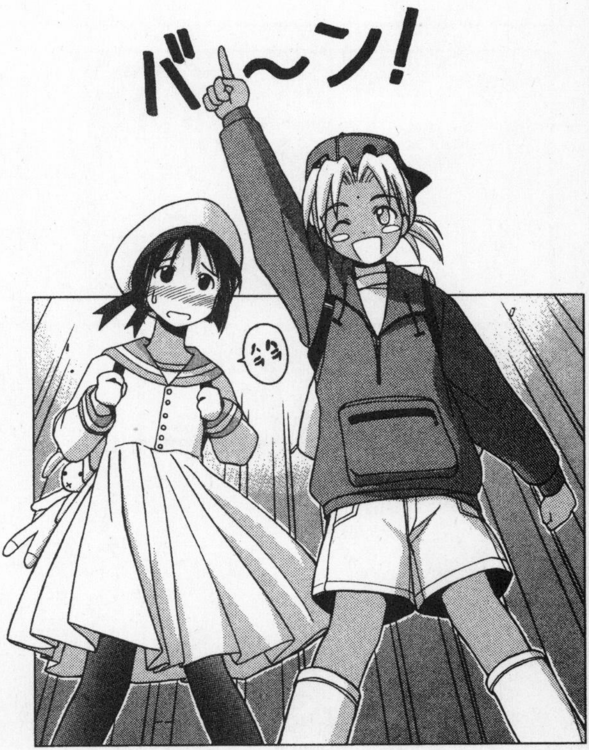
バ〜ン!
うう

LOVE ♥ HINA

HINATA. 20 A Virginal Night

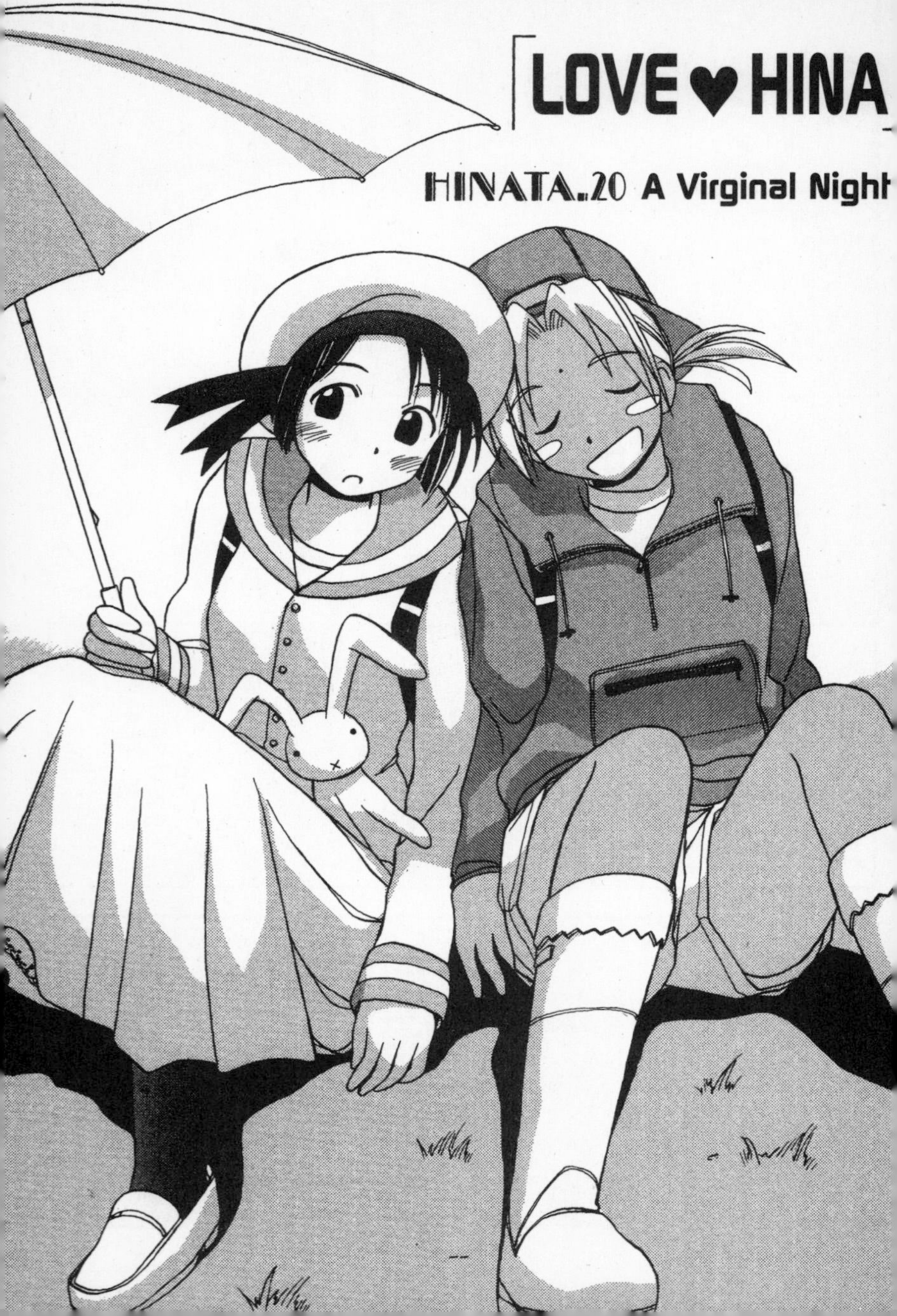

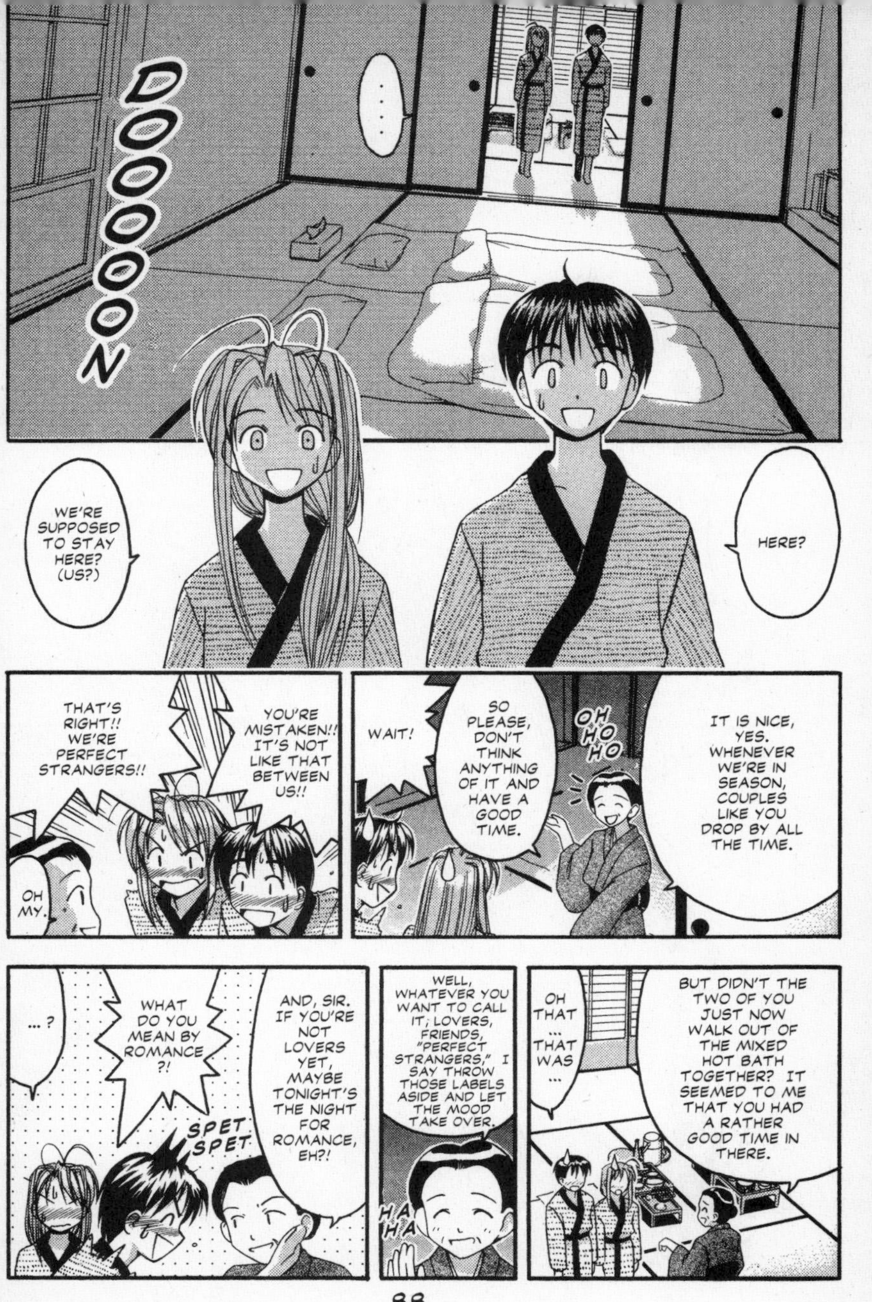

...
DOOOOOON
HERE?
WE'RE SUPPOSED TO STAY HERE? (US?)
IT IS NICE, YES. WHENEVER WE'RE IN SEASON, COUPLES LIKE YOU DROP BY ALL THE TIME.
OH HO HO
SO PLEASE, DON'T THINK ANYTHING OF IT AND HAVE A GOOD TIME.
WAIT!
YOU'RE MISTAKEN!! IT'S NOT LIKE THAT BETWEEN US!!
THAT'S RIGHT!! WE'RE PERFECT STRANGERS!!
OH MY.
BUT DIDN'T THE TWO OF YOU JUST NOW WALK OUT OF THE MIXED HOT BATH TOGETHER? IT SEEMED TO ME THAT YOU HAD A RATHER GOOD TIME IN THERE.
OH THAT ... THAT WAS ...
WELL, WHATEVER YOU WANT TO CALL IT, LOVERS, FRIENDS, "PERFECT STRANGERS," I SAY THROW THOSE LABELS ASIDE AND LET THE MOOD TAKE OVER.
HA HA
AND, SIR. IF YOU'RE NOT LOVERS YET, MAYBE TONIGHT'S THE NIGHT FOR ROMANCE, EH?!
SPET SPET
WHAT DO YOU MEAN BY ROMANCE ?!
... ?

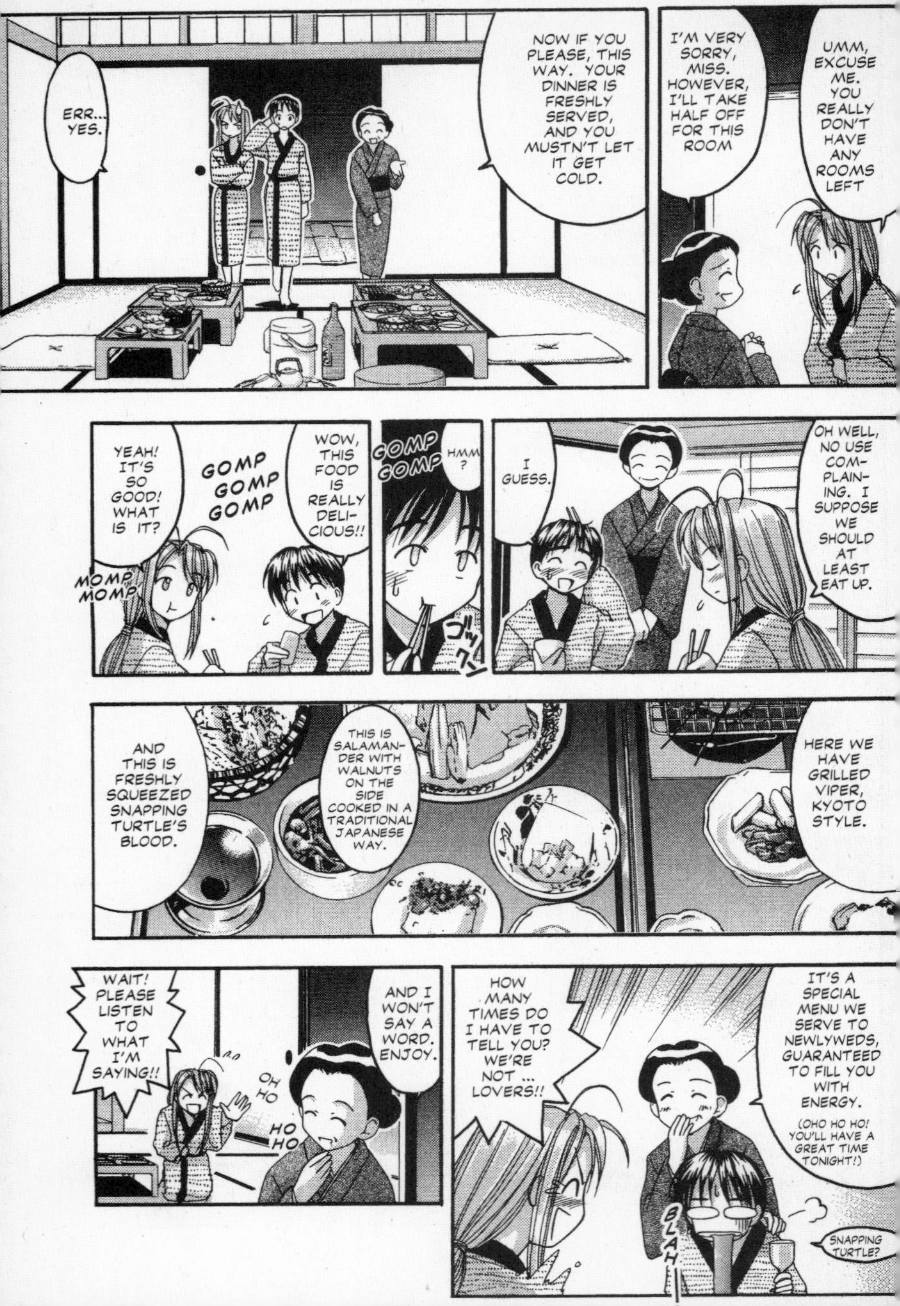
UMM, EXCUSE ME. YOU REALLY DON'T HAVE ANY ROOMS LEFT
I'M VERY SORRY, MISS. HOWEVER, I'LL TAKE HALF OFF FOR THIS ROOM
NOW IF YOU PLEASE, THIS WAY. YOUR DINNER IS FRESHLY SERVED, AND YOU MUSTN'T LET IT GET COLD.
ERR... YES.
OH WELL, NO USE COMPLAINING. I SUPPOSE WE SHOULD AT LEAST EAT UP.
I GUESS.
HMM?
GOMP GOMP
ゴックン
WOW, THIS FOOD IS REALLY DELICIOUS!!
GOMP GOMP GOMP
YEAH! IT'S SO GOOD! WHAT IS IT?
MOMP MOMP
HERE WE HAVE GRILLED VIPER, KYOTO STYLE.
THIS IS SALAMANDER WITH WALNUTS ON THE SIDE COOKED IN A TRADITIONAL JAPANESE WAY.
AND THIS IS FRESHLY SQUEEZED SNAPPING TURTLE'S BLOOD.
IT'S A SPECIAL MENU WE SERVE TO NEWLYWEDS, GUARANTEED TO FILL YOU WITH ENERGY.
(OHO HO HO! YOU'LL HAVE A GREAT TIME TONIGHT!)
SNAPPING TURTLE?
BLAH
HOW MANY TIMES DO I HAVE TO TELL YOU? WE'RE NOT ... LOVERS!!
AND I WON'T SAY A WORD. ENJOY.
OH HO
HO HO
WAIT! PLEASE LISTEN TO WHAT I'M SAYING!!

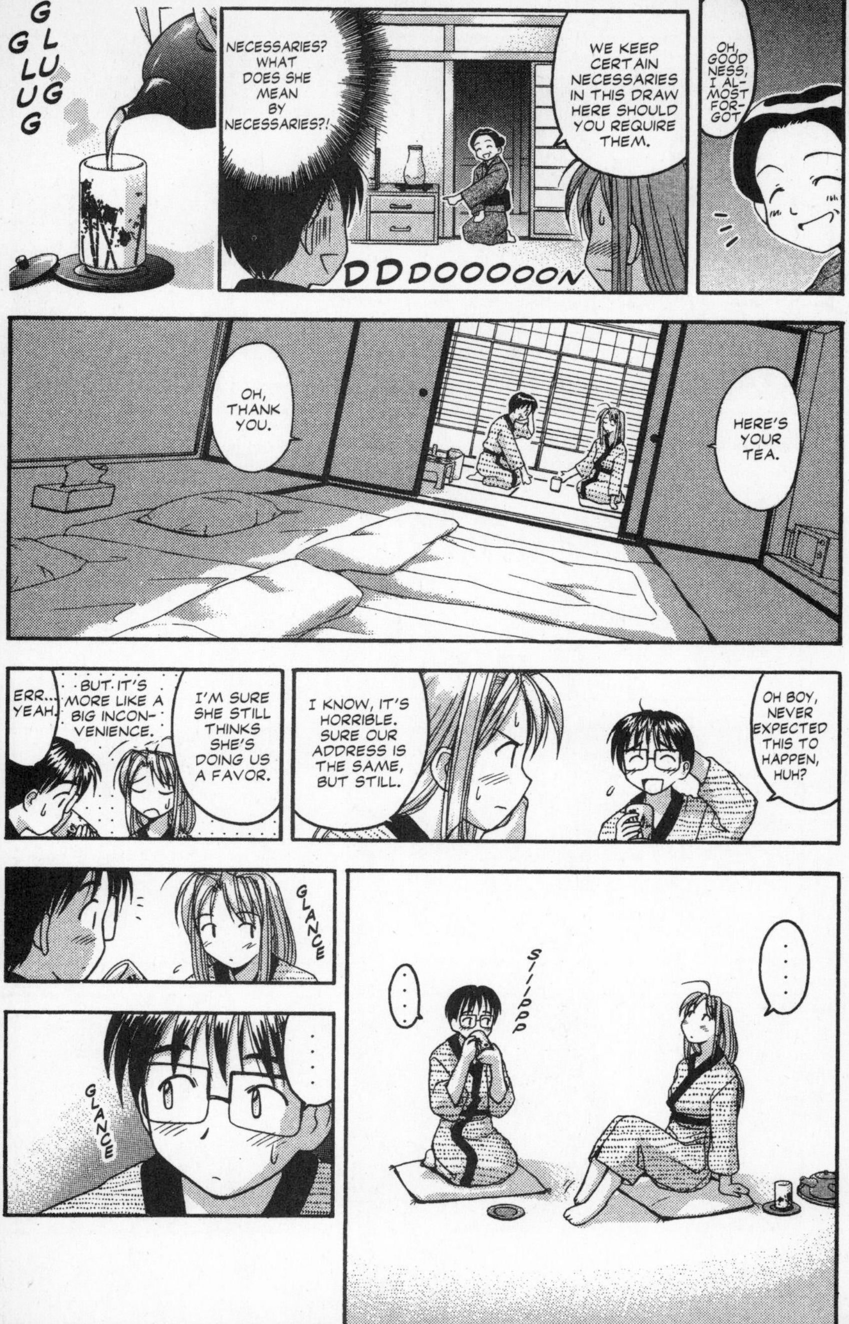

OH, GOODNESS, I ALMOST FORGOT
WE KEEP CERTAIN NECESSARIES IN THIS DRAW HERE SHOULD YOU REQUIRE THEM.
NECESSARIES? WHAT DOES SHE MEAN BY NECESSARIES?!
DDDOOOOON
GLUG GLUG
HERE'S YOUR TEA.
OH, THANK YOU.
OH BOY, NEVER EXPECTED THIS TO HAPPEN, HUH?
I KNOW, IT'S HORRIBLE. SURE OUR ADDRESS IS THE SAME, BUT STILL.
I'M SURE SHE STILL THINKS SHE'S DOING US A FAVOR.
BUT IT'S MORE LIKE A BIG INCONVENIENCE.
ERR... YEAH.
....
SIIIPPP
...
GLANCE
....
GLANCE

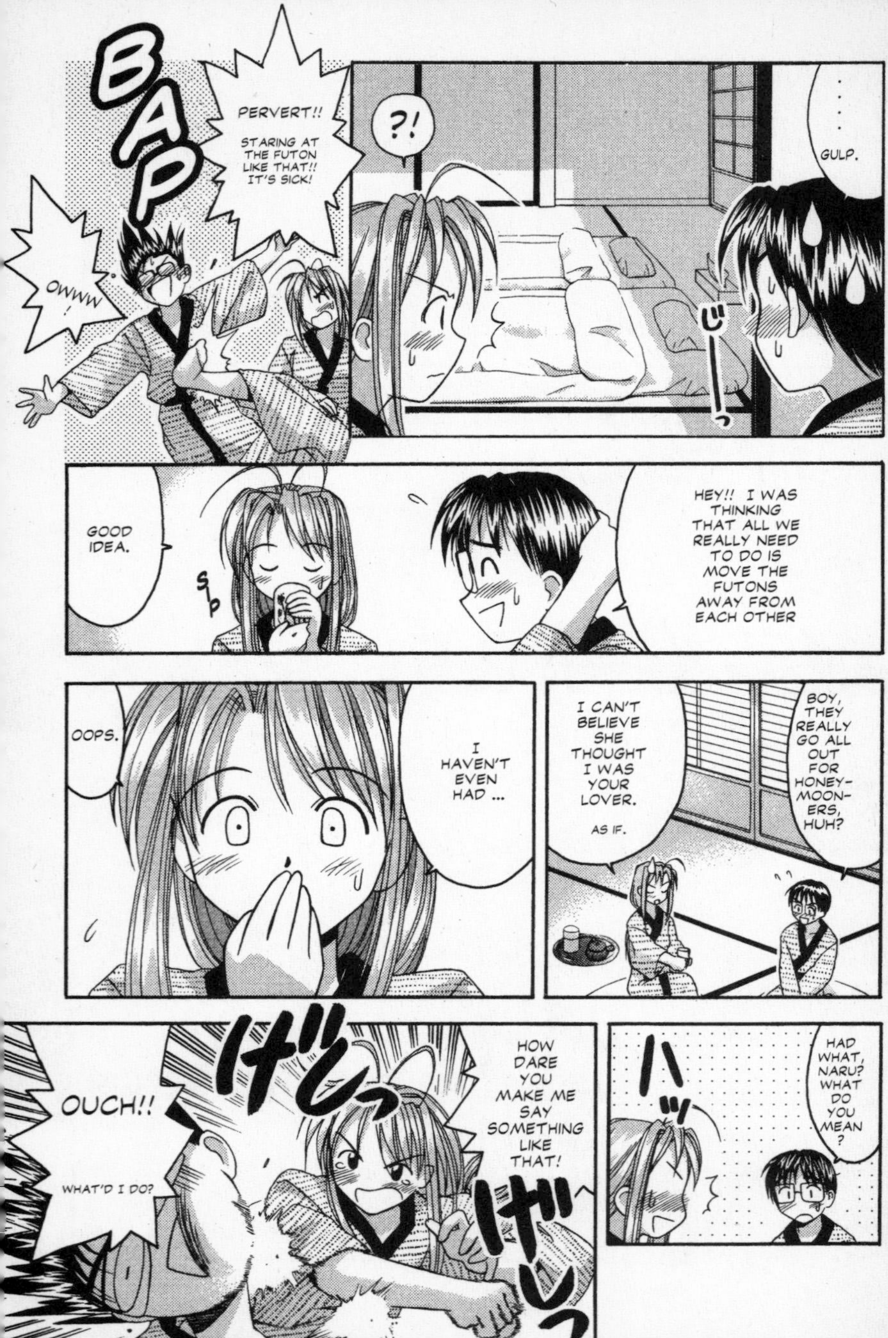
. . . .
GULP.
じーっ
?!
PERVERT!!
STARING AT THE FUTON LIKE THAT!! IT'S SICK!
BAP
OWWW!
HEY!! I WAS THINKING THAT ALL WE REALLY NEED TO DO IS MOVE THE FUTONS AWAY FROM EACH OTHER
SIP
GOOD IDEA.
BOY, THEY REALLY GO ALL OUT FOR HONEY-MOON-ERS, HUH?
I CAN'T BELIEVE SHE THOUGHT I WAS YOUR LOVER.
AS IF.
I HAVEN'T EVEN HAD ...
OOPS.
HAD WHAT, NARU? WHAT DO YOU MEAN?
ハッ
HOW DARE YOU MAKE ME SAY SOMETHING LIKE THAT!
げしっ
げしっ
OUCH!!
WHAT'D I DO?

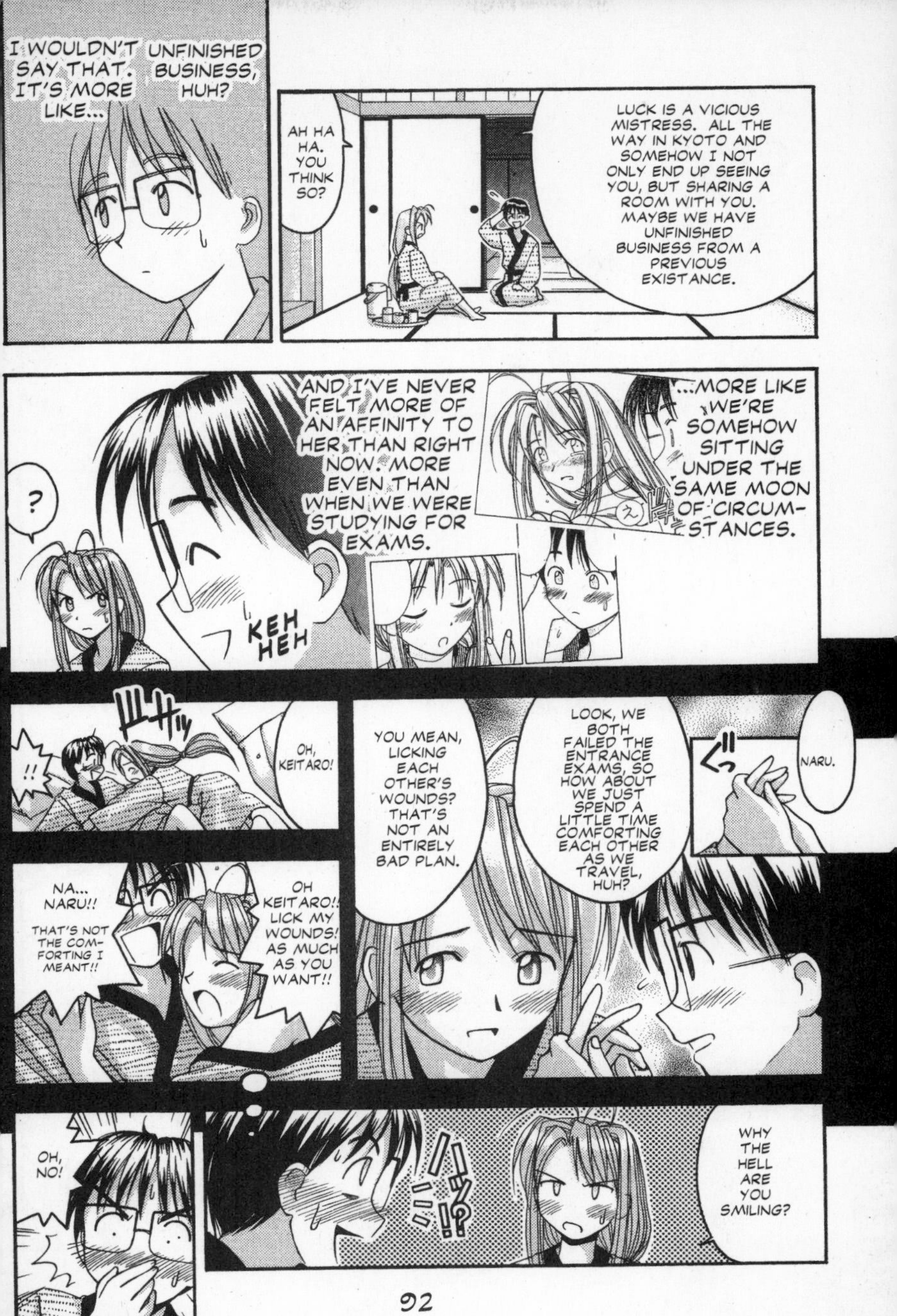
LUCK IS A VICIOUS MISTRESS. ALL THE WAY IN KYOTO AND SOMEHOW I NOT ONLY END UP SEEING YOU, BUT SHARING A ROOM WITH YOU. MAYBE WE HAVE UNFINISHED BUSINESS FROM A PREVIOUS EXISTANCE.
AH HA HA. YOU THINK SO?
UNFINISHED BUSINESS, HUH?
I WOULDN'T SAY THAT. IT'S MORE LIKE...
...MORE LIKE WE'RE SOMEHOW SITTING UNDER THE SAME MOON OF CIRCUM-STANCES.
AND I'VE NEVER FELT MORE OF AN AFFINITY TO HER THAN RIGHT NOW. MORE EVEN THAN WHEN WE WERE STUDYING FOR EXAMS.
?
KEH HEH
NARU.
LOOK, WE BOTH FAILED THE ENTRANCE EXAMS, SO HOW ABOUT WE JUST SPEND A LITTLE TIME COMFORTING EACH OTHER AS WE TRAVEL, HUH?
YOU MEAN, LICKING EACH OTHER'S WOUNDS? THAT'S NOT AN ENTIRELY BAD PLAN.
OH, KEITARO!
!!
OH KEITARO!! LICK MY WOUNDS! AS MUCH AS YOU WANT!!
NA... NARU!!
THAT'S NOT THE COM-FORTING I MEANT!!
WHY THE HELL ARE YOU SMILING?
!!?
OH, NO!

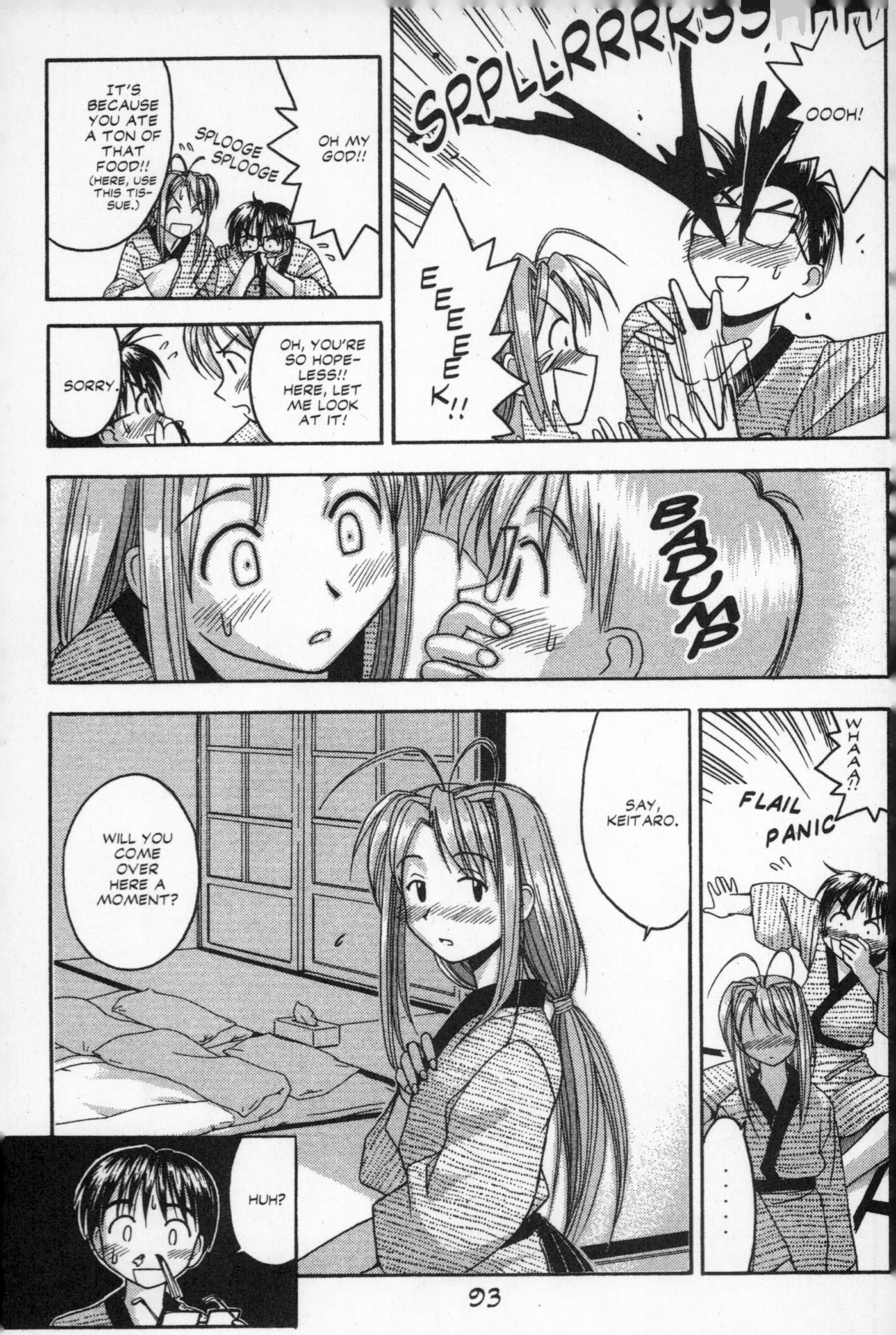

SPPLLRRRKSS
OOOH!
EEEEEK!!
OH MY GOD!!
SPLOOGE SPLOOGE
IT'S BECAUSE YOU ATE A TON OF THAT FOOD!! (HERE, USE THIS TIS-SUE.)
OH, YOU'RE SO HOPE-LESS!! HERE, LET ME LOOK AT IT!
SORRY.
BADUMP
WHAAA!!
FLAIL PANIC
....
SAY, KEITARO.
WILL YOU COME OVER HERE A MOMENT?
HUH?

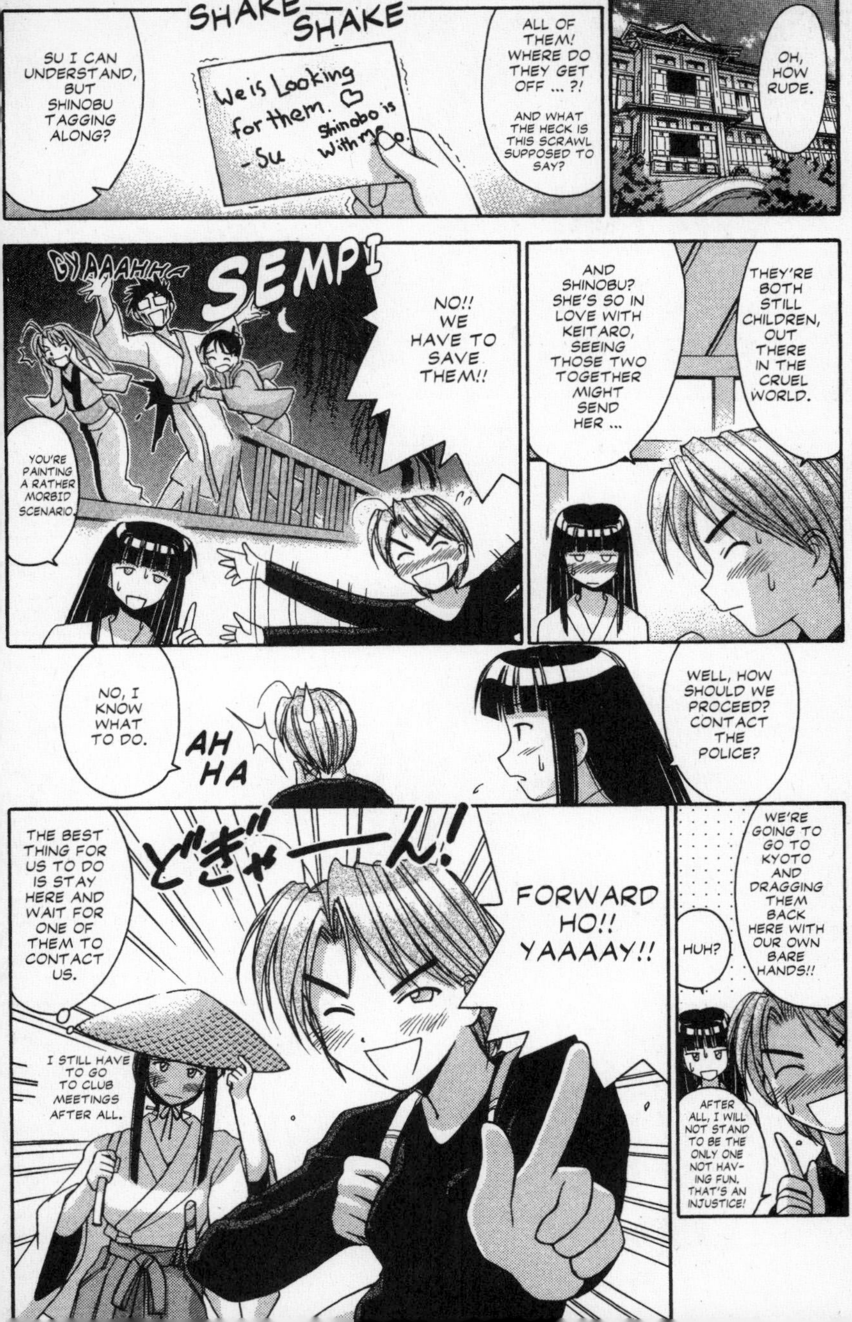
OH, HOW RUDE.
ALL OF THEM! WHERE DO THEY GET OFF ... ?!
AND WHAT THE HECK IS THIS SCRAWL SUPPOSED TO SAY?
SHAKE SHAKE
We is Looking for them. ♡ -Su
Shinobo is with me.
SU I CAN UNDERSTAND, BUT SHINOBU TAGGING ALONG?
THEY'RE BOTH STILL CHILDREN, OUT THERE IN THE CRUEL WORLD.
AND SHINOBU? SHE'S SO IN LOVE WITH KEITARO, SEEING THOSE TWO TOGETHER MIGHT SEND HER ...
NO!! WE HAVE TO SAVE THEM!!
SEMPI
GYAAAHHA
YOU'RE PAINTING A RATHER MORBID SCENARIO.
WELL, HOW SHOULD WE PROCEED? CONTACT THE POLICE?
AH HA
NO, I KNOW WHAT TO DO.
WE'RE GOING TO GO TO KYOTO AND DRAGGING THEM BACK HERE WITH OUR OWN BARE HANDS!!
HUH?
AFTER ALL, I WILL NOT STAND TO BE THE ONLY ONE NOT HAVING FUN. THAT'S AN INJUSTICE!
FORWARD HO!! YAAAAY!!
どぎゃーーん!
THE BEST THING FOR US TO DO IS STAY HERE AND WAIT FOR ONE OF THEM TO CONTACT US.
I STILL HAVE TO GO TO CLUB MEETINGS AFTER ALL.

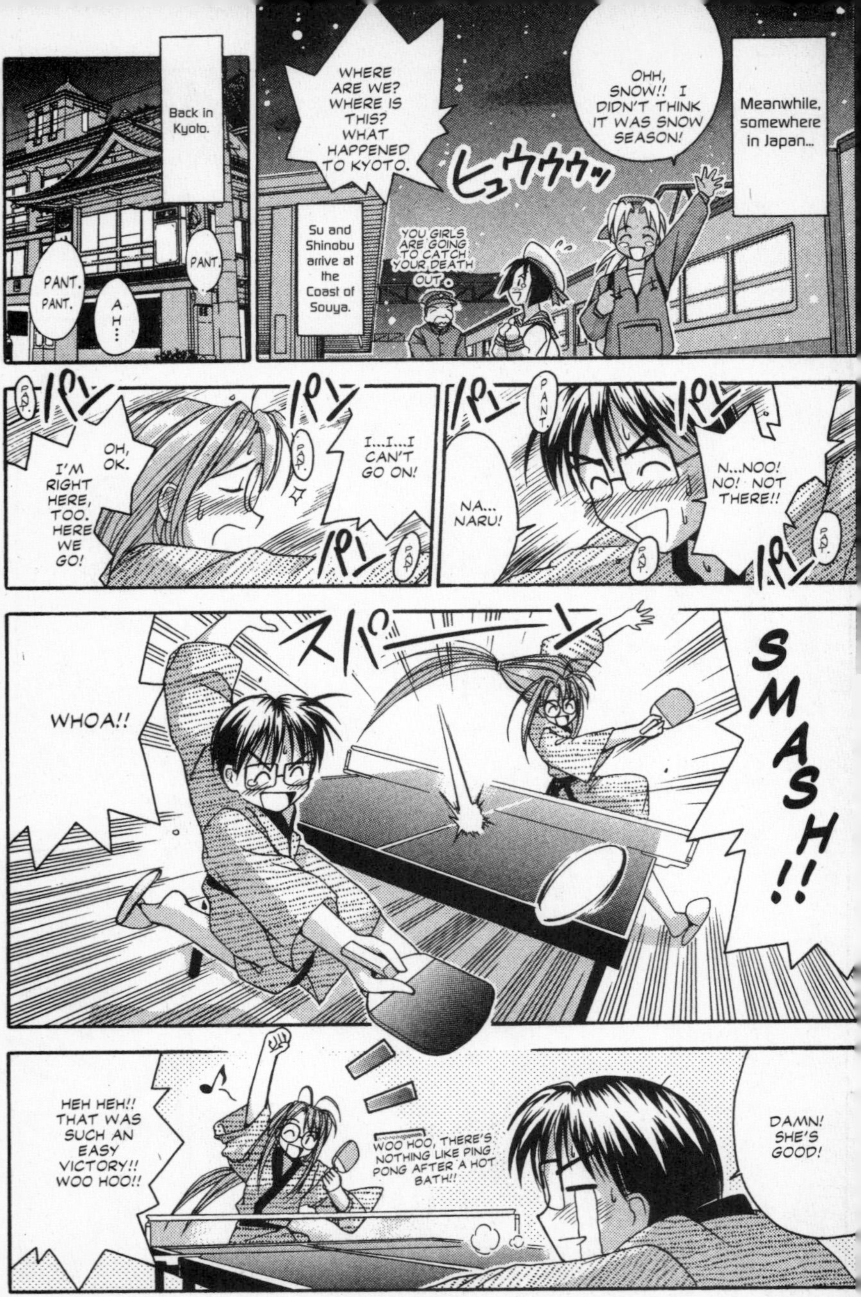
Meanwhile, somewhere in Japan...
OHH, SNOW!! I DIDN'T THINK IT WAS SNOW SEASON!
WHERE ARE WE? WHERE IS THIS? WHAT HAPPENED TO KYOTO.
ヒュウウウッ
YOU GIRLS ARE GOING TO CATCH YOUR DEATH OUT...
Su and Shinobu arrive at the Coast of Souya.
Back in Kyoto.
PANT.
A H...
PANT. PANT.
パン
N...NOO! NO! NOT THERE!!
PANT.
パン
NA... NARU!
PANT.
パン
PANT.
パン
PANT.
パン
I...I...I CAN'T GO ON!
PANT.
パン
OH, OK.
I'M RIGHT HERE, TOO. HERE WE GO!
PANT.
SMASH!!
スパーーン
WHOA!!
DAMN! SHE'S GOOD!
WOO HOO, THERE'S NOTHING LIKE PING PONG AFTER A HOT BATH!!
HEH HEH!! THAT WAS SUCH AN EASY VICTORY!! WOO HOO!!

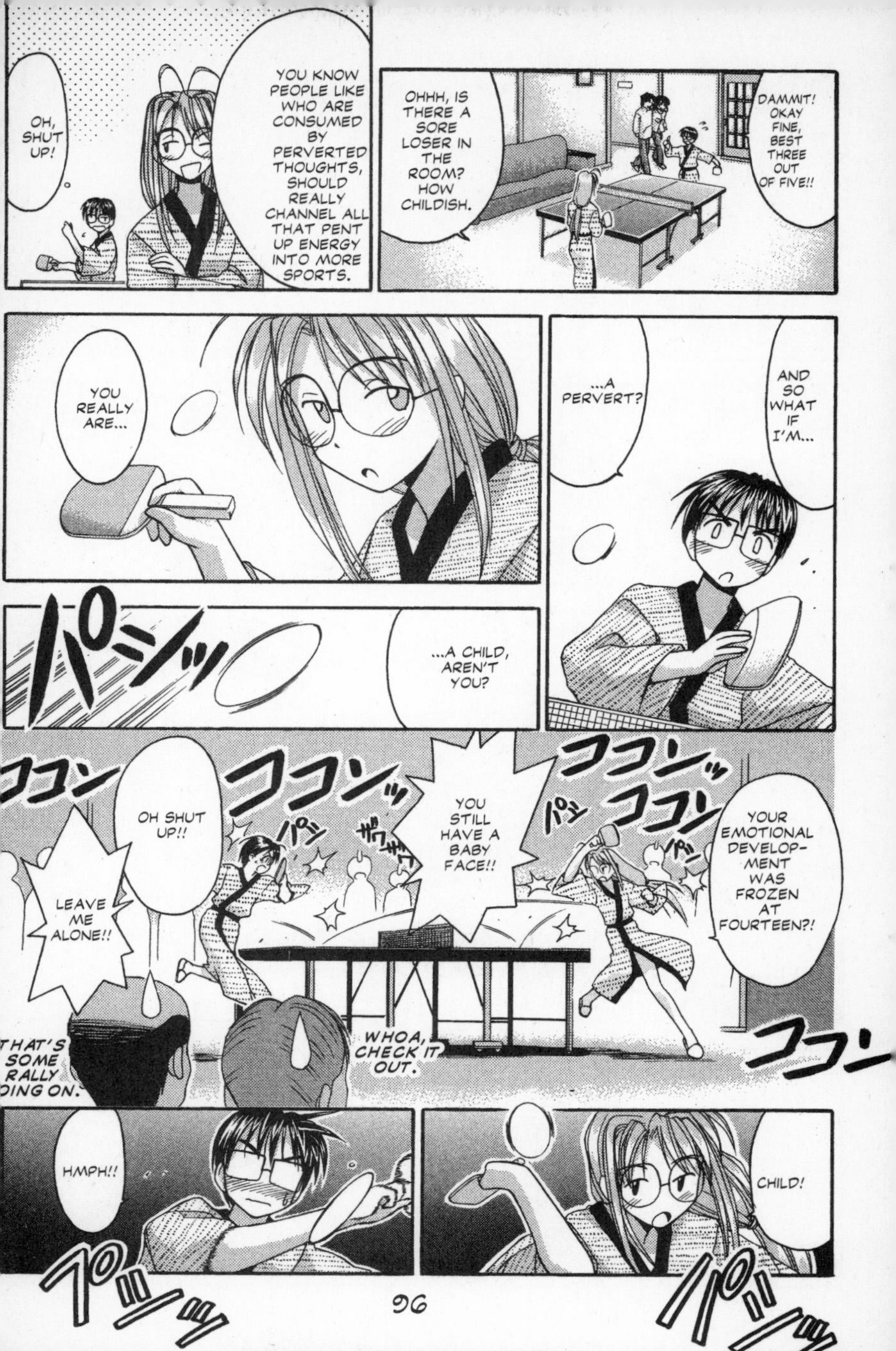

DAMMIT! OKAY FINE, BEST THREE OUT OF FIVE!!
OHHH, IS THERE A SORE LOSER IN THE ROOM? HOW CHILDISH.
YOU KNOW PEOPLE LIKE WHO ARE CONSUMED BY PERVERTED THOUGHTS, SHOULD REALLY CHANNEL ALL THAT PENT UP ENERGY INTO MORE SPORTS.
OH, SHUT UP!
AND SO WHAT IF I'M...
...A PERVERT?
YOU REALLY ARE...
...A CHILD, AREN'T YOU?
ココンッ
ココン
YOUR EMOTIONAL DEVELOP-MENT WAS FROZEN AT FOURTEEN?!
YOU STILL HAVE A BABY FACE!!
ココンッ
OH SHUT UP!!
LEAVE ME ALONE!!
ココン
ココン
WHOA, CHECK IT OUT.
THAT'S SOME RALLY
CHILD!
HMPH!!

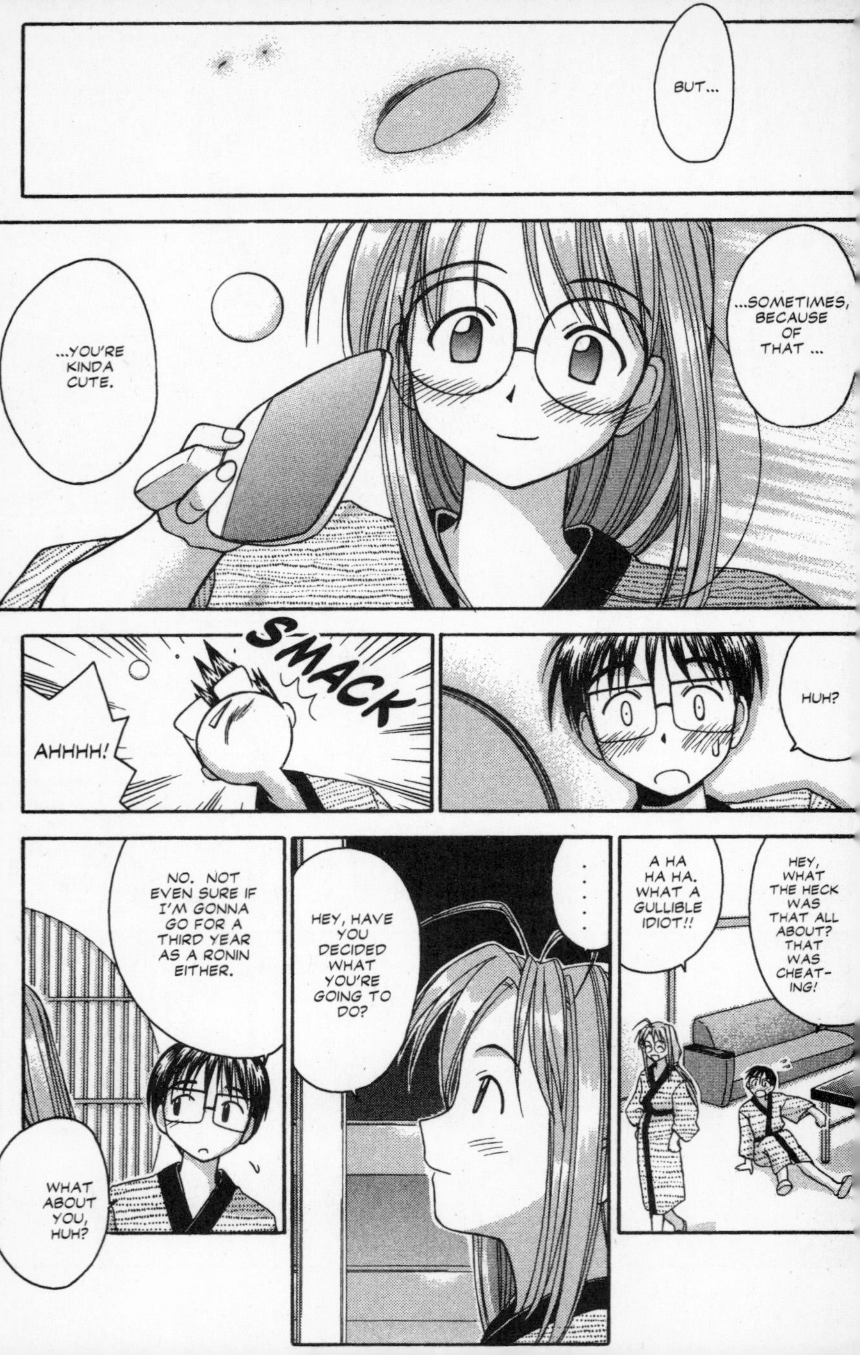
BUT...
...SOMETIMES, BECAUSE OF THAT ...
...YOU'RE KINDA CUTE.
HUH?
S'MACK
AHHHH!
HEY, WHAT THE HECK WAS THAT ALL ABOUT? THAT WAS CHEAT-ING!
A HA HA HA. WHAT A GULLIBLE IDIOT!!
.....
HEY, HAVE YOU DECIDED WHAT YOU'RE GOING TO DO?
NO. NOT EVEN SURE IF I'M GONNA GO FOR A THIRD YEAR AS A RONIN EITHER.
WHAT ABOUT YOU, HUH?

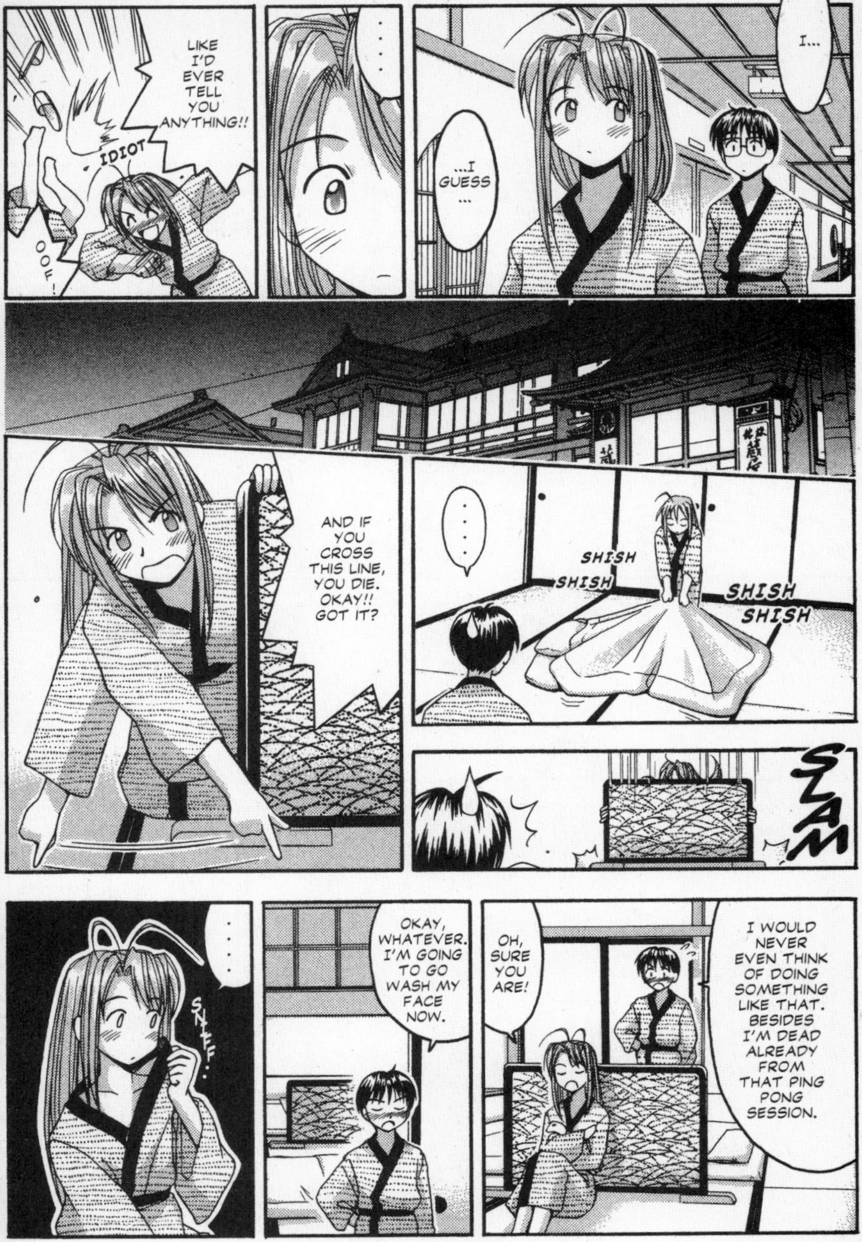
I...
...I GUESS ...
....
LIKE I'D EVER TELL YOU ANYTHING!!
IDIOT
OOF!
....
SHISH
SHISH
SHISH
SHISH
SLAM
AND IF YOU CROSS THIS LINE, YOU DIE. OKAY!! GOT IT?
I WOULD NEVER EVEN THINK OF DOING SOMETHING LIKE THAT. BESIDES I'M DEAD ALREADY FROM THAT PING PONG SESSION.
OH, SURE YOU ARE!
OKAY, WHATEVER. I'M GOING TO GO WASH MY FACE NOW.
....
SNIFF..

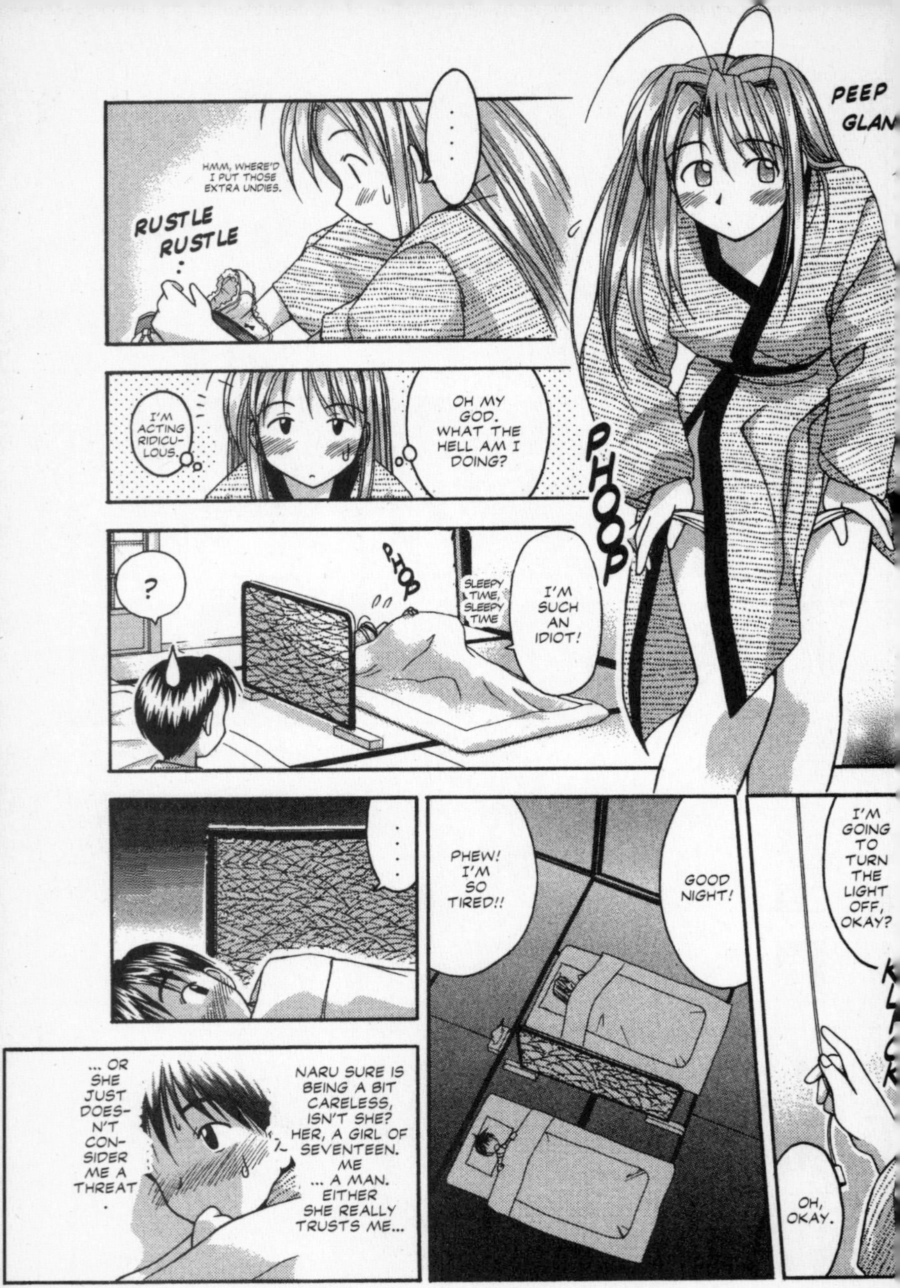
PEEP
GLAN
PHOOP
....
HMM, WHERE'D I PUT THOSE EXTRA UNDIES.
RUSTLE RUSTLE
OH MY GOD. WHAT THE HELL AM I DOING?
I'M ACTING RIDICULOUS.
I'M SUCH AN IDIOT!
SLEEPY TIME, SLEEPY TIME
PHOOP
?
I'M GOING TO TURN THE LIGHT OFF, OKAY?
KLACK
OH, OKAY.
GOOD NIGHT!
PHEW! I'M SO TIRED!!
....
NARU SURE IS BEING A BIT CARELESS, ISN'T SHE? HER, A GIRL OF SEVENTEEN. ME ... A MAN. EITHER SHE REALLY TRUSTS ME...
... OR SHE JUST DOESN'T CONSIDER ME A THREAT.

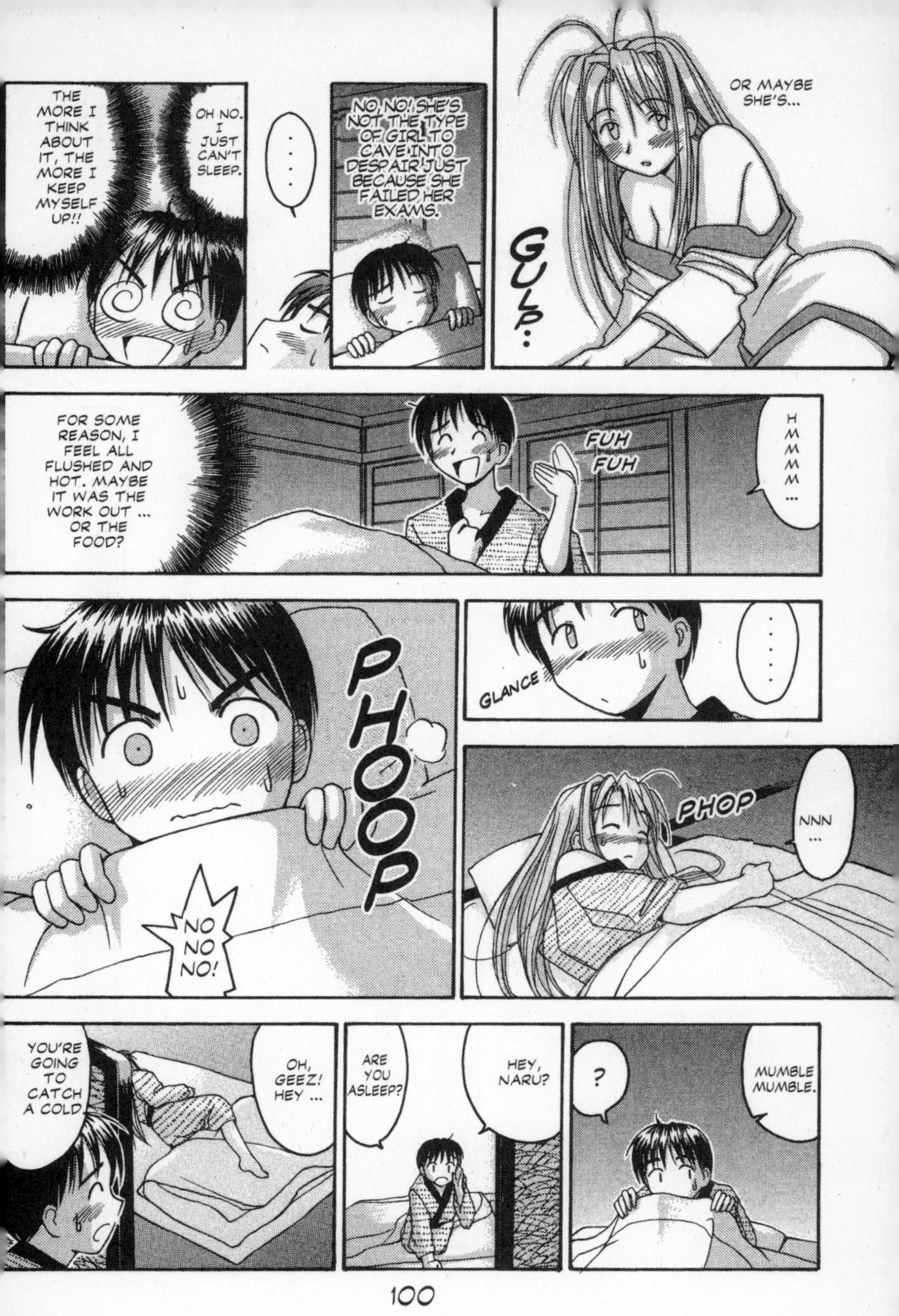
OR MAYBE SHE'S...
GULP..
NO, NO! SHE'S NOT THE TYPE OF GIRL TO CAVE INTO DESPAIR JUST BECAUSE SHE FAILED HER EXAMS.
.....
OH NO. I JUST CAN'T SLEEP.
THE MORE I THINK ABOUT IT, THE MORE I KEEP MYSELF UP!!
HMMMM...
FUH FUH
FOR SOME REASON, I FEEL ALL FLUSHED AND HOT.. MAYBE IT WAS THE WORK OUT ... OR THE FOOD?
......
GLANCE
NNN...
PHOP
PHOOP
NO NO NO!
MUMBLE MUMBLE.
?
HEY, NARU?
ARE YOU ASLEEP?
OH, GEEZ! HEY ...
YOU'RE GOING TO CATCH A COLD.

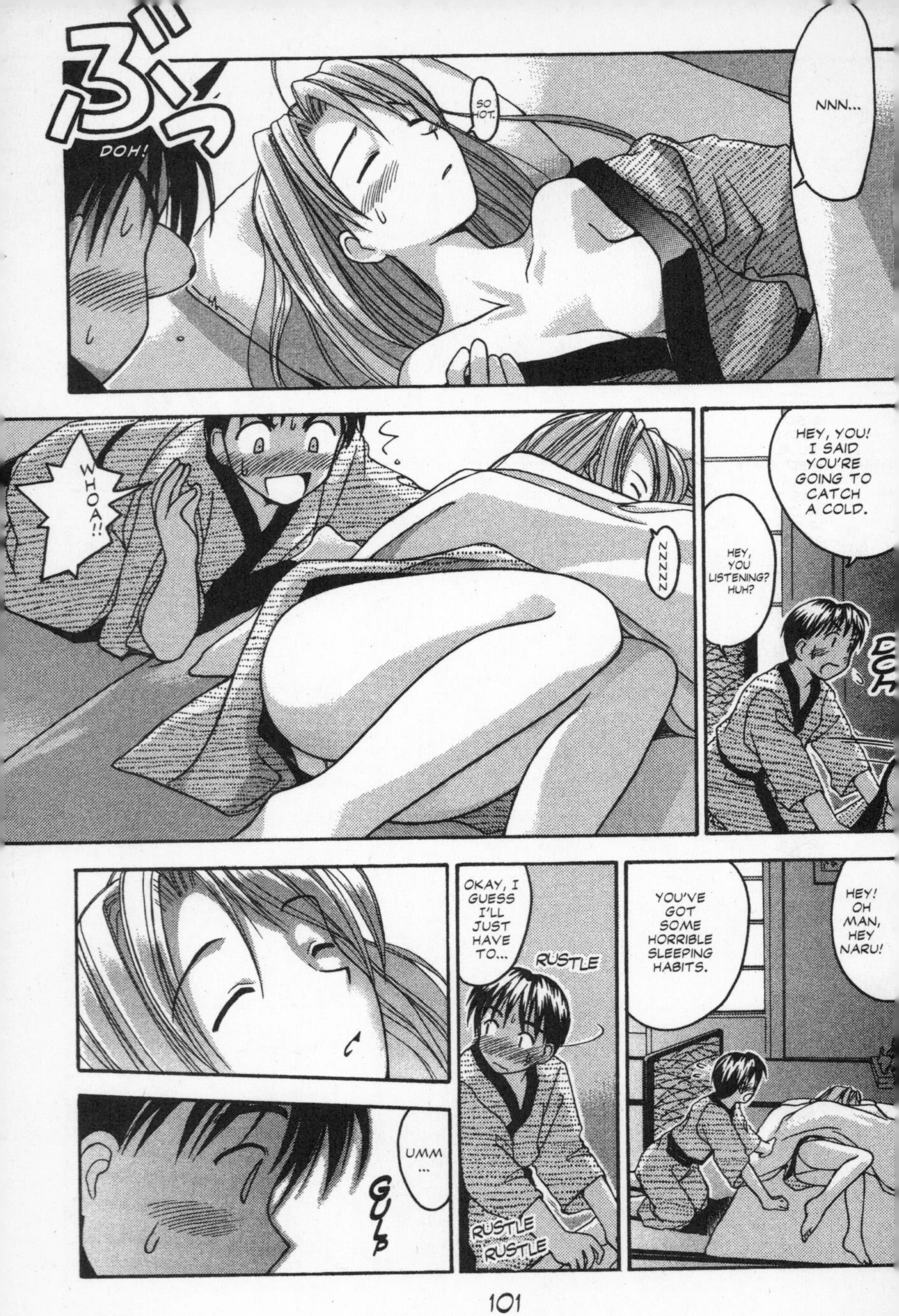
NNN...
SO HOT.
DOH!
HEY, YOU! I SAID YOU'RE GOING TO CATCH A COLD.
HEY, YOU LISTENING? HUH?
NNNNN
WHOA!!
HEY! OH MAN, HEY NARU!
YOU'VE GOT SOME HORRIBLE SLEEPING HABITS.
OKAY, I GUESS I'LL JUST HAVE TO...
RUSTLE
RUSTLE RUSTLE
UMM ...
GULP

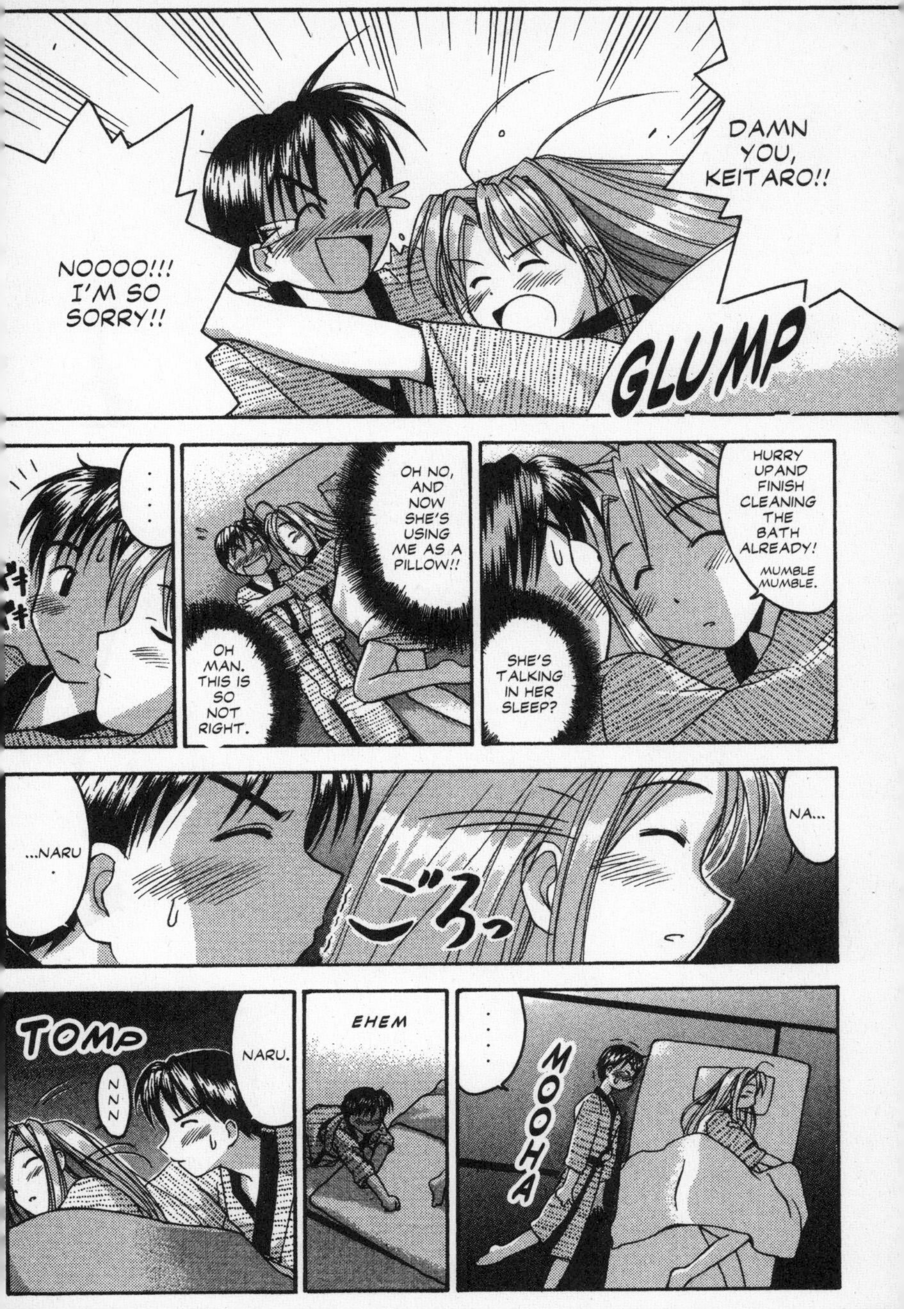

DAMN YOU, KEITARO!!
NOOOO!!! I'M SO SORRY!!
GLUMP
HURRY UP AND FINISH CLEANING THE BATH ALREADY!
MUMBLE MUMBLE.
SHE'S TALKING IN HER SLEEP?
OH NO, AND NOW SHE'S USING ME AS A PILLOW!!
OH MAN. THIS IS SO NOT RIGHT.
....
NA...
ごろっ
...NARU.
....
MOOHA
EHEM
NARU.
TOMP
NNN

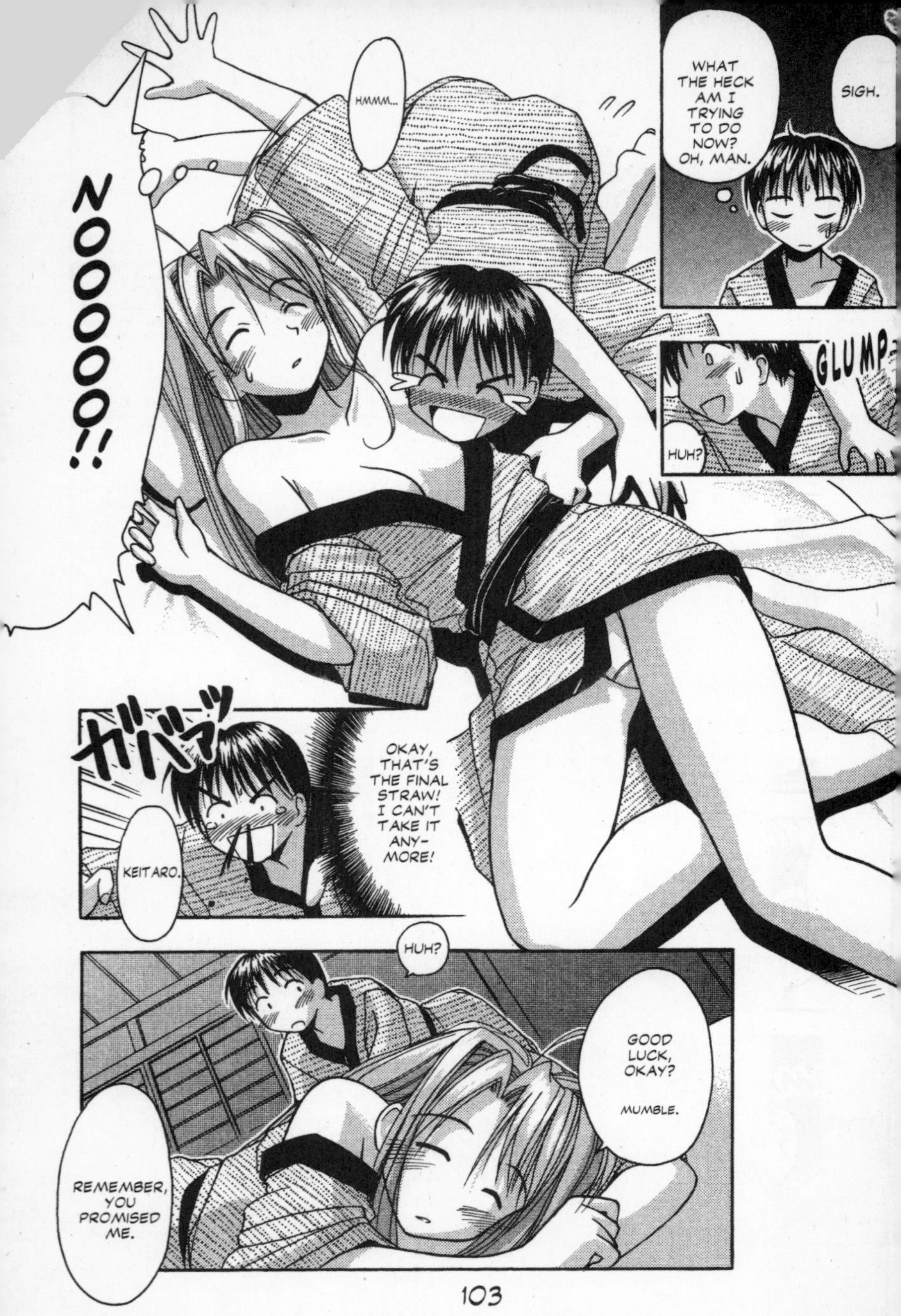
WHAT THE HECK AM I TRYING TO DO NOW? OH, MAN.
SIGH.
GLUMP
HUH?
HMMM...
NOOOOOO!!
ガバァッ
OKAY, THAT'S THE FINAL STRAW! I CAN'T TAKE IT ANY-MORE!
KEITARO.
HUH?
GOOD LUCK, OKAY?
MUMBLE.
REMEMBER, YOU PROMISED ME.

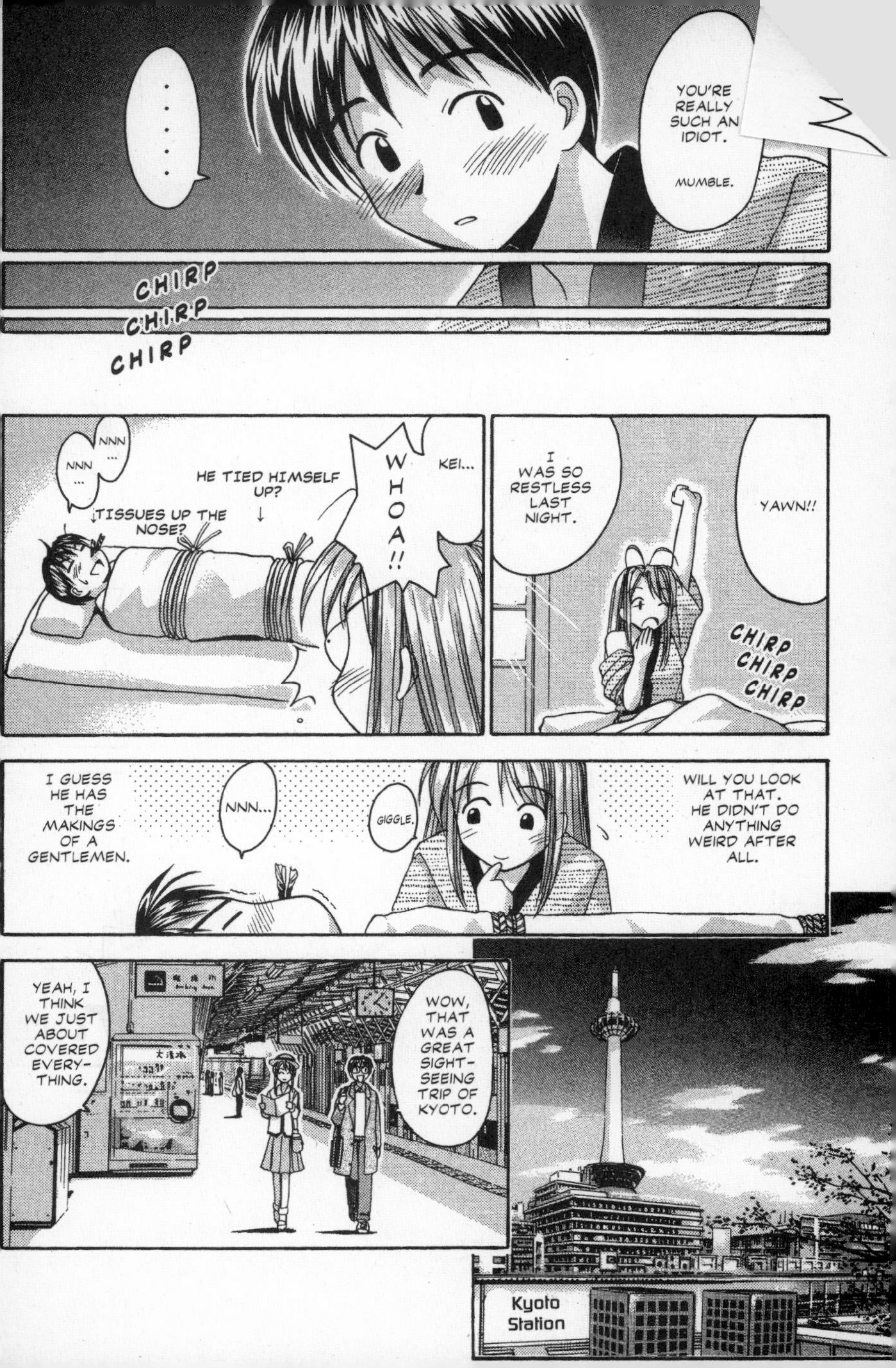
YOU'RE REALLY SUCH AN IDIOT.
MUMBLE.
. . . . . .
CHIRP
CHIRP
CHIRP
YAWN!!
I WAS SO RESTLESS LAST NIGHT.
CHIRP
CHIRP
CHIRP
KEI...
WHOA!!
HE TIED HIMSELF UP?
TISSUES UP THE NOSE?
NNN...
NNN...
WILL YOU LOOK AT THAT. HE DIDN'T DO ANYTHING WEIRD AFTER ALL.
GIGGLE.
NNN...
I GUESS HE HAS THE MAKINGS OF A GENTLEMEN.
Kyoto Station
WOW, THAT WAS A GREAT SIGHT-SEEING TRIP OF KYOTO.
YEAH, I THINK WE JUST ABOUT COVERED EVERY-THING.

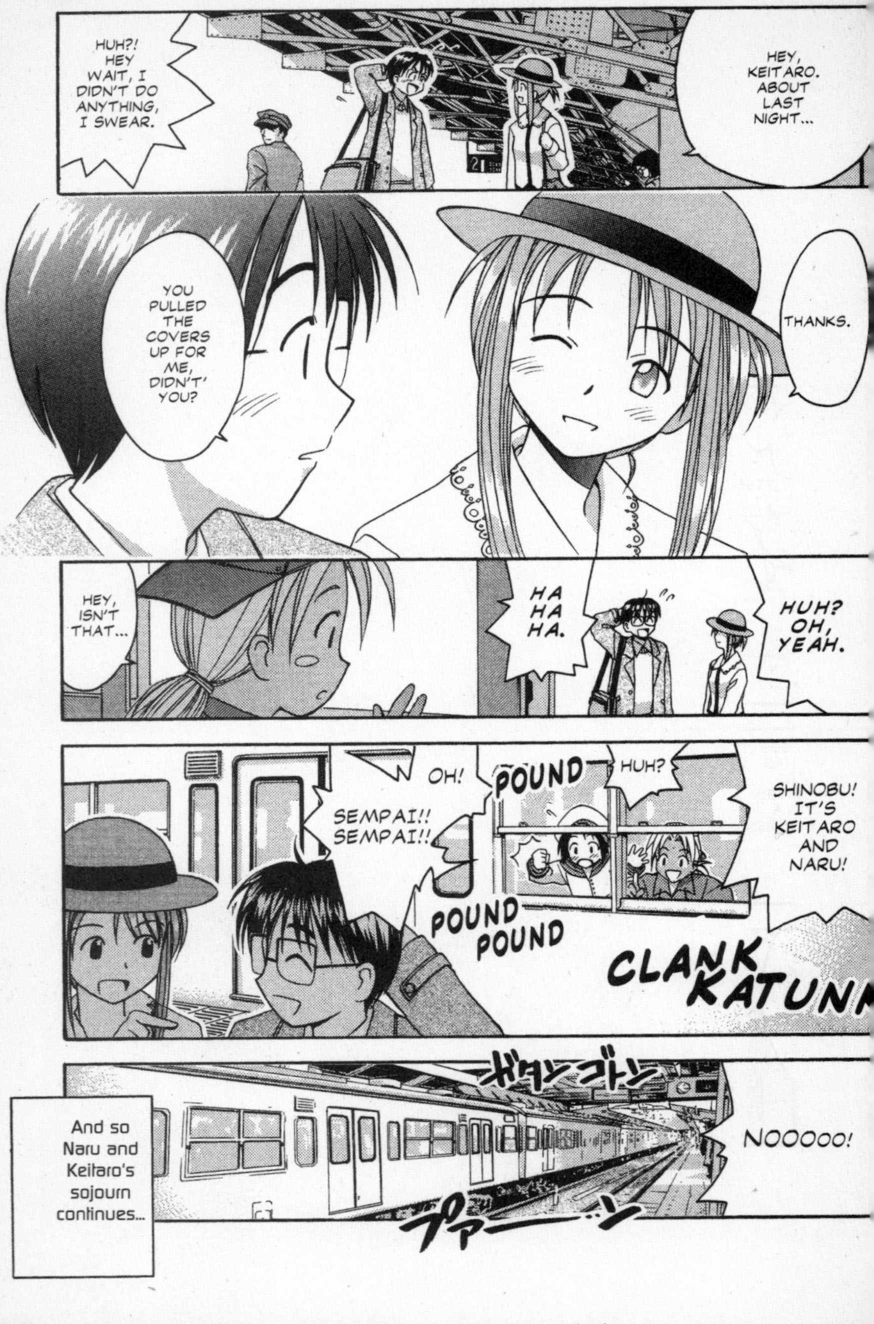
HEY, KEITARO. ABOUT LAST NIGHT...
HUH?! HEY WAIT, I DIDN'T DO ANYTHING, I SWEAR.
THANKS.
YOU PULLED THE COVERS UP FOR ME, DIDN'T' YOU?
HUH? OH, YEAH.
HA HA HA.
HEY, ISN'T THAT...
SHINOBU! IT'S KEITARO AND NARU!
HUH?
POUND
OH!
SEMPAI!! SEMPAI!!
POUND POUND
CLANK KATUNN
ガタンゴトン
NOOOOO!
プァーン
And so Naru and Keitaro's sojourn continues...

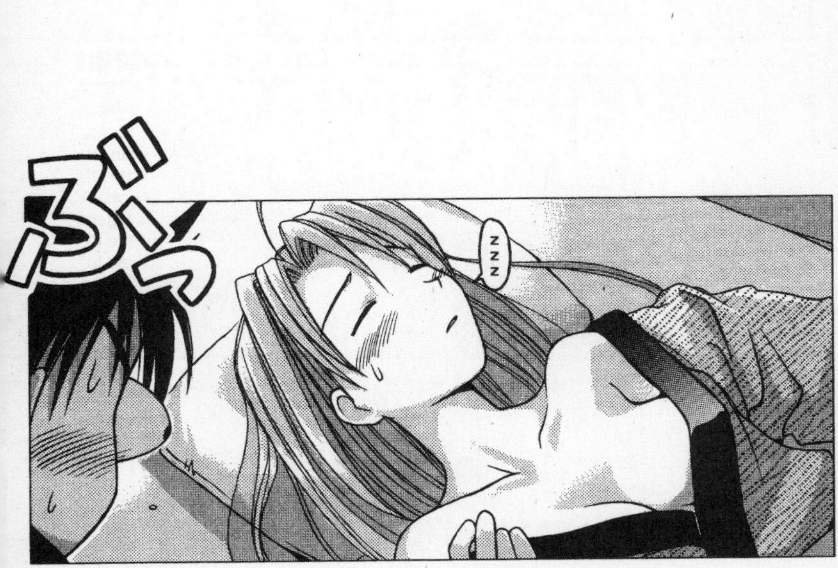
ぶ
NNN

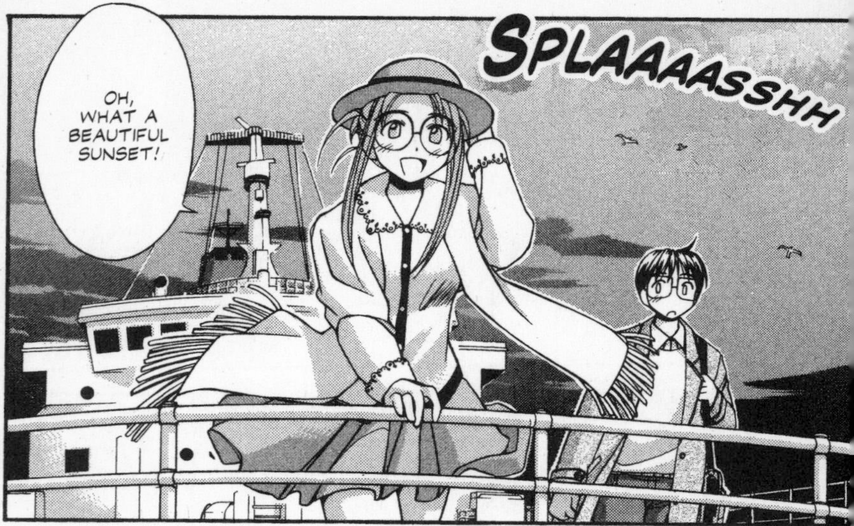
SPLAAAASSHH
OH, WHAT A BEAUTIFUL SUNSET!

LOVE ♥ HINA

HINATA..21 Oh Me, Oh My! Otohime Appears!!

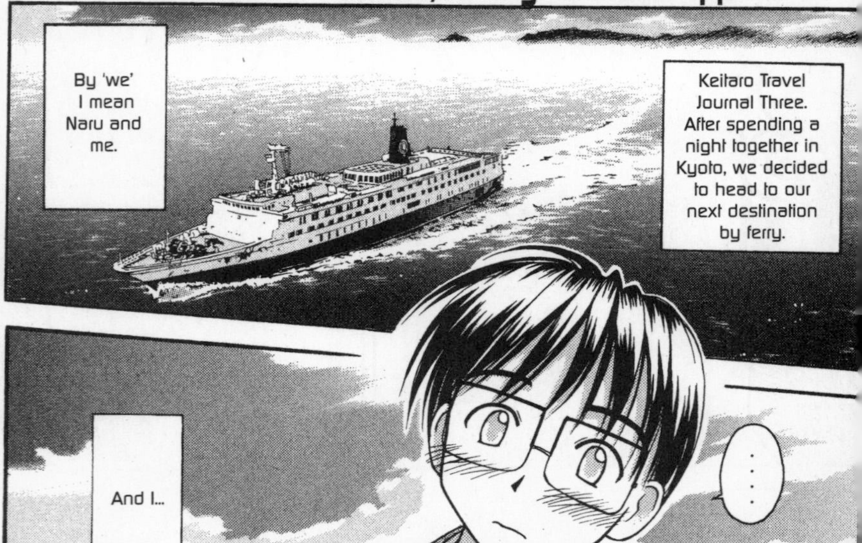
Keitaro Travel Journal Three. After spending a night together in Kyoto, we decided to head to our next destination by ferry.
By 'we' I mean Naru and me.
....
And I...

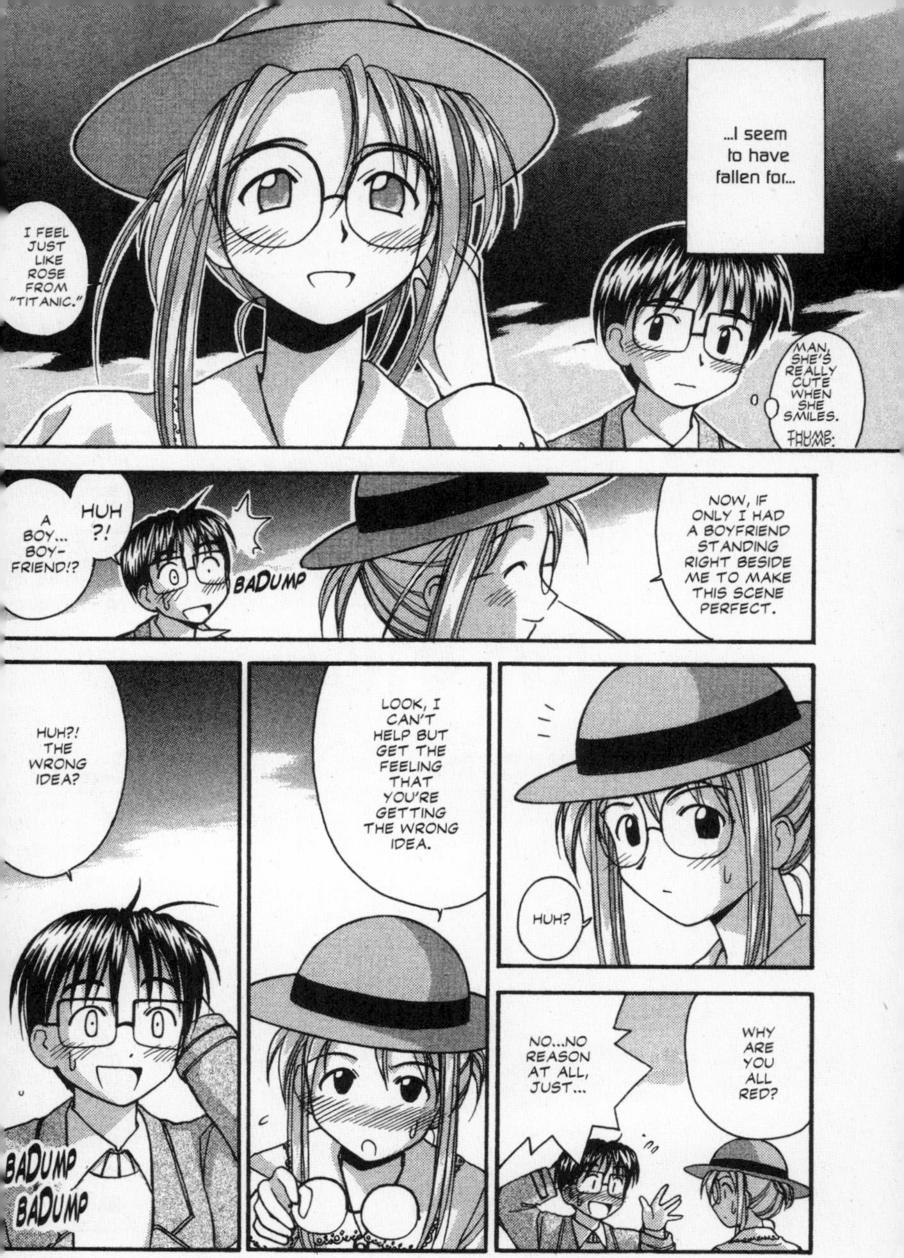
...I seem to have fallen for...
MAN, SHE'S REALLY CUTE WHEN SHE SMILES.
THUMP THUMP
I FEEL JUST LIKE ROSE FROM "TITANIC."
NOW, IF ONLY I HAD A BOYFRIEND STANDING RIGHT BESIDE ME TO MAKE THIS SCENE PERFECT.
BADUMP
HUH ?!
A BOY... BOY-FRIEND!?
HUH?
WHY ARE YOU ALL RED?
NO...NO REASON AT ALL, JUST...
LOOK, I CAN'T HELP BUT GET THE FEELING THAT YOU'RE GETTING THE WRONG IDEA.
HUH?! THE WRONG IDEA?
BADUMP BADUMP

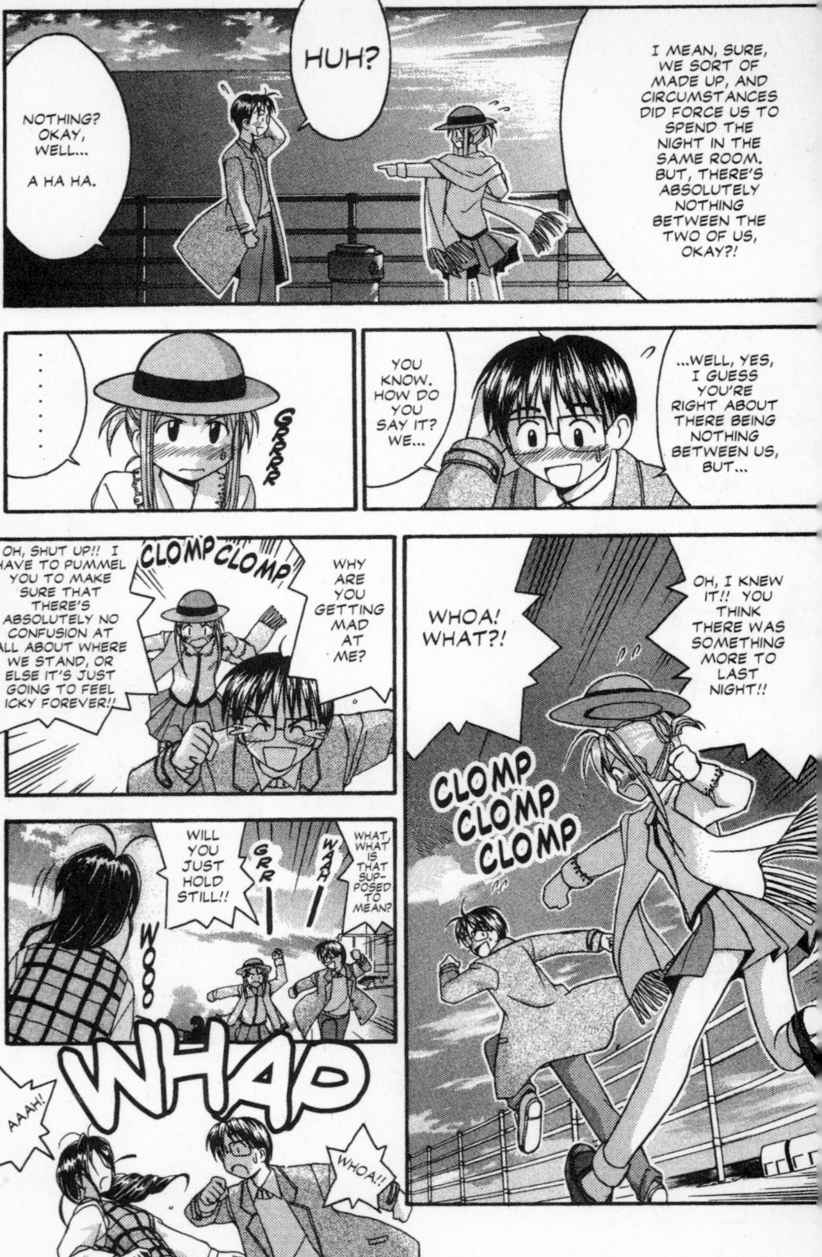
I MEAN, SURE, WE SORT OF MADE UP, AND CIRCUMSTANCES DID FORCE US TO SPEND THE NIGHT IN THE SAME ROOM. BUT, THERE'S ABSOLUTELY NOTHING BETWEEN THE TWO OF US, OKAY?!
HUH?
NOTHING? OKAY, WELL... A HA HA.
...WELL, YES, I GUESS YOU'RE RIGHT ABOUT THERE BEING NOTHING BETWEEN US, BUT...
YOU KNOW. HOW DO YOU SAY IT? WE...
GRRRR
......
OH, I KNEW IT!! YOU THINK THERE WAS SOMETHING MORE TO LAST NIGHT!!
WHOA! WHAT?!
CLOMP CLOMP CLOMP
WHY ARE YOU GETTING MAD AT ME?
CLOMP CLOMP
OH, SHUT UP!! I HAVE TO PUMMEL YOU TO MAKE SURE THAT THERE'S ABSOLUTELY NO CONFUSION AT ALL ABOUT WHERE WE STAND, OR ELSE IT'S JUST GOING TO FEEL ICKY FOREVER!!
WHAT, WHAT IS THAT SUP-POSED TO MEAN?
WAAH
GRR
WILL YOU JUST HOLD STILL!!
WOOO
WHAP
WHOA!!
AAAH!

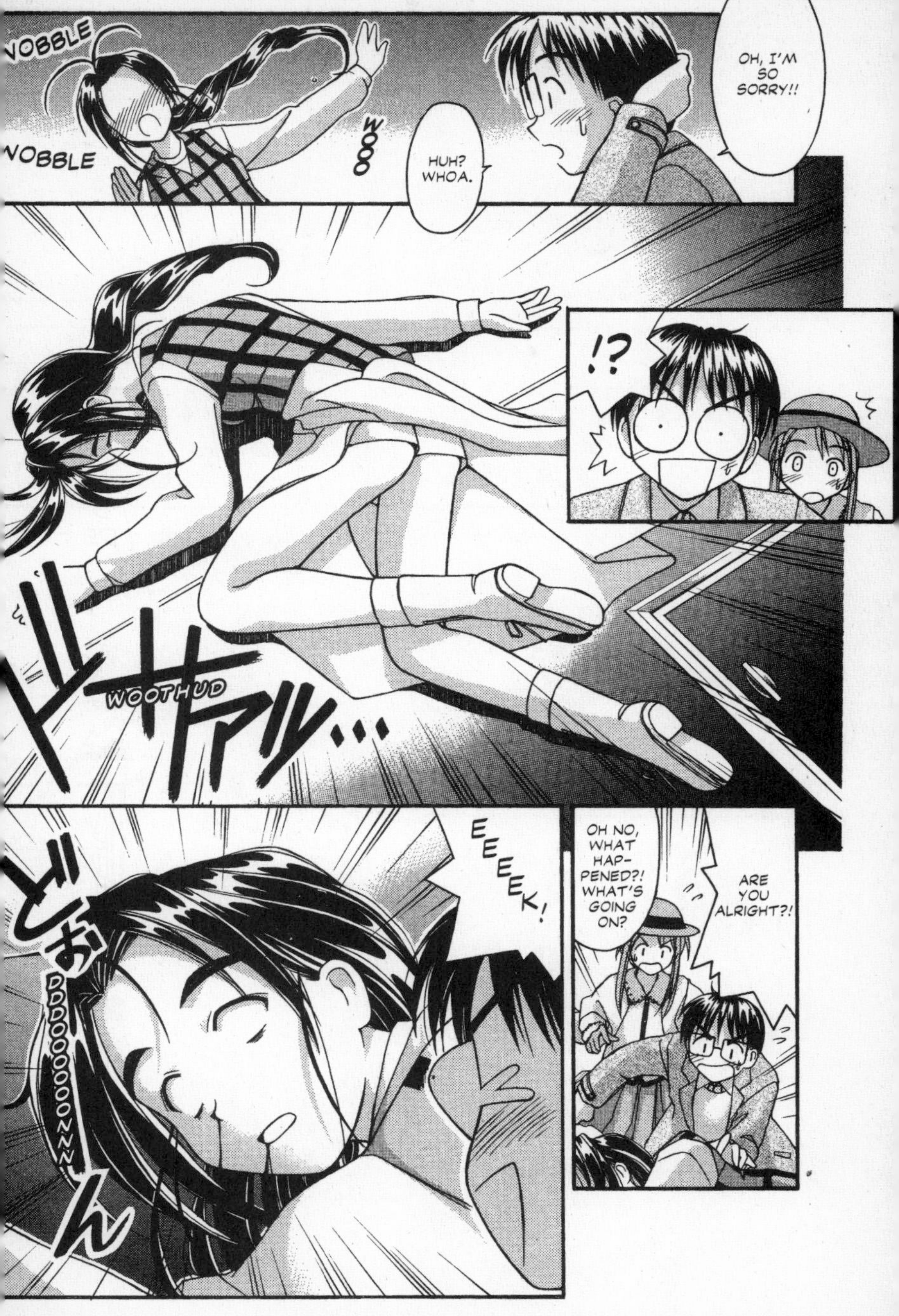

OH, I'M SO SORRY!!
HUH? WHOA.
WOOO
WOBBLE
WOBBLE
!?
WOOTHUD
ARE YOU ALRIGHT?!
OH NO, WHAT HAP-PENED?! WHAT'S GOING ON?
EEEEK!
DDDOOOOOOONNN

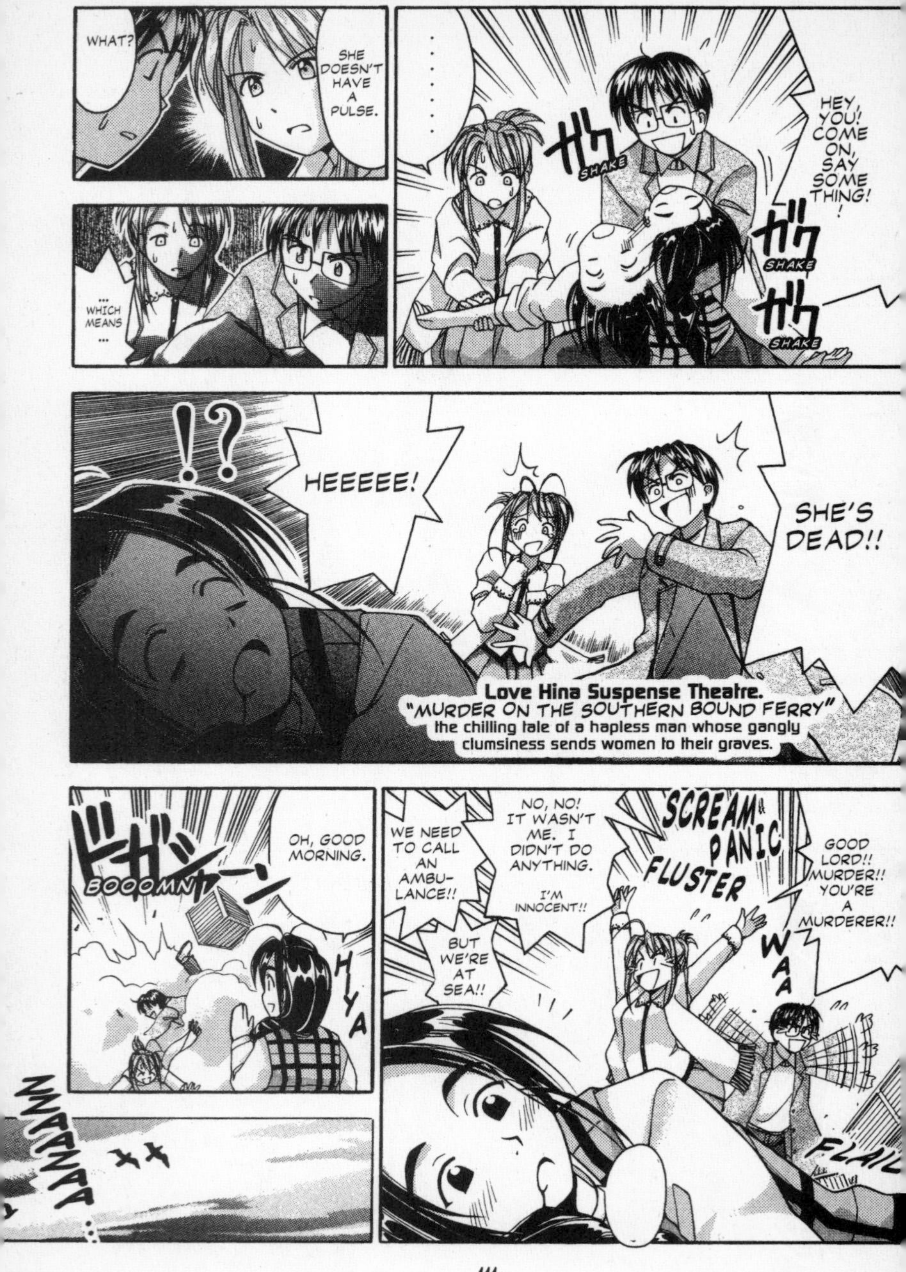
WHAT?
SHE DOESN'T HAVE A PULSE.
...WHICH MEANS...
....
SHAKE
HEY, YOU! COME ON, SAY SOME THING!
SHAKE
SHAKE
!?
HEEEEEE!
SHE'S DEAD!!
Love Hina Suspense Theatre.
"MURDER ON THE SOUTHERN BOUND FERRY"
the chilling tale of a hapless man whose gangly clumsiness sends women to their graves.
NO, NO! IT WASN'T ME. I DIDN'T DO ANYTHING.
I'M INNOCENT!!
WE NEED TO CALL AN AMBULANCE!!
BUT WE'RE AT SEA!!
SCREAM
PANIC
FLUSTER
GOOD LORD!! MURDER!! YOU'RE A MURDERER!!
WAA
FLAIL
BOOOMN
OH, GOOD MORNING.
HIYA

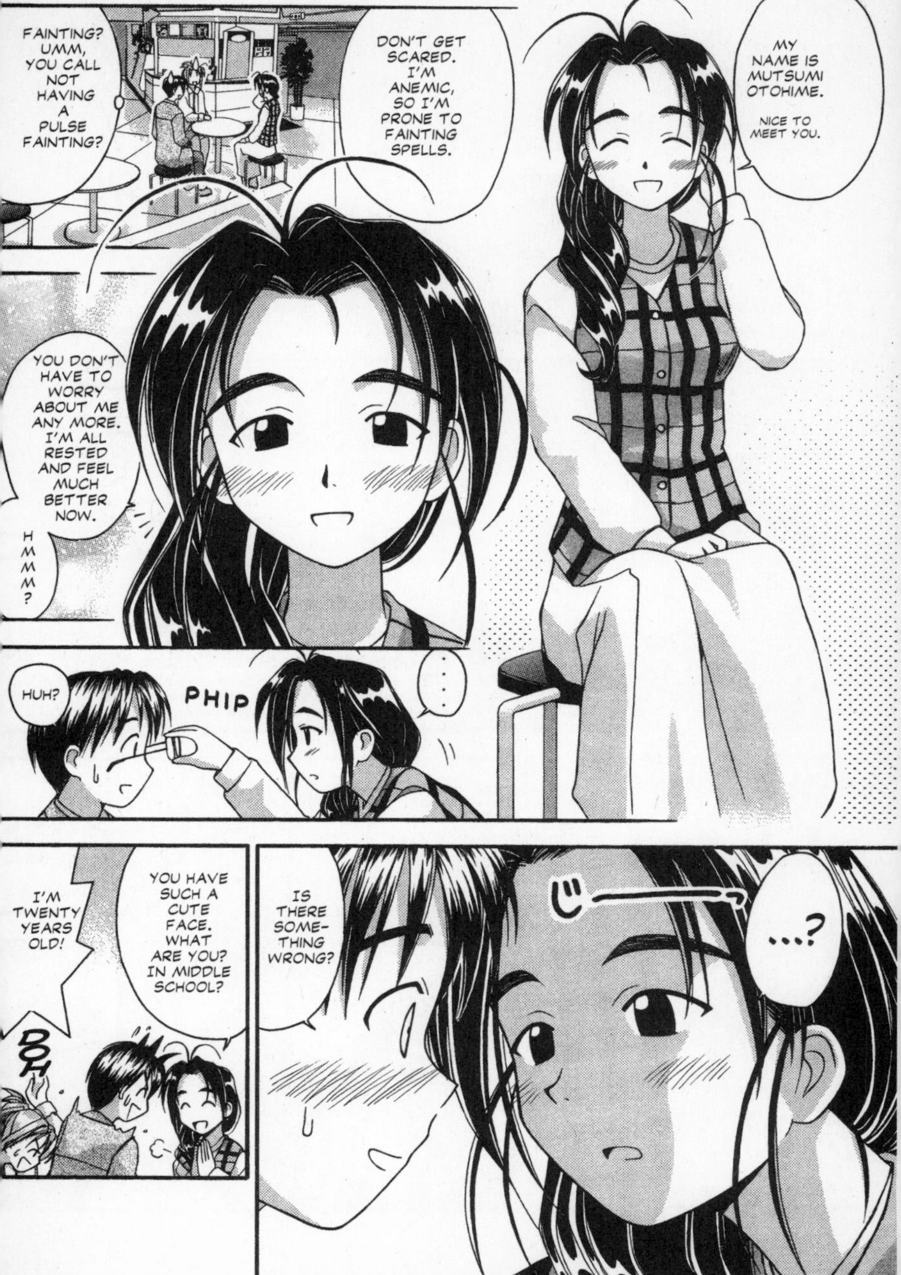
MY NAME IS MUTSUMI OTOHIME.
NICE TO MEET YOU.
DON'T GET SCARED. I'M ANEMIC, SO I'M PRONE TO FAINTING SPELLS.
FAINTING? UMM, YOU CALL NOT HAVING A PULSE FAINTING?
YOU DON'T HAVE TO WORRY ABOUT ME ANY MORE. I'M ALL RESTED AND FEEL MUCH BETTER NOW.
HMMMM?
....
PHIP
HUH?
じ—
...?
IS THERE SOME-THING WRONG?
YOU HAVE SUCH A CUTE FACE. WHAT ARE YOU? IN MIDDLE SCHOOL?
I'M TWENTY YEARS OLD!
DOH

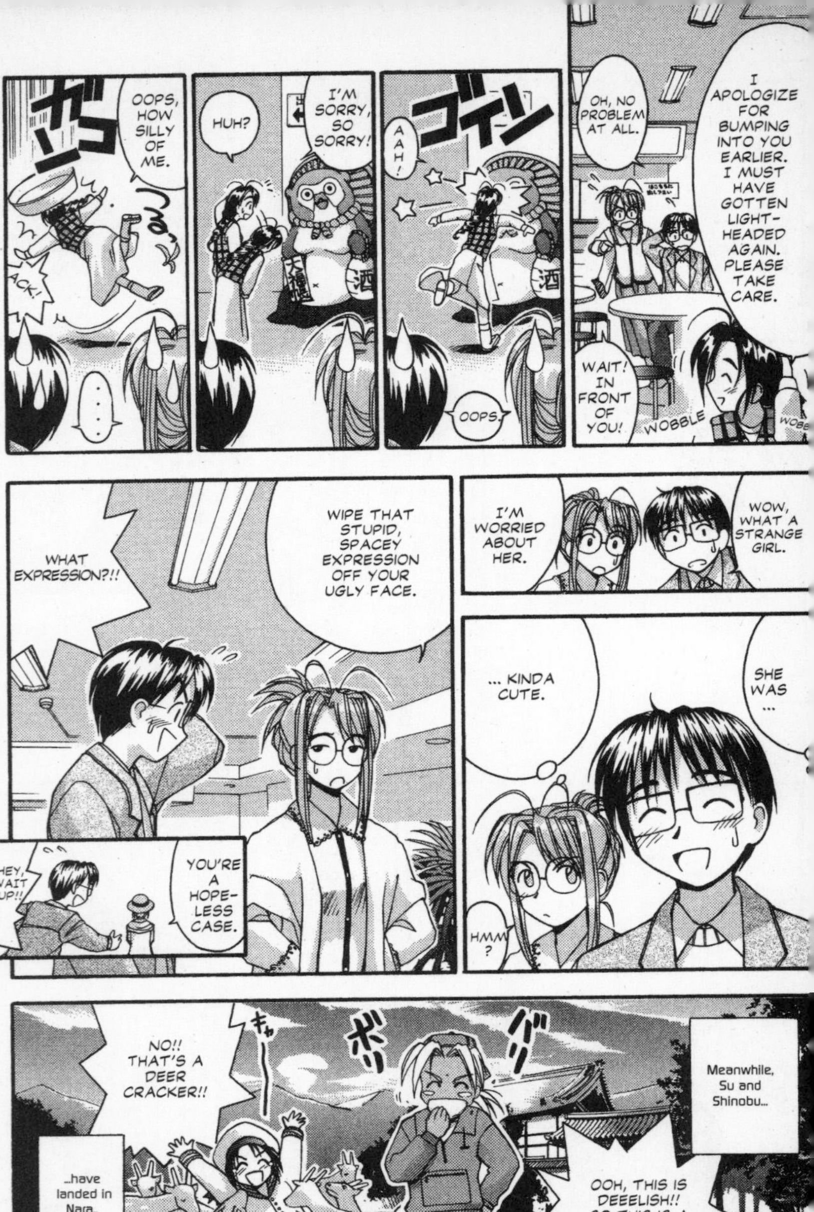
I APOLOGIZE FOR BUMPING INTO YOU EARLIER. I MUST HAVE GOTTEN LIGHT-HEADED AGAIN. PLEASE TAKE CARE.
OH, NO PROBLEM AT ALL.
WAIT! IN FRONT OF YOU!
WOBBLE
AAH!
OOPS.
I'M SORRY, SO SORRY!
HUH?
OOPS, HOW SILLY OF ME.
ACK!
...
WOW, WHAT A STRANGE GIRL.
I'M WORRIED ABOUT HER.
SHE WAS ...
... KINDA CUTE.
HMM?
WIPE THAT STUPID, SPACEY EXPRESSION OFF YOUR UGLY FACE.
WHAT EXPRESSION?!!
YOU'RE A HOPE-LESS CASE.
HEY, WAIT UP!!
Meanwhile, Su and Shinobu...
OOH, THIS IS DEEELISH!! SO THIS IS A CINNAMON COOKIE, HUH?
NO!! THAT'S A DEER CRACKER!!
...have landed in Nara..

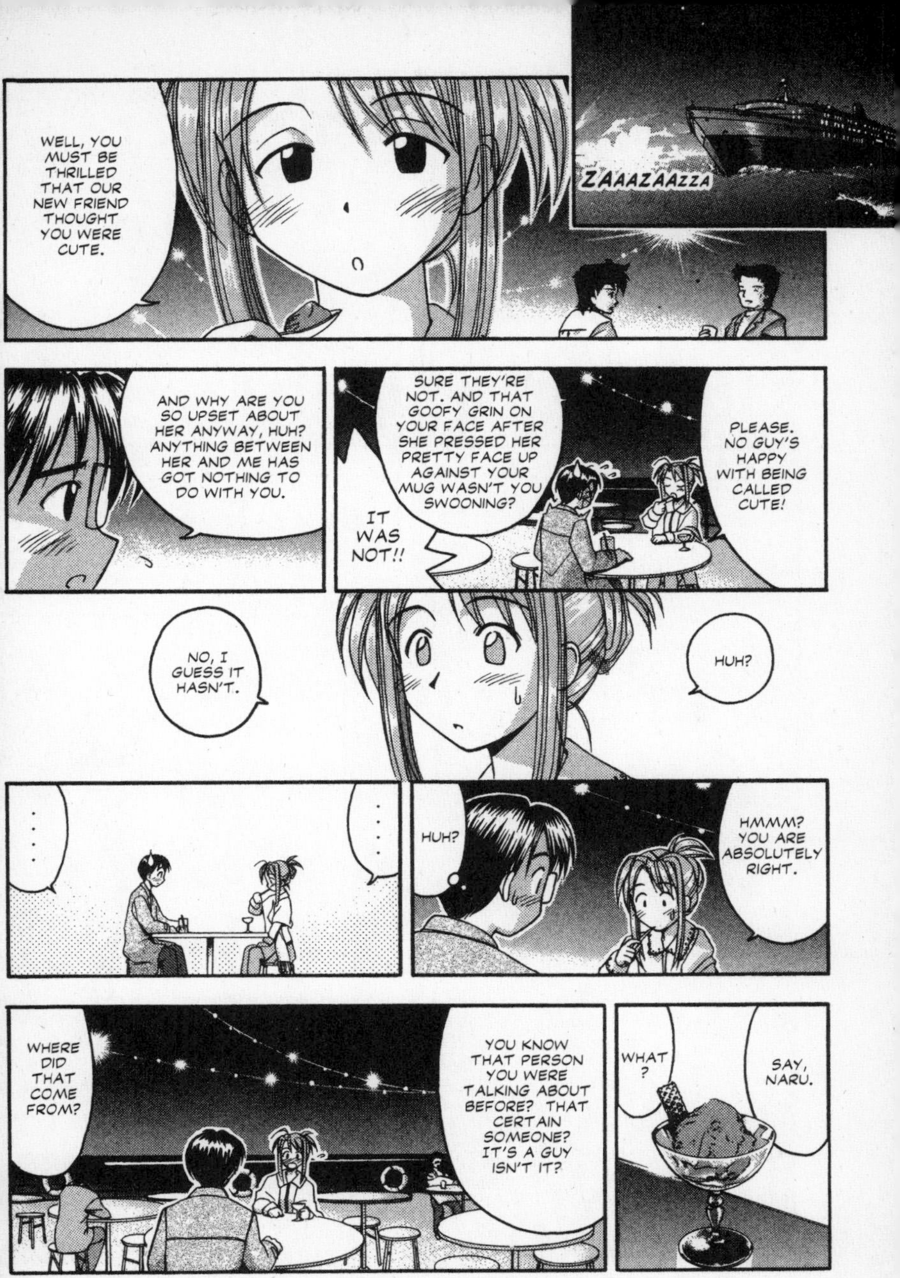
ZAAAZAAZZA
WELL, YOU MUST BE THRILLED THAT OUR NEW FRIEND THOUGHT YOU WERE CUTE.
PLEASE. NO GUY'S HAPPY WITH BEING CALLED CUTE!
SURE THEY'RE NOT. AND THAT GOOFY GRIN ON YOUR FACE AFTER SHE PRESSED HER PRETTY FACE UP AGAINST YOUR MUG WASN'T YOU SWOONING?
IT WAS NOT!!
AND WHY ARE YOU SO UPSET ABOUT HER ANYWAY, HUH? ANYTHING BETWEEN HER AND ME HAS GOT NOTHING TO DO WITH YOU.
HUH?
NO, I GUESS IT HASN'T.
HMMM? YOU ARE ABSOLUTELY RIGHT.
HUH?
....
....
SAY, NARU.
WHAT?
YOU KNOW THAT PERSON YOU WERE TALKING ABOUT BEFORE? THAT CERTAIN SOMEONE? IT'S A GUY ISN'T IT?
WHERE DID THAT COME FROM?

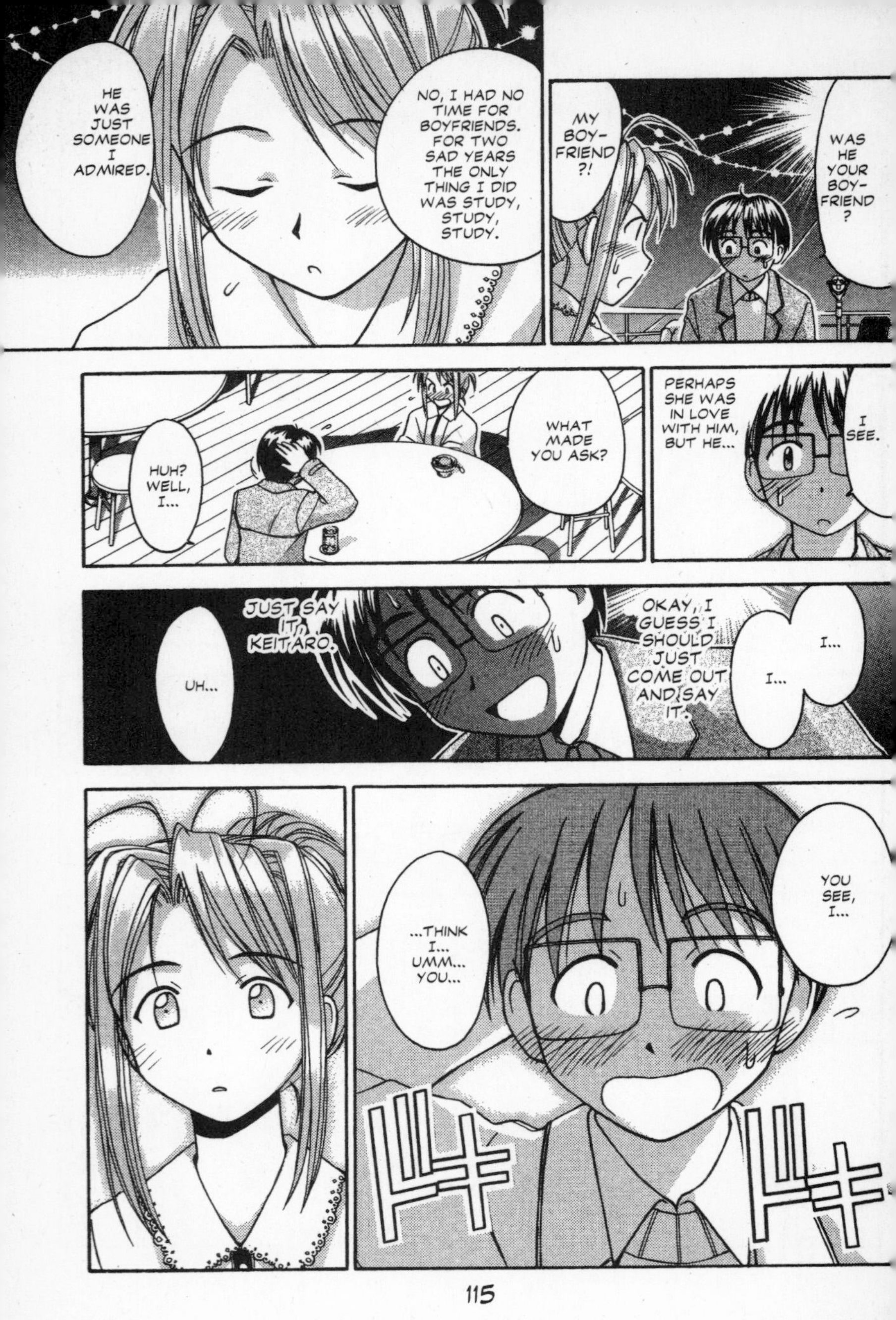
WAS HE YOUR BOY-FRIEND?
MY BOY-FRIEND?!
NO, I HAD NO TIME FOR BOYFRIENDS. FOR TWO SAD YEARS THE ONLY THING I DID WAS STUDY, STUDY, STUDY.
HE WAS JUST SOMEONE I ADMIRED.
I SEE.
PERHAPS SHE WAS IN LOVE WITH HIM, BUT HE...
WHAT MADE YOU ASK?
HUH? WELL, I...
I...
I...
OKAY, I GUESS I SHOULD JUST COME OUT AND SAY IT.
JUST SAY IT, KEITARO.
UH...
YOU SEE, I...
...THINK I... UMM... YOU...
ドキ
ドキ

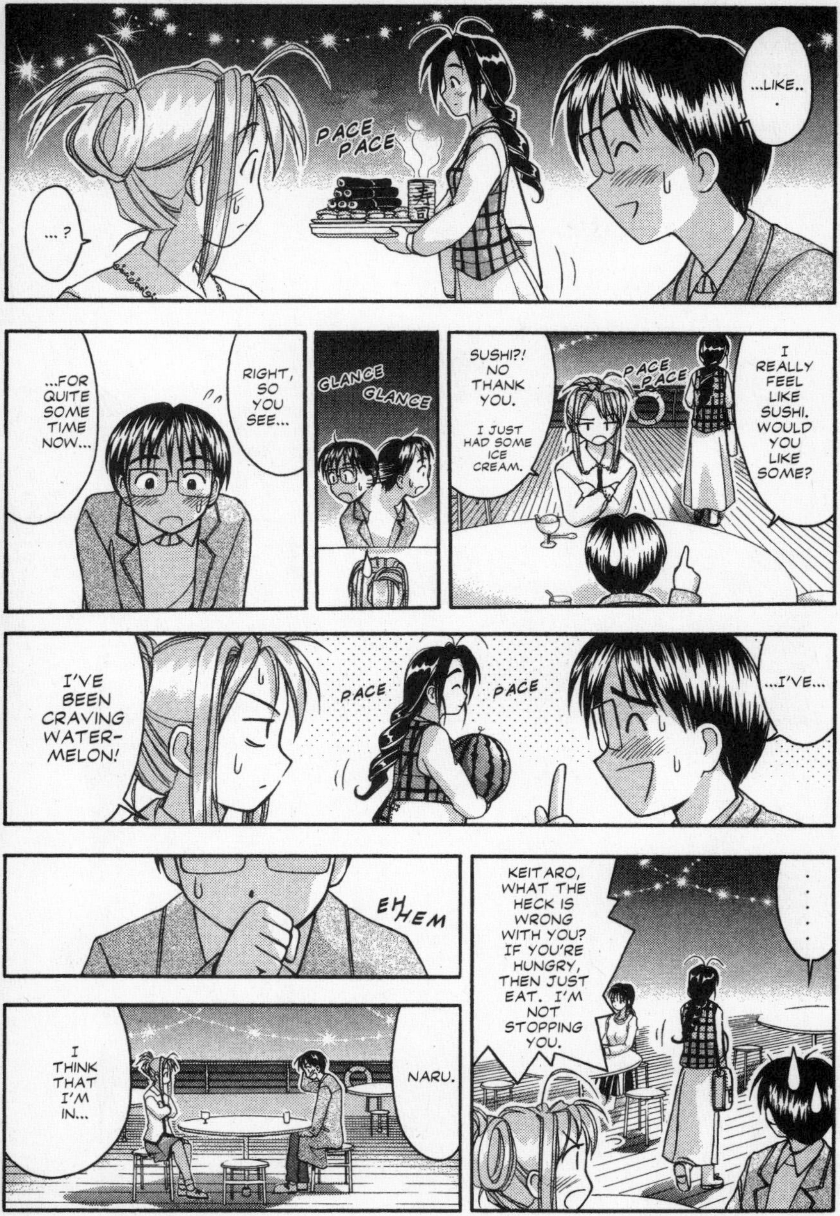
...LIKE.. .
PACE PACE
...?
I REALLY FEEL LIKE SUSHI. WOULD YOU LIKE SOME?
PACE PACE
SUSHI?! NO THANK YOU.
I JUST HAD SOME ICE CREAM.
GLANCE GLANCE
RIGHT, SO YOU SEE...
...FOR QUITE SOME TIME NOW...
...I'VE...
PACE PACE
I'VE BEEN CRAVING WATER-MELON!
......
KEITARO, WHAT THE HECK IS WRONG WITH YOU? IF YOU'RE HUNGRY, THEN JUST EAT. I'M NOT STOPPING YOU.
EH HEM
NARU.
I THINK THAT I'M IN...

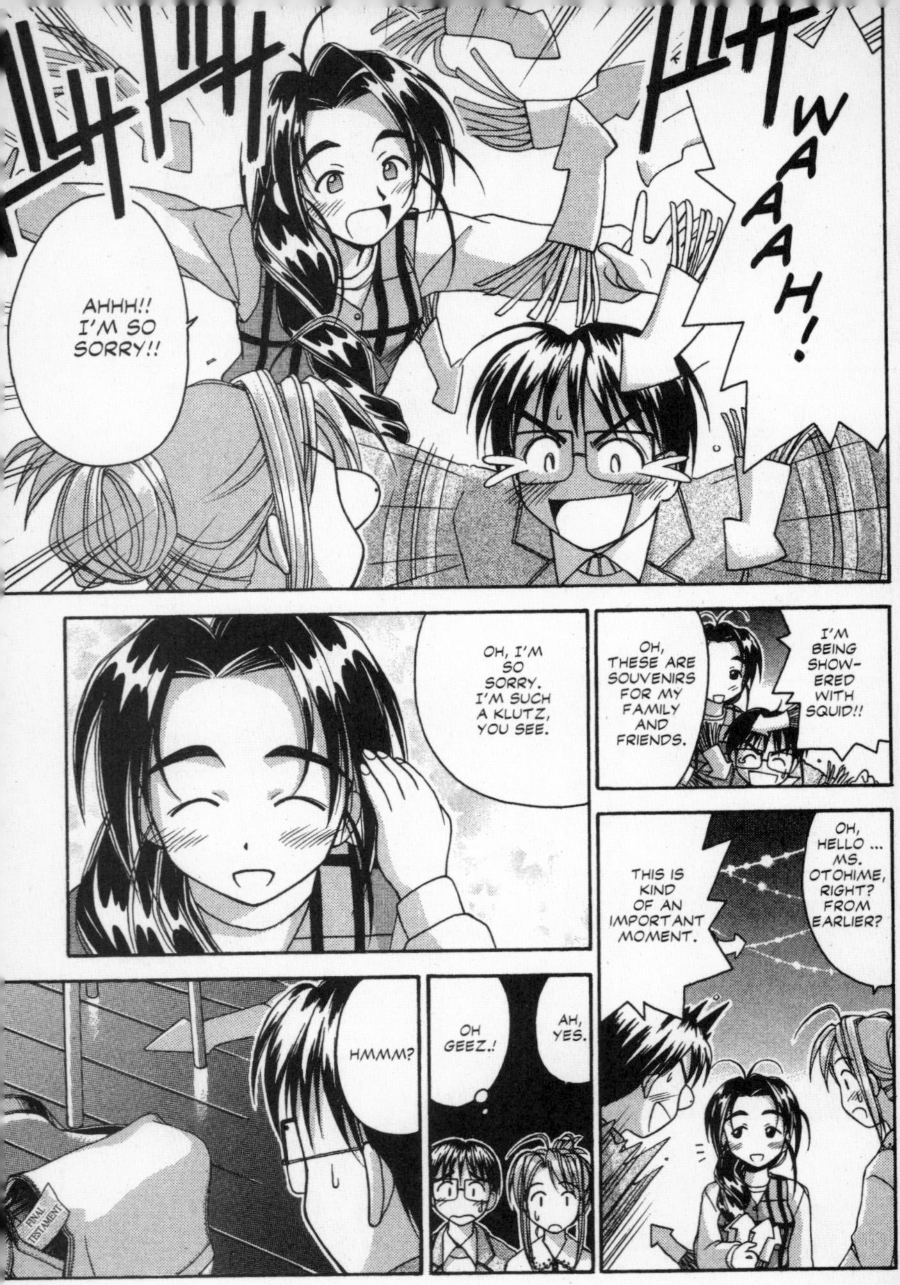
WAAAAH!
AHHH!! I'M SO SORRY!!
I'M BEING SHOWERED WITH SQUID!!
OH, THESE ARE SOUVENIRS FOR MY FAMILY AND FRIENDS.
OH, I'M SO SORRY. I'M SUCH A KLUTZ, YOU SEE.
OH, HELLO ... MS. OTOHIME, RIGHT? FROM EARLIER?
THIS IS KIND OF AN IMPORTANT MOMENT.
AH, YES.
OH GEEZ..!
HMMM?
FINAL TESTAMENT

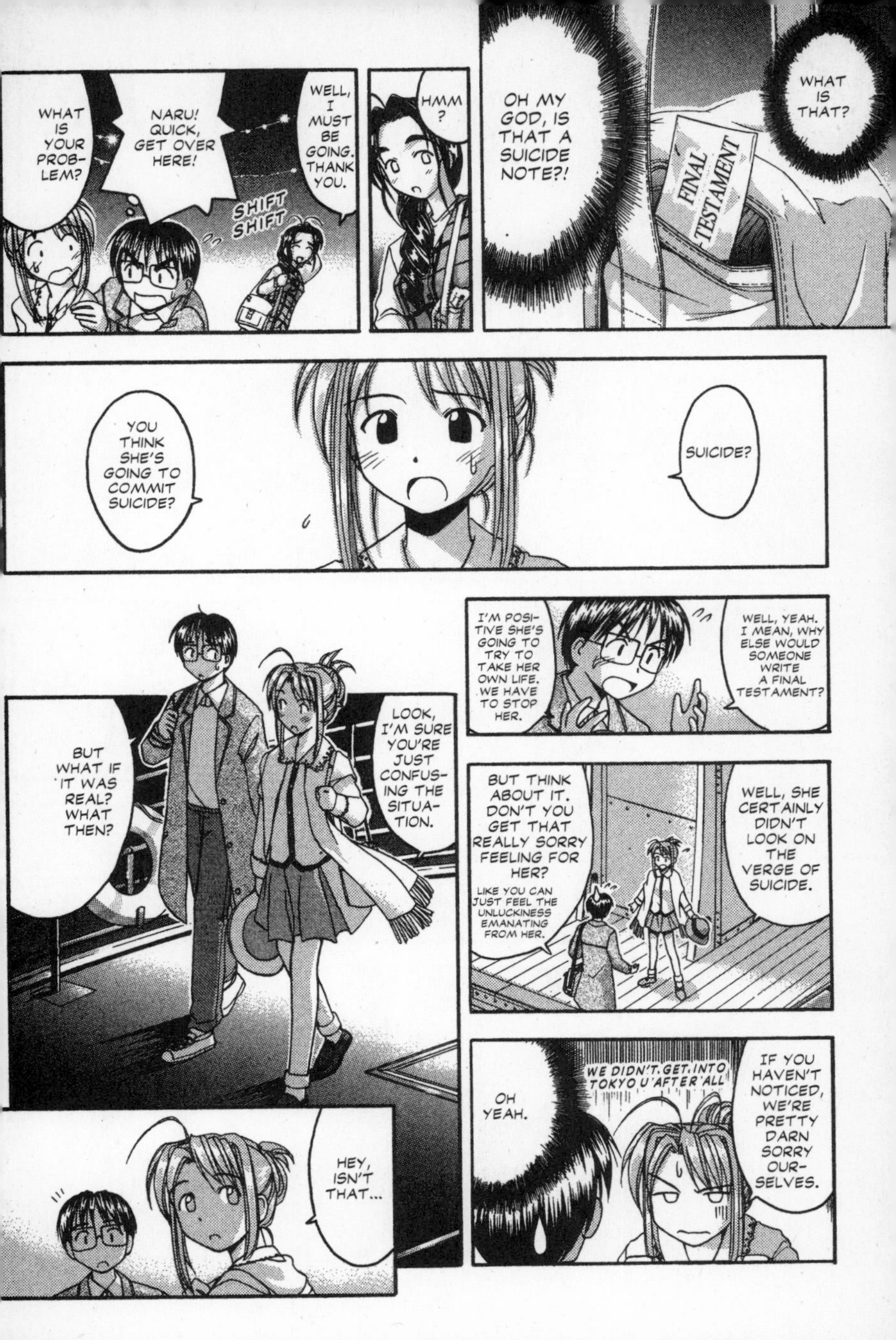

WHAT IS THAT?
OH MY GOD, IS THAT A SUICIDE NOTE?!
FINAL TESTAMENT
HMM?
WELL, I MUST BE GOING. THANK YOU.
NARU! QUICK, GET OVER HERE!
SHIFT SHIFT
WHAT IS YOUR PROB-LEM?
SUICIDE?
YOU THINK SHE'S GOING TO COMMIT SUICIDE?
WELL, YEAH. I MEAN, WHY ELSE WOULD SOMEONE WRITE A FINAL TESTAMENT?
I'M POSI-TIVE SHE'S GOING TO TRY TO TAKE HER OWN LIFE. WE HAVE TO STOP HER.
WELL, SHE CERTAINLY DIDN'T LOOK ON THE VERGE OF SUICIDE.
BUT THINK ABOUT IT. DON'T YOU GET THAT REALLY SORRY FEELING FOR HER?
LIKE YOU CAN JUST FEEL THE UNLUCKINESS EMANATING FROM HER.
IF YOU HAVEN'T NOTICED, WE'RE PRETTY DARN SORRY OUR-SELVES.
WE DIDN'T GET INTO TOKYO U AFTER ALL
OH YEAH.
LOOK, I'M SURE YOU'RE JUST CONFUS-ING THE SITUA-TION.
BUT WHAT IF IT WAS REAL? WHAT THEN?
HEY, ISN'T THAT...

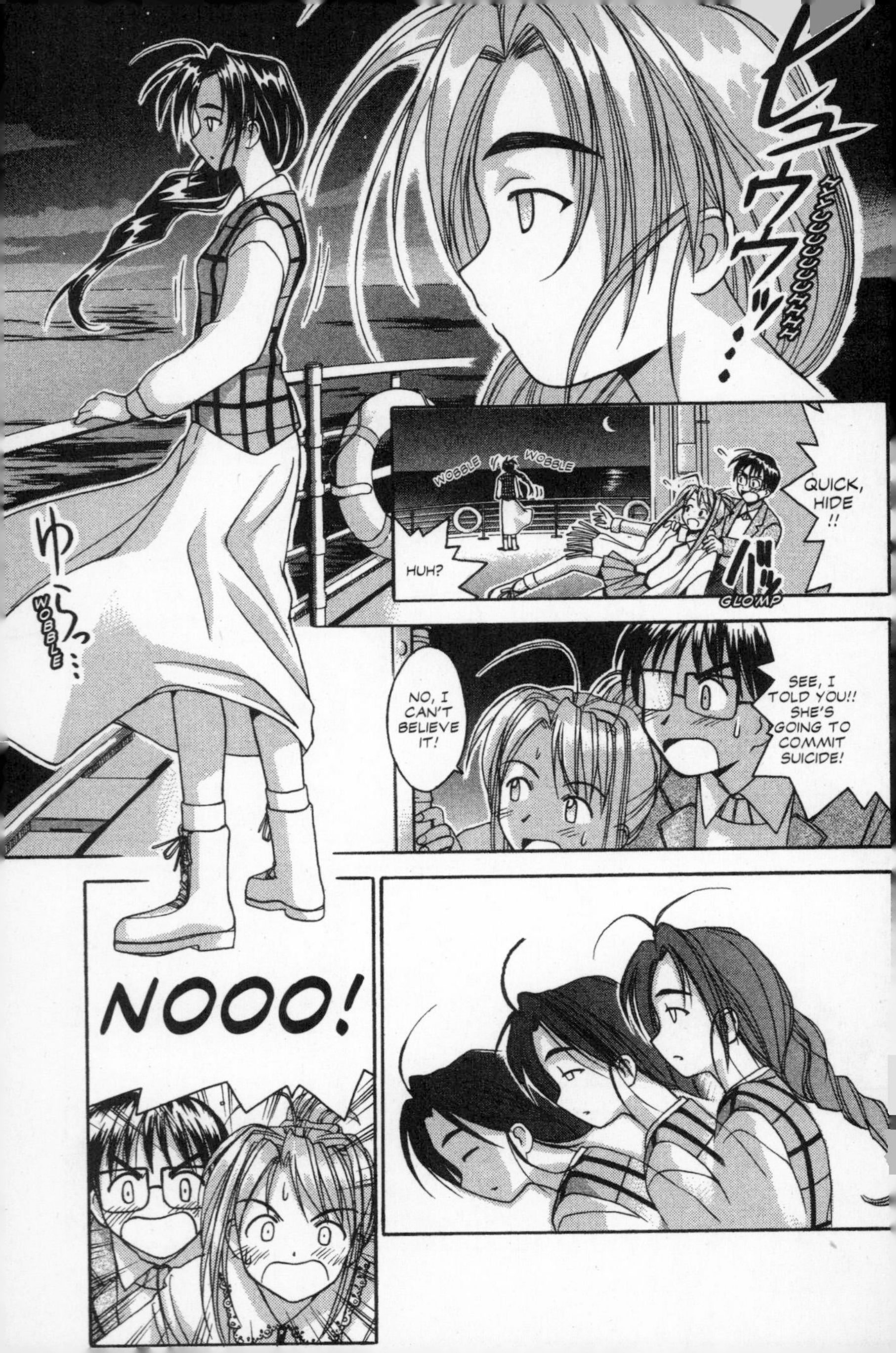
ヒュウウッ…
WOBBLE
WOBBLE
QUICK, HIDE !!
HUH?
バッ
GLOMP
SEE, I TOLD YOU!! SHE'S GOING TO COMMIT SUICIDE!
NO, I CAN'T BELIEVE IT!
ゆらっ…
WOBBLE
NOOO!

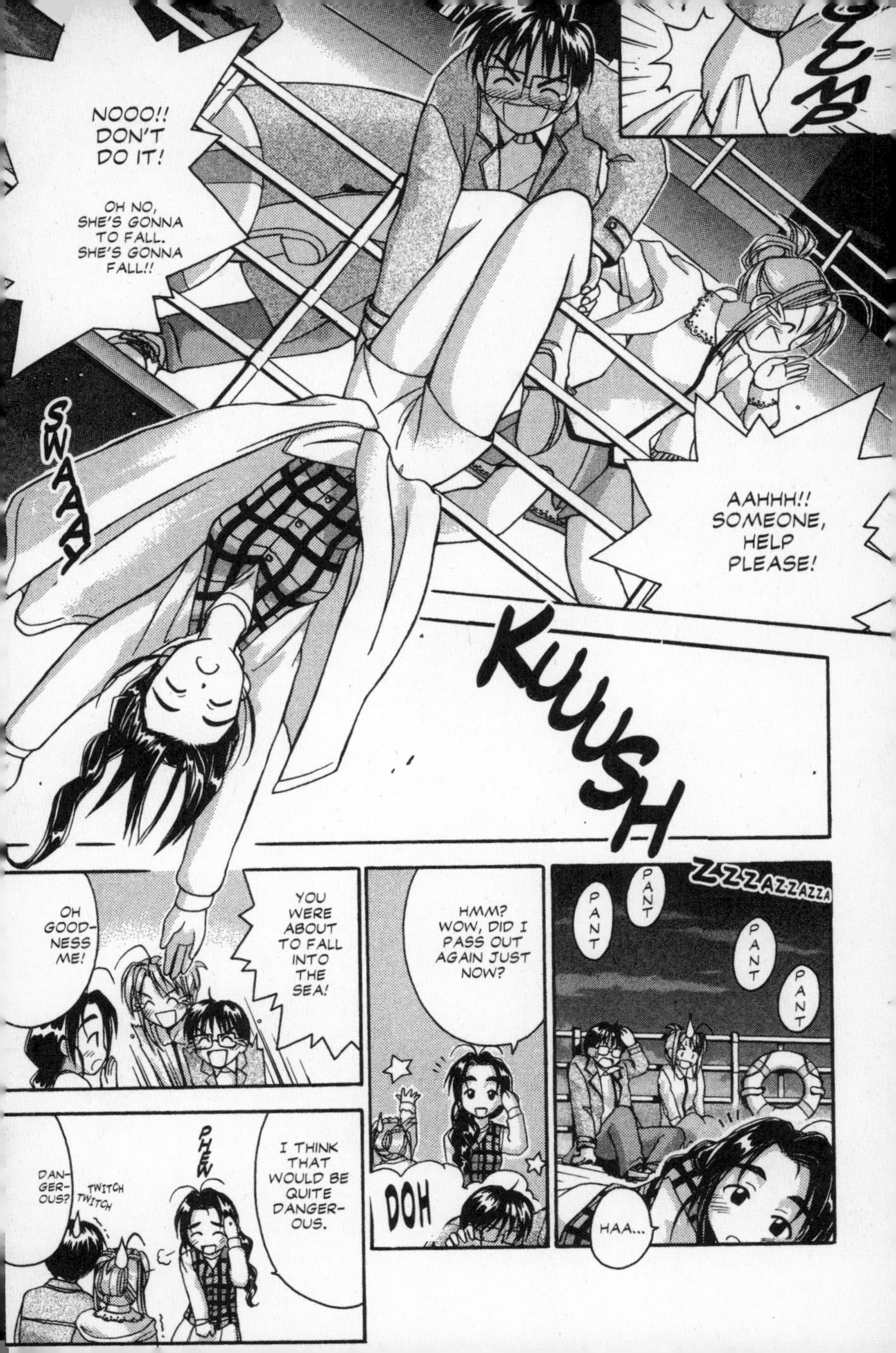
AAHHH!! SOMEONE, HELP PLEASE!
NOOO!! DON'T DO IT!
OH NO, SHE'S GONNA TO FALL. SHE'S GONNA FALL!!
SWAAAY
KUUUSH
ZZZAZZAZZA
PANT
PANT
PANT
PANT
HAA...
HMM? WOW, DID I PASS OUT AGAIN JUST NOW?
DOH
YOU WERE ABOUT TO FALL INTO THE SEA!
OH GOODNESS ME!
I THINK THAT WOULD BE QUITE DANGER-OUS.
PHEW
DAN-GER-OUS?
TWITCH TWITCH

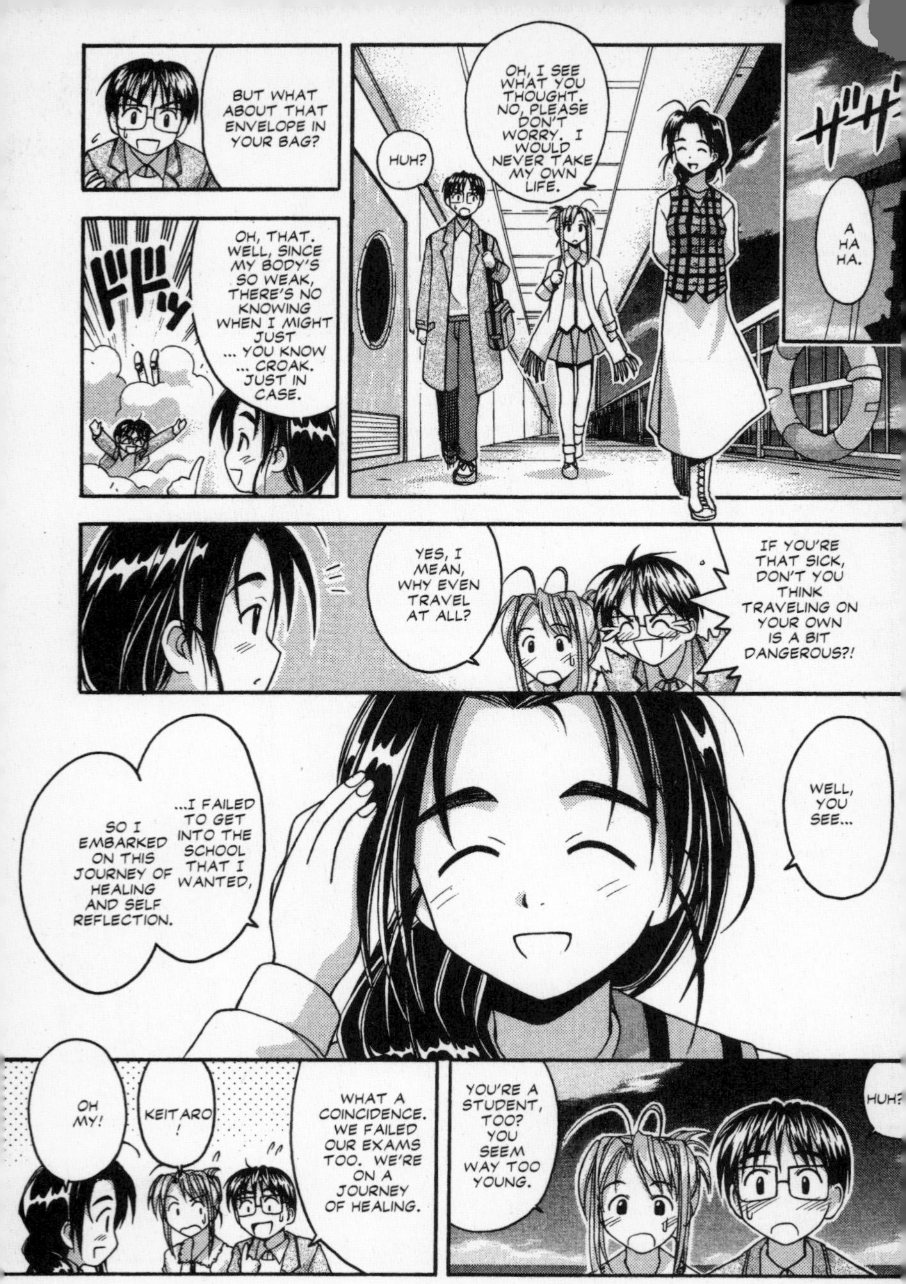
ザザ
A HA HA.
OH, I SEE WHAT YOU THOUGHT. NO, PLEASE DON'T WORRY. I WOULD NEVER TAKE MY OWN LIFE.
HUH?
BUT WHAT ABOUT THAT ENVELOPE IN YOUR BAG?
OH, THAT. WELL, SINCE MY BODY'S SO WEAK, THERE'S NO KNOWING WHEN I MIGHT JUST ... YOU KNOW ... CROAK. JUST IN CASE.
ドドッ
IF YOU'RE THAT SICK, DON'T YOU THINK TRAVELING ON YOUR OWN IS A BIT DANGEROUS?!
YES, I MEAN, WHY EVEN TRAVEL AT ALL?
WELL, YOU SEE...
...I FAILED TO GET INTO THE SCHOOL THAT I WANTED,
SO I EMBARKED ON THIS JOURNEY OF HEALING AND SELF REFLECTION.
HUH?
YOU'RE A STUDENT, TOO? YOU SEEM WAY TOO YOUNG.
WHAT A COINCIDENCE. WE FAILED OUR EXAMS TOO. WE'RE ON A JOURNEY OF HEALING.
KEITARO!
OH MY!

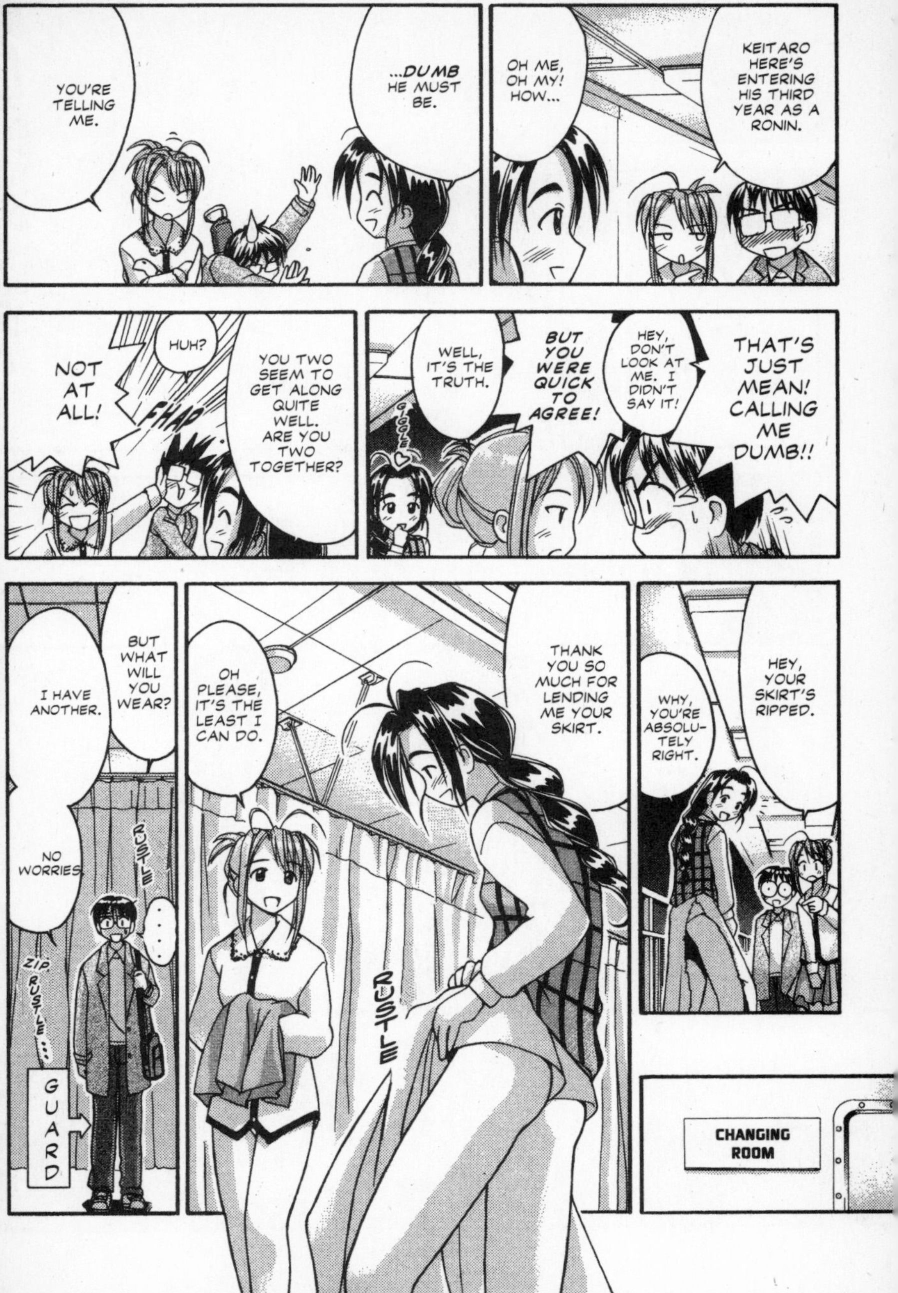
KEITARO HERE'S ENTERING HIS THIRD YEAR AS A RONIN.
OH ME, OH MY! HOW...
...DUMB HE MUST BE.
YOU'RE TELLING ME.
THAT'S JUST MEAN! CALLING ME DUMB!!
HEY, DON'T LOOK AT ME. I DIDN'T SAY IT!
BUT YOU WERE QUICK TO AGREE!
WELL, IT'S THE TRUTH.
GIGGLE
YOU TWO SEEM TO GET ALONG QUITE WELL. ARE YOU TWO TOGETHER?
HUH?
NOT AT ALL!
FHAP
HEY, YOUR SKIRT'S RIPPED.
WHY, YOU'RE ABSOLUTELY RIGHT.
CHANGING ROOM
THANK YOU SO MUCH FOR LENDING ME YOUR SKIRT.
OH PLEASE, IT'S THE LEAST I CAN DO.
RUSTLE
BUT WHAT WILL YOU WEAR?
I HAVE ANOTHER.
RUSTLE
...
NO WORRIES.
ZIP RUSTLE...
GUARD

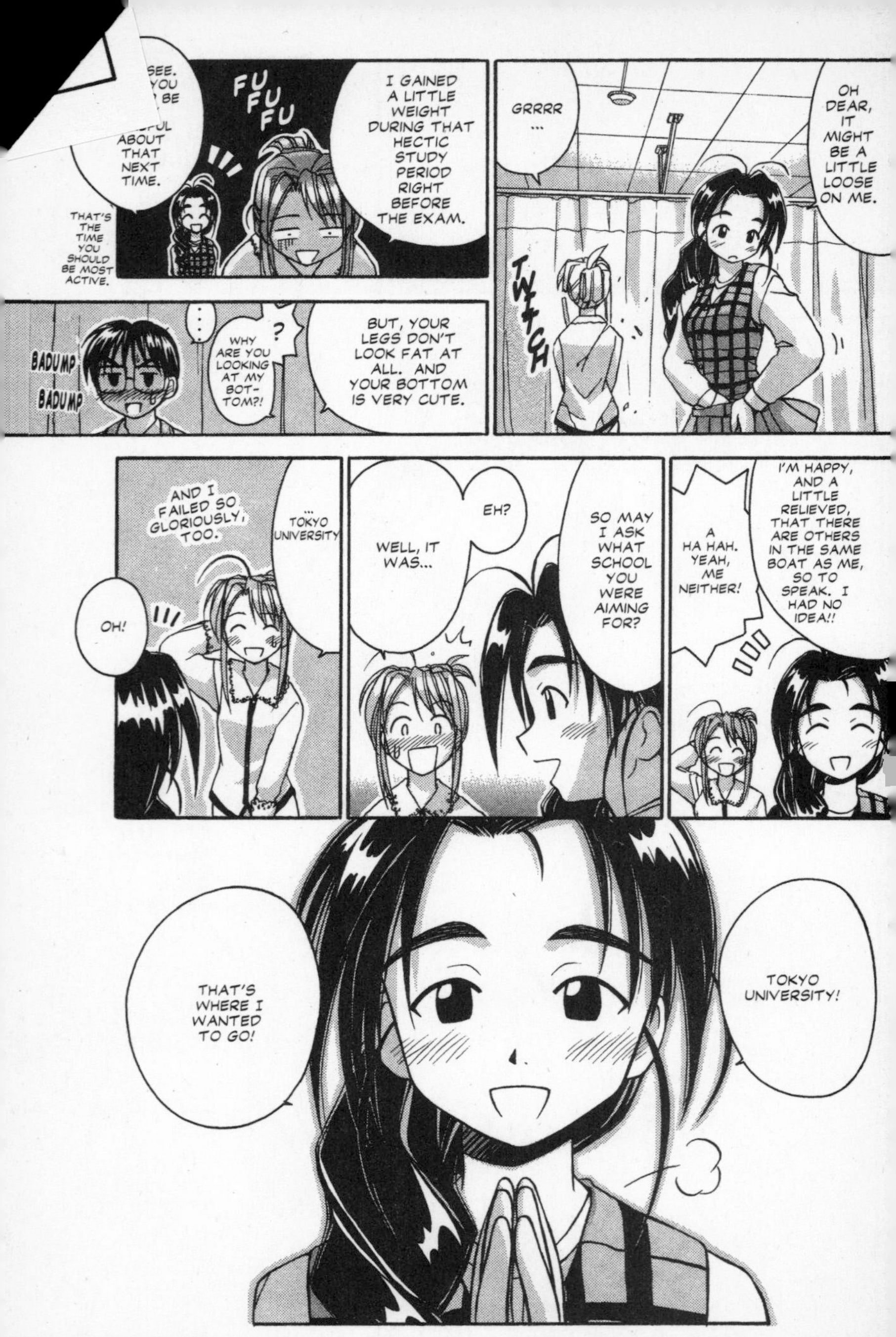
OH DEAR, IT MIGHT BE A LITTLE LOOSE ON ME.
GRRRR ...
TWITCH
I GAINED A LITTLE WEIGHT DURING THAT HECTIC STUDY PERIOD RIGHT BEFORE THE EXAM.
FU FU FU
SEE. YOU BE ABOUT THAT NEXT TIME.
THAT'S THE TIME YOU SHOULD BE MOST ACTIVE.
BUT, YOUR LEGS DON'T LOOK FAT AT ALL. AND YOUR BOTTOM IS VERY CUTE.
?
WHY ARE YOU LOOKING AT MY BOT-TOM?!
...
BADUMP
BADUMP
I'M HAPPY, AND A LITTLE RELIEVED, THAT THERE ARE OTHERS IN THE SAME BOAT AS ME, SO TO SPEAK. I HAD NO IDEA!!
A HA HAH. YEAH, ME NEITHER!
SO MAY I ASK WHAT SCHOOL YOU WERE AIMING FOR?
EH?
WELL, IT WAS...
... TOKYO UNIVERSITY
AND I FAILED SO GLORIOUSLY, TOO.
OH!
TOKYO UNIVERSITY!
THAT'S WHERE I WANTED TO GO!

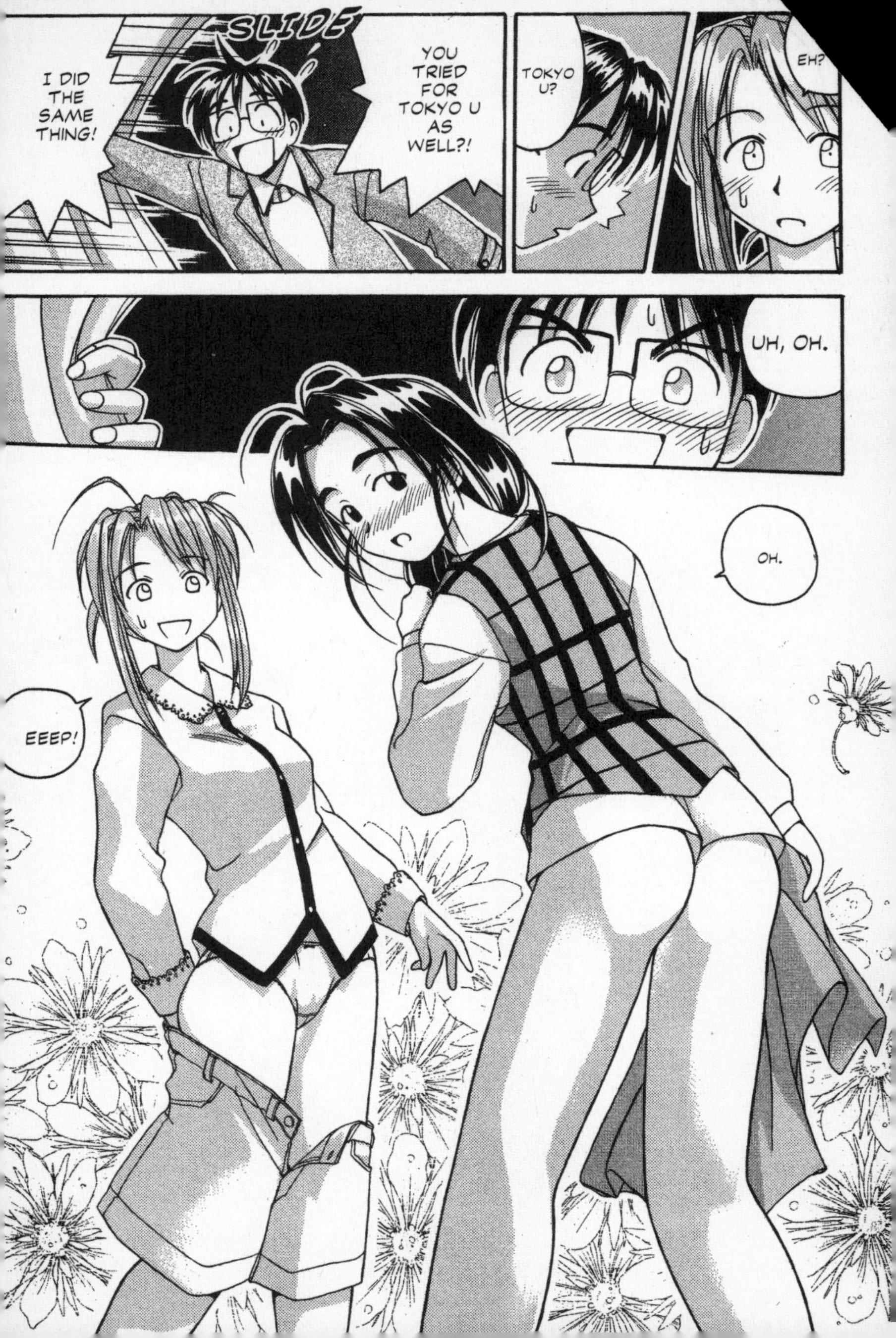
EH?
TOKYO U?
SLIDE
YOU TRIED FOR TOKYO U AS WELL?!
I DID THE SAME THING!
UH, OH.
OH.
EEEP!

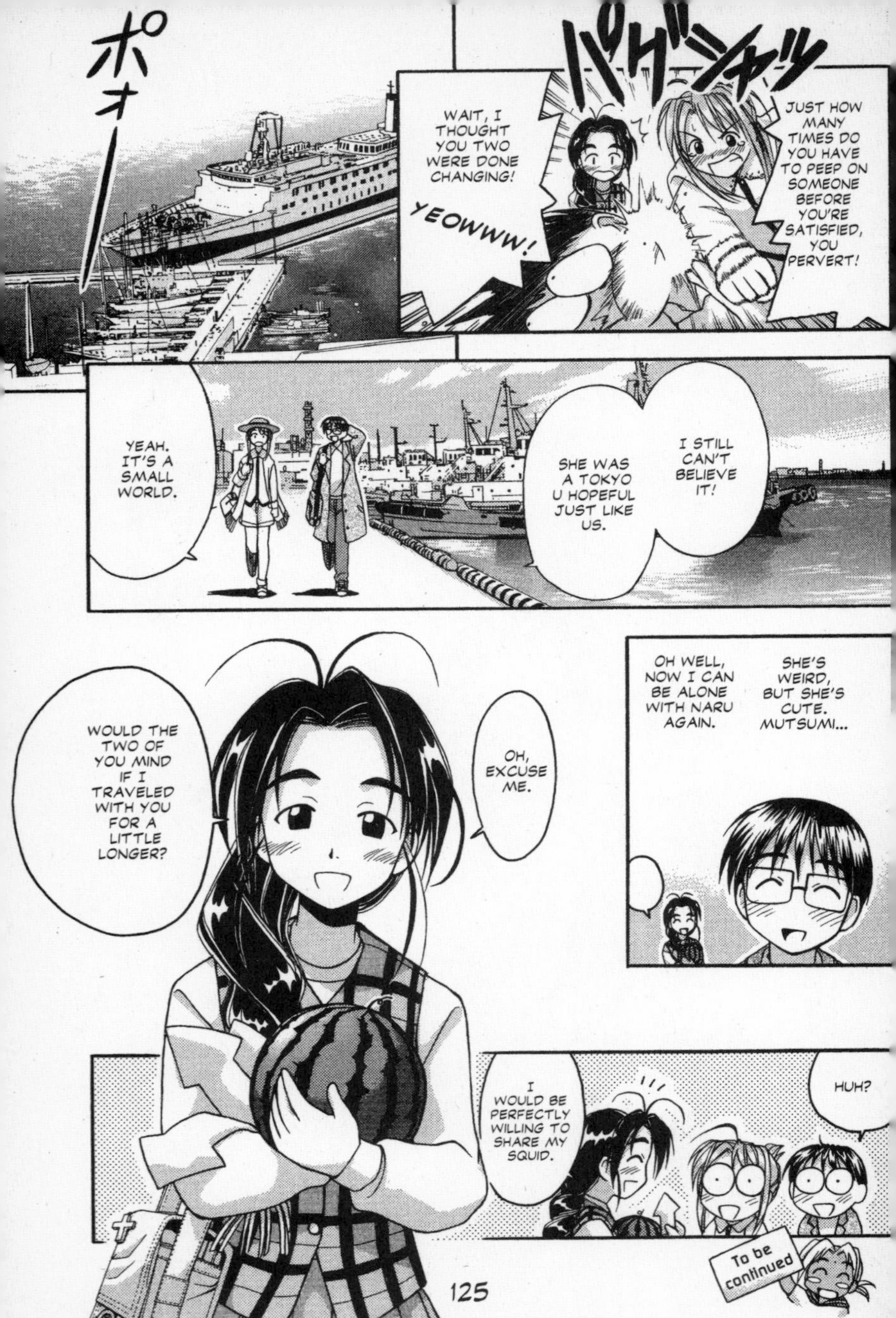
JUST HOW MANY TIMES DO YOU HAVE TO PEEP ON SOMEONE BEFORE YOU'RE SATISFIED, YOU PERVERT!
WAIT, I THOUGHT YOU TWO WERE DONE CHANGING!
YEOWWW!
ポォー
I STILL CAN'T BELIEVE IT!
SHE WAS A TOKYO U HOPEFUL JUST LIKE US.
YEAH. IT'S A SMALL WORLD.
SHE'S WEIRD, BUT SHE'S CUTE. MUTSUMI...
OH WELL, NOW I CAN BE ALONE WITH NARU AGAIN.
OH, EXCUSE ME.
WOULD THE TWO OF YOU MIND IF I TRAVELED WITH YOU FOR A LITTLE LONGER?
HUH?
I WOULD BE PERFECTLY WILLING TO SHARE MY SQUID.
To be continued

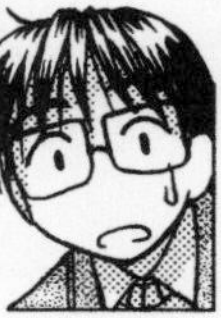
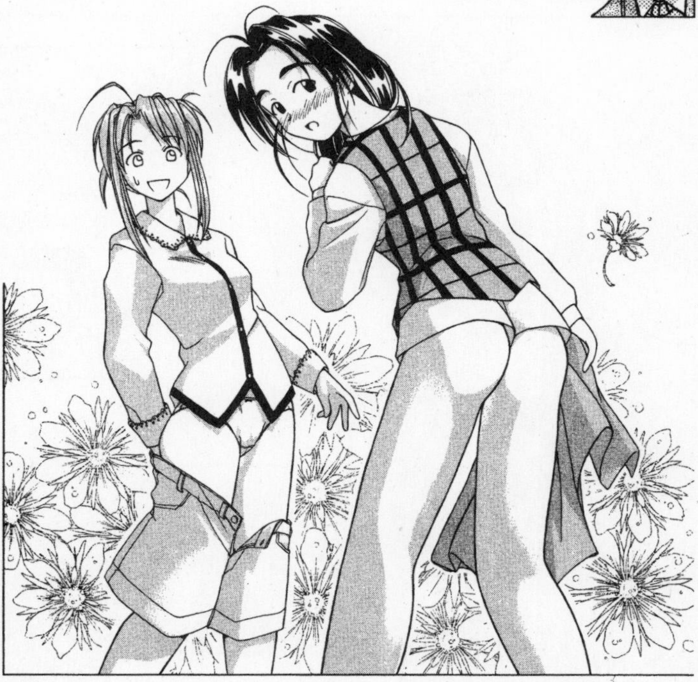

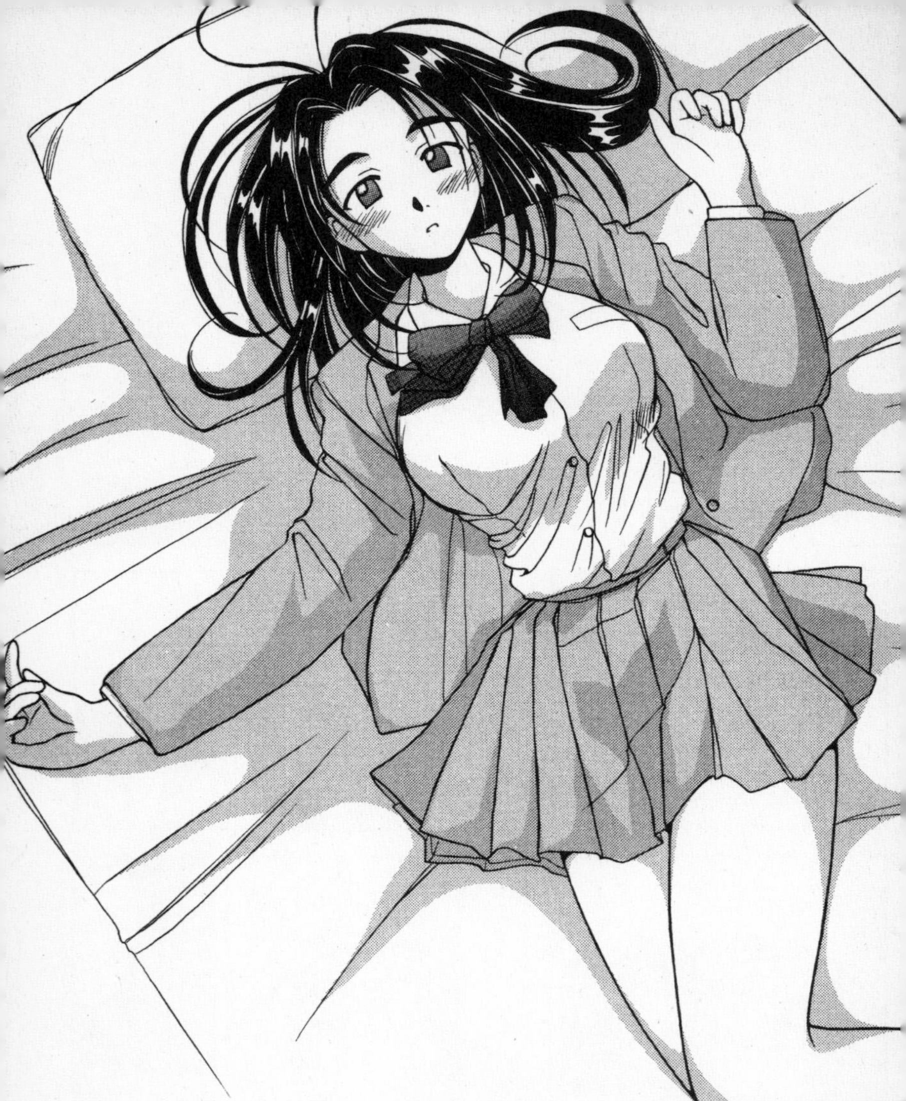

「LOVE ♥ HINA」

HINATA.22 Sorry For Being So Alike ♥

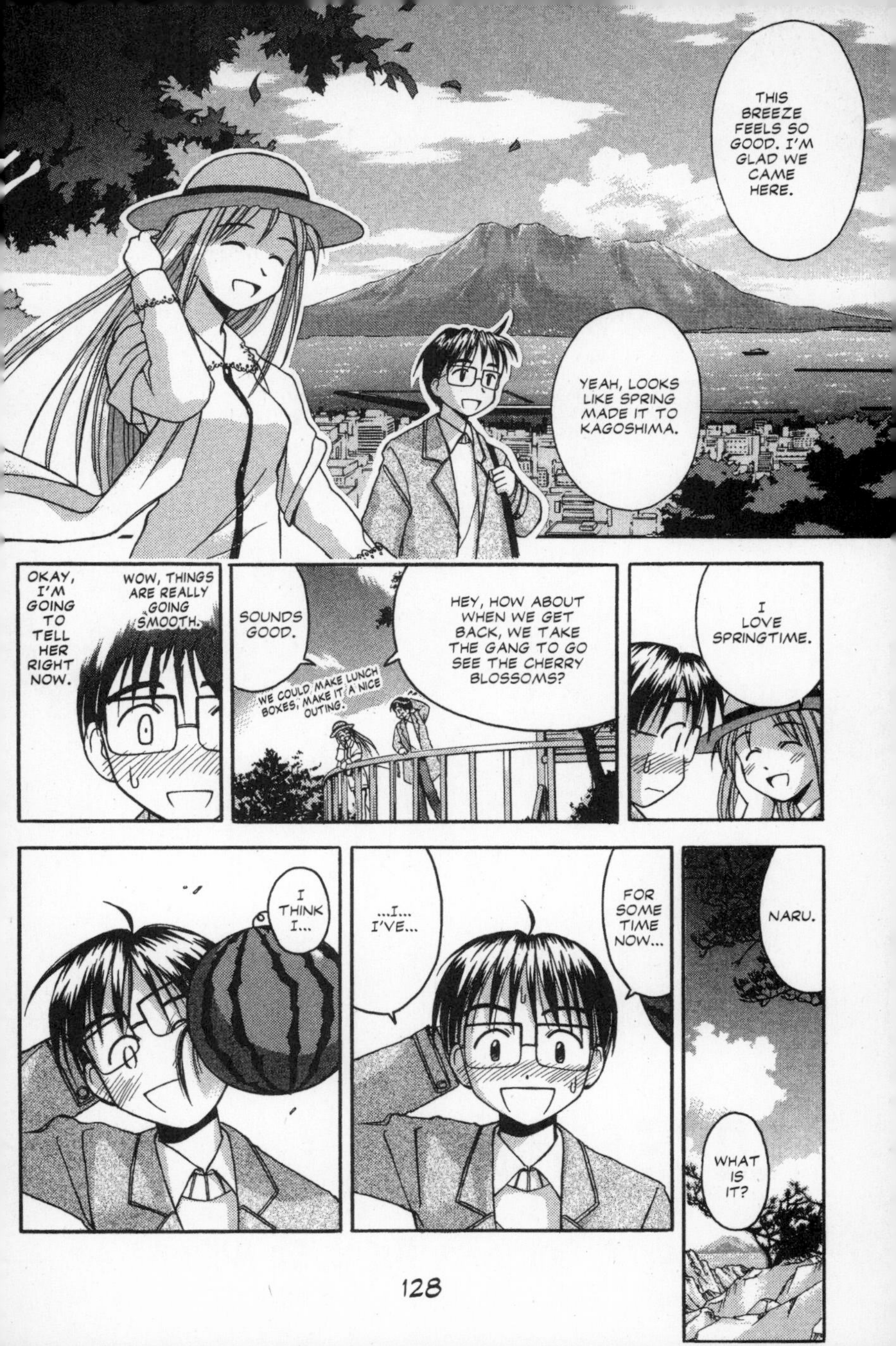

THIS BREEZE FEELS SO GOOD. I'M GLAD WE CAME HERE.
YEAH, LOOKS LIKE SPRING MADE IT TO KAGOSHIMA.
I LOVE SPRINGTIME.
HEY, HOW ABOUT WHEN WE GET BACK, WE TAKE THE GANG TO GO SEE THE CHERRY BLOSSOMS?
SOUNDS GOOD.
WE COULD MAKE LUNCH BOXES, MAKE IT A NICE OUTING.
WOW, THINGS ARE REALLY GOING SMOOTH.
OKAY, I'M GOING TO TELL HER RIGHT NOW.
NARU.
WHAT IS IT?
FOR SOME TIME NOW...
...I... I'VE...
I THINK I...

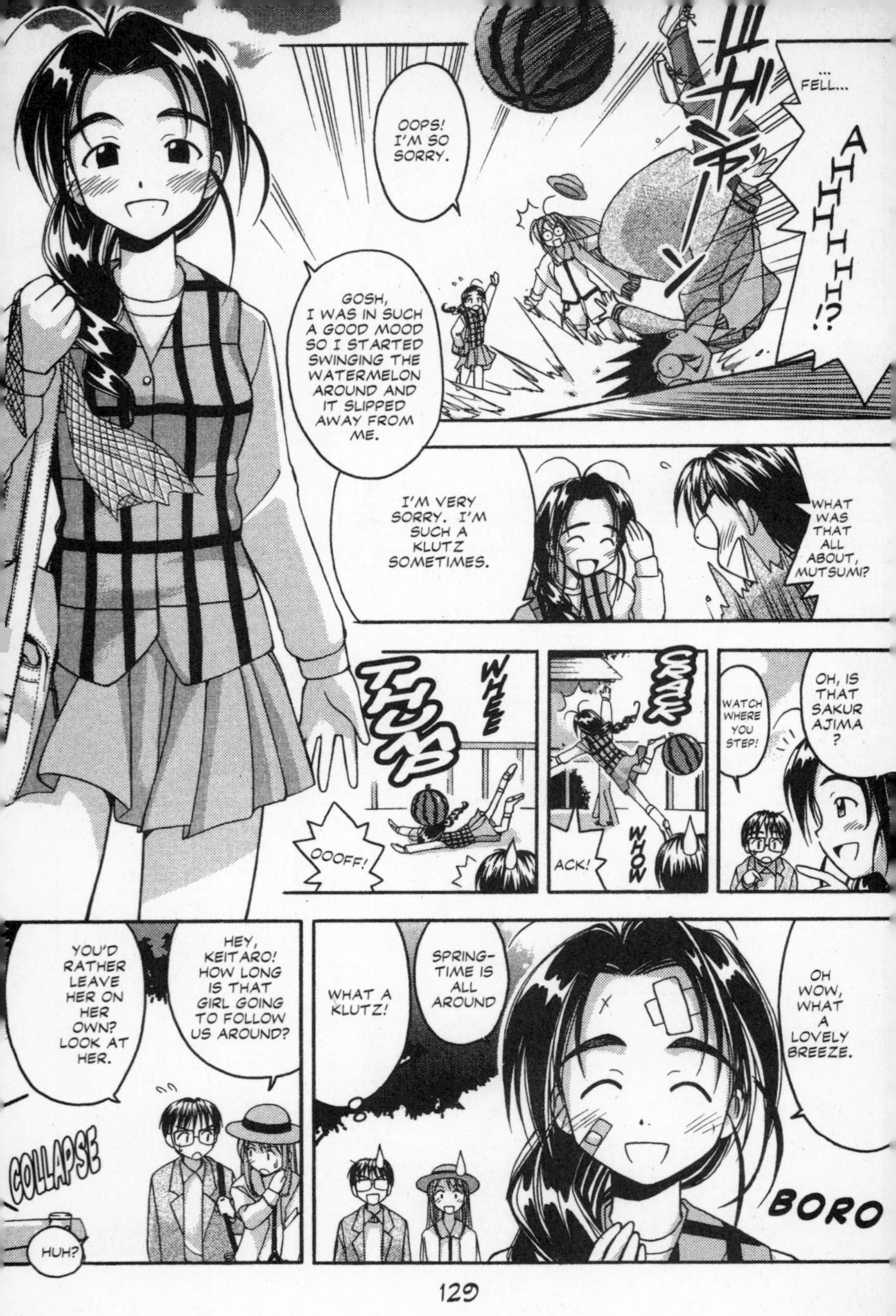
...FELL...
AHHHHHH!?
OOPS! I'M SO SORRY.
GOSH, I WAS IN SUCH A GOOD MOOD SO I STARTED SWINGING THE WATERMELON AROUND AND IT SLIPPED AWAY FROM ME.
WHAT WAS THAT ALL ABOUT, MUTSUMI?
I'M VERY SORRY. I'M SUCH A KLUTZ SOMETIMES.
OH, IS THAT SAKUR AJIMA?
WATCH WHERE YOU STEP!
CRACK
WHOW
ACK!
WHEE
THUD
OOOFF!
OH WOW, WHAT A LOVELY BREEZE.
BORO
SPRING-TIME IS ALL AROUND
WHAT A KLUTZ!
HEY, KEITARO! HOW LONG IS THAT GIRL GOING TO FOLLOW US AROUND?
YOU'D RATHER LEAVE HER ON HER OWN? LOOK AT HER.
COLLAPSE
HUH?

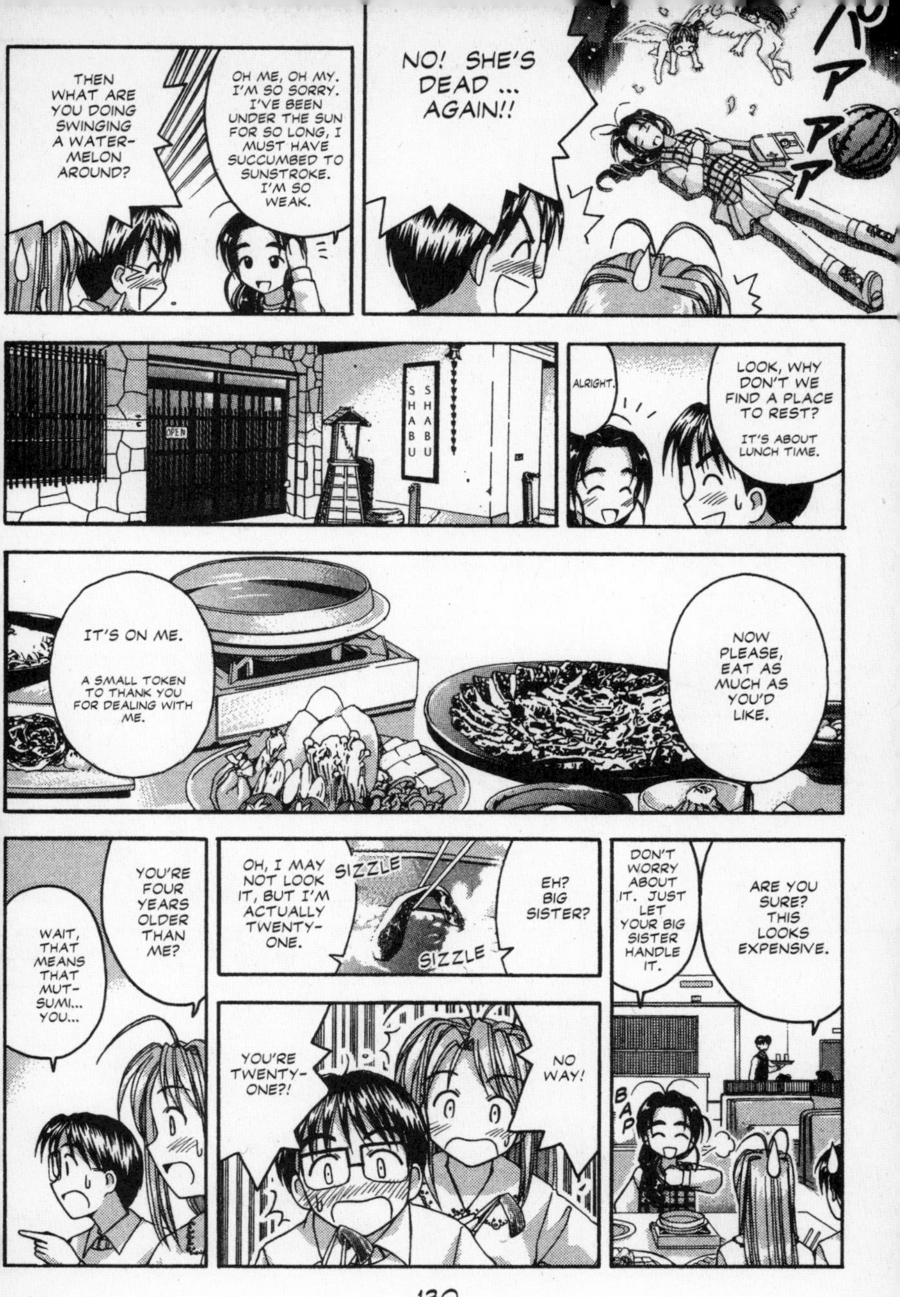
パアア
NO! SHE'S DEAD ... AGAIN!!
OH ME, OH MY. I'M SO SORRY. I'VE BEEN UNDER THE SUN FOR SO LONG, I MUST HAVE SUCCUMBED TO SUNSTROKE. I'M SO WEAK.
THEN WHAT ARE YOU DOING SWINGING A WATER-MELON AROUND?
LOOK, WHY DON'T WE FIND A PLACE TO REST?
IT'S ABOUT LUNCH TIME.
ALRIGHT.
SHABU SHABU
OPEN
NOW PLEASE, EAT AS MUCH AS YOU'D LIKE.
IT'S ON ME.
A SMALL TOKEN TO THANK YOU FOR DEALING WITH ME.
ARE YOU SURE? THIS LOOKS EXPENSIVE.
DON'T WORRY ABOUT IT. JUST LET YOUR BIG SISTER HANDLE IT.
BAP
EH? BIG SISTER?
OH, I MAY NOT LOOK IT, BUT I'M ACTUALLY TWENTY-ONE.
SIZZLE
SIZZLE
NO WAY!
YOU'RE TWENTY-ONE?!
YOU'RE FOUR YEARS OLDER THAN ME?
WAIT, THAT MEANS THAT MUT-SUMI... YOU...

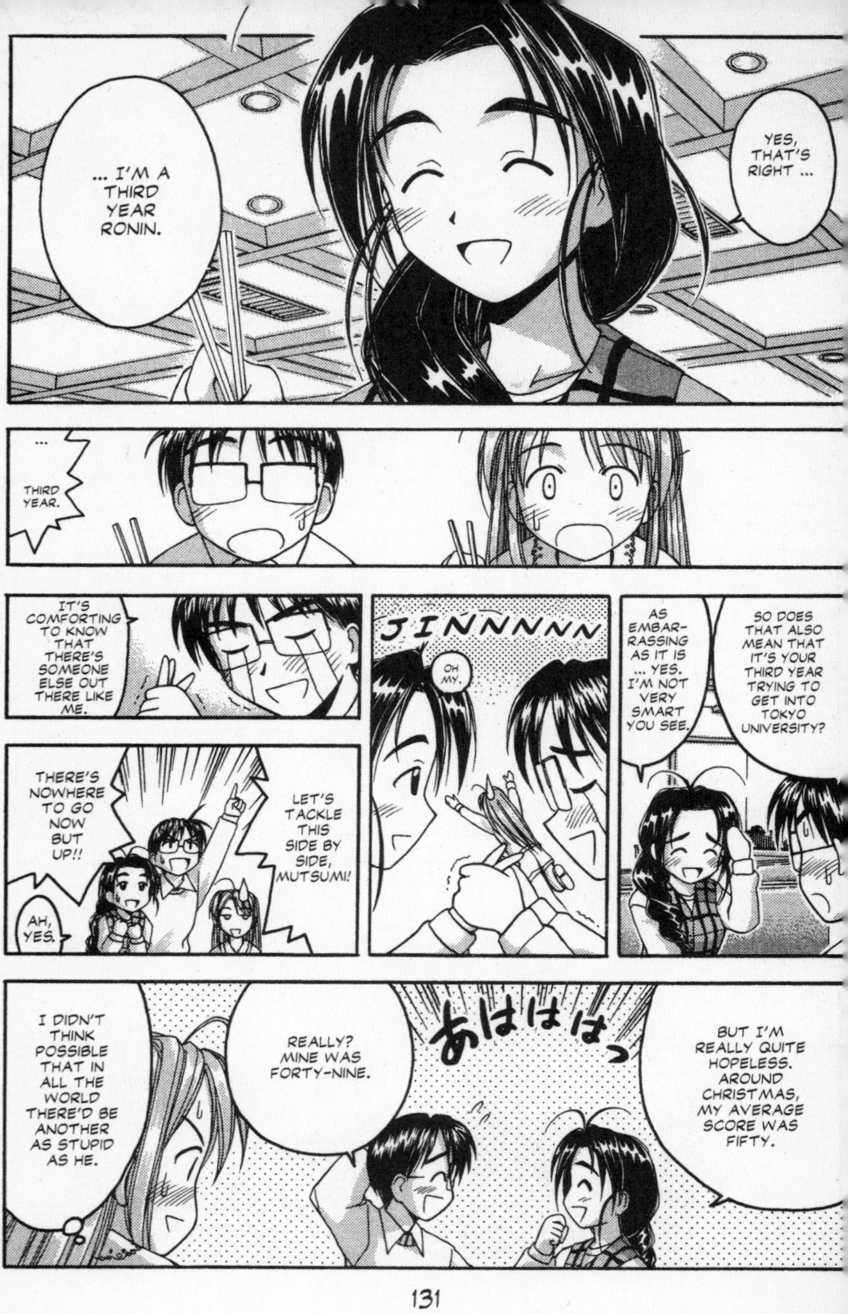
YES, THAT'S RIGHT ...
... I'M A THIRD YEAR RONIN.
... THIRD YEAR.
SO DOES THAT ALSO MEAN THAT IT'S YOUR THIRD YEAR TRYING TO GET INTO TOKYO UNIVERSITY?
AS EMBARRASSING AS IT IS ... YES. I'M NOT VERY SMART YOU SEE.
JINNNNNN
OH MY.
IT'S COMFORTING TO KNOW THAT THERE'S SOMEONE ELSE OUT THERE LIKE ME.
LET'S TACKLE THIS SIDE BY SIDE, MUTSUMI!
THERE'S NOWHERE TO GO NOW BUT UP!!
AH, YES.
BUT I'M REALLY QUITE HOPELESS. AROUND CHRISTMAS, MY AVERAGE SCORE WAS FIFTY.
あはははっ
REALLY? MINE WAS FORTY-NINE.
I DIDN'T THINK POSSIBLE THAT IN ALL THE WORLD THERE'D BE ANOTHER AS STUPID AS HE.

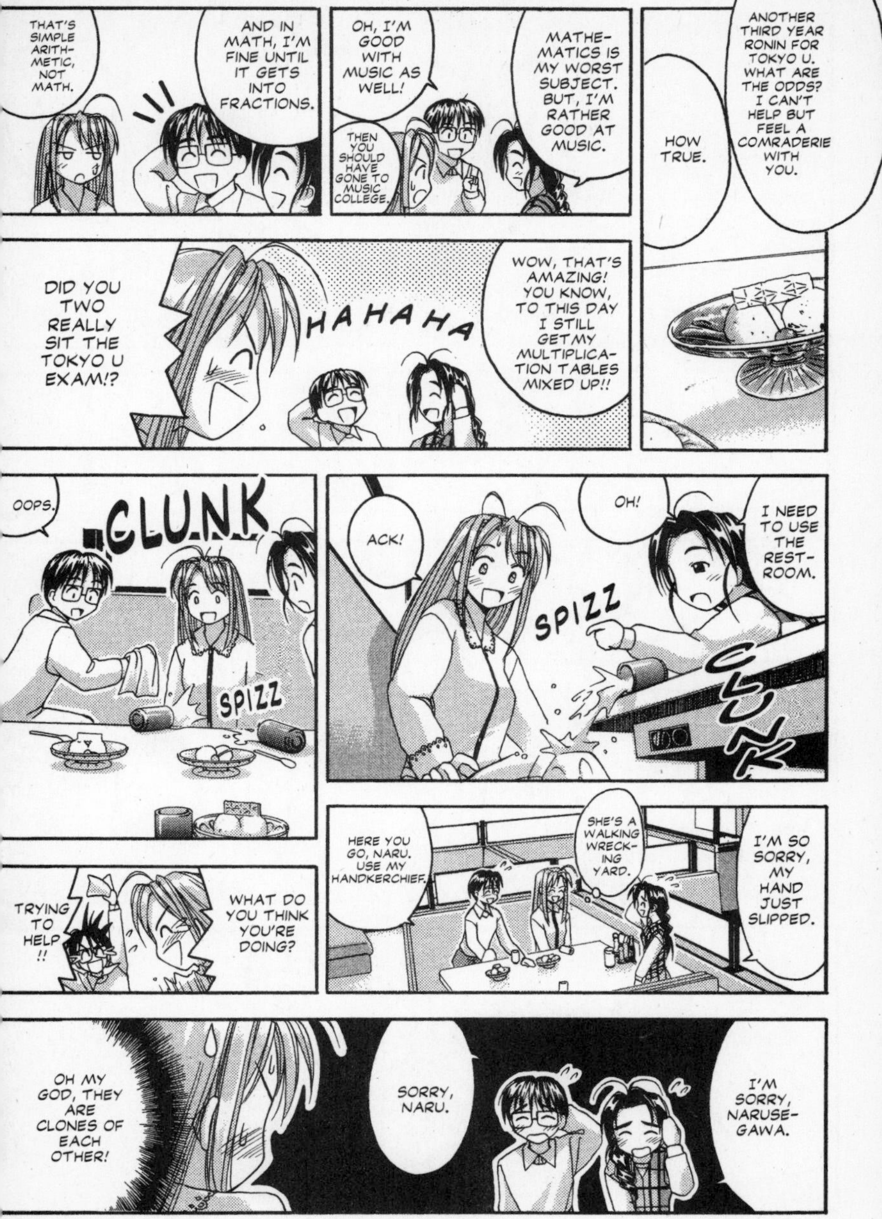
ANOTHER THIRD YEAR RONIN FOR TOKYO U. WHAT ARE THE ODDS? I CAN'T HELP BUT FEEL A COMRADERIE WITH YOU.
HOW TRUE.
MATHEMATICS IS MY WORST SUBJECT. BUT, I'M RATHER GOOD AT MUSIC.
OH, I'M GOOD WITH MUSIC AS WELL!
THEN YOU SHOULD HAVE GONE TO MUSIC COLLEGE.
AND IN MATH, I'M FINE UNTIL IT GETS INTO FRACTIONS.
THAT'S SIMPLE ARITHMETIC, NOT MATH.
WOW, THAT'S AMAZING! YOU KNOW, TO THIS DAY I STILL GETMY MULTIPLICATION TABLES MIXED UP!!
HAHAHA
DID YOU TWO REALLY SIT THE TOKYO U EXAM!?
I NEED TO USE THE REST-ROOM.
OH!
SPIZZ
CLUNK
ACK!
CLUNK
OOPS.
SPIZZ
I'M SO SORRY, MY HAND JUST SLIPPED.
SHE'S A WALKING WRECK-ING YARD.
HERE YOU GO, NARU. USE MY HANDKERCHIEF.
WHAT DO YOU THINK YOU'RE DOING?
TRYING TO HELP !!
I'M SORRY, NARUSE-GAWA.
SORRY, NARU.
OH MY GOD, THEY ARE CLONES OF EACH OTHER!

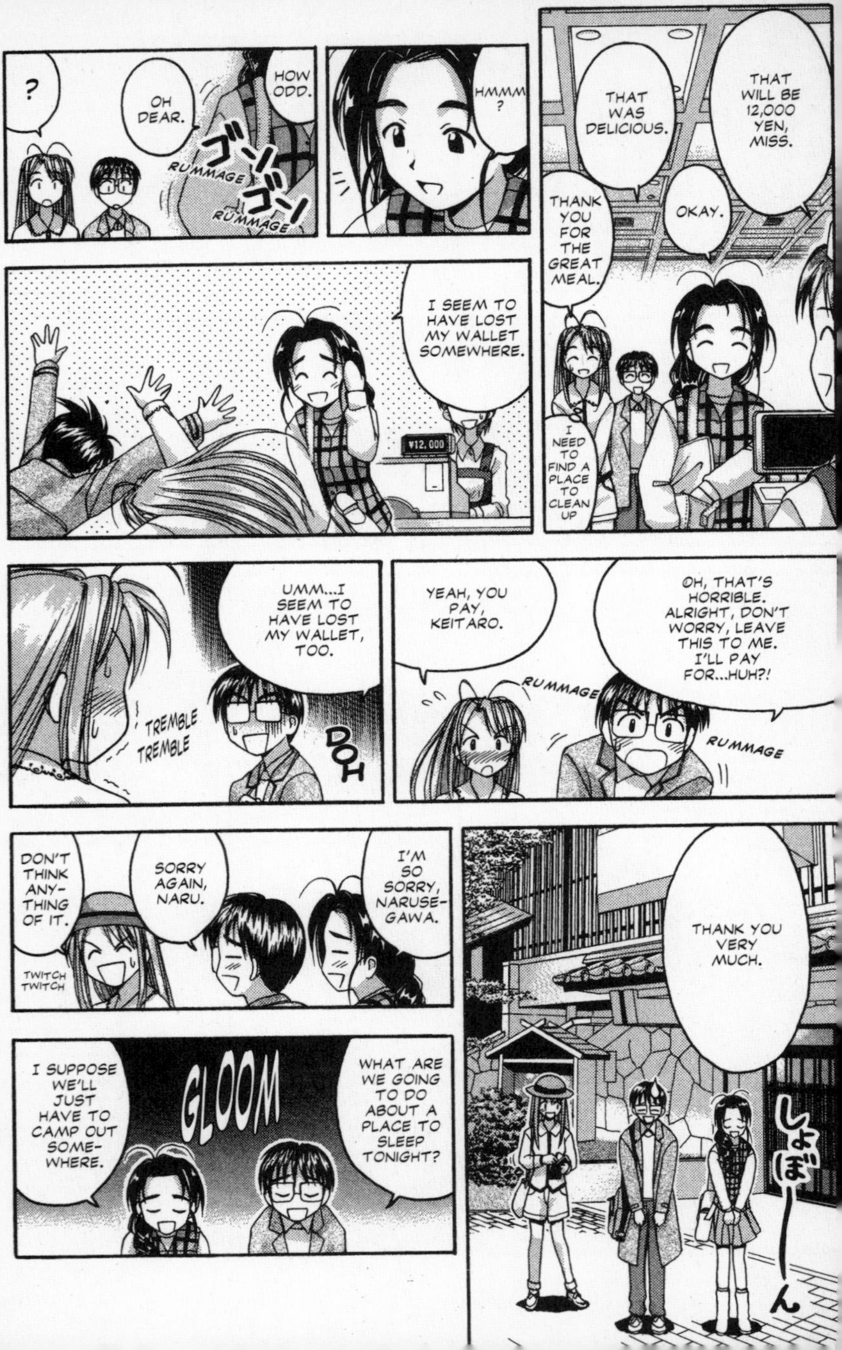
THAT WILL BE 12,000 YEN, MISS.
THAT WAS DELICIOUS.
OKAY.
THANK YOU FOR THE GREAT MEAL.
I NEED TO FIND A PLACE TO CLEAN UP
HMMM ?
HOW ODD.
OH DEAR.
ゴソゴソ
RUMMAGE
RUMMAGE
?
I SEEM TO HAVE LOST MY WALLET SOMEWHERE.
¥12,000
OH, THAT'S HORRIBLE. ALRIGHT, DON'T WORRY, LEAVE THIS TO ME. I'LL PAY FOR...HUH?!
RUMMAGE
RUMMAGE
YEAH, YOU PAY, KEITARO.
UMM...I SEEM TO HAVE LOST MY WALLET, TOO.
DOH
TREMBLE TREMBLE
THANK YOU VERY MUCH.
しょぼーん
I'M SO SORRY, NARUSE-GAWA.
SORRY AGAIN, NARU.
DON'T THINK ANY-THING OF IT.
TWITCH TWITCH
WHAT ARE WE GOING TO DO ABOUT A PLACE TO SLEEP TONIGHT?
GLOOM
I SUPPOSE WE'LL JUST HAVE TO CAMP OUT SOME-WHERE.

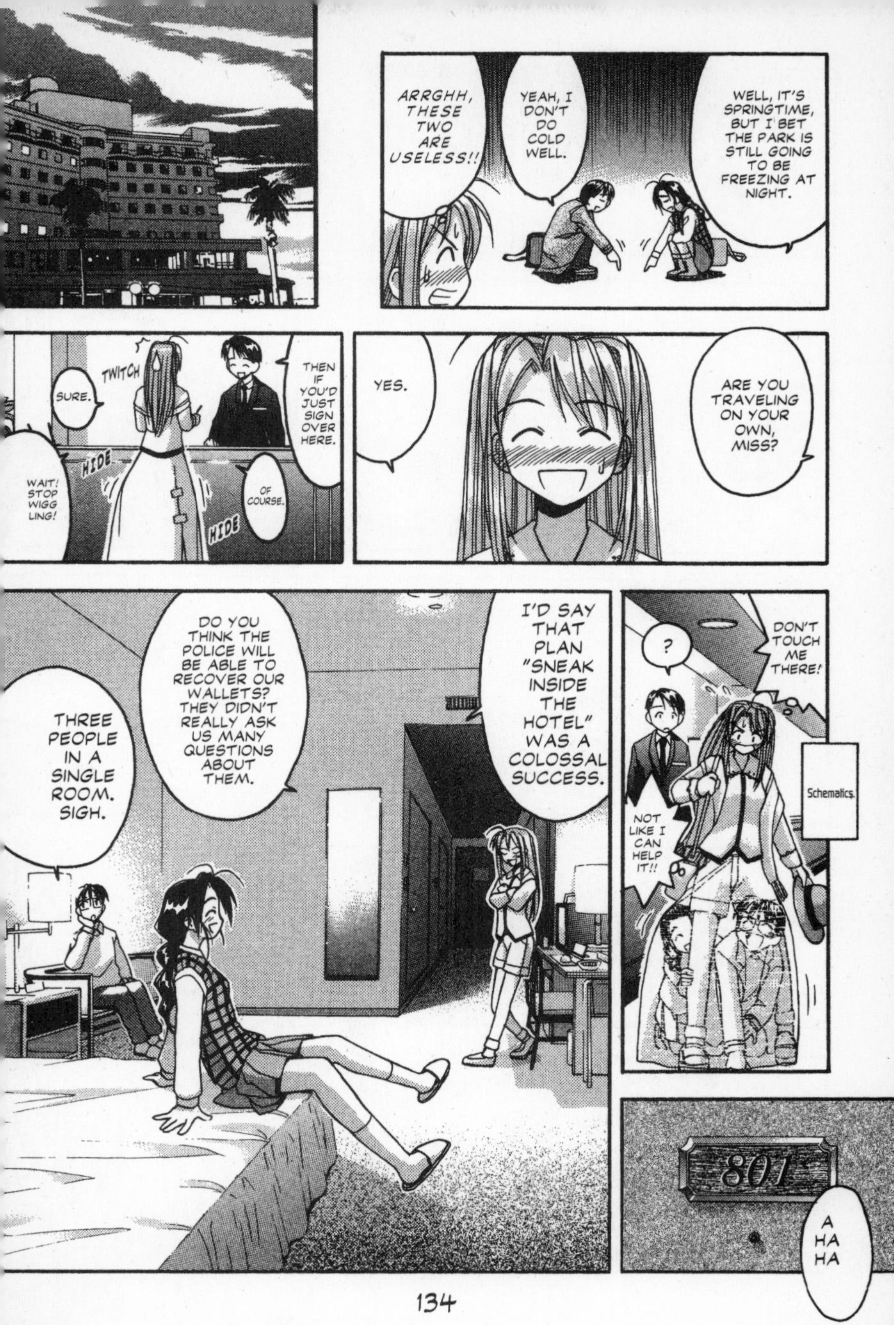
WELL, IT'S SPRINGTIME, BUT I BET THE PARK IS STILL GOING TO BE FREEZING AT NIGHT.
YEAH, I DON'T DO COLD WELL.
ARRGHH, THESE TWO ARE USELESS!!
ARE YOU TRAVELING ON YOUR OWN, MISS?
YES.
THEN IF YOU'D JUST SIGN OVER HERE.
TWITCH
SURE.
OF COURSE.
HIDE
HIDE
WAIT! STOP WIGG LING!
DON'T TOUCH ME THERE!
?
Schematics.
NOT LIKE I CAN HELP IT!!
801
A HA HA
I'D SAY THAT PLAN "SNEAK INSIDE THE HOTEL" WAS A COLOSSAL SUCCESS.
DO YOU THINK THE POLICE WILL BE ABLE TO RECOVER OUR WALLETS? THEY DIDN'T REALLY ASK US MANY QUESTIONS ABOUT THEM.
THREE PEOPLE IN A SINGLE ROOM. SIGH.

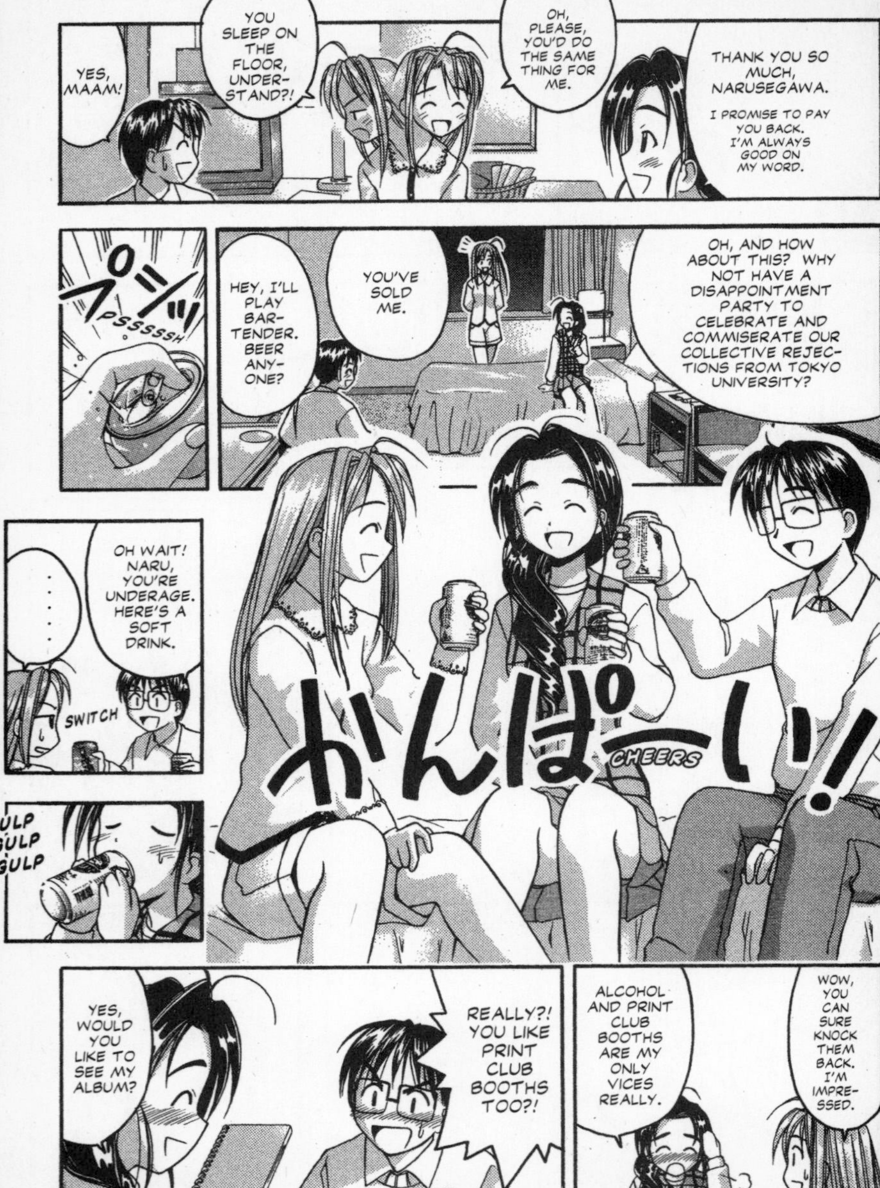

THANK YOU SO MUCH, NARUSEGAWA.
I PROMISE TO PAY YOU BACK. I'M ALWAYS GOOD ON MY WORD.
OH, PLEASE, YOU'D DO THE SAME THING FOR ME.
YOU SLEEP ON THE FLOOR, UNDER-STAND?!
YES, MAAM!
OH, AND HOW ABOUT THIS? WHY NOT HAVE A DISAPPOINTMENT PARTY TO CELEBRATE AND COMMISERATE OUR COLLECTIVE REJEC-TIONS FROM TOKYO UNIVERSITY?
YOU'VE SOLD ME.
HEY, I'LL PLAY BAR-TENDER. BEER ANY-ONE?
PSSSSSH
かんぱーい!!
CHEERS
OH WAIT! NARU, YOU'RE UNDERAGE. HERE'S A SOFT DRINK.
......
SWITCH
GULP GULP GULP
WOW, YOU CAN SURE KNOCK THEM BACK. I'M IMPRE-SSED.
ALCOHOL AND PRINT CLUB BOOTHS ARE MY ONLY VICES REALLY.
REALLY?! YOU LIKE PRINT CLUB BOOTHS TOO?!
YES, WOULD YOU LIKE TO SEE MY ALBUM?

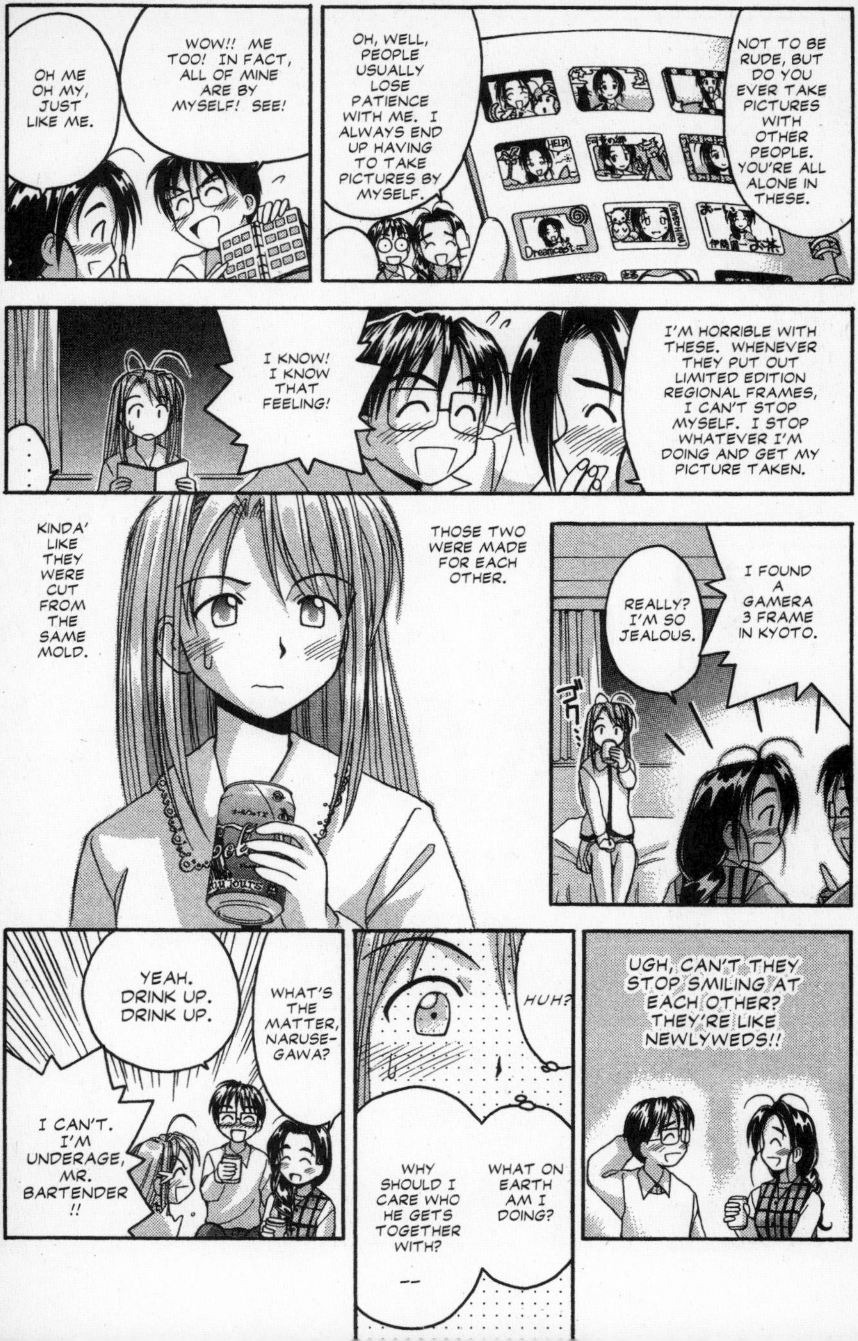
NOT TO BE RUDE, BUT DO YOU EVER TAKE PICTURES WITH OTHER PEOPLE. YOU'RE ALL ALONE IN THESE.
OH, WELL, PEOPLE USUALLY LOSE PATIENCE WITH ME. I ALWAYS END UP HAVING TO TAKE PICTURES BY MYSELF.
WOW!! ME TOO! IN FACT, ALL OF MINE ARE BY MYSELF! SEE!
OH ME OH MY, JUST LIKE ME.
I'M HORRIBLE WITH THESE. WHENEVER THEY PUT OUT LIMITED EDITION REGIONAL FRAMES, I CAN'T STOP MYSELF. I STOP WHATEVER I'M DOING AND GET MY PICTURE TAKEN.
I KNOW! I KNOW THAT FEELING!
I FOUND A GAMERA 3 FRAME IN KYOTO.
REALLY? I'M SO JEALOUS.
THOSE TWO WERE MADE FOR EACH OTHER.
KINDA' LIKE THEY WERE CUT FROM THE SAME MOLD.
UGH, CAN'T THEY STOP SMILING AT EACH OTHER? THEY'RE LIKE NEWLYWEDS!!
HUH?
WHAT ON EARTH AM I DOING?
WHY SHOULD I CARE WHO HE GETS TOGETHER WITH?
--
WHAT'S THE MATTER, NARUSE-GAWA?
YEAH. DRINK UP. DRINK UP.
I CAN'T. I'M UNDERAGE, MR. BARTENDER!!

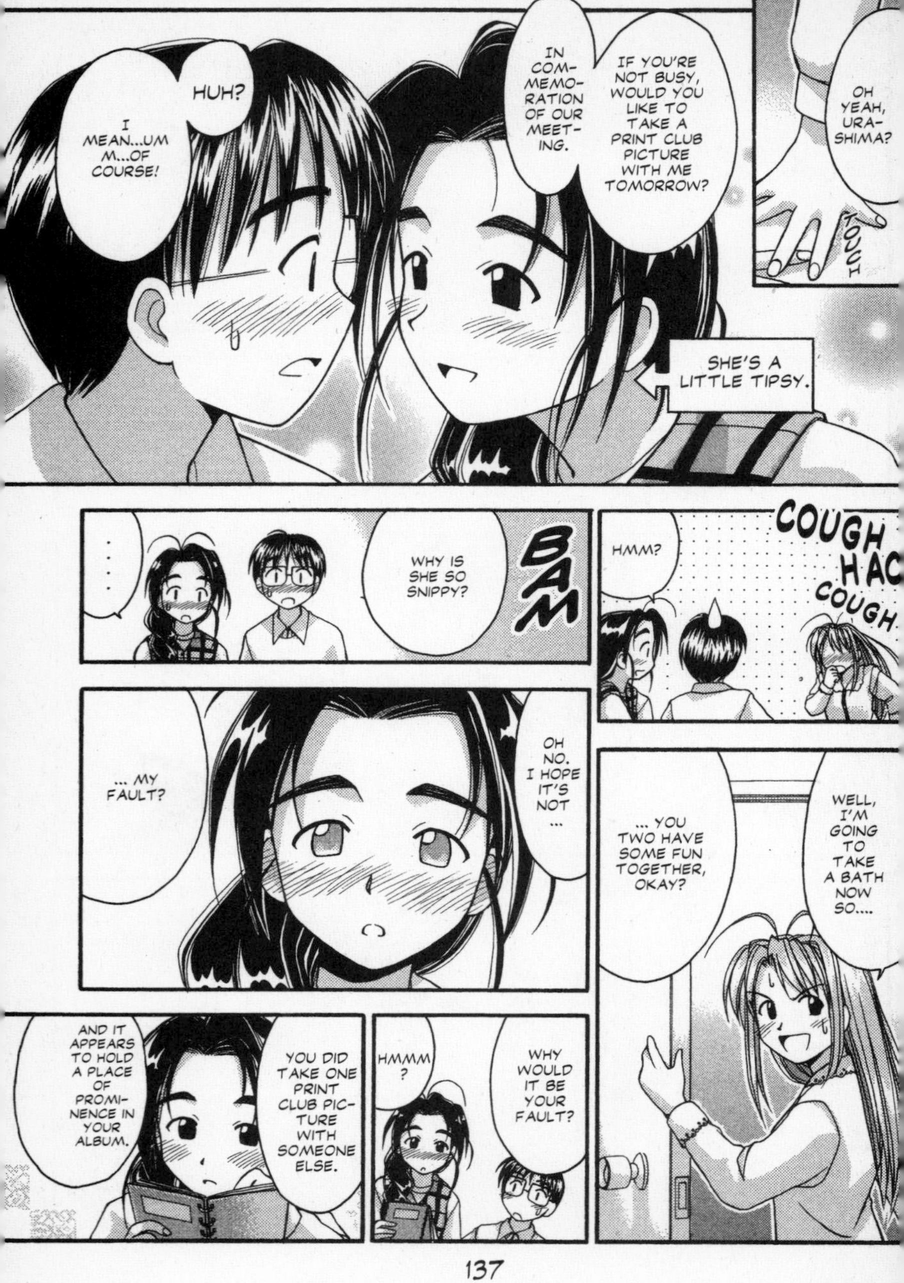
OH YEAH, URA-SHIMA?
TOUCH
IF YOU'RE NOT BUSY, WOULD YOU LIKE TO TAKE A PRINT CLUB PICTURE WITH ME TOMORROW?
IN COM-MEMO-RATION OF OUR MEET-ING.
HUH?
I MEAN...UM M...OF COURSE!
SHE'S A LITTLE TIPSY.
COUGH
HAC
COUGH
HMM?
BAM
WHY IS SHE SO SNIPPY?
. . . .
WELL, I'M GOING TO TAKE A BATH NOW SO....
... YOU TWO HAVE SOME FUN TOGETHER, OKAY?
OH NO. I HOPE IT'S NOT ...
... MY FAULT?
WHY WOULD IT BE YOUR FAULT?
HMMM ?
YOU DID TAKE ONE PRINT CLUB PIC-TURE WITH SOMEONE ELSE.
AND IT APPEARS TO HOLD A PLACE OF PROMI-NENCE IN YOUR ALBUM.

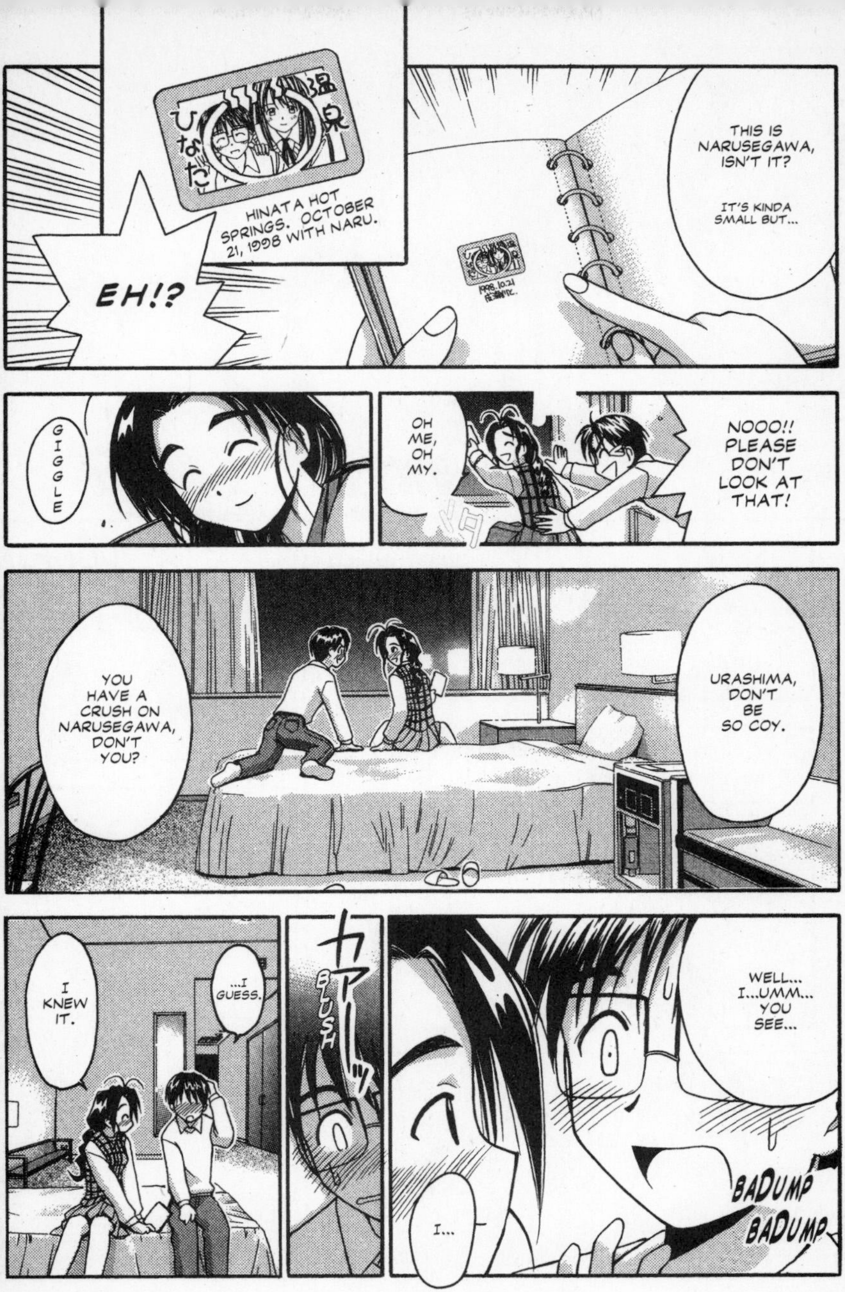
THIS IS NARUSEGAWA, ISN'T IT?
IT'S KINDA SMALL BUT...
HINATA HOT SPRINGS. OCTOBER 21, 1998 WITH NARU.
EH!?
NOOO!! PLEASE DON'T LOOK AT THAT!
OH ME, OH MY.
GIGGLE
URASHIMA, DON'T BE SO COY.
YOU HAVE A CRUSH ON NARUSEGAWA, DON'T YOU?
WELL... I...UMM... YOU SEE...
BADUMP BADUMP
I...
BLUSH
...I GUESS.
I KNEW IT.

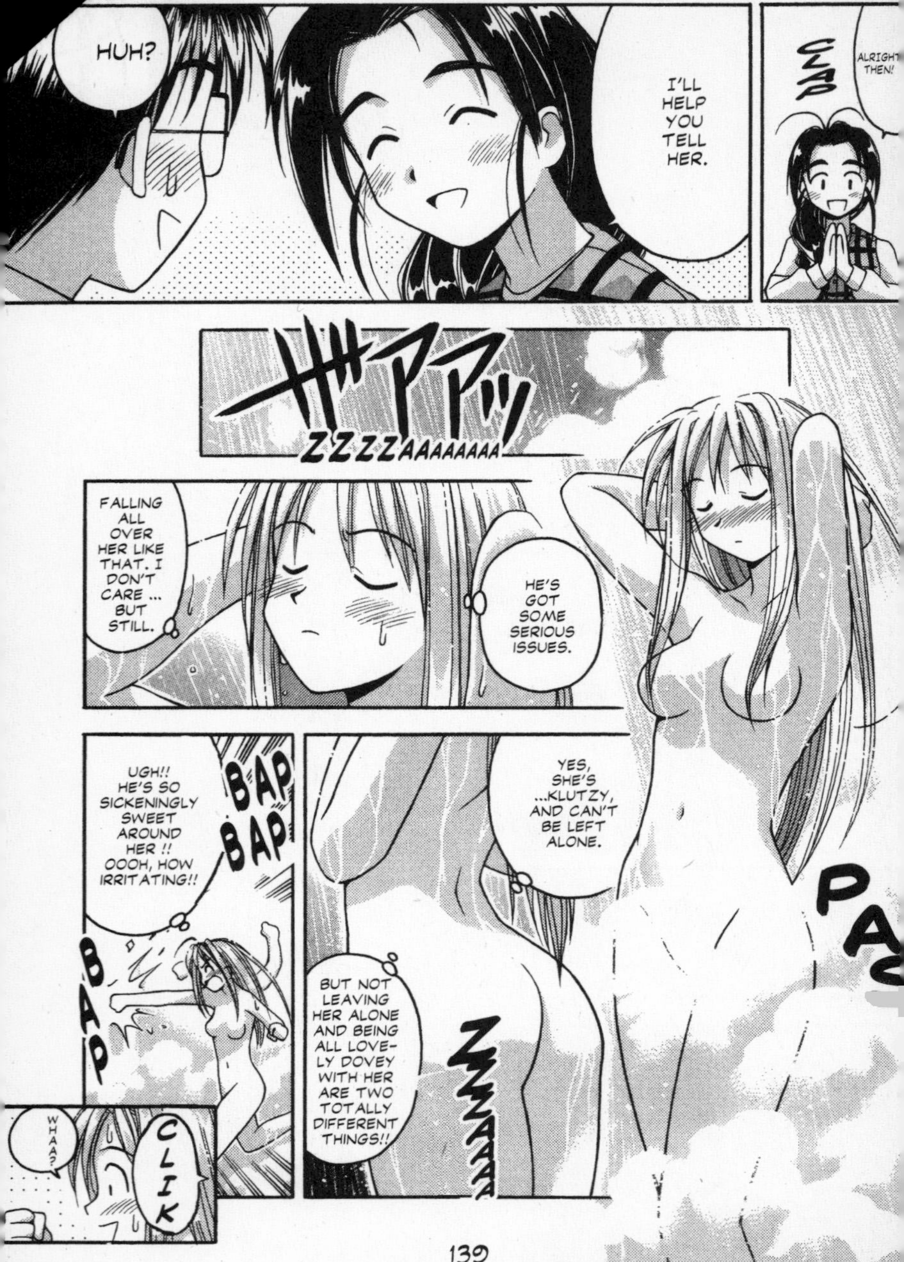

CLAP
ALRIGHT THEN!
I'LL HELP YOU TELL HER.
HUH?
PA
ザアアッ
ZZZZAAAAAAA
HE'S GOT SOME SERIOUS ISSUES.
FALLING ALL OVER HER LIKE THAT. I DON'T CARE ... BUT STILL.
YES, SHE'S ...KLUTZY, AND CAN'T BE LEFT ALONE.
BUT NOT LEAVING HER ALONE AND BEING ALL LOVE-LY DOVEY WITH HER ARE TWO TOTALLY DIFFERENT THINGS!!
ZZZAAAA
UGH!! HE'S SO SICKENINGLY SWEET AROUND HER !! OOOH, HOW IRRITATING!!
BAP BAP
BAP
CLIK
WHAA?

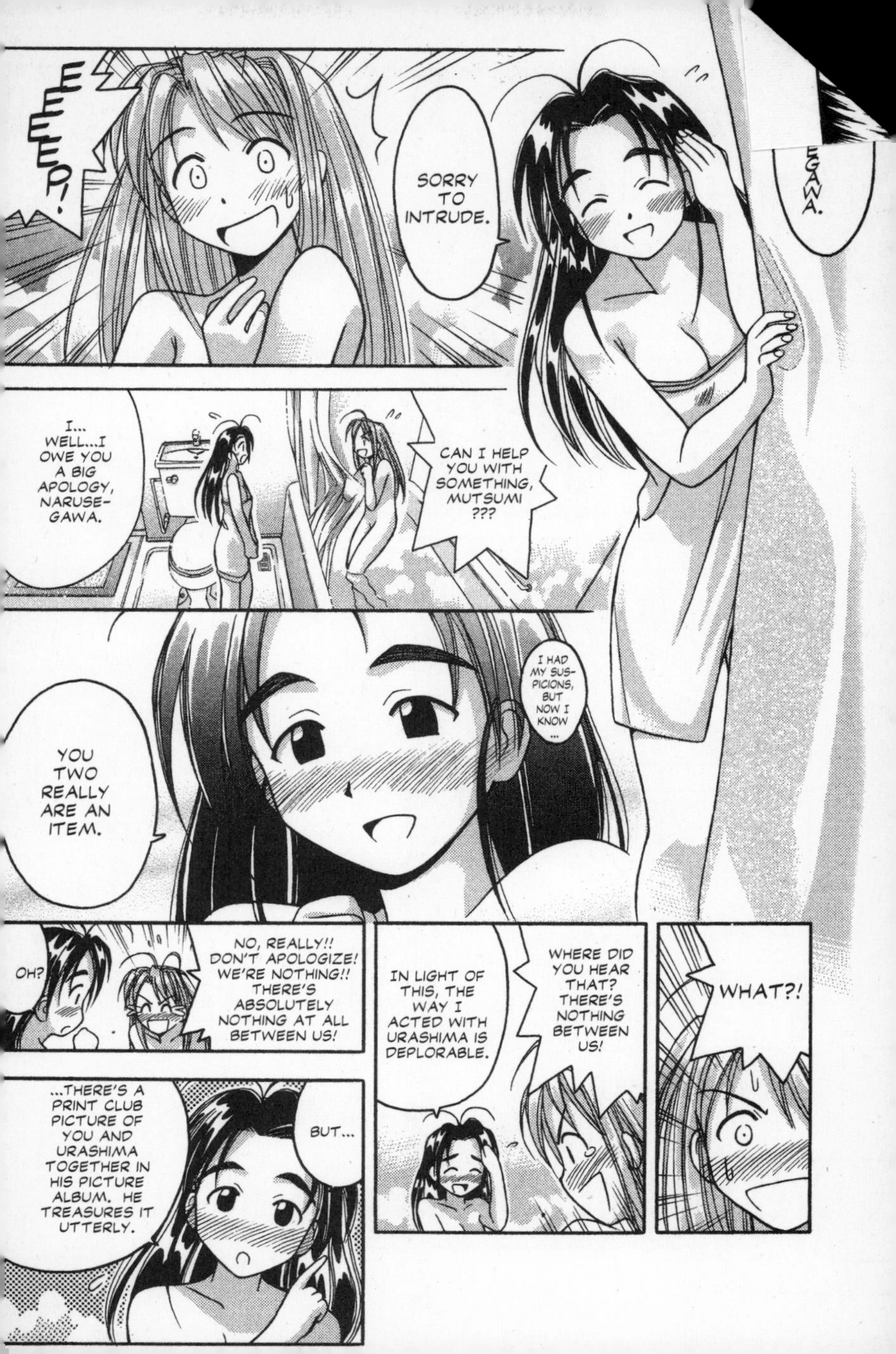
EGAWA.
EEEEEP!
SORRY TO INTRUDE.
CAN I HELP YOU WITH SOMETHING, MUTSUMI ???
I... WELL...I OWE YOU A BIG APOLOGY, NARUSE-GAWA.
I HAD MY SUS-PICIONS, BUT NOW I KNOW ...
YOU TWO REALLY ARE AN ITEM.
WHAT?!
WHERE DID YOU HEAR THAT? THERE'S NOTHING BETWEEN US!
IN LIGHT OF THIS, THE WAY I ACTED WITH URASHIMA IS DEPLORABLE.
NO, REALLY!! DON'T APOLOGIZE! WE'RE NOTHING!! THERE'S ABSOLUTELY NOTHING AT ALL BETWEEN US!
OH?
BUT...
...THERE'S A PRINT CLUB PICTURE OF YOU AND URASHIMA TOGETHER IN HIS PICTURE ALBUM. HE TREASURES IT UTTERLY.

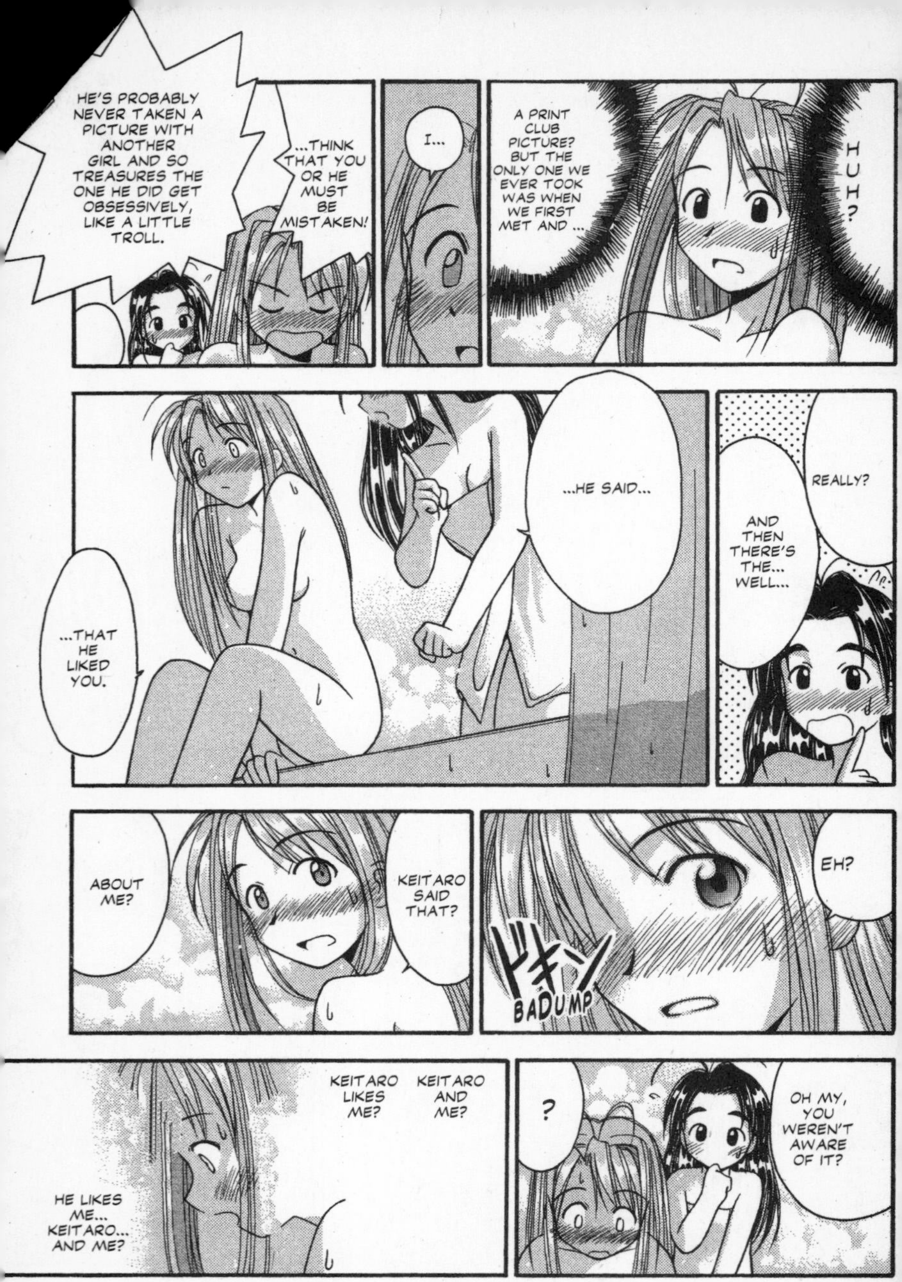
HUH?
A PRINT CLUB PICTURE? BUT THE ONLY ONE WE EVER TOOK WAS WHEN WE FIRST MET AND ...
I...
...THINK THAT YOU OR HE MUST BE MISTAKEN!
HE'S PROBABLY NEVER TAKEN A PICTURE WITH ANOTHER GIRL AND SO TREASURES THE ONE HE DID GET OBSESSIVELY, LIKE A LITTLE TROLL.
REALLY?
AND THEN THERE'S THE... WELL...
...HE SAID...
...THAT HE LIKED YOU.
EH?
ドキン
BADUMP
KEITARO SAID THAT?
ABOUT ME?
OH MY, YOU WEREN'T AWARE OF IT?
?
KEITARO AND ME?
KEITARO LIKES ME?
HE LIKES ME... KEITARO... AND ME?

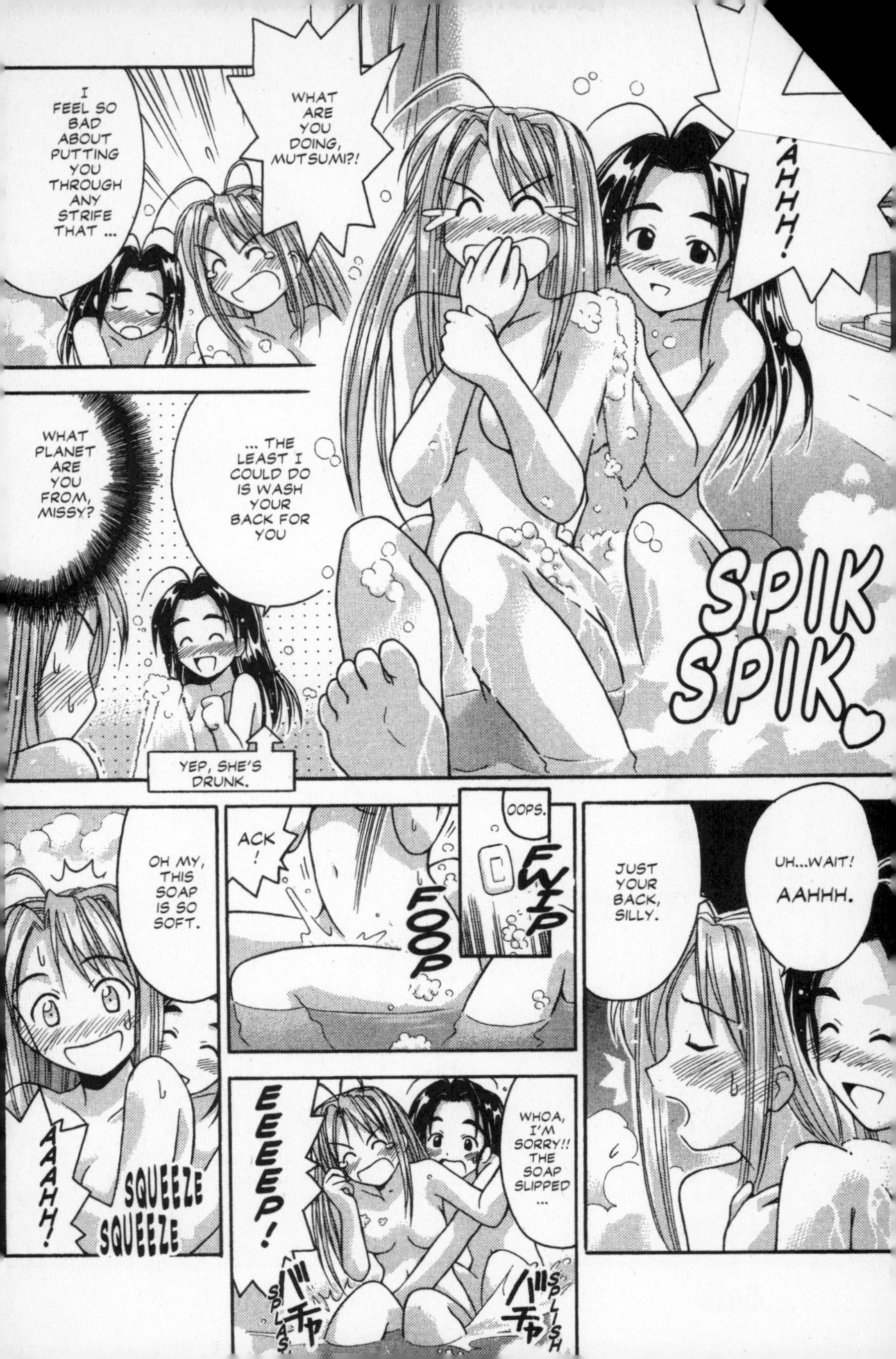
AHHH!
WHAT ARE YOU DOING, MUTSUMI?!
SPIK SPIK
I FEEL SO BAD ABOUT PUTTING YOU THROUGH ANY STRIFE THAT ...
... THE LEAST I COULD DO IS WASH YOUR BACK FOR YOU
WHAT PLANET ARE YOU FROM, MISSY?
YEP, SHE'S DRUNK.
UH...WAIT!
AAHHH.
JUST YOUR BACK, SILLY.
OOPS.
FWIP
ACK!
FOOP
WHOA, I'M SORRY!! THE SOAP SLIPPED ...
EEEEP!
SPLISH
SPLAS
OH MY, THIS SOAP IS SO SOFT.
AAAHH!
SQUEEZE SQUEEZE

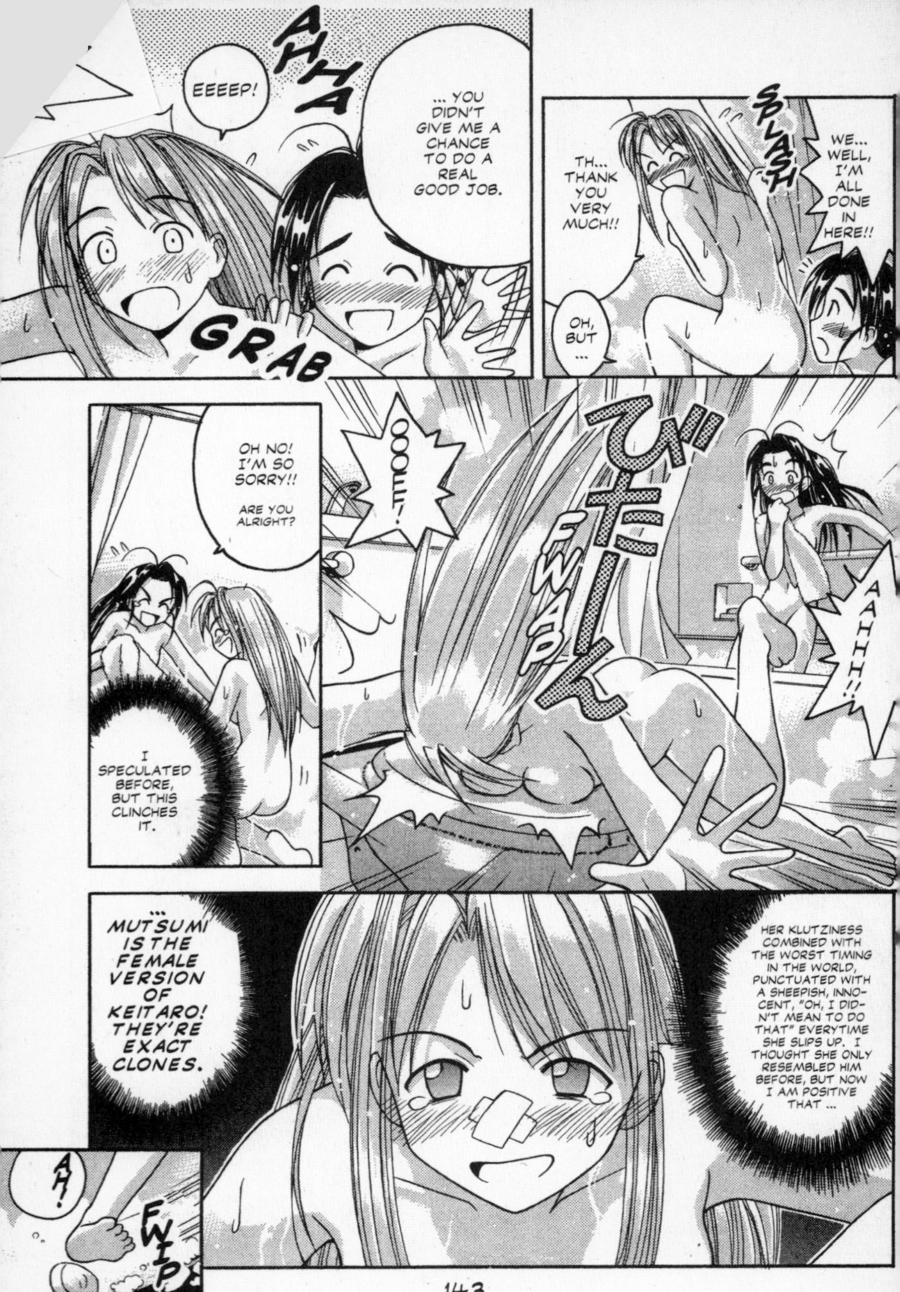
SPLASH
WE... WELL, I'M ALL DONE IN HERE!!
TH... THANK YOU VERY MUCH!!
OH, BUT ...
AHHA
... YOU DIDN'T GIVE ME A CHANCE TO DO A REAL GOOD JOB.
EEEEP!
GRAB
びたーん
FWAP
AAHHH!!
OOOF!
OH NO! I'M SO SORRY!!
ARE YOU ALRIGHT?
I SPECULATED BEFORE, BUT THIS CLINCHES IT.
HER KLUTZINESS COMBINED WITH THE WORST TIMING IN THE WORLD, PUNCTUATED WITH A SHEEPISH, INNOCENT, "OH, I DIDN'T MEAN TO DO THAT" EVERYTIME SHE SLIPS UP. I THOUGHT SHE ONLY RESEMBLED HIM BEFORE, BUT NOW I AM POSITIVE THAT ...
... MUTSUMI IS THE FEMALE VERSION OF KEITARO! THEY'RE EXACT CLONES.
AH!
FWIP

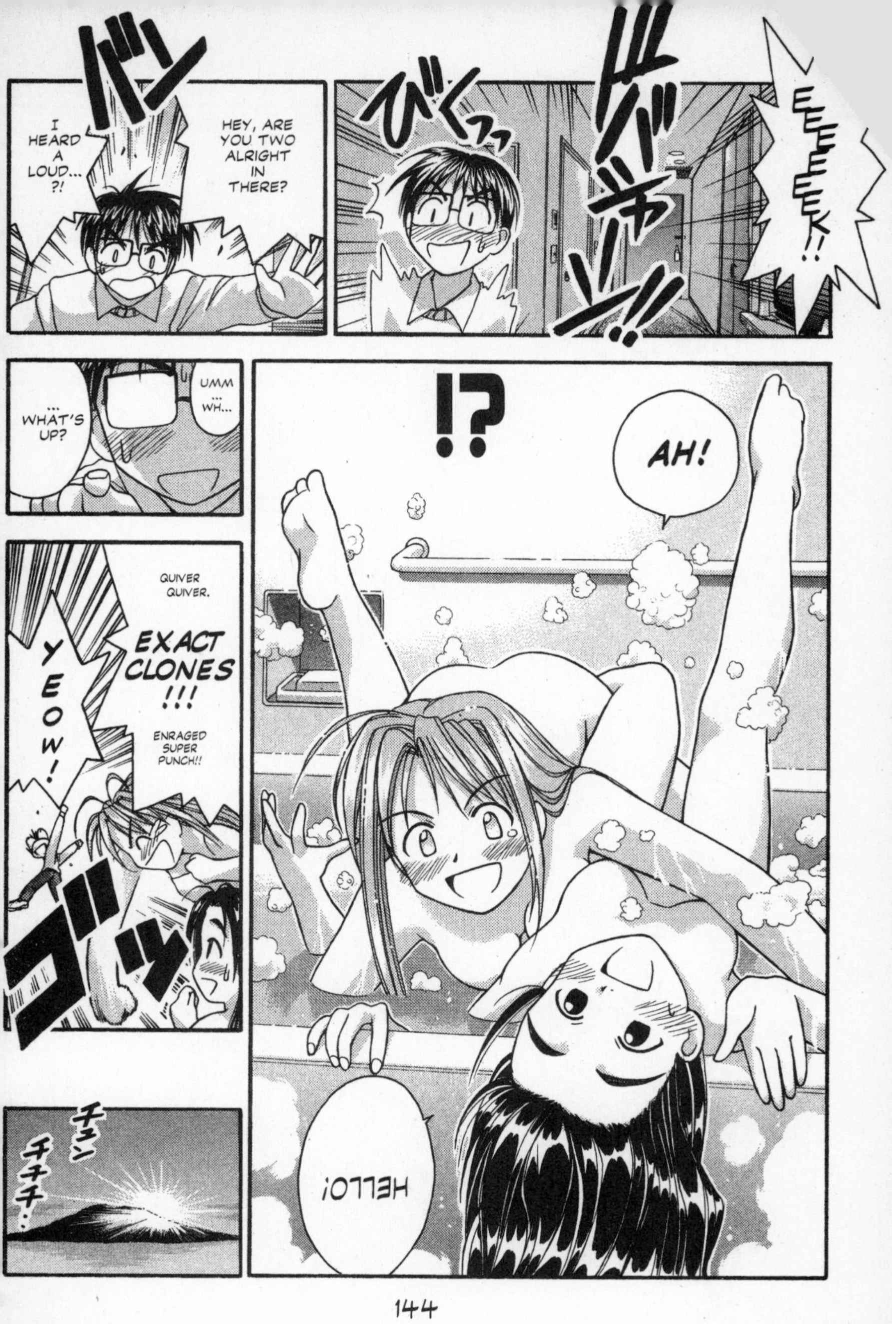
EEEEEEK!!
ザバシャーン!!
びくっ
バン
HEY, ARE YOU TWO ALRIGHT IN THERE?
I HEARD A LOUD...?!
!?
AH!
HELLO!
UMM... WH...
...WHAT'S UP?
QUIVER QUIVER.
EXACT CLONES!!!
ENRAGED SUPER PUNCH!!
YEOW!
ゴッ
チュン
チチチ…

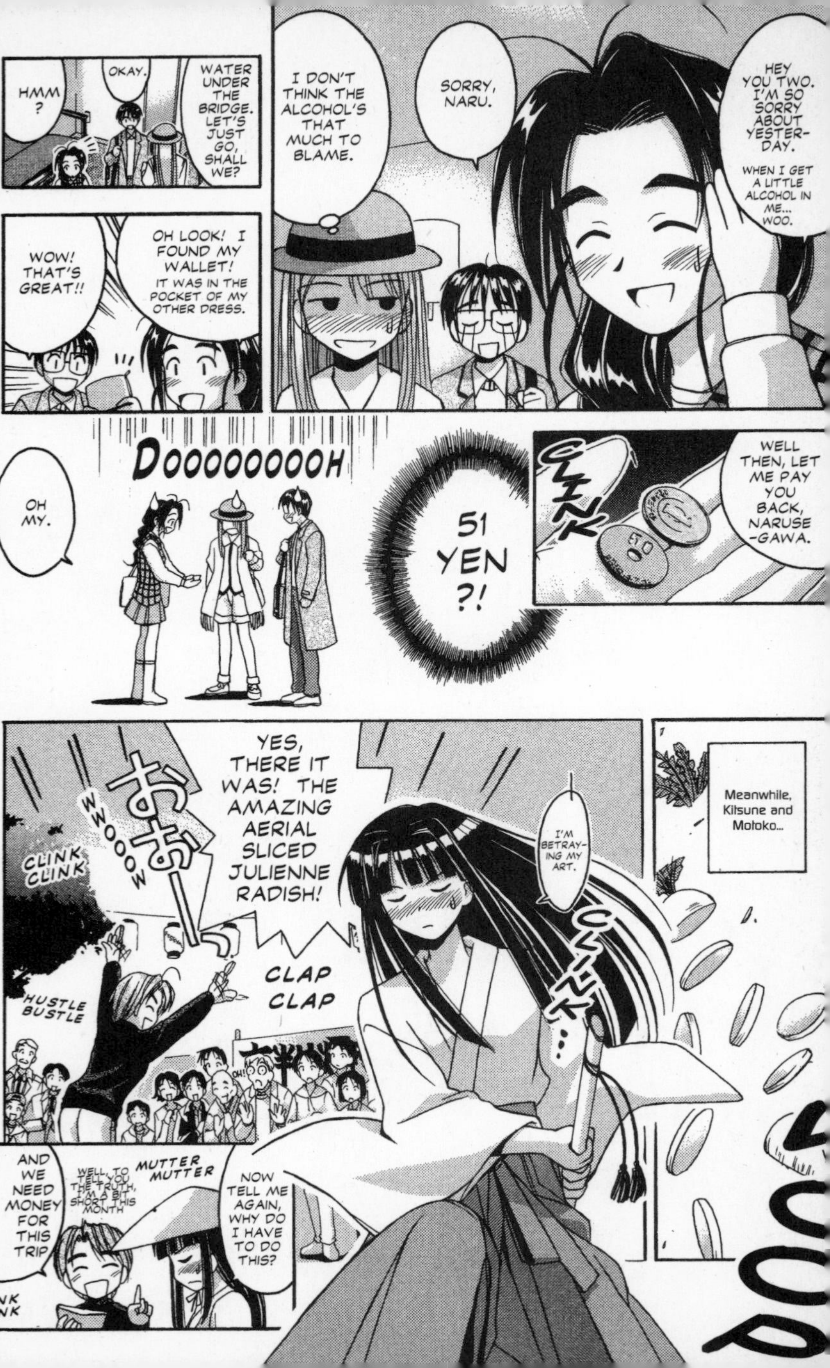
HEY YOU TWO. I'M SO SORRY ABOUT YESTER-DAY.
WHEN I GET A LITTLE ALCOHOL IN ME... WOO.
SORRY, NARU.
I DON'T THINK THE ALCOHOL'S THAT MUCH TO BLAME.
WATER UNDER THE BRIDGE. LET'S JUST GO, SHALL WE?
OKAY.
HMM?
OH LOOK! I FOUND MY WALLET! IT WAS IN THE POCKET OF MY OTHER DRESS.
WOW! THAT'S GREAT!!
WELL THEN, LET ME PAY YOU BACK, NARUSE-GAWA.
CLINK
51 YEN ?!
DOOOOOOOOH
OH MY.
Meanwhile, Kitsune and Motoko...
CLINK...
I'M BETRAYING MY ART.
YES, THERE IT WAS! THE AMAZING AERIAL SLICED JULIENNE RADISH!
おぉー
WWOOOOW
CLINK CLINK
CLAP CLAP
HUSTLE BUSTLE
OH!
NOW TELL ME AGAIN, WHY DO I HAVE TO DO THIS?
MUTTER MUTTER
WELL, TO TELL YOU THE TRUTH, I'M A BIT SHORT THIS MONTH
AND WE NEED MONEY FOR THIS TRIP
CLINK CLINK

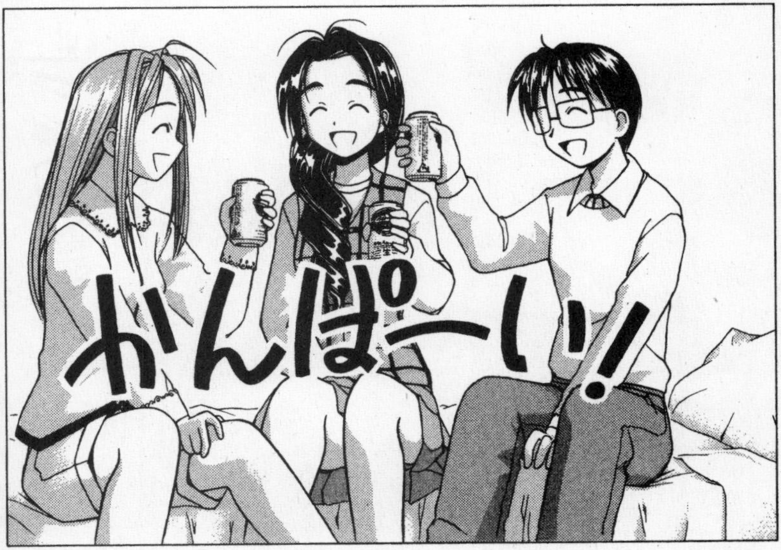
かんぱーい!!

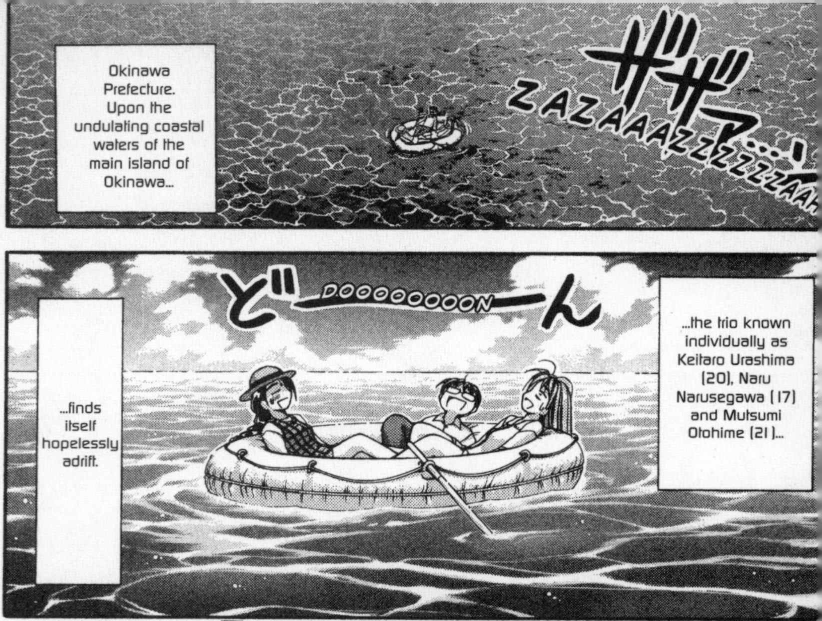
ザザァ…
ZAZAAAAZZZZZZZAAAH
Okinawa Prefecture. Upon the undulating coastal waters of the main island of Okinawa...
...the trio known individually as Keitaro Urashima (20), Naru Narusegawa (17) and Mutsumi Otohime (21)...
どー ん
DOOOOOOOON
...finds itself hopelessly adrift.

LOVE ♥ HINA

HINATA.23 Palpitations While Floating Away!

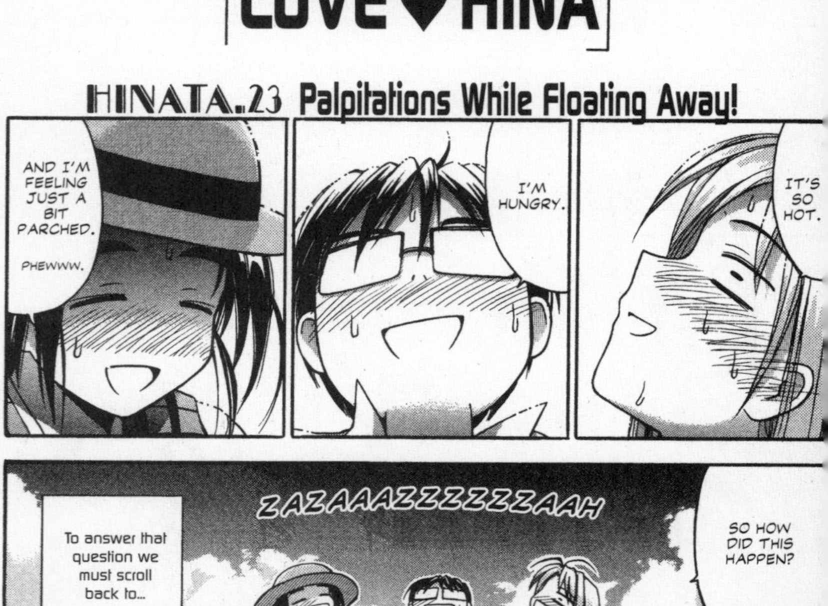
IT'S SO HOT.
I'M HUNGRY.
AND I'M FEELING JUST A BIT PARCHED.
PHEWWW.
SO HOW DID THIS HAPPEN?
ZAZAAAZZZZZZZAAH
To answer that question we must scroll back to...

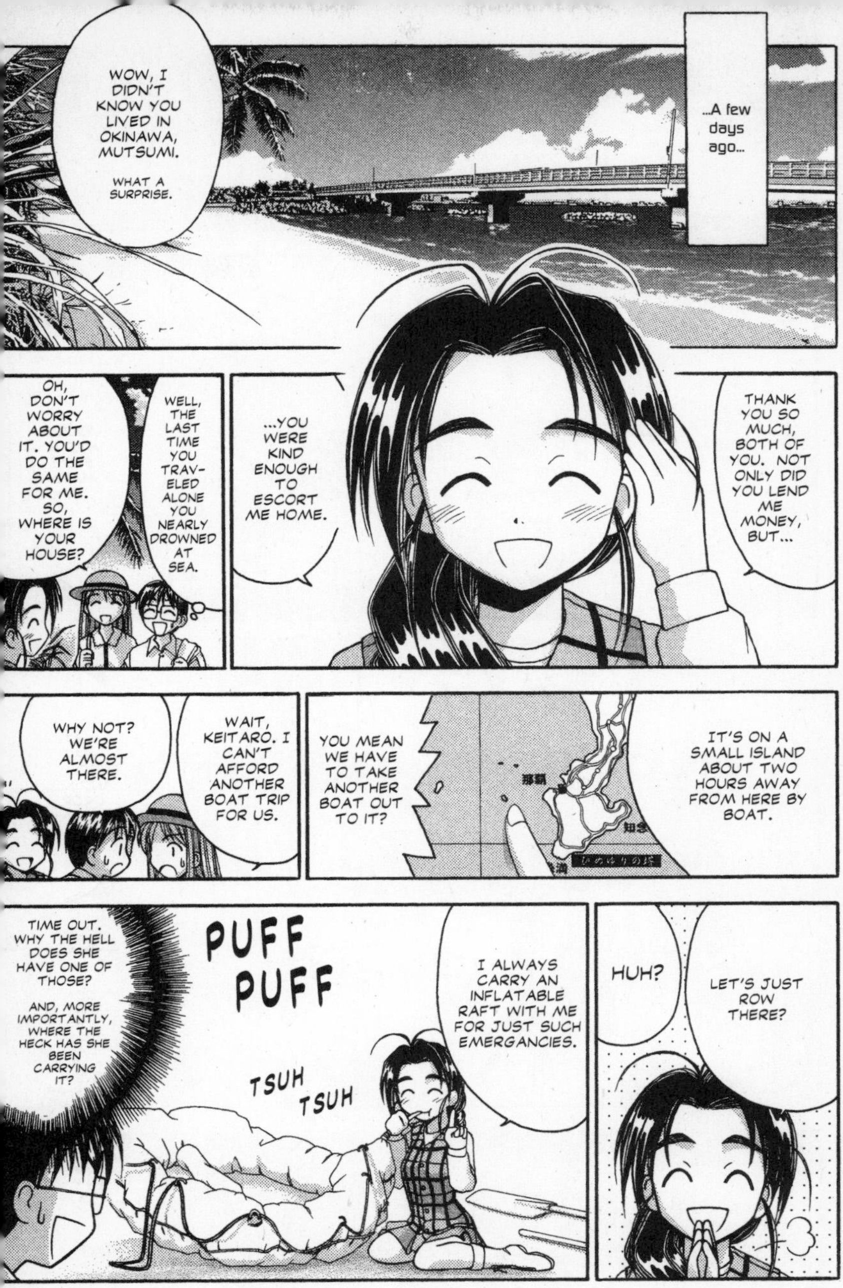
...A few days ago...
WOW, I DIDN'T KNOW YOU LIVED IN OKINAWA, MUTSUMI. WHAT A SURPRISE.
THANK YOU SO MUCH, BOTH OF YOU. NOT ONLY DID YOU LEND ME MONEY, BUT...
...YOU WERE KIND ENOUGH TO ESCORT ME HOME.
WELL, THE LAST TIME YOU TRAV-ELED ALONE YOU NEARLY DROWNED AT SEA.
OH, DON'T WORRY ABOUT IT. YOU'D DO THE SAME FOR ME. SO, WHERE IS YOUR HOUSE?
IT'S ON A SMALL ISLAND ABOUT TWO HOURS AWAY FROM HERE BY BOAT.
那覇
知念
ひめゆりの塔
YOU MEAN WE HAVE TO TAKE ANOTHER BOAT OUT TO IT?
WAIT, KEITARO. I CAN'T AFFORD ANOTHER BOAT TRIP FOR US.
WHY NOT? WE'RE ALMOST THERE.
LET'S JUST ROW THERE?
HUH?
I ALWAYS CARRY AN INFLATABLE RAFT WITH ME FOR JUST SUCH EMERGANCIES.
PUFF PUFF
TIME OUT. WHY THE HELL DOES SHE HAVE ONE OF THOSE?
AND, MORE IMPORTANTLY, WHERE THE HECK HAS SHE BEEN CARRYING IT?
TSUH TSUH

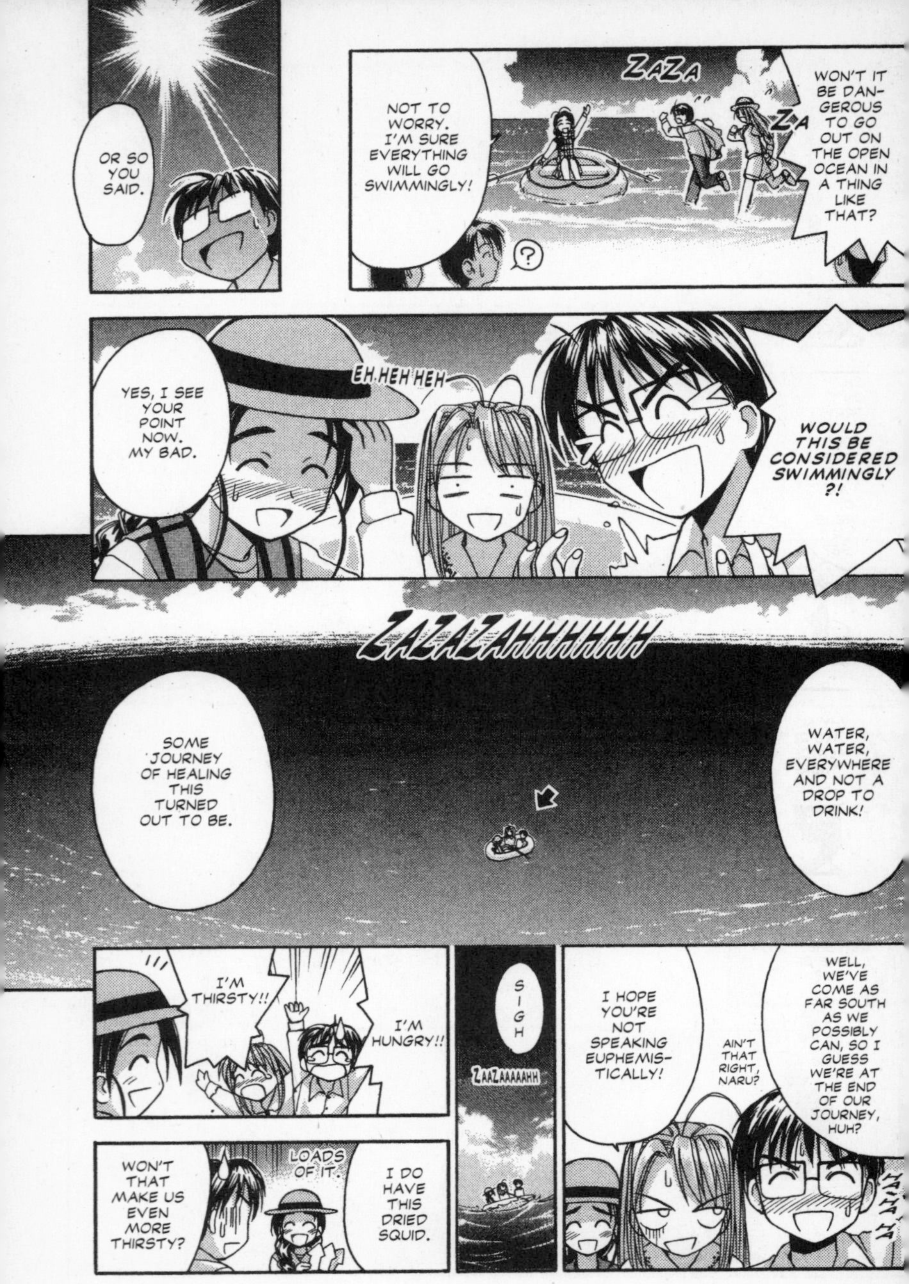
WON'T IT BE DANGEROUS TO GO OUT ON THE OPEN OCEAN IN A THING LIKE THAT?
ZAZA
ZA
NOT TO WORRY. I'M SURE EVERYTHING WILL GO SWIMMINGLY!
?
OR SO YOU SAID.
WOULD THIS BE CONSIDERED SWIMMINGLY?!
EH HEH HEH
YES, I SEE YOUR POINT NOW. MY BAD.
ZAZAZAHHHHHH
WATER, WATER, EVERYWHERE AND NOT A DROP TO DRINK!
SOME JOURNEY OF HEALING THIS TURNED OUT TO BE.
WELL, WE'VE COME AS FAR SOUTH AS WE POSSIBLY CAN, SO I GUESS WE'RE AT THE END OF OUR JOURNEY, HUH?
AIN'T THAT RIGHT, NARU?
I HOPE YOU'RE NOT SPEAKING EUPHEMISTICALLY!
SIGH
ZAAZAAAAAHH
I'M HUNGRY!!
I'M THIRSTY!!
I DO HAVE THIS DRIED SQUID.
LOADS OF IT.
WON'T THAT MAKE US EVEN MORE THIRSTY?

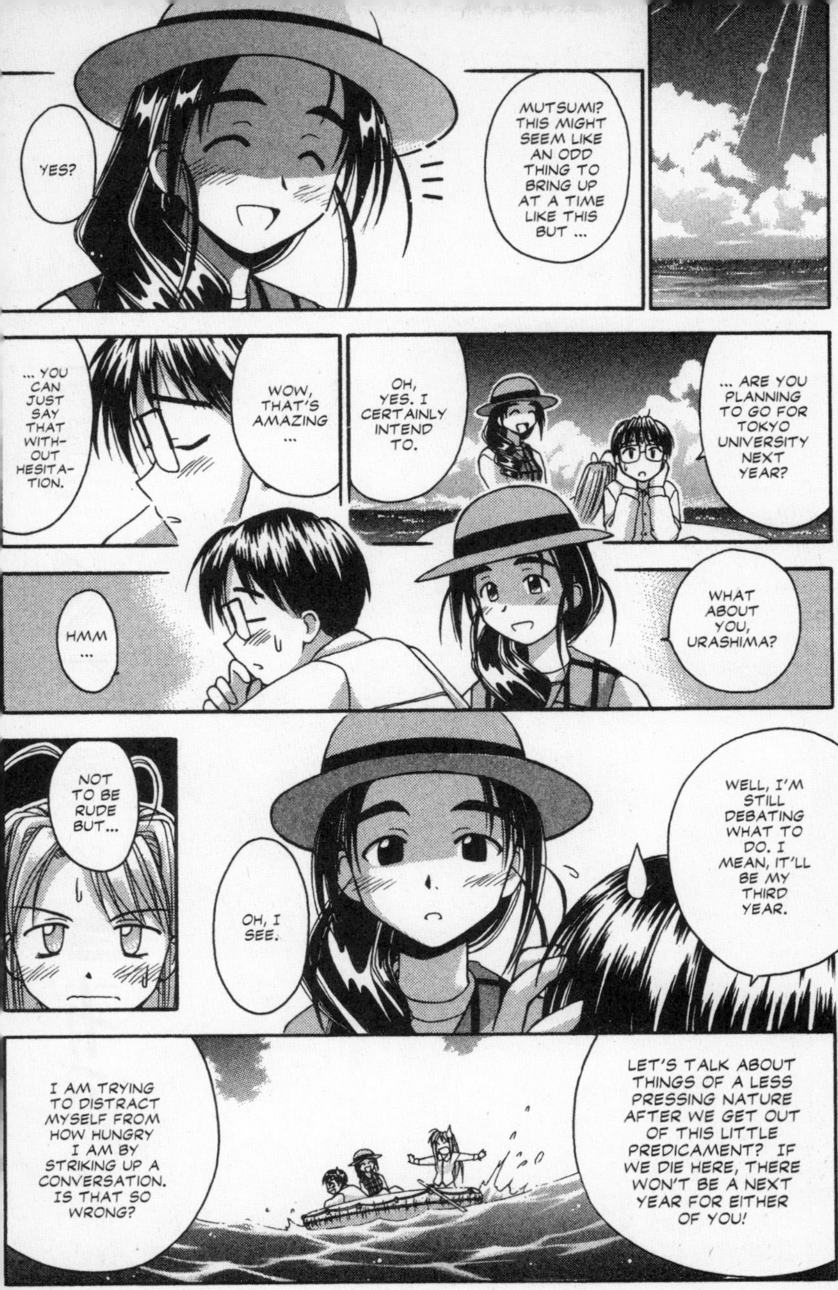
MUTSUMI? THIS MIGHT SEEM LIKE AN ODD THING TO BRING UP AT A TIME LIKE THIS BUT ...
YES?
... ARE YOU PLANNING TO GO FOR TOKYO UNIVERSITY NEXT YEAR?
OH, YES. I CERTAINLY INTEND TO.
WOW, THAT'S AMAZING ...
... YOU CAN JUST SAY THAT WITH-OUT HESITA-TION.
WHAT ABOUT YOU, URASHIMA?
HMM ...
WELL, I'M STILL DEBATING WHAT TO DO. I MEAN, IT'LL BE MY THIRD YEAR.
OH, I SEE.
NOT TO BE RUDE BUT...
LET'S TALK ABOUT THINGS OF A LESS PRESSING NATURE AFTER WE GET OUT OF THIS LITTLE PREDICAMENT? IF WE DIE HERE, THERE WON'T BE A NEXT YEAR FOR EITHER OF YOU!
I AM TRYING TO DISTRACT MYSELF FROM HOW HUNGRY I AM BY STRIKING UP A CONVERSATION. IS THAT SO WRONG?

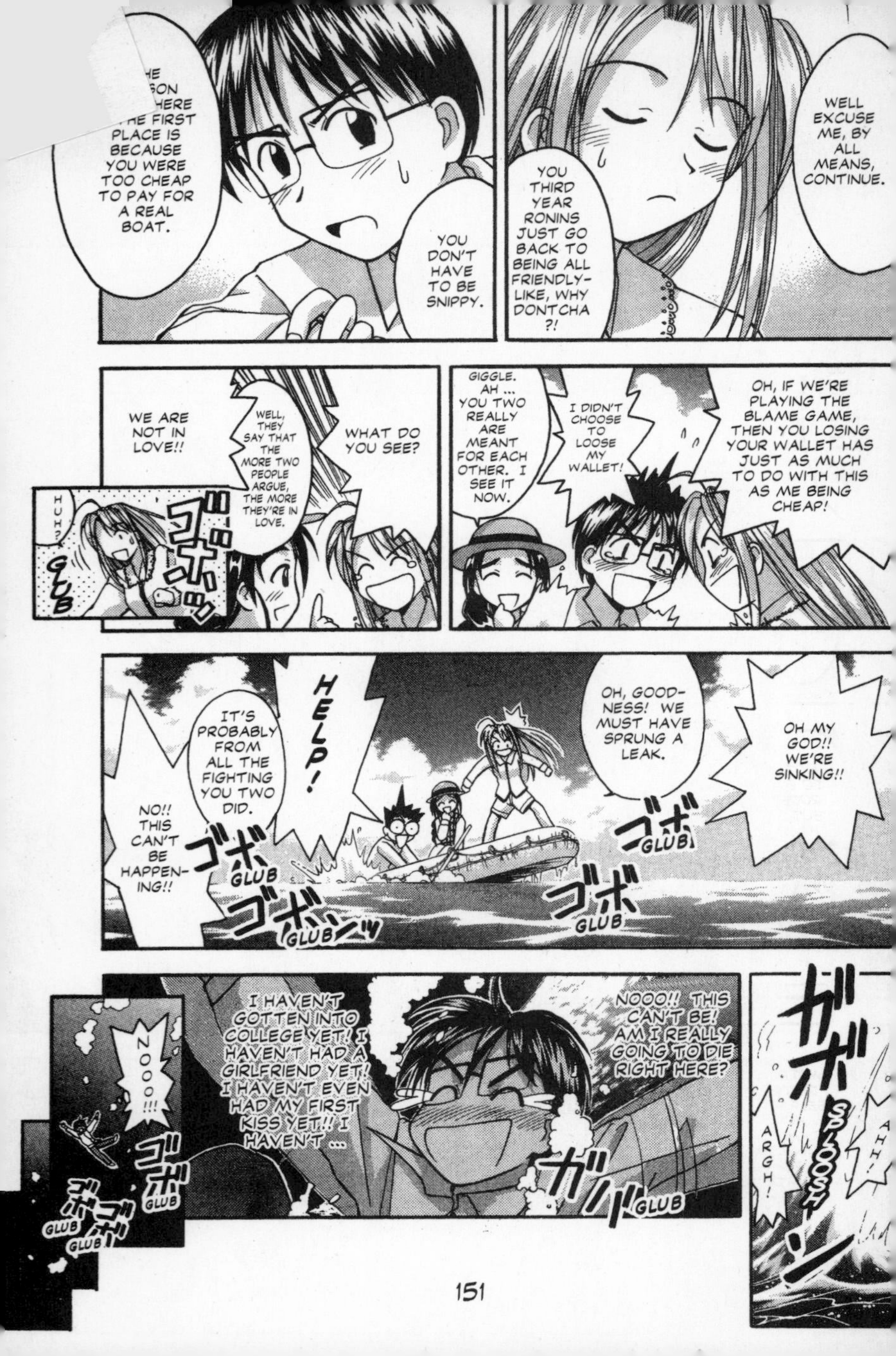
WELL EXCUSE ME, BY ALL MEANS, CONTINUE.
YOU THIRD YEAR RONINS JUST GO BACK TO BEING ALL FRIENDLY-LIKE, WHY DONTCHA ?!
YOU DON'T HAVE TO BE SNIPPY.
HE SON HERE THE FIRST PLACE IS BECAUSE YOU WERE TOO CHEAP TO PAY FOR A REAL BOAT.
OH, IF WE'RE PLAYING THE BLAME GAME, THEN YOU LOSING YOUR WALLET HAS JUST AS MUCH TO DO WITH THIS AS ME BEING CHEAP!
I DIDN'T CHOOSE TO LOOSE MY WALLET!
GIGGLE. AH ... YOU TWO REALLY ARE MEANT FOR EACH OTHER. I SEE IT NOW.
WHAT DO YOU SEE?
WELL, THEY SAY THAT THE MORE TWO PEOPLE ARGUE, THE MORE THEY'RE IN LOVE.
WE ARE NOT IN LOVE!!
ゴボッ
HUH?
GLUB
OH MY GOD!! WE'RE SINKING!!
OH, GOODNESS! WE MUST HAVE SPRUNG A LEAK.
ゴボ GLUB
ゴボ GLUB
HELP!
IT'S PROBABLY FROM ALL THE FIGHTING YOU TWO DID.
NO!! THIS CAN'T BE HAPPENING!!
ゴボ GLUB
ゴボンッ GLUB
ガボ SPLOOSH ン
AHH!
ARGH!
NOOO!! THIS CAN'T BE! AM I REALLY GOING TO DIE RIGHT HERE?
I HAVEN'T GOTTEN INTO COLLEGE YET! I HAVEN'T HAD A GIRLFRIEND YET! I HAVEN'T EVEN HAD MY FIRST KISS YET!! I HAVEN'T ...
ガバ GLUB
NOOO!!!
ゴボ GLUB
ゴボ GLUB
ゴボ GLUB

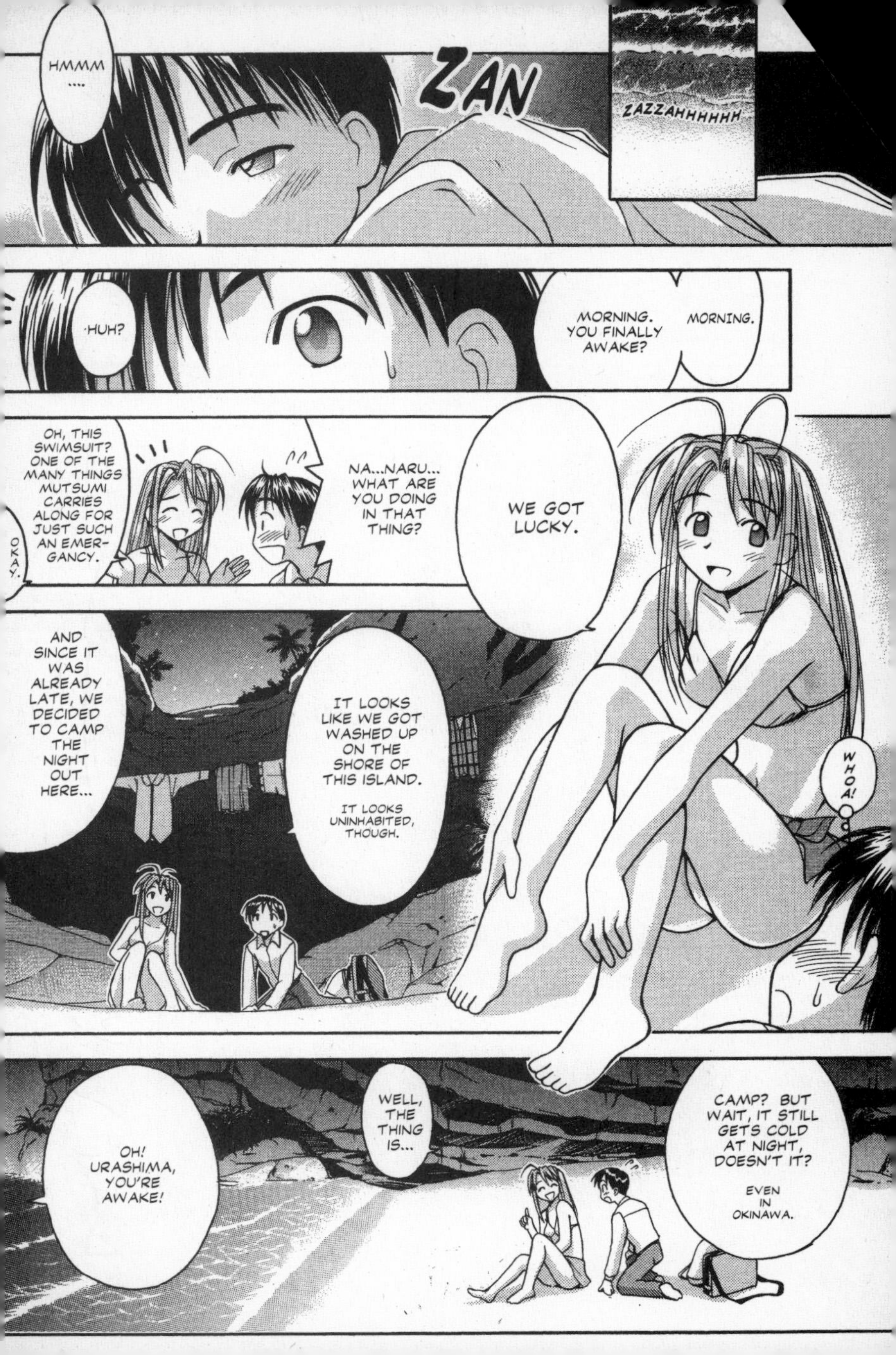

ZAZZAHHHHHH
ZAN
HMMM ....
MORNING.
MORNING. YOU FINALLY AWAKE?
·HUH?
WE GOT LUCKY.
WHOA!
NA...NARU... WHAT ARE YOU DOING IN THAT THING?
OH, THIS SWIMSUIT? ONE OF THE MANY THINGS MUTSUMI CARRIES ALONG FOR JUST SUCH AN EMER-GANCY.
OKAY.
IT LOOKS LIKE WE GOT WASHED UP ON THE SHORE OF THIS ISLAND.
IT LOOKS UNINHABITED, THOUGH.
AND SINCE IT WAS ALREADY LATE, WE DECIDED TO CAMP THE NIGHT OUT HERE...
CAMP? BUT WAIT, IT STILL GETS COLD AT NIGHT, DOESN'T IT?
EVEN IN OKINAWA.
WELL, THE THING IS...
OH! URASHIMA, YOU'RE AWAKE!

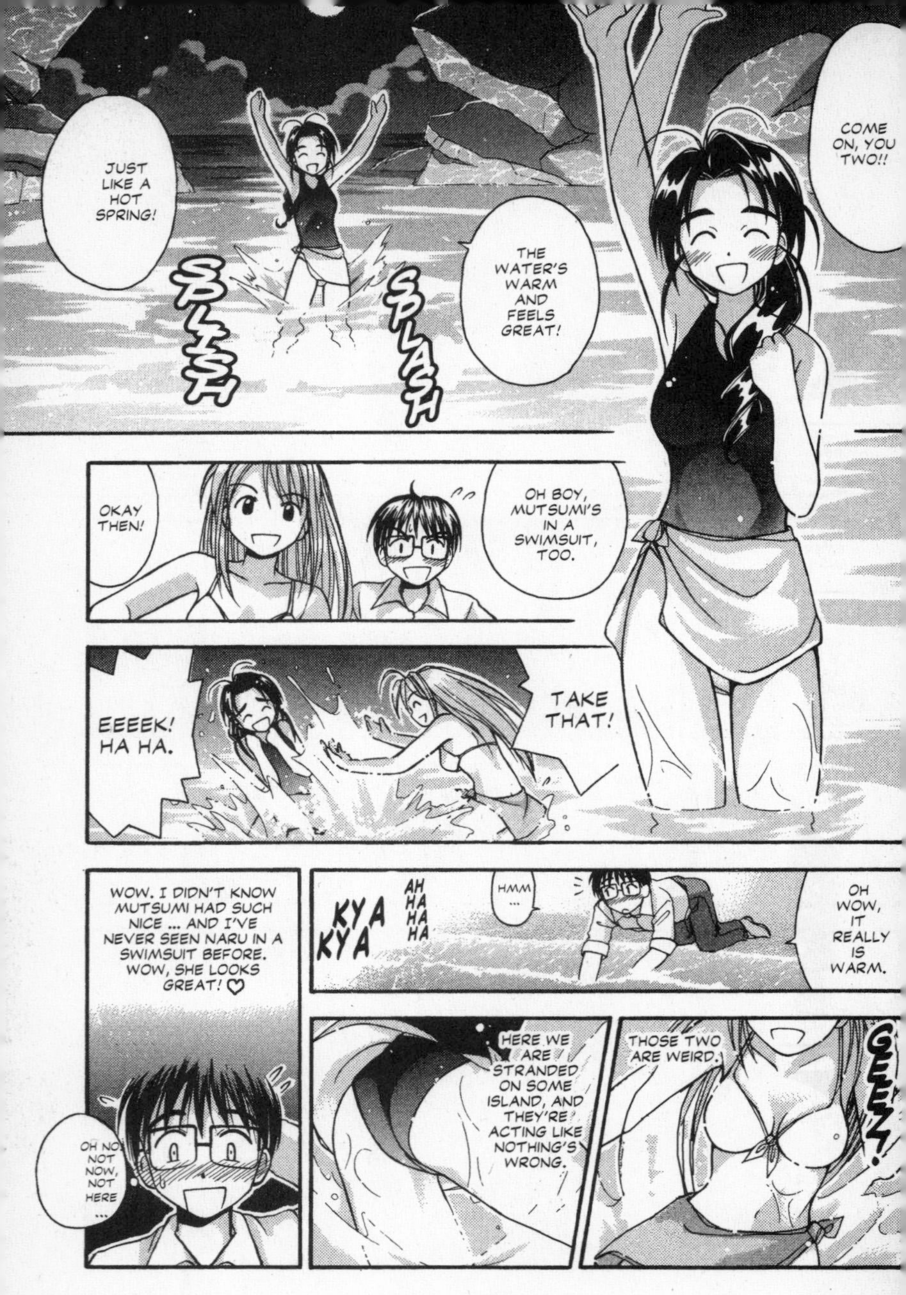
COME ON, YOU TWO!!
THE WATER'S WARM AND FEELS GREAT!
SPLASH
JUST LIKE A HOT SPRING!
SPLISH
OH BOY, MUTSUMI'S IN A SWIMSUIT, TOO.
OKAY THEN!
TAKE THAT!
EEEEK! HA HA.
OH WOW, IT REALLY IS WARM.
HMM ...
AH HA HA HA HA
KYA KYA
GEEZ!
THOSE TWO ARE WEIRD.
HERE WE ARE STRANDED ON SOME ISLAND, AND THEY'RE ACTING LIKE NOTHING'S WRONG.
WOW. I DIDN'T KNOW MUTSUMI HAD SUCH NICE ... AND I'VE NEVER SEEN NARU IN A SWIMSUIT BEFORE. WOW, SHE LOOKS GREAT! ♡
OH NO NOT NOW, NOT HERE ...

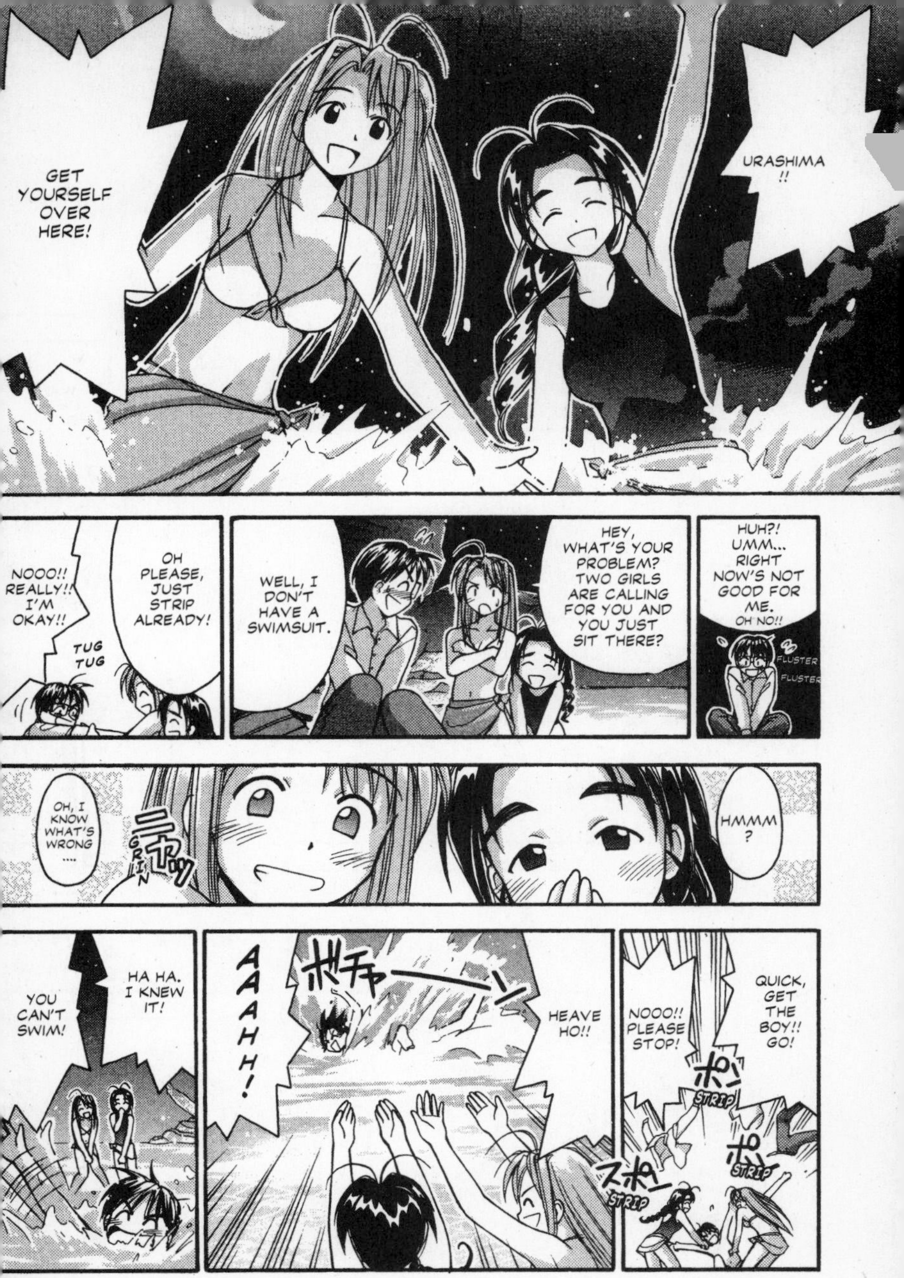
URASHIMA !!
GET YOURSELF OVER HERE!
HUH?! UMM... RIGHT NOW'S NOT GOOD FOR ME.
OH NO!!
FLUSTER
FLUSTER
HEY, WHAT'S YOUR PROBLEM? TWO GIRLS ARE CALLING FOR YOU AND YOU JUST SIT THERE?
WELL, I DON'T HAVE A SWIMSUIT.
OH PLEASE, JUST STRIP ALREADY!
NOOO!! REALLY!! I'M OKAY!!
TUG TUG
HMMM ?
GRIN
OH, I KNOW WHAT'S WRONG ....
QUICK, GET THE BOY!! GO!
NOOO!! PLEASE STOP!
STRIP
STRIP
STRIP
HEAVE HO!!
AAAHH!
HA HA. I KNEW IT!
YOU CAN'T SWIM!

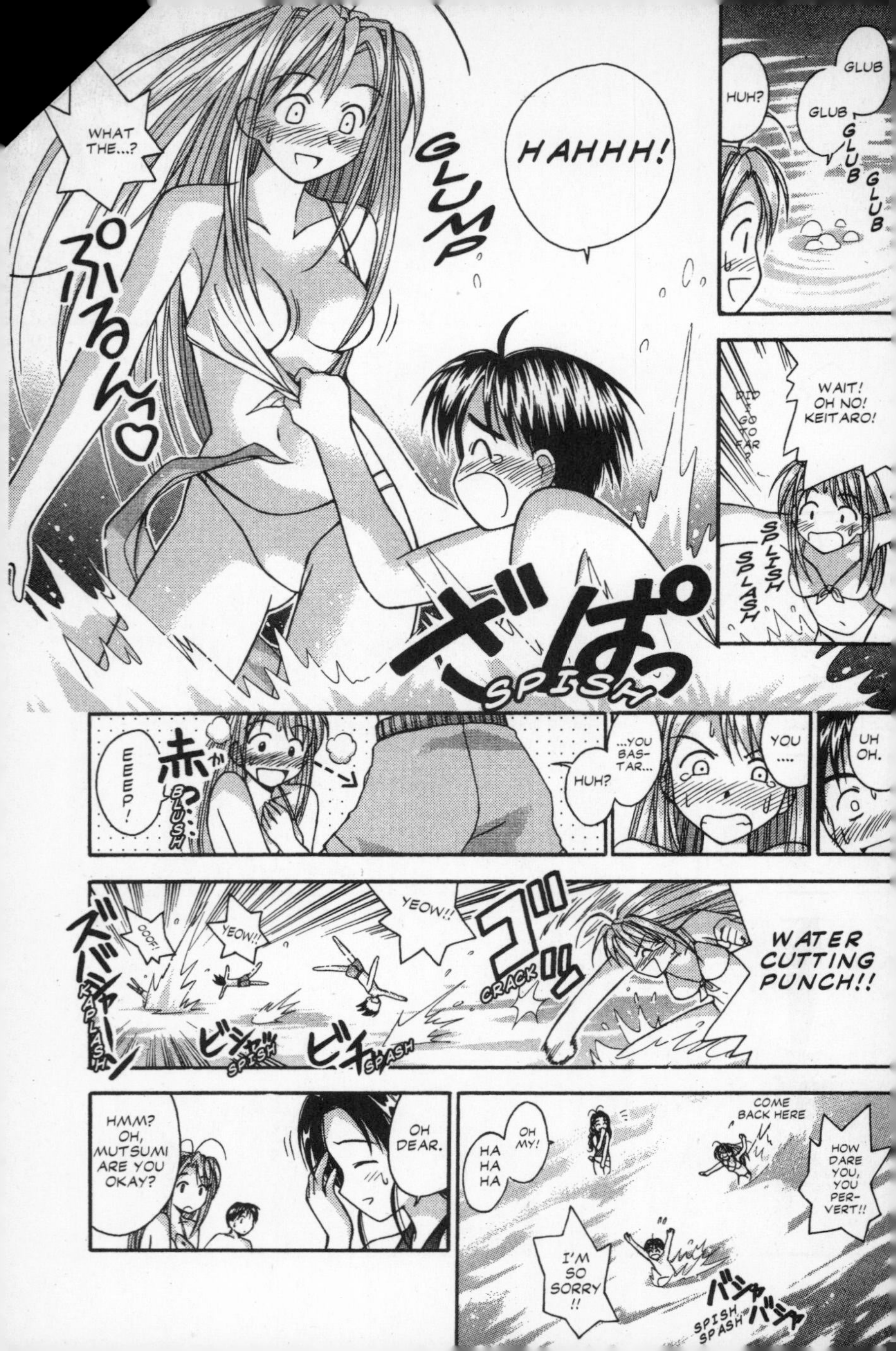
GLUB
HUH?
GLUB GLUB GLUB GLUB
WAIT! OH NO! KEITARO!
DID I GO TO FAR?
SPLISH SPLASH
HAHHH!
GLUMP
WHAT THE...?
ぷるんっ♡
ざぱっ
SPISH
UH OH.
YOU ....
...YOU BASTAR...
HUH?
EEEEP!
赤っ
BLUSH
WATER CUTTING PUNCH!!
ゴッ
CRACK
YEOW!!
YEOW!!
OOOF!
ズバシャー
KAPLASH
ビシャ
SPISH
ビチ
SPASH
COME BACK HERE
HOW DARE YOU, YOU PER-VERT!!
OH MY!
HA HA HA
I'M SO SORRY!!
バシャバシャ
SPISH SPASH
OH DEAR.
HMM? OH, MUTSUMI ARE YOU OKAY?

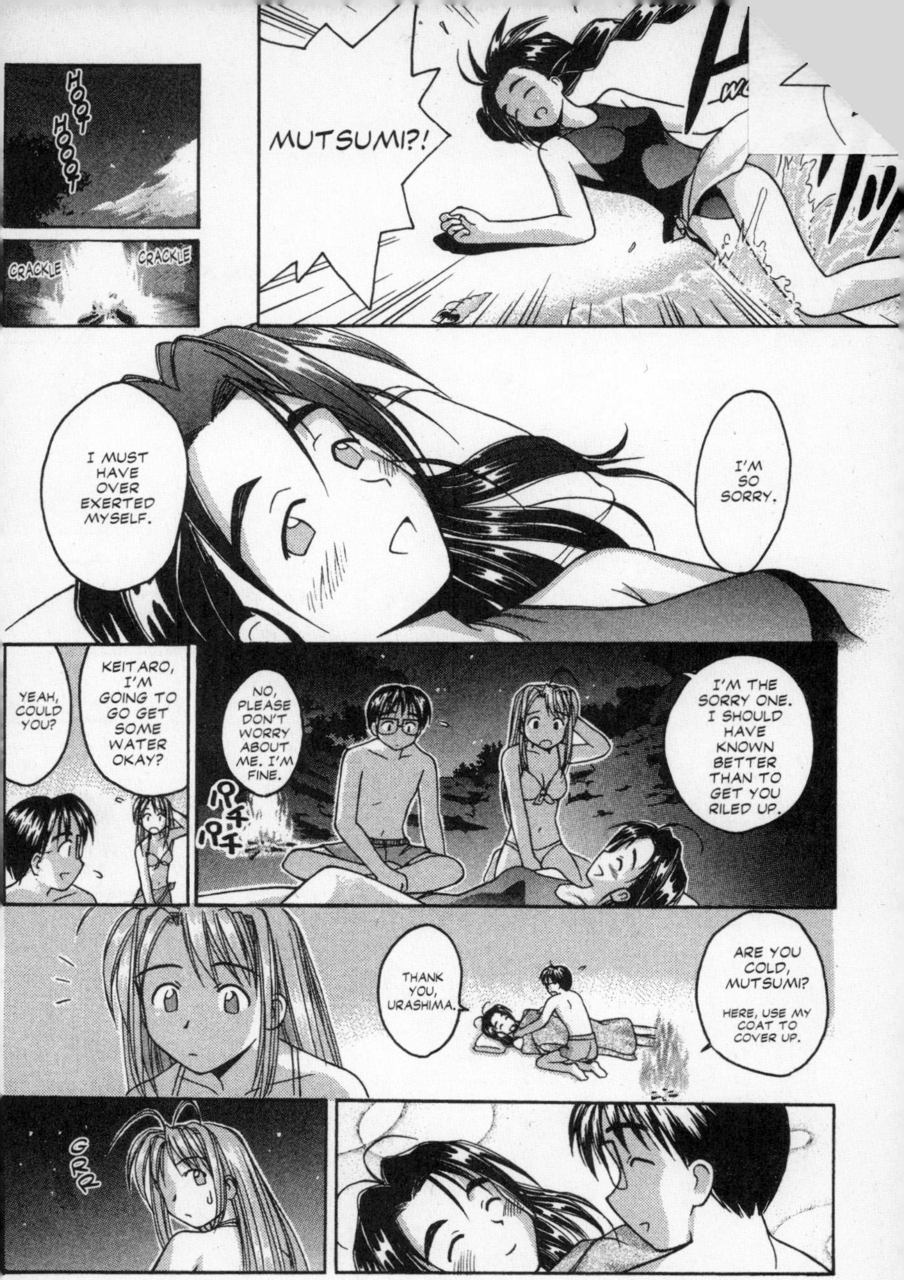
MUTSUMI?!
HOOT HOOOT
CRACKLE
CRACKLE
I'M SO SORRY.
I MUST HAVE OVER EXERTED MYSELF.
I'M THE SORRY ONE. I SHOULD HAVE KNOWN BETTER THAN TO GET YOU RILED UP.
NO, PLEASE DON'T WORRY ABOUT ME. I'M FINE.
パチ
パチ
KEITARO, I'M GOING TO GO GET SOME WATER OKAY?
YEAH, COULD YOU?
ARE YOU COLD, MUTSUMI?
HERE, USE MY COAT TO COVER UP.
THANK YOU, URASHIMA.
GRR

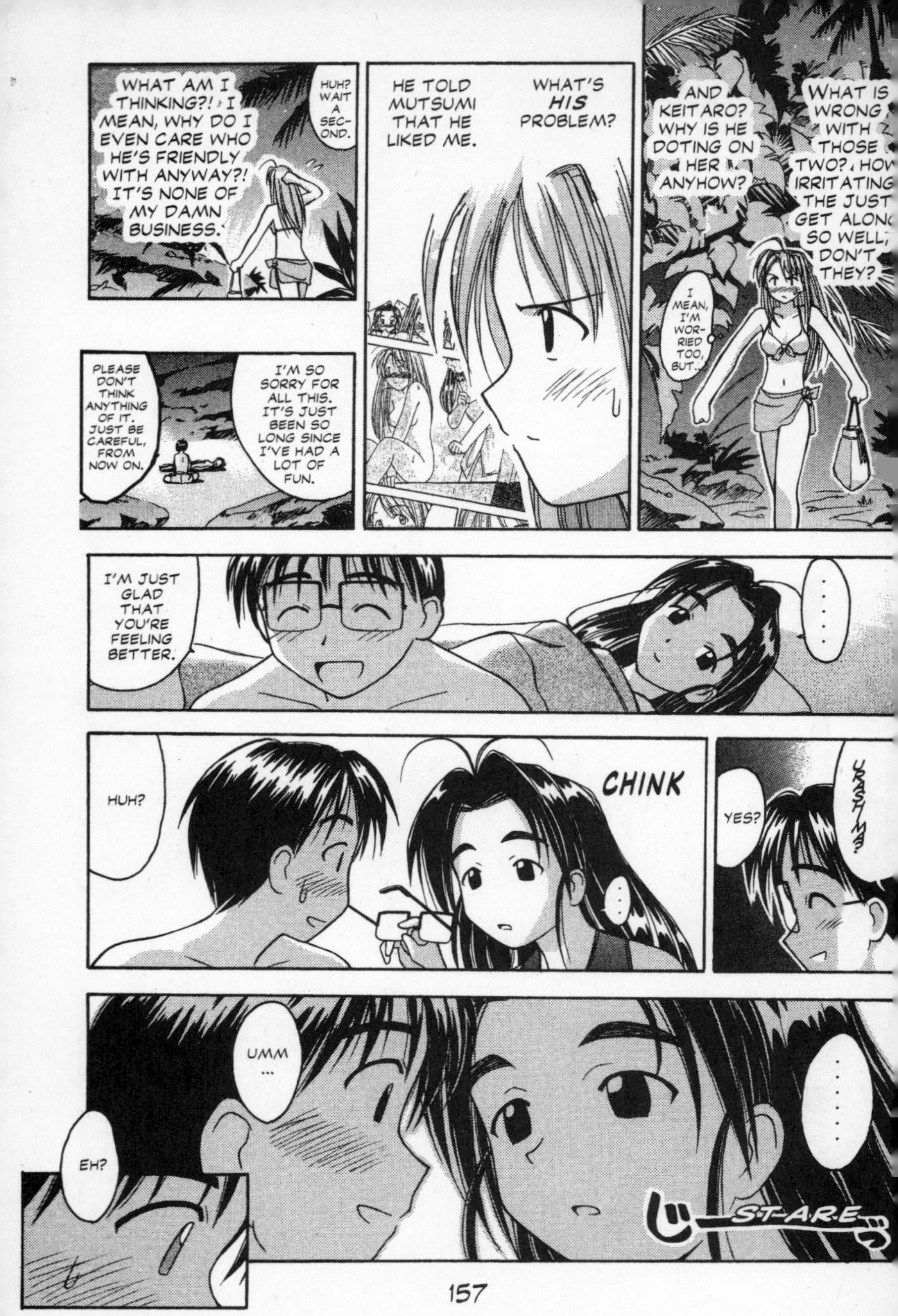
WHAT IS WRONG WITH THOSE TWO?, HOW IRRITATING THE JUST GET ALON SO WELL, DON'T THEY?
AND KEITARO? WHY IS HE DOTING ON HER ANYHOW?
I MEAN, I'M WORRIED TOO, BUT...
WHAT'S **HIS** PROBLEM?
HE TOLD MUTSUMI THAT HE LIKED ME.
HUH? WAIT A SECOND.
WHAT AM I THINKING?! I MEAN, WHY DO I EVEN CARE WHO HE'S FRIENDLY WITH ANYWAY?! IT'S NONE OF MY DAMN BUSINESS.
I'M SO SORRY FOR ALL THIS. IT'S JUST BEEN SO LONG SINCE I'VE HAD A LOT OF FUN.
PLEASE DON'T THINK ANYTHING OF IT. JUST BE CAREFUL, FROM NOW ON.
......
I'M JUST GLAD THAT YOU'RE FEELING BETTER.
URASHIMA?
YES?
CHINK
...
HUH?
......
S-T-A-R-E
UMM...
EH?

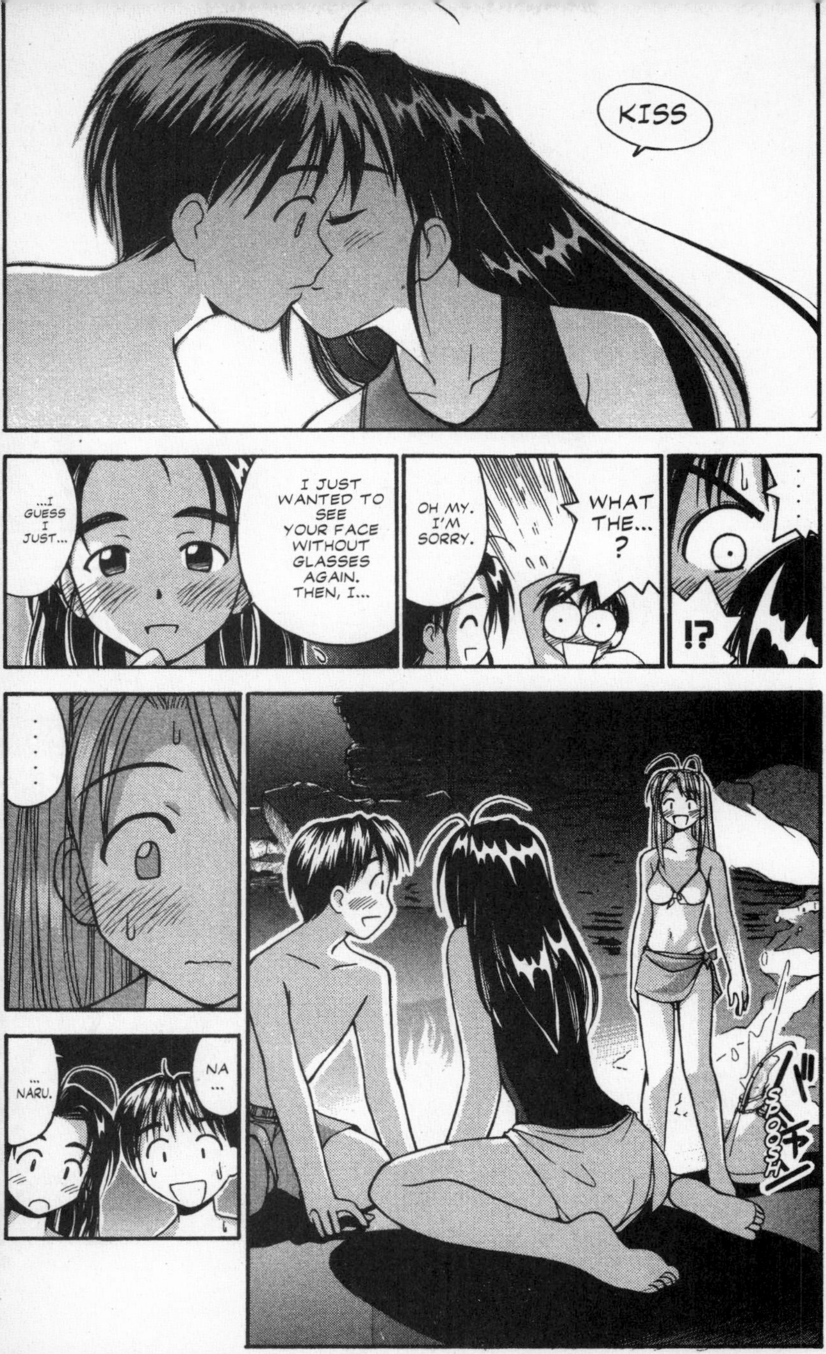
KISS
. . .
!?
WHAT THE... ?
OH MY. I'M SORRY.
I JUST WANTED TO SEE YOUR FACE WITHOUT GLASSES AGAIN. THEN, I...
...I GUESS I JUST...
SPOOSH
. . . . . .
NA ...
... NARU.

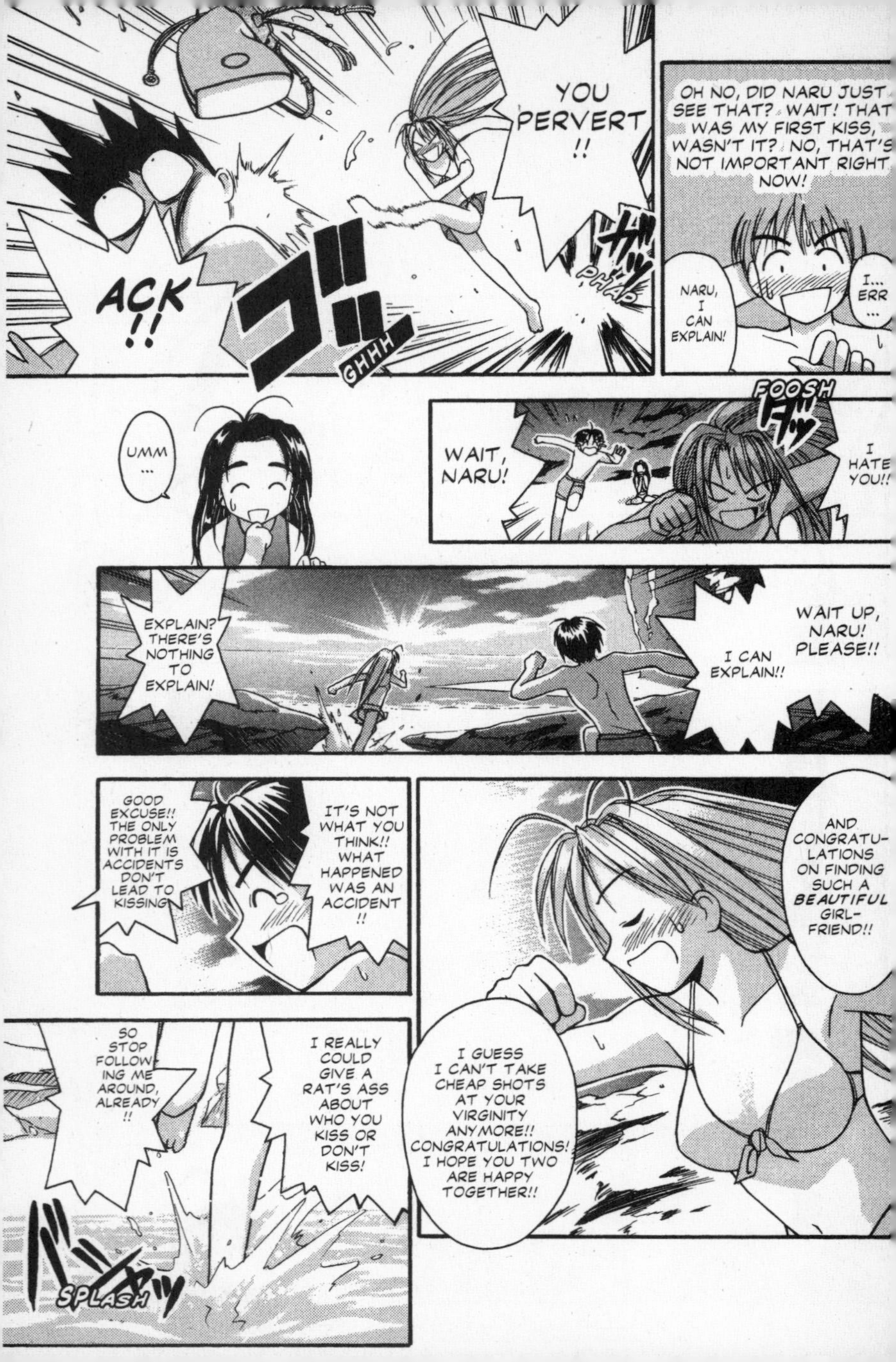
OH NO, DID NARU JUST SEE THAT? WAIT! THAT WAS MY FIRST KISS, WASN'T IT? NO, THAT'S NOT IMPORTANT RIGHT NOW!
I... ERR ...
NARU, I CAN EXPLAIN!
YOU PERVERT !!
PHAP
ACK !!
GHHH
FOOSH
I HATE YOU!!
WAIT, NARU!
UMM ...
WAIT UP, NARU! PLEASE!!
I CAN EXPLAIN!!
EXPLAIN? THERE'S NOTHING TO EXPLAIN!
AND CONGRATULATIONS ON FINDING SUCH A BEAUTIFUL GIRLFRIEND!!
I GUESS I CAN'T TAKE CHEAP SHOTS AT YOUR VIRGINITY ANYMORE!! CONGRATULATIONS! I HOPE YOU TWO ARE HAPPY TOGETHER!!
IT'S NOT WHAT YOU THINK!! WHAT HAPPENED WAS AN ACCIDENT !!
GOOD EXCUSE!! THE ONLY PROBLEM WITH IT IS ACCIDENTS DON'T LEAD TO KISSING
I REALLY COULD GIVE A RAT'S ASS ABOUT WHO YOU KISS OR DON'T KISS!
SO STOP FOLLOWING ME AROUND, ALREADY !!
SPLASH

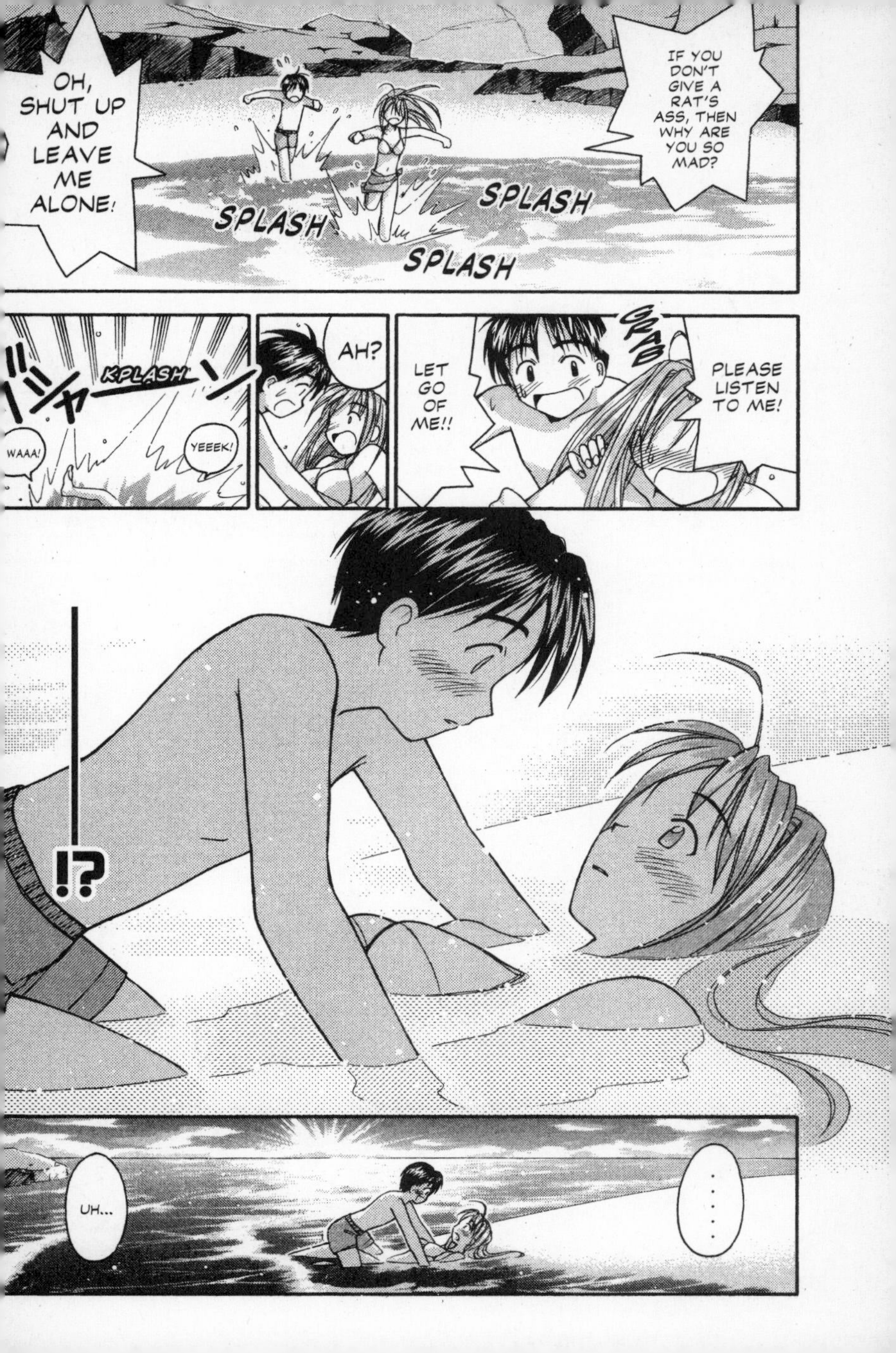
IF YOU DON'T GIVE A RAT'S ASS, THEN WHY ARE YOU SO MAD?
OH, SHUT UP AND LEAVE ME ALONE!
SPLASH
SPLASH
SPLASH
PLEASE LISTEN TO ME!
GRAB
LET GO OF ME!!
AH?
KPLASH
YEEEK!
WAAA!
!?
.....
UH...

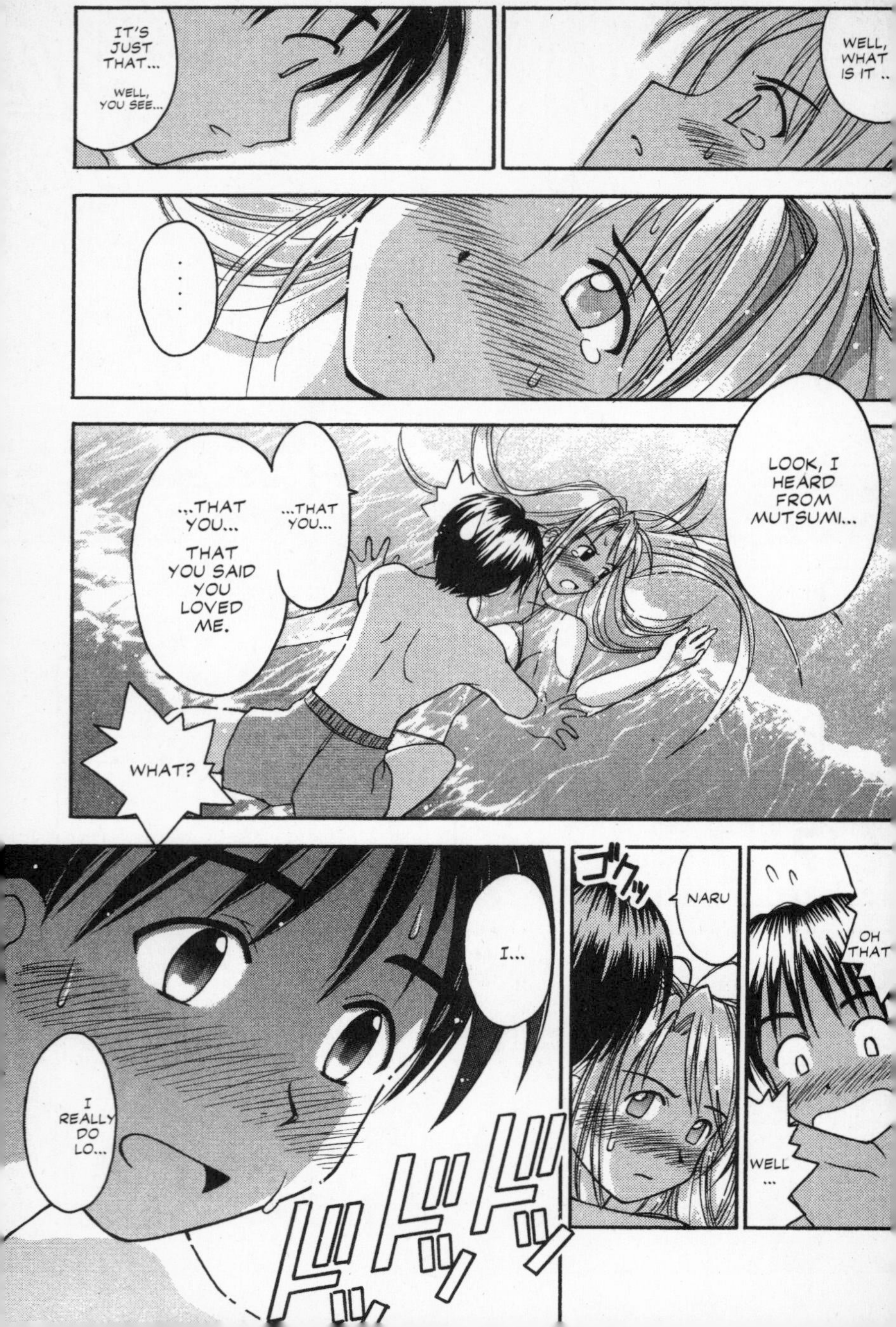
WELL, WHAT IS IT ..
IT'S JUST THAT...
WELL, YOU SEE...
....
LOOK, I HEARD FROM MUTSUMI...
...THAT YOU...
...THAT YOU... THAT YOU SAID YOU LOVED ME.
WHAT?
OH THAT
WELL ...
NARU
ゴクッ
I...
I REALLY DO LO...
ドッドッドッ

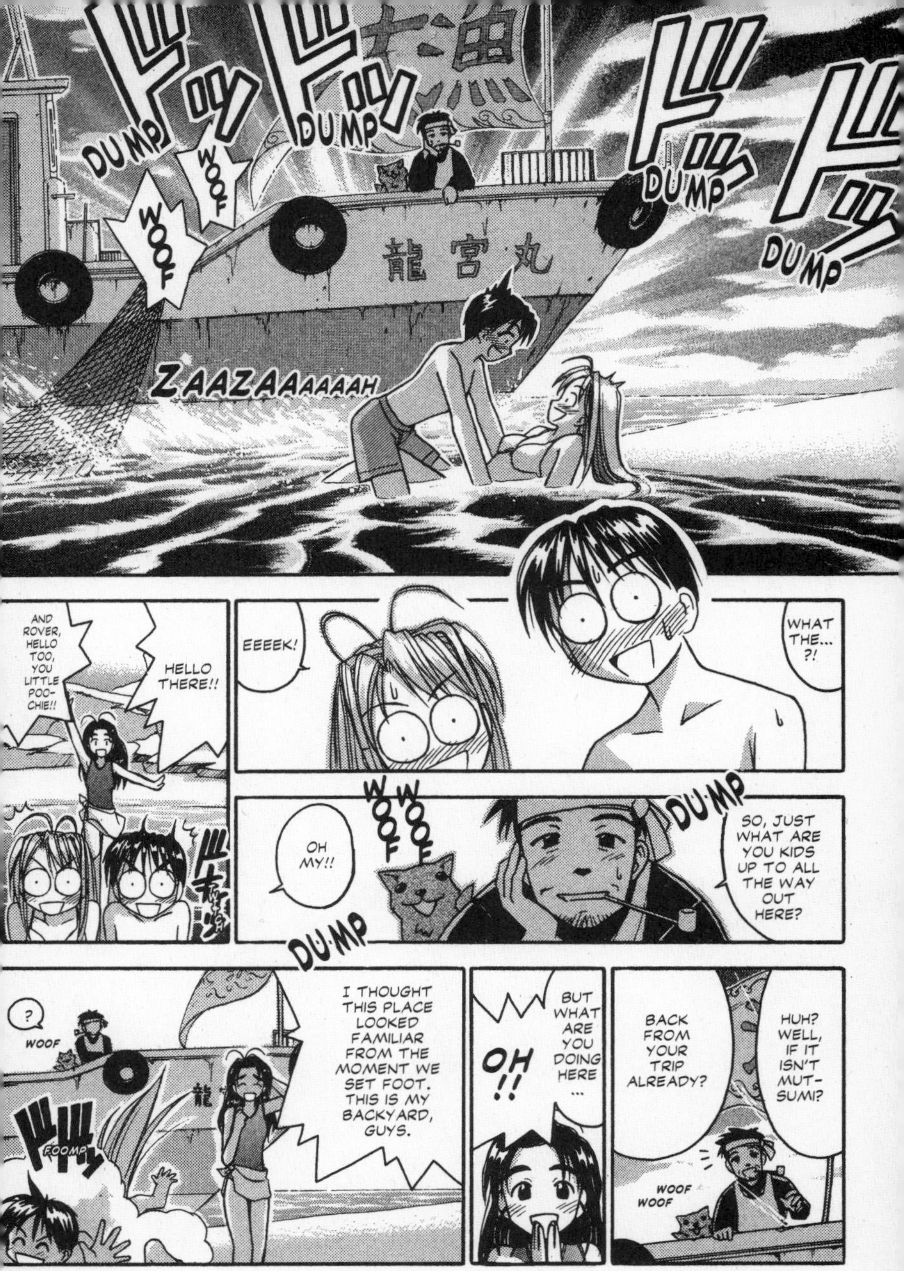
DUMP
DUMP
DUMP
DUMP
WOOF
WOOF
ZAAZAAAAAAH
WHAT THE... ?!
EEEEK!
SO, JUST WHAT ARE YOU KIDS UP TO ALL THE WAY OUT HERE?
DUMP
WOOF WOOF
OH MY!!
DUMP
HELLO THERE!!
AND ROVER, HELLO TOO, YOU LITTLE POO-CHIE!!
HUH? WELL, IF IT ISN'T MUT-SUMI?
BACK FROM YOUR TRIP ALREADY?
WOOF WOOF
BUT WHAT ARE YOU DOING HERE ...
OH !!
I THOUGHT THIS PLACE LOOKED FAMILIAR FROM THE MOMENT WE SET FOOT. THIS IS MY BACKYARD, GUYS.
?
WOOF
FOOMP

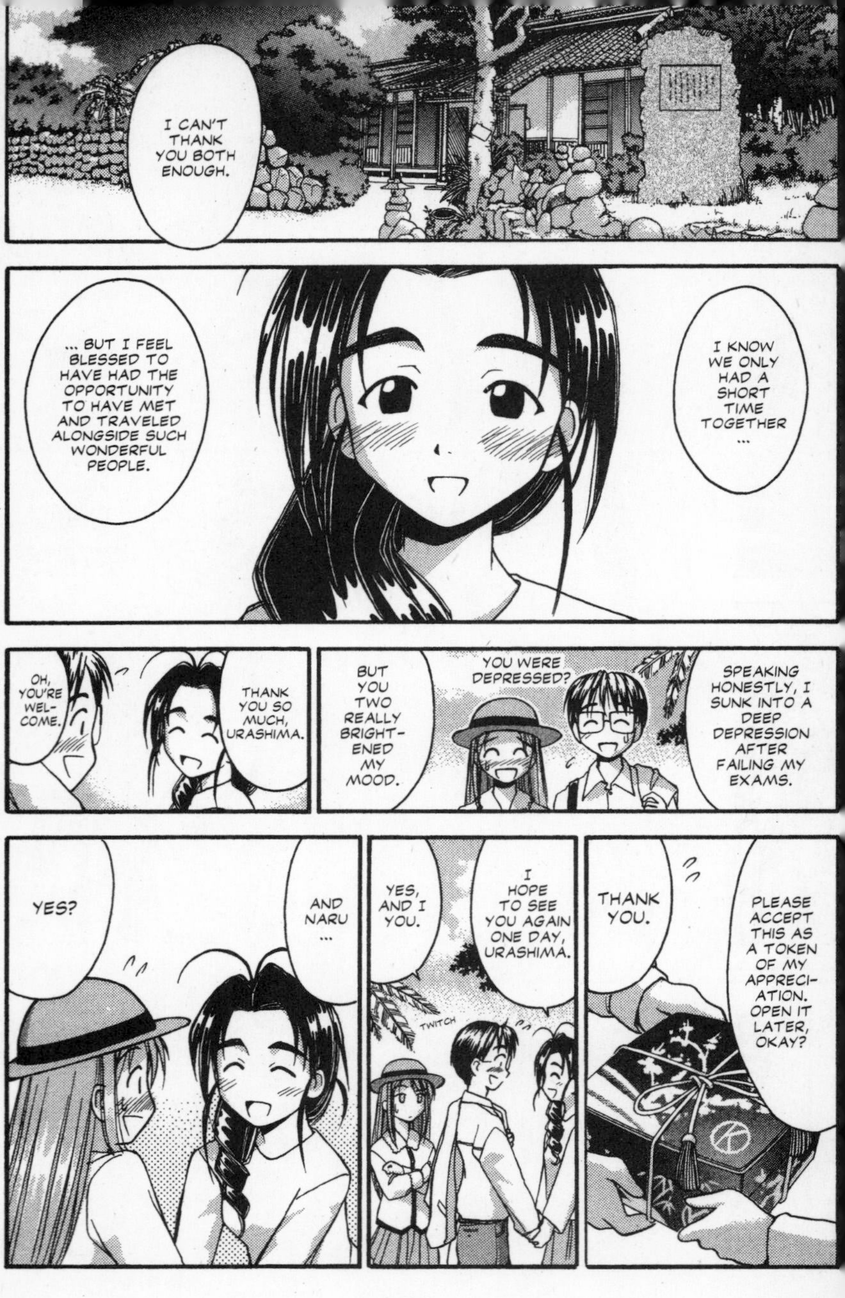
I CAN'T THANK YOU BOTH ENOUGH.
I KNOW WE ONLY HAD A SHORT TIME TOGETHER ...
... BUT I FEEL BLESSED TO HAVE HAD THE OPPORTUNITY TO HAVE MET AND TRAVELED ALONGSIDE SUCH WONDERFUL PEOPLE.
SPEAKING HONESTLY, I SUNK INTO A DEEP DEPRESSION AFTER FAILING MY EXAMS.
YOU WERE DEPRESSED?
BUT YOU TWO REALLY BRIGHT-ENED MY MOOD.
THANK YOU SO MUCH, URASHIMA.
OH, YOU'RE WEL-COME.
PLEASE ACCEPT THIS AS A TOKEN OF MY APPRECI-ATION. OPEN IT LATER, OKAY?
THANK YOU.
I HOPE TO SEE YOU AGAIN ONE DAY, URASHIMA.
YES, AND I YOU.
TWITCH
AND NARU ...
YES?

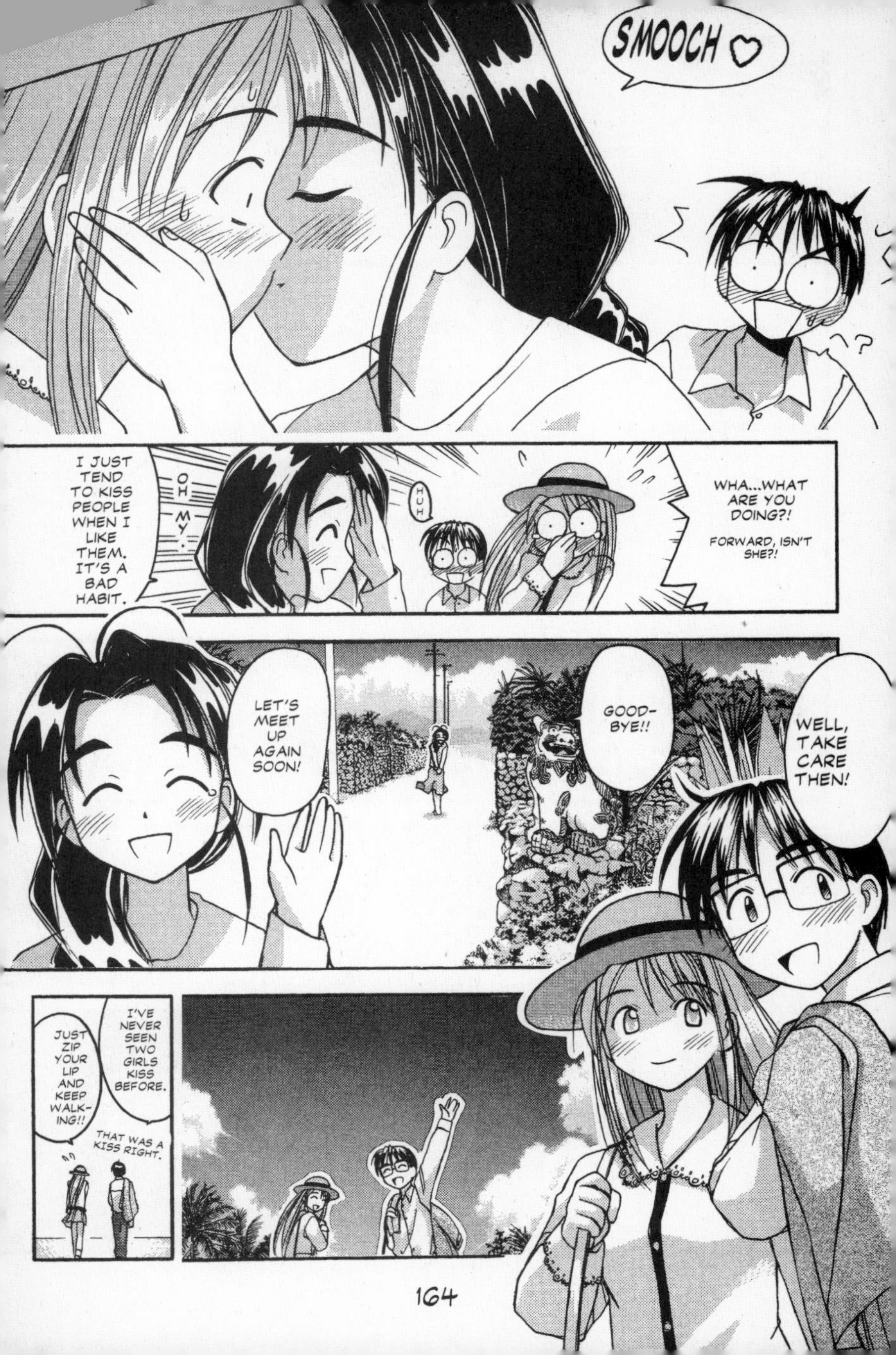
SMOOCH ♡
WHA...WHAT ARE YOU DOING?!
FORWARD, ISN'T SHE?!
HUH
OH MY...
I JUST TEND TO KISS PEOPLE WHEN I LIKE THEM. IT'S A BAD HABIT.
WELL, TAKE CARE THEN!
GOOD-BYE!!
LET'S MEET UP AGAIN SOON!
I'VE NEVER SEEN TWO GIRLS KISS BEFORE.
JUST ZIP YOUR LIP AND KEEP WALKING!!
THAT WAS A KISS RIGHT.

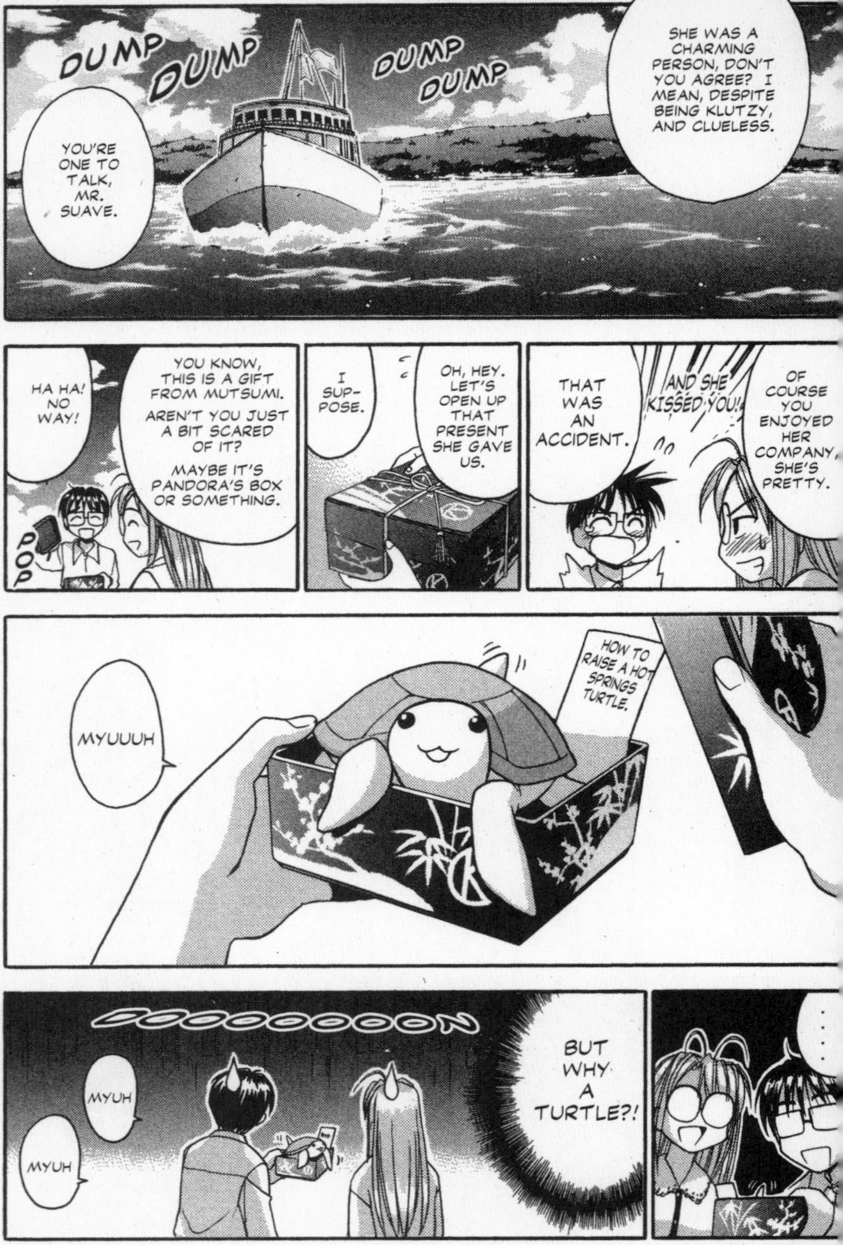
SHE WAS A CHARMING PERSON, DON'T YOU AGREE? I MEAN, DESPITE BEING KLUTZY, AND CLUELESS.
DUMP DUMP
DUMP DUMP
YOU'RE ONE TO TALK, MR. SUAVE.
OF COURSE YOU ENJOYED HER COMPANY, SHE'S PRETTY.
AND SHE KISSED YOU!
THAT WAS AN ACCIDENT.
OH, HEY. LET'S OPEN UP THAT PRESENT SHE GAVE US.
I SUPPOSE.
YOU KNOW, THIS IS A GIFT FROM MUTSUMI.
AREN'T YOU JUST A BIT SCARED OF IT?
MAYBE IT'S PANDORA'S BOX OR SOMETHING.
HA HA! NO WAY!
POP
HOW TO RAISE A HOT SPRINGS TURTLE.
MYUUUH
. . . .
BUT WHY A TURTLE?!
DOOOOOOOON
MYUH
MYUH

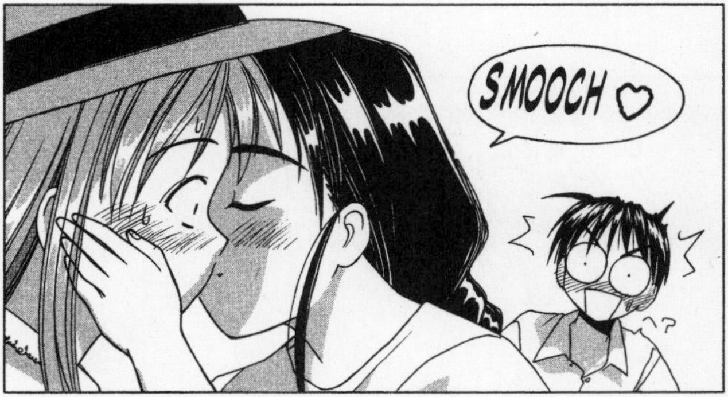
SMOOCH ♡

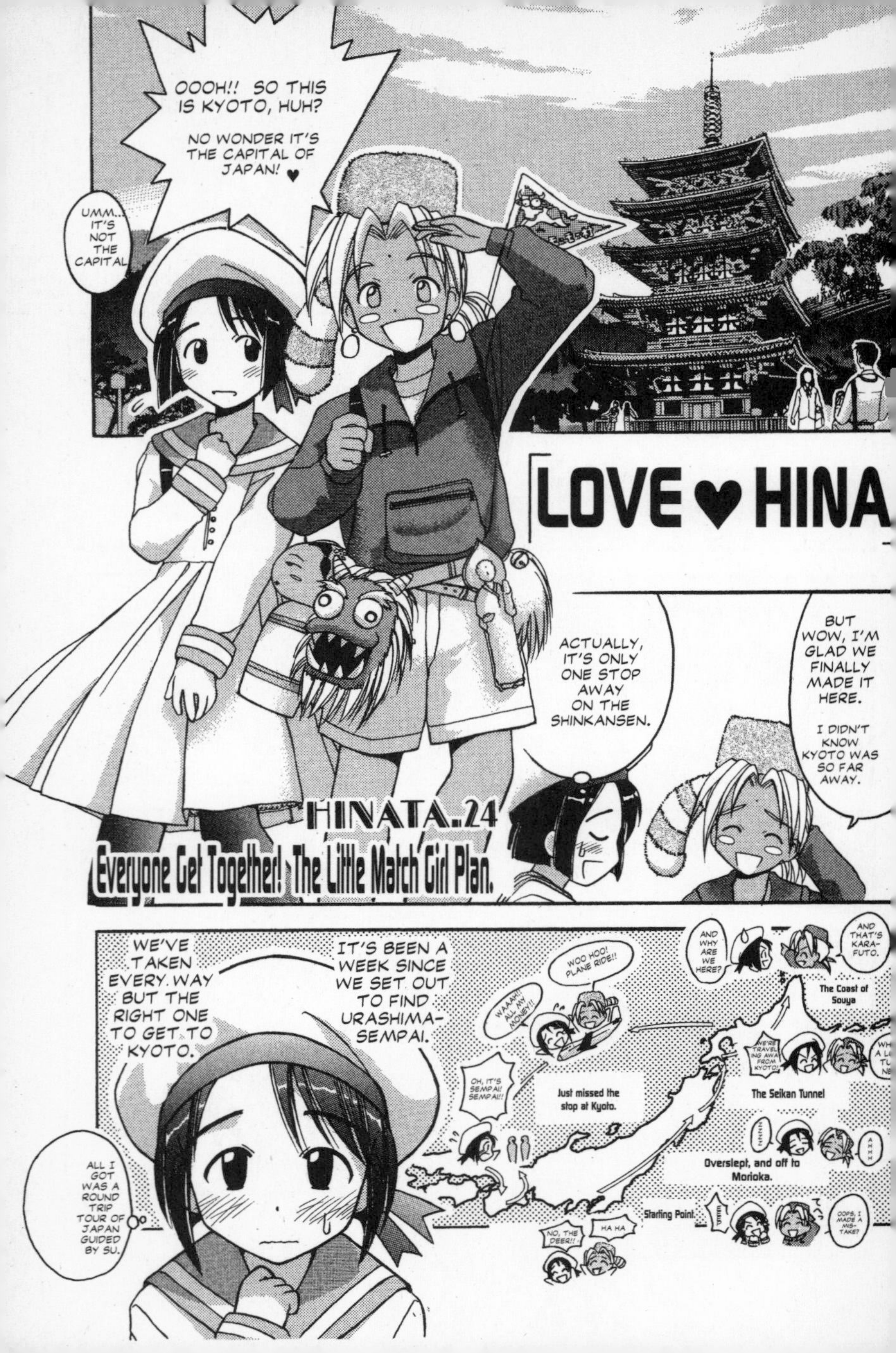
OOOH!! SO THIS IS KYOTO, HUH?
NO WONDER IT'S THE CAPITAL OF JAPAN! ♥
UMM... IT'S NOT THE CAPITAL
LOVE ♥ HINA
BUT WOW, I'M GLAD WE FINALLY MADE IT HERE.
I DIDN'T KNOW KYOTO WAS SO FAR AWAY.
ACTUALLY, IT'S ONLY ONE STOP AWAY ON THE SHINKANSEN.
HINATA. 24
Everyone Get Together! The Little Match Girl Plan.
IT'S BEEN A WEEK SINCE WE SET OUT TO FIND URASHIMA-SEMPAI.
WE'VE TAKEN EVERY WAY BUT THE RIGHT ONE TO GET TO KYOTO.
AND THAT'S KARA-FUTO.
AND WHY ARE WE HERE?
The Coast of Souya
WOO HOO! PLANE RIDE!!
WAAAH!! ALL MY MONEY!!
The Seikan Tunnel
Just missed the stop at Kyoto.
OH, IT'S SEMPAI! SEMPAI!!
Overslept, and off to Morioka.
Starting Point.
OOPS, I MADE A MIS-TAKE?
HA HA
NO, THE DEER!!
ALL I GOT WAS A ROUND TRIP TOUR OF JAPAN GUIDED BY SU.

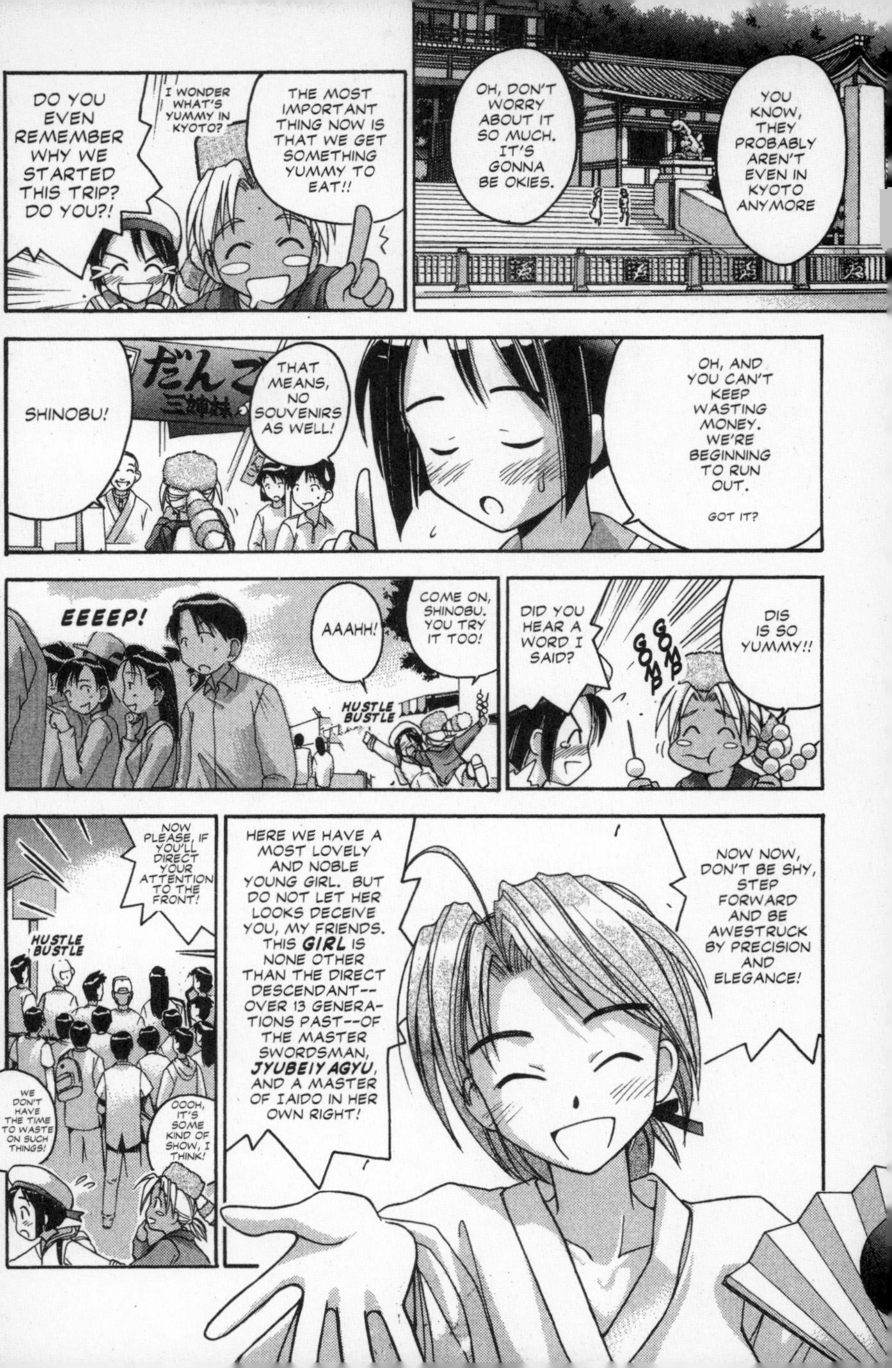
YOU KNOW, THEY PROBABLY AREN'T EVEN IN KYOTO ANYMORE
OH, DON'T WORRY ABOUT IT SO MUCH. IT'S GONNA BE OKIES.
THE MOST IMPORTANT THING NOW IS THAT WE GET SOMETHING YUMMY TO EAT!!
I WONDER WHAT'S YUMMY IN KYOTO?
DO YOU EVEN REMEMBER WHY WE STARTED THIS TRIP? DO YOU?!
OH, AND YOU CAN'T KEEP WASTING MONEY. WE'RE BEGINNING TO RUN OUT.
GOT IT?
THAT MEANS, NO SOUVENIRS AS WELL!
だんご
三姉妹
SHINOBU!
DIS IS SO YUMMY!!
GOMP GOMP
DID YOU HEAR A WORD I SAID?
COME ON, SHINOBU. YOU TRY IT TOO!
AAAHH!
HUSTLE BUSTLE
EEEEP!
NOW NOW, DON'T BE SHY, STEP FORWARD AND BE AWESTRUCK BY PRECISION AND ELEGANCE!
HERE WE HAVE A MOST LOVELY AND NOBLE YOUNG GIRL. BUT DO NOT LET HER LOOKS DECEIVE YOU, MY FRIENDS. THIS GIRL IS NONE OTHER THAN THE DIRECT DESCENDANT--OVER 13 GENERATIONS PAST--OF THE MASTER SWORDSMAN, JYUBEIY AGYU, AND A MASTER OF IAIDO IN HER OWN RIGHT!
NOW PLEASE, IF YOU'LL DIRECT YOUR ATTENTION TO THE FRONT!
HUSTLE BUSTLE
OOOH, IT'S SOME KIND OF SHOW, I THINK!
WE DON'T HAVE THE TIME TO WASTE ON SUCH THINGS!

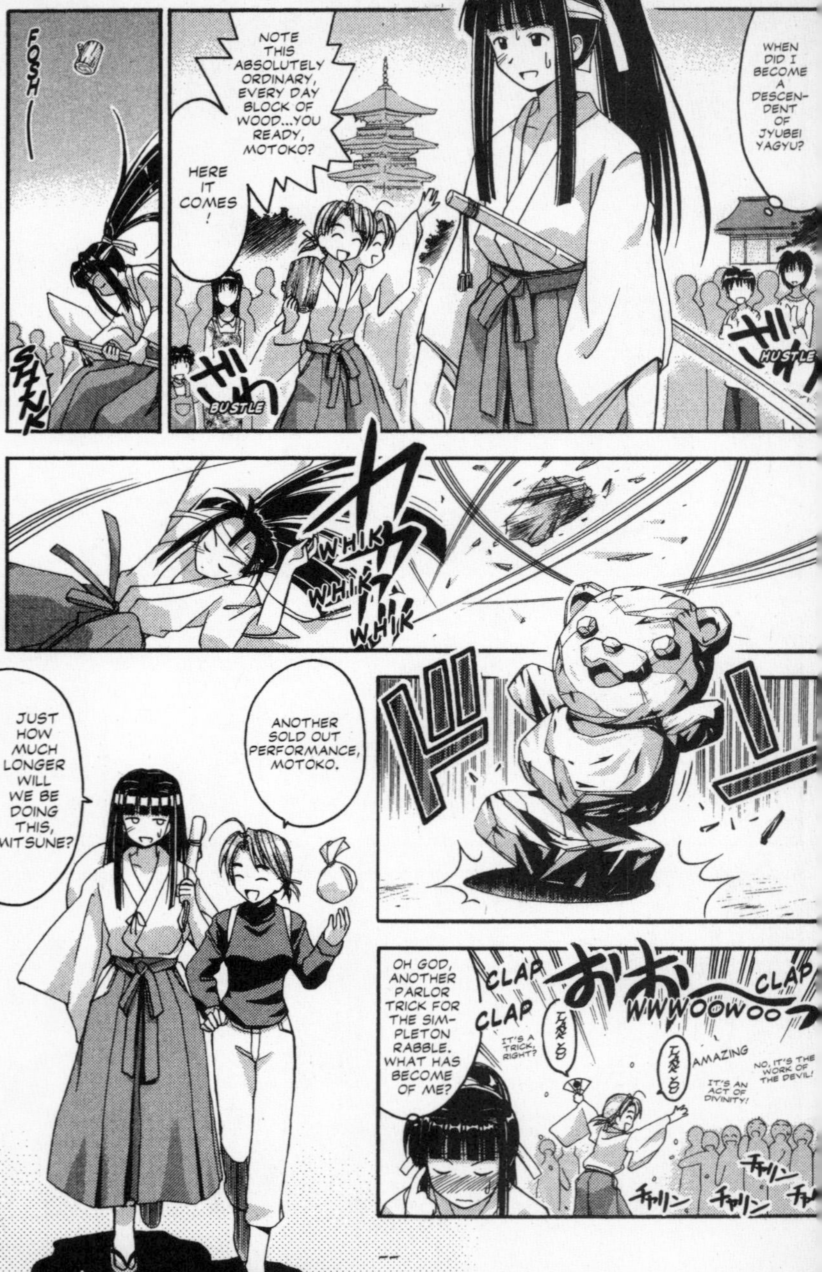
WHEN DID I BECOME A DESCENDENT OF JYUBEI YAGYU?
NOTE THIS ABSOLUTELY ORDINARY, EVERY DAY BLOCK OF WOOD...YOU READY, MOTOKO?
HERE IT COMES!
HUSTLE
BUSTLE
FOSH
SHIKK
WHIK
WHIK
WHIK
OH GOD, ANOTHER PARLOR TRICK FOR THE SIMPLETON RABBLE. WHAT HAS BECOME OF ME?
CLAP
CLAP
CLAP
WWWOOWOO
IT'S A TRICK, RIGHT?
AMAZING
IT'S AN ACT OF DIVINITY!
NO, IT'S THE WORK OF THE DEVIL!
チャリン
チャリン
チャリン
ANOTHER SOLD OUT PERFORMANCE, MOTOKO.
JUST HOW MUCH LONGER WILL WE BE DOING THIS, MITSUNE?

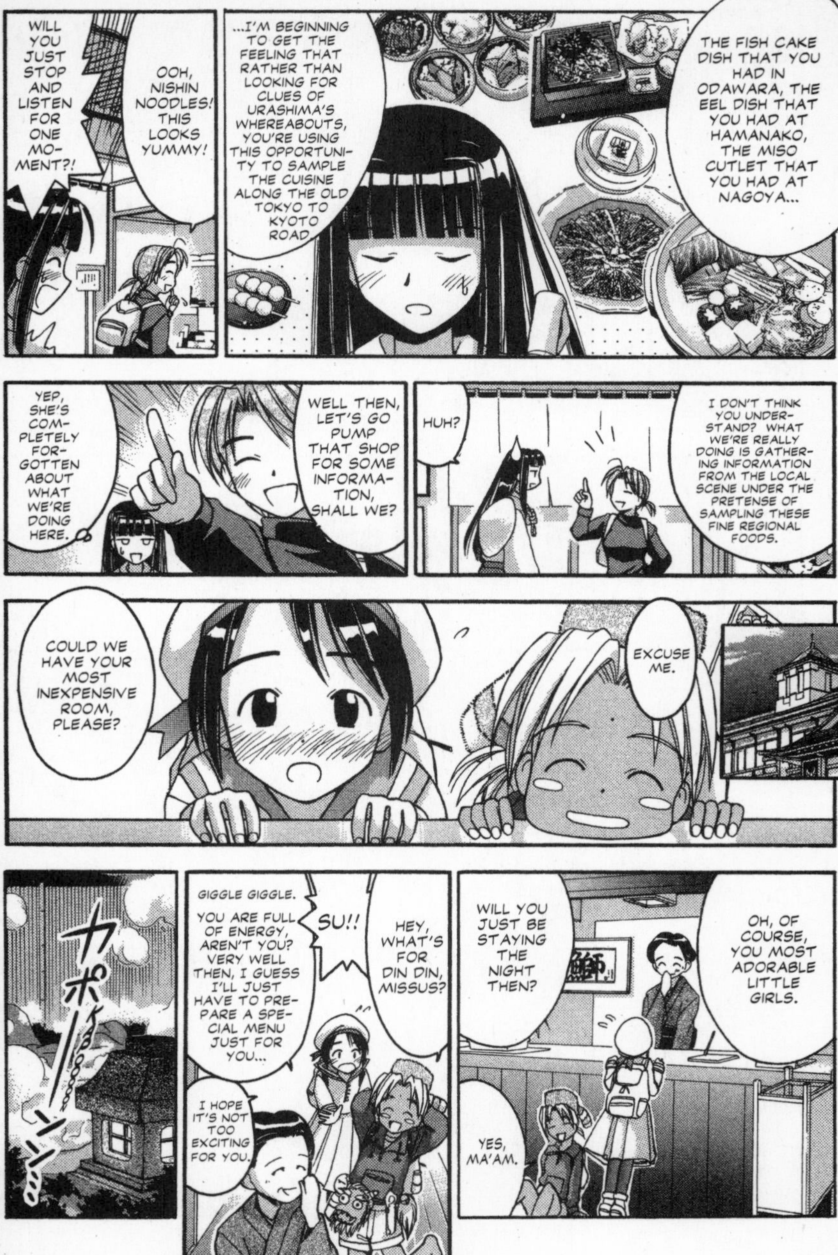

THE FISH CAKE DISH THAT YOU HAD IN ODAWARA, THE EEL DISH THAT YOU HAD AT HAMANAKO, THE MISO CUTLET THAT YOU HAD AT NAGOYA...
...I'M BEGINNING TO GET THE FEELING THAT RATHER THAN LOOKING FOR CLUES OF URASHIMA'S WHEREABOUTS, YOU'RE USING THIS OPPORTUNITY TO SAMPLE THE CUISINE ALONG THE OLD TOKYO TO KYOTO ROAD
OOH, NISHIN NOODLES! THIS LOOKS YUMMY!
WILL YOU JUST STOP AND LISTEN FOR ONE MOMENT?!
I DON'T THINK YOU UNDERSTAND? WHAT WE'RE REALLY DOING IS GATHERING INFORMATION FROM THE LOCAL SCENE UNDER THE PRETENSE OF SAMPLING THESE FINE REGIONAL FOODS.
HUH?
WELL THEN, LET'S GO PUMP THAT SHOP FOR SOME INFORMATION, SHALL WE?
YEP, SHE'S COMPLETELY FORGOTTEN ABOUT WHAT WE'RE DOING HERE.
EXCUSE ME.
COULD WE HAVE YOUR MOST INEXPENSIVE ROOM, PLEASE?
OH, OF COURSE, YOU MOST ADORABLE LITTLE GIRLS.
WILL YOU JUST BE STAYING THE NIGHT THEN?
YES, MA'AM.
HEY, WHAT'S FOR DIN DIN, MISSUS?
SU!!
GIGGLE GIGGLE.
YOU ARE FULL OF ENERGY, AREN'T YOU? VERY WELL THEN, I GUESS I'LL JUST HAVE TO PREPARE A SPECIAL MENU JUST FOR YOU...
I HOPE IT'S NOT TOO EXCITING FOR YOU.

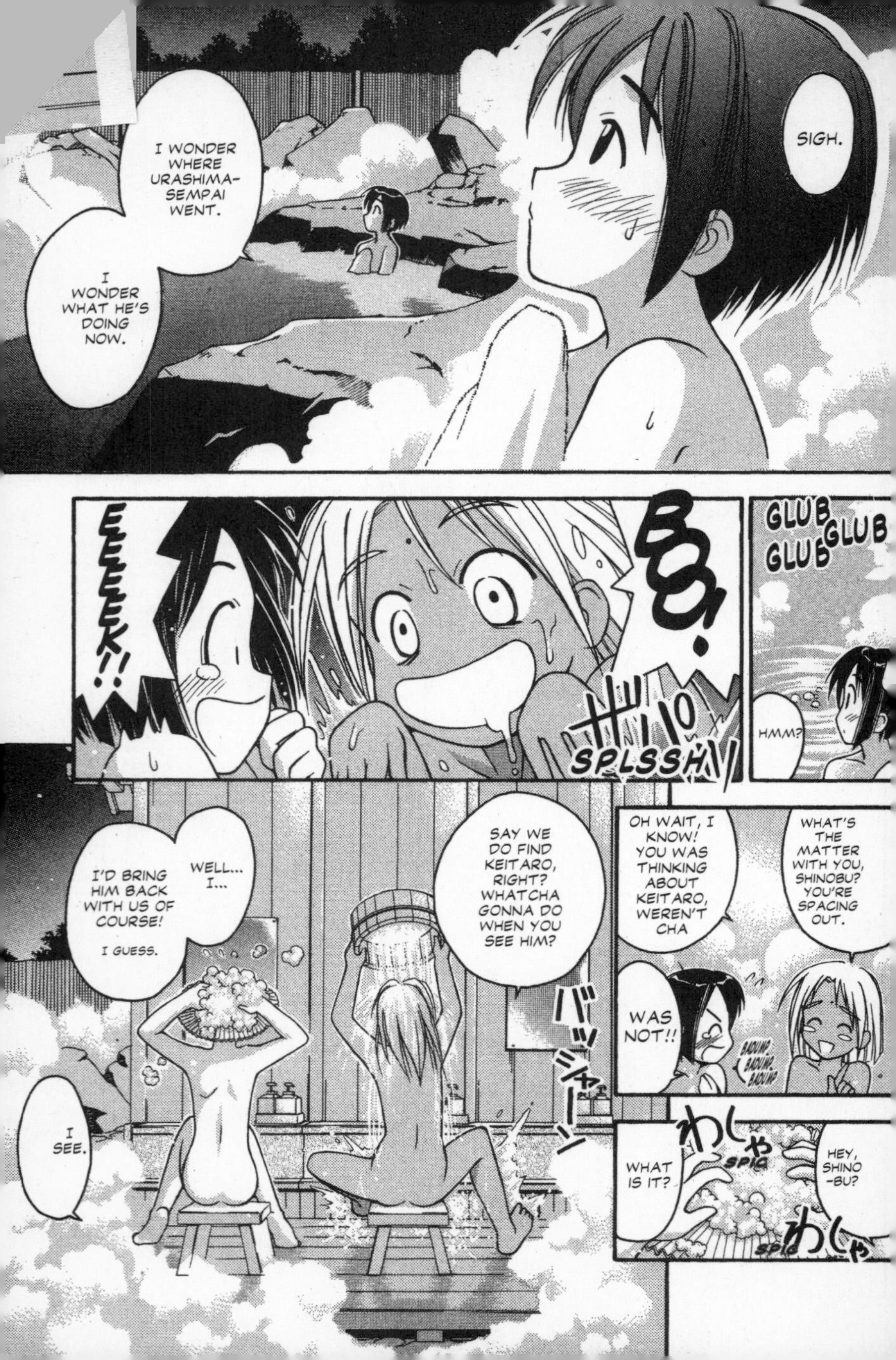
SIGH.
I WONDER WHERE URASHIMA-SEMPAI WENT.
I WONDER WHAT HE'S DOING NOW.
GLUB GLUB GLUB
HMM?
BOO!
SPLSSH
EEEEEK!!
WHAT'S THE MATTER WITH YOU, SHINOBU? YOU'RE SPACING OUT.
OH WAIT, I KNOW! YOU WAS THINKING ABOUT KEITARO, WEREN'T CHA
WAS NOT!!
BADUMP BADUMP BADUMP
HEY, SHINO-BU?
わしゃ
SPIC
WHAT IS IT?
わしゃ
SPIC
SAY WE DO FIND KEITARO, RIGHT? WHATCHA GONNA DO WHEN YOU SEE HIM?
WELL... I...
I'D BRING HIM BACK WITH US OF COURSE!
I GUESS.
バッシャーン
I SEE.

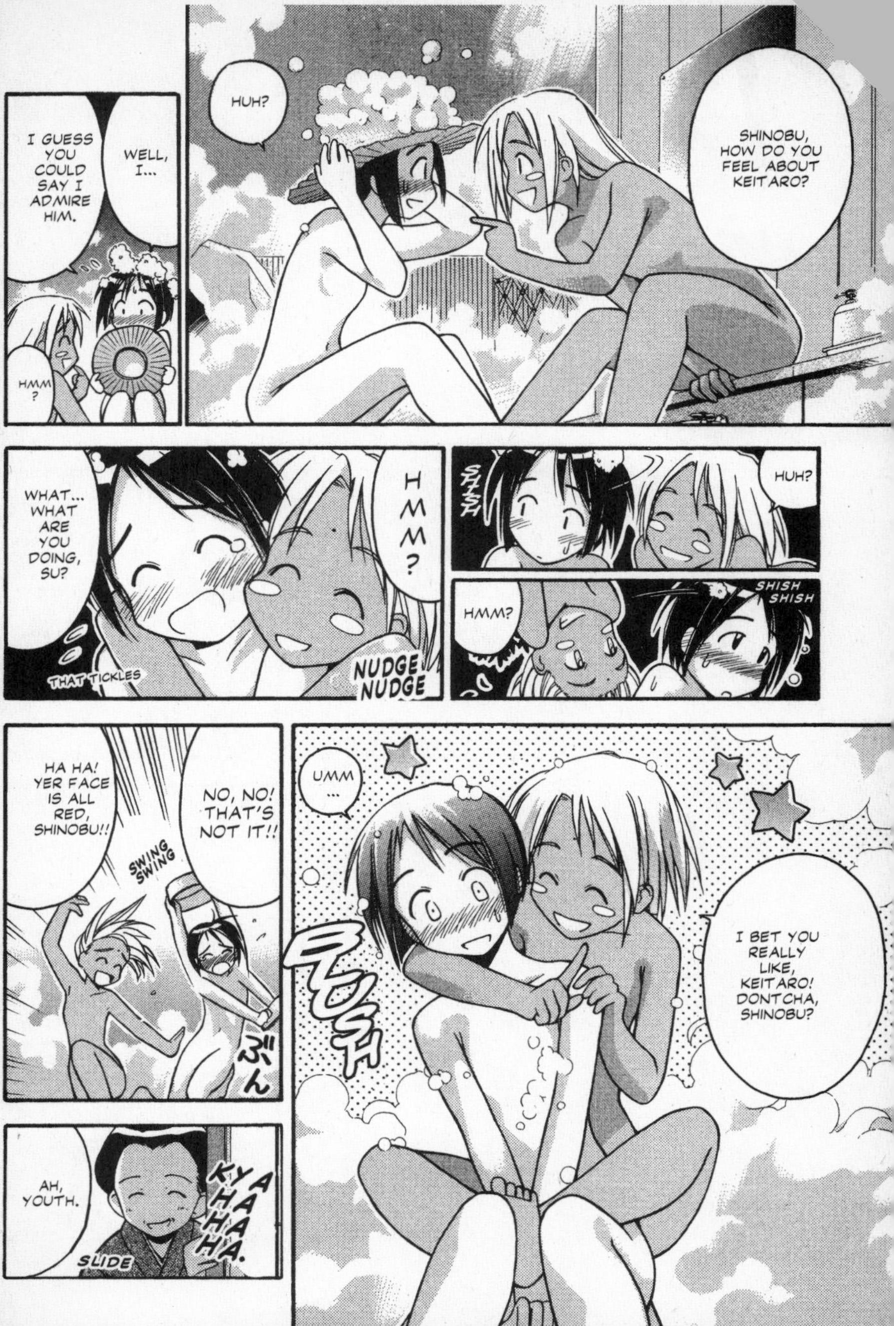
SHINOBU, HOW DO YOU FEEL ABOUT KEITARO?
HUH?
WELL, I...
I GUESS YOU COULD SAY I ADMIRE HIM.
HMM?
HUH?
SHISH
SHISH SHISH
HMM?
HMMM?
WHAT... WHAT ARE YOU DOING, SU?
NUDGE NUDGE
THAT TICKLES
I BET YOU REALLY LIKE, KEITARO! DONTCHA, SHINOBU?
UMM ...
NO, NO! THAT'S NOT IT!!
HA HA! YER FACE IS ALL RED, SHINOBU!!
SWING SWING
ぶん
KYAHAHAHA.
AH, YOUTH.
SLIDE

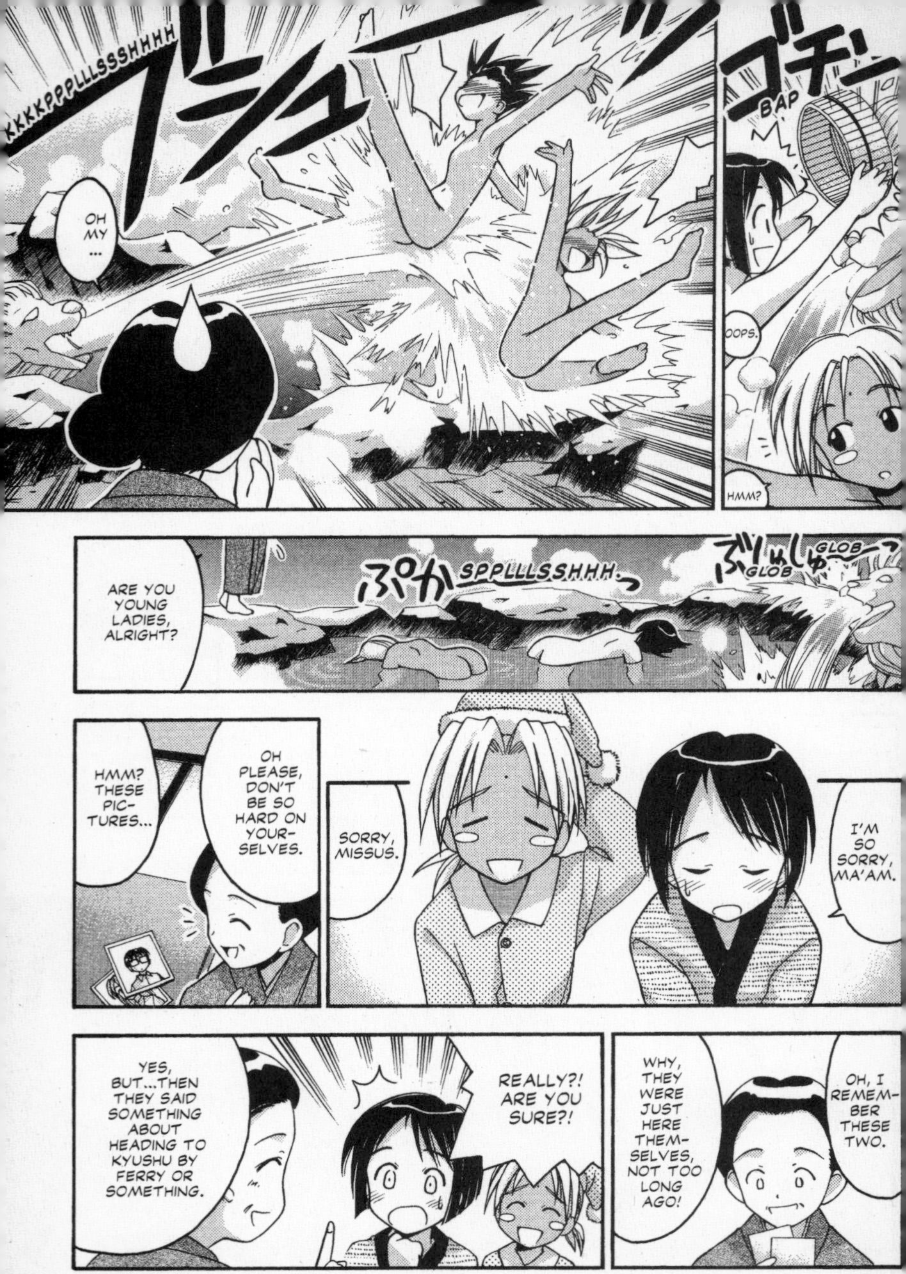

ゴチン
BAP
OOPS.
HMM?
ブシューッ
KKKKPPPLLLSSSHHHH
OH MY ...
ぶりゅしゅ
GLOB
GLOB
ぷか
SPPLLLSSHHHH
ARE YOU YOUNG LADIES, ALRIGHT?
I'M SO SORRY, MA'AM.
SORRY, MISSUS.
OH PLEASE, DON'T BE SO HARD ON YOUR-SELVES.
HMM? THESE PIC-TURES...
OH, I REMEM-BER THESE TWO.
WHY, THEY WERE JUST HERE THEM-SELVES, NOT TOO LONG AGO!
REALLY?! ARE YOU SURE?!
YES, BUT...THEN THEY SAID SOMETHING ABOUT HEADING TO KYUSHU BY FERRY OR SOMETHING.

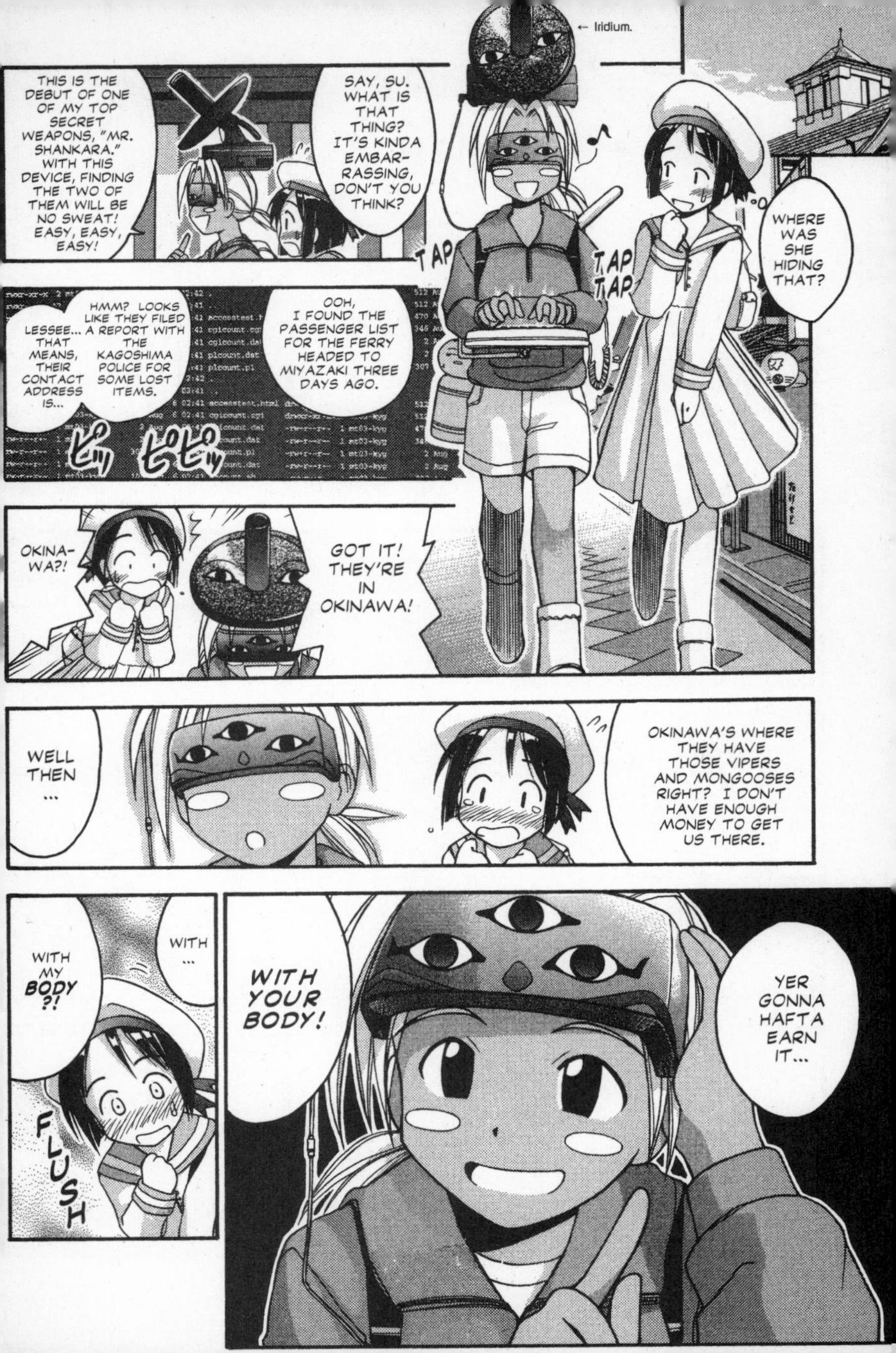
← Iridium.
SAY, SU. WHAT IS THAT THING? IT'S KINDA EMBARRASSING, DON'T YOU THINK?
THIS IS THE DEBUT OF ONE OF MY TOP SECRET WEAPONS, "MR. SHANKARA." WITH THIS DEVICE, FINDING THE TWO OF THEM WILL BE NO SWEAT! EASY, EASY, EASY!
WHERE WAS SHE HIDING THAT?
TAP
TAP TAP
OOH, I FOUND THE PASSENGER LIST FOR THE FERRY HEADED TO MIYAZAKI THREE DAYS AGO.
HMM? LOOKS LIKE THEY FILED A REPORT WITH THE KAGOSHIMA POLICE FOR SOME LOST ITEMS.
LESSEE... THAT MEANS, THEIR CONTACT ADDRESS IS...
ピッ ピピピッ
GOT IT! THEY'RE IN OKINAWA!
OKINAWA?!
OKINAWA'S WHERE THEY HAVE THOSE VIPERS AND MONGOOSES RIGHT? I DON'T HAVE ENOUGH MONEY TO GET US THERE.
WELL THEN ...
YER GONNA HAFTA EARN IT...
WITH YOUR BODY!
WITH ...
WITH MY BODY ?!
FLUSH

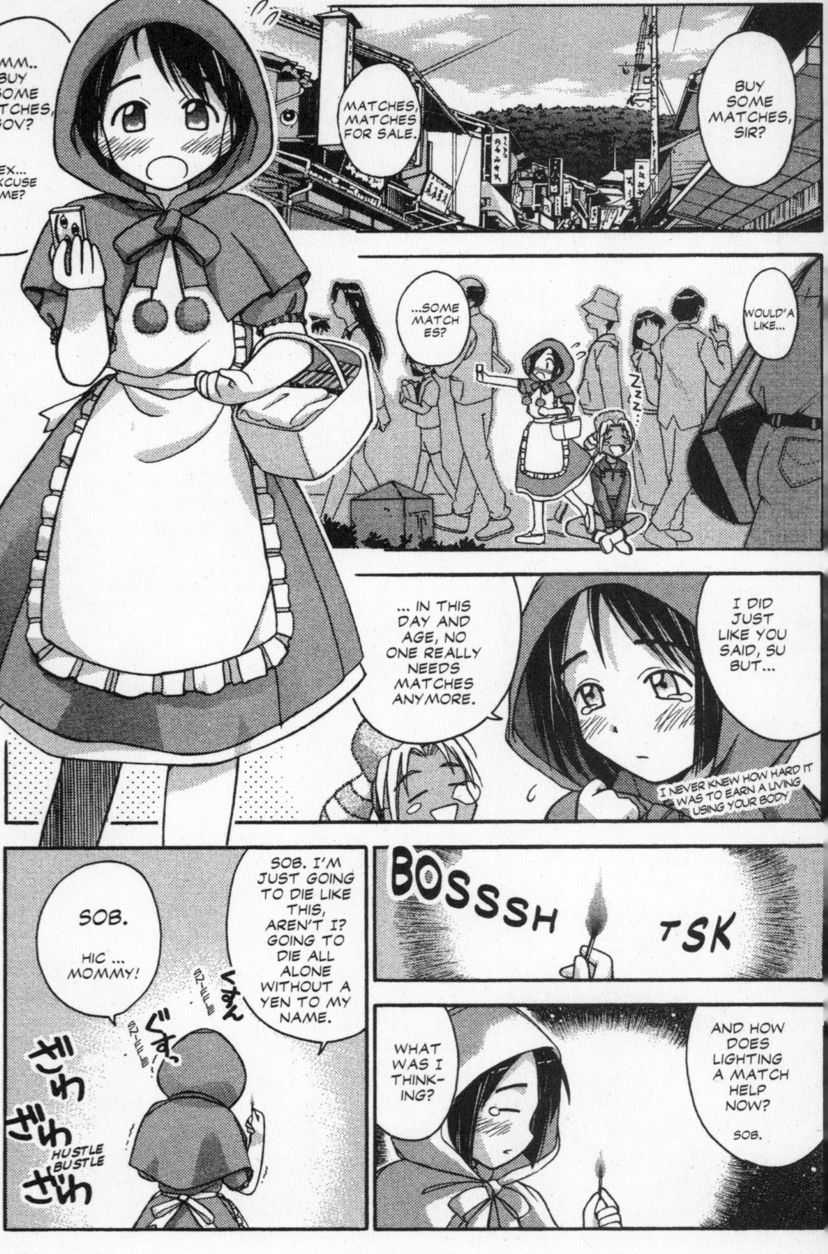
BUY SOME MATCHES, SIR?
MATCHES, MATCHES FOR SALE.
WOULD'A LIKE...
ZZZ...
...SOME MATCH ES?
I DID JUST LIKE YOU SAID, SU BUT...
... IN THIS DAY AND AGE, NO ONE REALLY NEEDS MATCHES ANYMORE.
I NEVER KNEW HOW HARD IT WAS TO EARN A LIVING USING YOUR BODY
UMM.. BUY SOME MATCHES, GOV?
EX... EXCUSE ME?
BOSSSH
TSK
AND HOW DOES LIGHTING A MATCH HELP NOW?
SOB.
WHAT WAS I THINKING?
SOB. I'M JUST GOING TO DIE LIKE THIS, AREN'T I? GOING TO DIE ALL ALONE WITHOUT A YEN TO MY NAME.
SOB.
HIC ... MOMMY!
くすん
ぐすっ
ざわ ざわ ざわ
HUSTLE BUSTLE

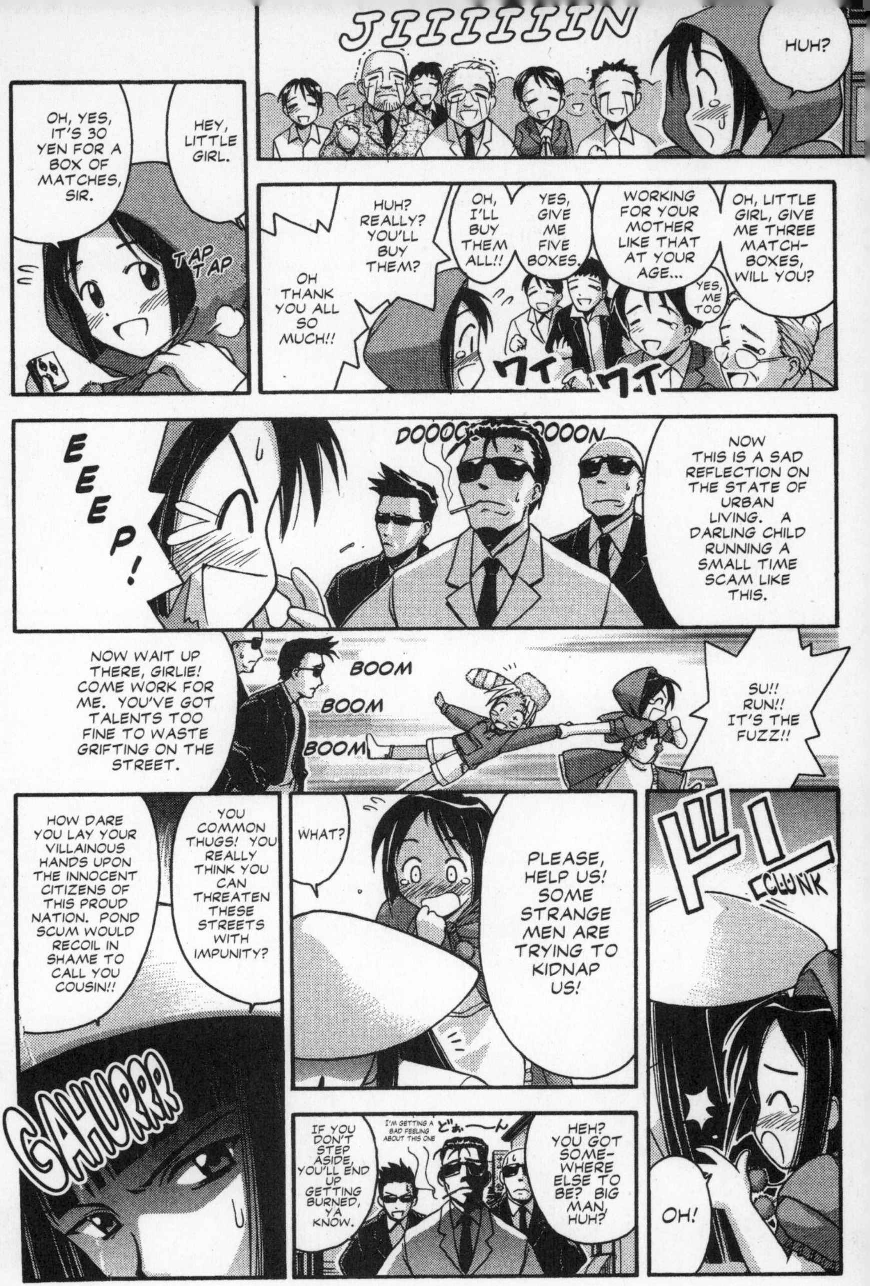
JIIIIIIN
HUH?
OH, LITTLE GIRL, GIVE ME THREE MATCH-BOXES, WILL YOU?
YES, ME TOO
WORKING FOR YOUR MOTHER LIKE THAT AT YOUR AGE...
YES, GIVE ME FIVE BOXES.
OH, I'LL BUY THEM ALL!!
HUH? REALLY? YOU'LL BUY THEM?
OH THANK YOU ALL SO MUCH!!
ワイ ワイ
HEY, LITTLE GIRL.
OH, YES, IT'S 30 YEN FOR A BOX OF MATCHES, SIR.
TAP TAP
NOW THIS IS A SAD REFLECTION ON THE STATE OF URBAN LIVING. A DARLING CHILD RUNNING A SMALL TIME SCAM LIKE THIS.
EEEEP!
SU!! RUN!! IT'S THE FUZZ!!
BOOM
BOOM
BOOM
NOW WAIT UP THERE, GIRLIE! COME WORK FOR ME. YOU'VE GOT TALENTS TOO FINE TO WASTE GRIFTING ON THE STREET.
CLUNK
OH!
PLEASE, HELP US! SOME STRANGE MEN ARE TRYING TO KIDNAP US!
WHAT?
HEH? YOU GOT SOME-WHERE ELSE TO BE? BIG MAN, HUH?
どぉーん
I'M GETTING A BAD FEELING ABOUT THIS ONE
IF YOU DON'T STEP ASIDE, YOU'LL END UP GETTING BURNED, YA KNOW.
YOU COMMON THUGS! YOU REALLY THINK YOU CAN THREATEN THESE STREETS WITH IMPUNITY?
HOW DARE YOU LAY YOUR VILLAINOUS HANDS UPON THE INNOCENT CITIZENS OF THIS PROUD NATION. POND SCUM WOULD RECOIL IN SHAME TO CALL YOU COUSIN!!
GAHURRR

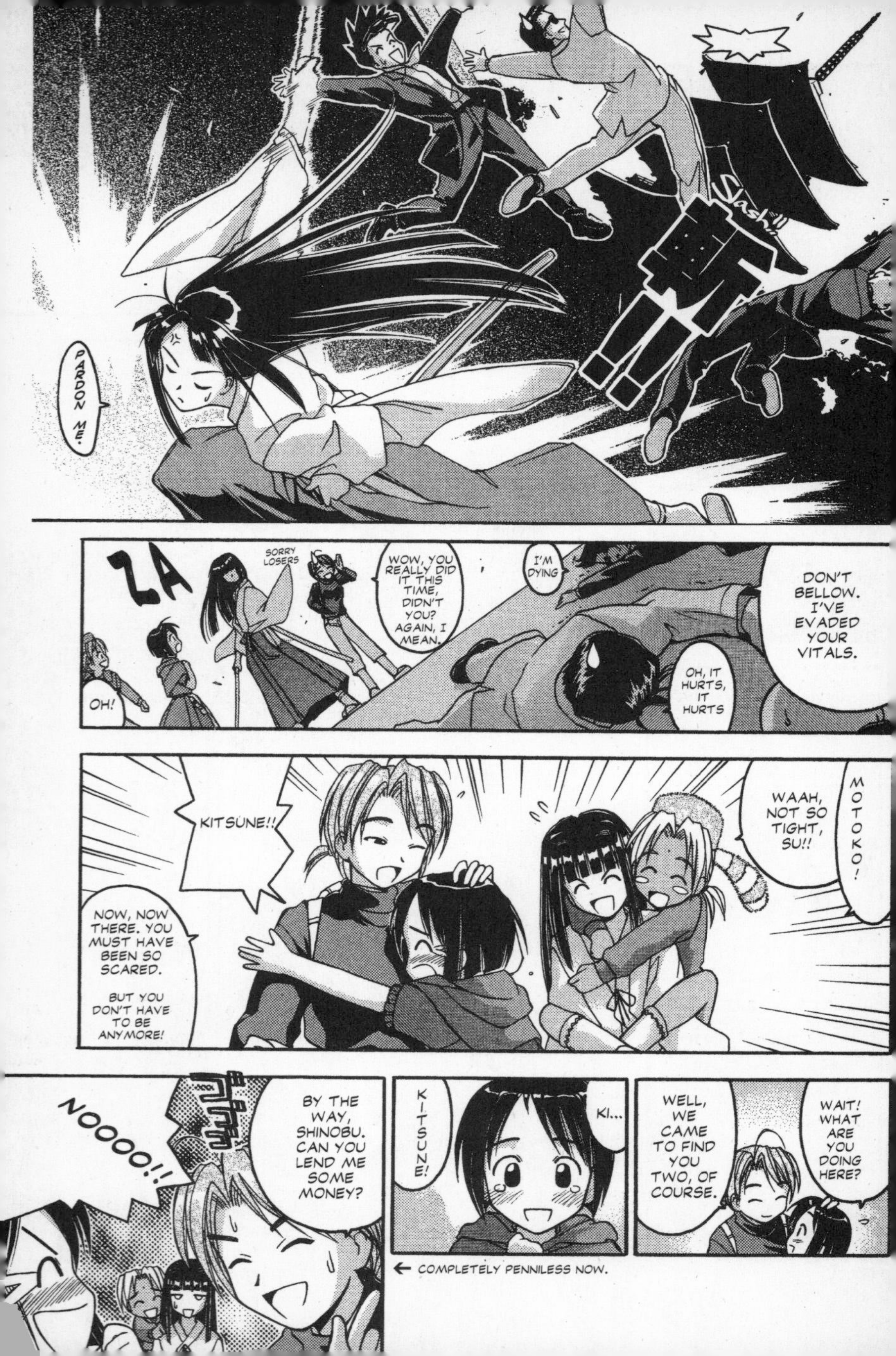
Slash!!
PARDON ME.
DON'T BELLOW. I'VE EVADED YOUR VITALS.
OH, IT HURTS, IT HURTS
I'M DYING
WOW, YOU REALLY DID IT THIS TIME, DIDN'T YOU? AGAIN, I MEAN.
SORRY LOSERS
ZA
OH!
MOTOKO!
WAAH, NOT SO TIGHT, SU!!
KITSUNE!!
NOW, NOW THERE. YOU MUST HAVE BEEN SO SCARED.
BUT YOU DON'T HAVE TO BE ANYMORE!
WAIT! WHAT ARE YOU DOING HERE?
WELL, WE CAME TO FIND YOU TWO, OF COURSE.
KI...
KITSUNE!
BY THE WAY, SHINOBU. CAN YOU LEND ME SOME MONEY?
NOOOO!!
← COMPLETELY PENNILESS NOW.

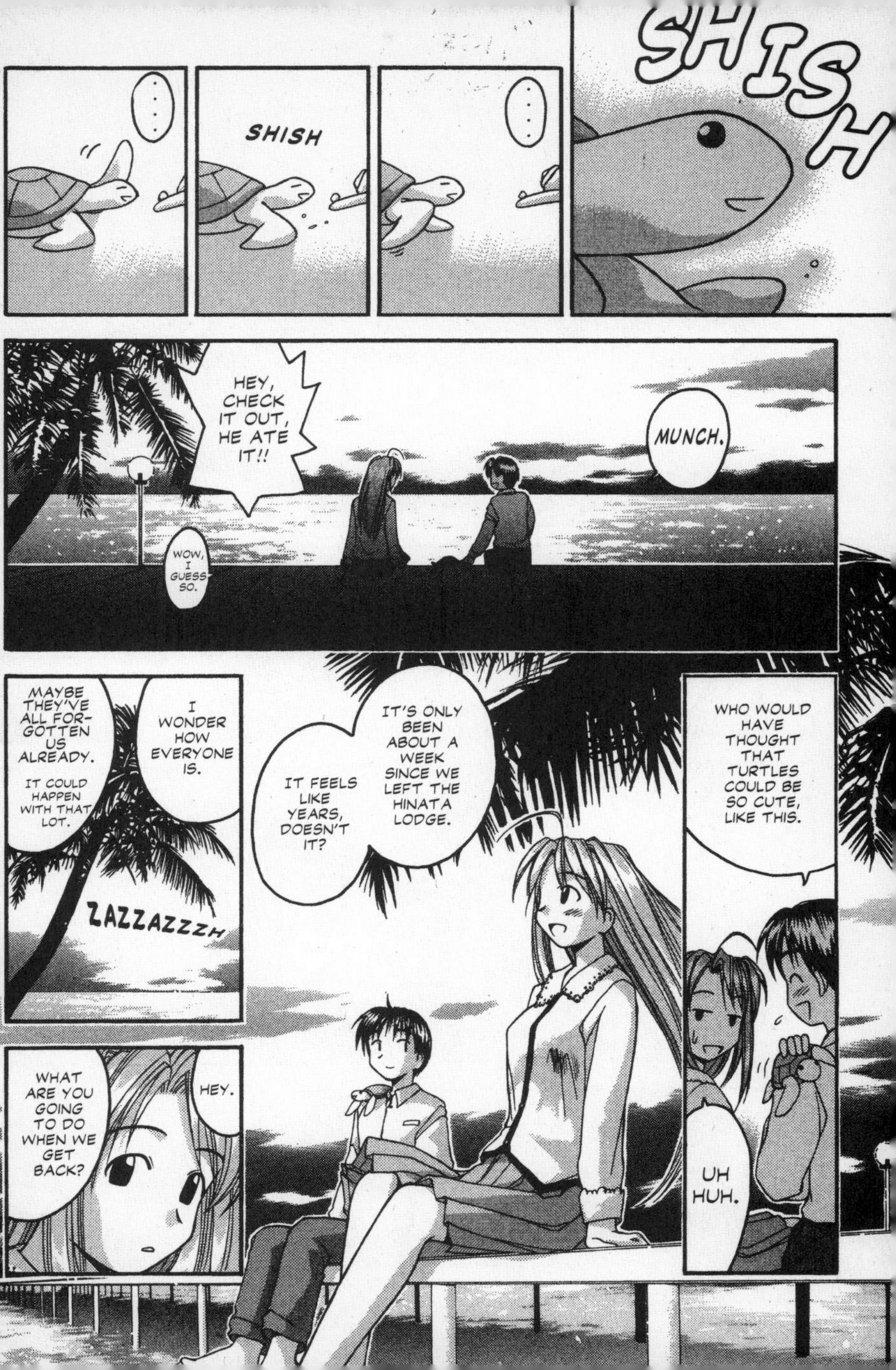
SHISH
...
SHISH
...
MUNCH.
HEY, CHECK IT OUT, HE ATE IT!!
WOW, I GUESS SO.
WHO WOULD HAVE THOUGHT THAT TURTLES COULD BE SO CUTE, LIKE THIS.
UH HUH.
IT'S ONLY BEEN ABOUT A WEEK SINCE WE LEFT THE HINATA LODGE.
IT FEELS LIKE YEARS, DOESN'T IT?
I WONDER HOW EVERYONE IS.
MAYBE THEY'VE ALL FORGOTTEN US ALREADY.
IT COULD HAPPEN WITH THAT LOT.
ZAZZAZZZH
HEY.
WHAT ARE YOU GOING TO DO WHEN WE GET BACK?

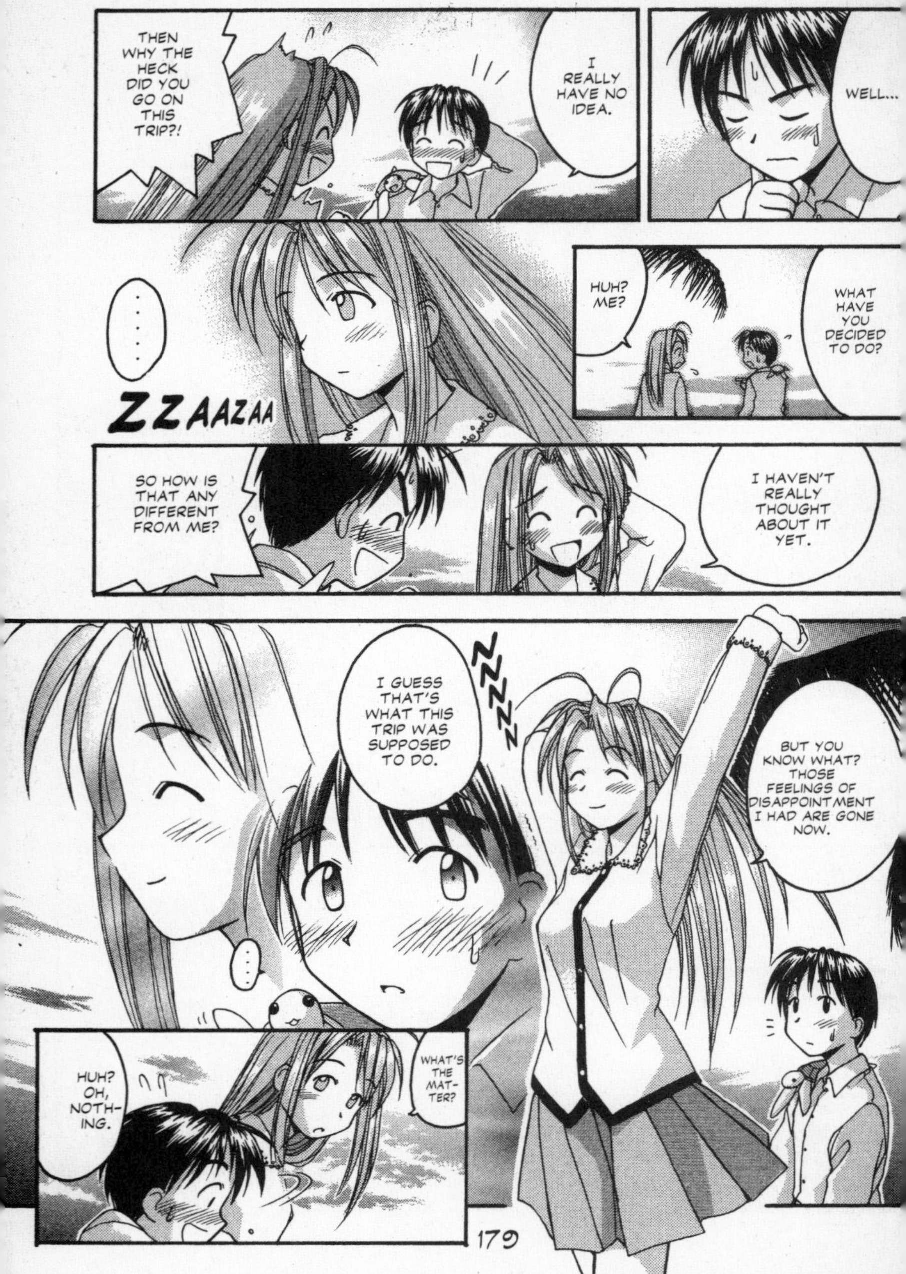
WELL...
I REALLY HAVE NO IDEA.
THEN WHY THE HECK DID YOU GO ON THIS TRIP?!
WHAT HAVE YOU DECIDED TO DO?
HUH? ME?
......
ZZAAZAA
I HAVEN'T REALLY THOUGHT ABOUT IT YET.
SO HOW IS THAT ANY DIFFERENT FROM ME?
BUT YOU KNOW WHAT? THOSE FEELINGS OF DISAPPOINTMENT I HAD ARE GONE NOW.
NNNNN
I GUESS THAT'S WHAT THIS TRIP WAS SUPPOSED TO DO.
...
WHAT'S THE MATTER?
HUH? OH, NOTHING.

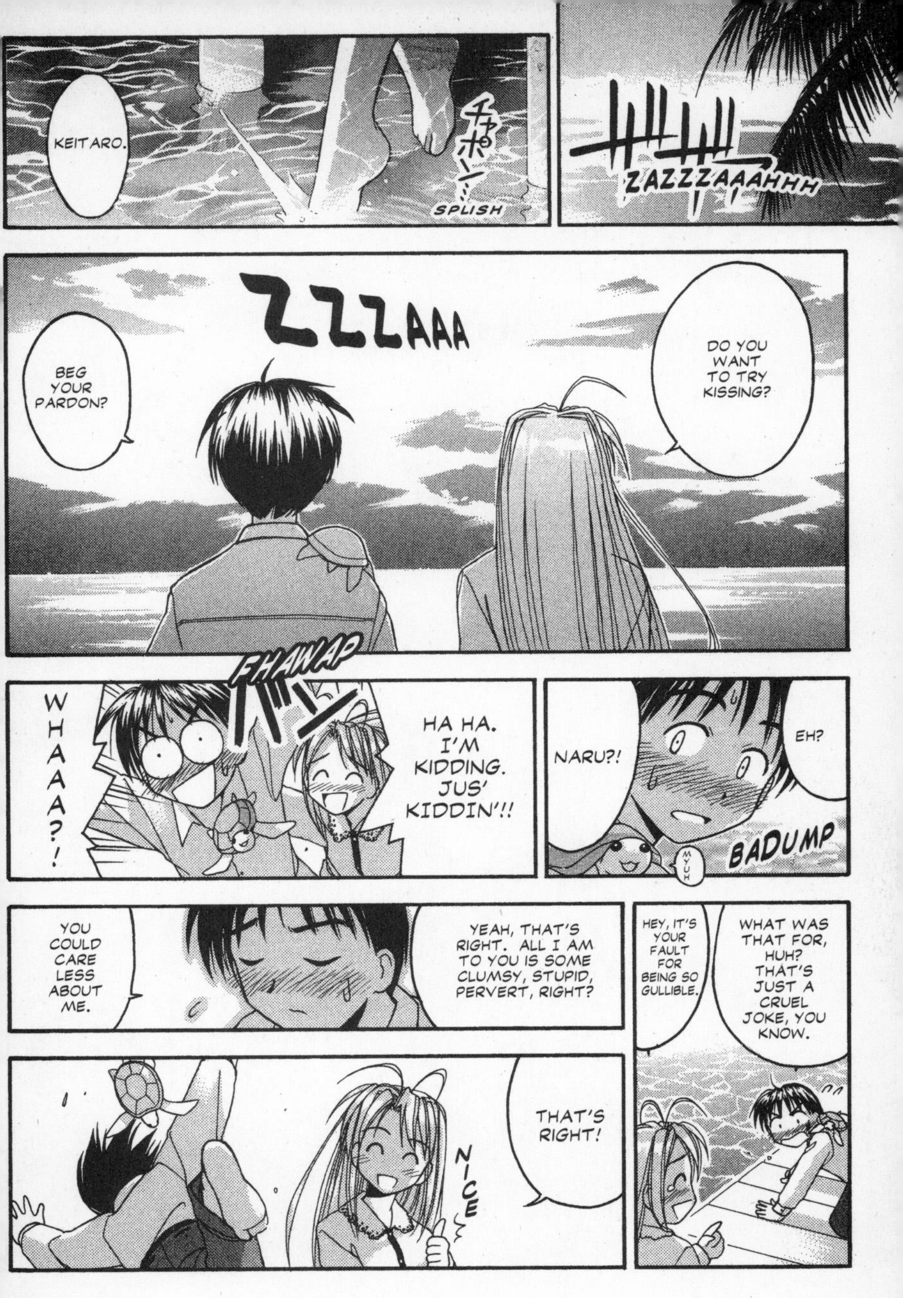
ZAZZZAAAHHH
チャポーン…
SPLISH
KEITARO.
DO YOU WANT TO TRY KISSING?
ZZZAAA
BEG YOUR PARDON?
EH?
NARU?!
BADUMP
MYUH
FHAWAP
HA HA. I'M KIDDING. JUS' KIDDIN'!!
WHAAAA?!
WHAT WAS THAT FOR, HUH? THAT'S JUST A CRUEL JOKE, YOU KNOW.
HEY, IT'S YOUR FAULT FOR BEING SO GULLIBLE.
YEAH, THAT'S RIGHT. ALL I AM TO YOU IS SOME CLUMSY, STUPID, PERVERT, RIGHT?
YOU COULD CARE LESS ABOUT ME.
THAT'S RIGHT!
NICE

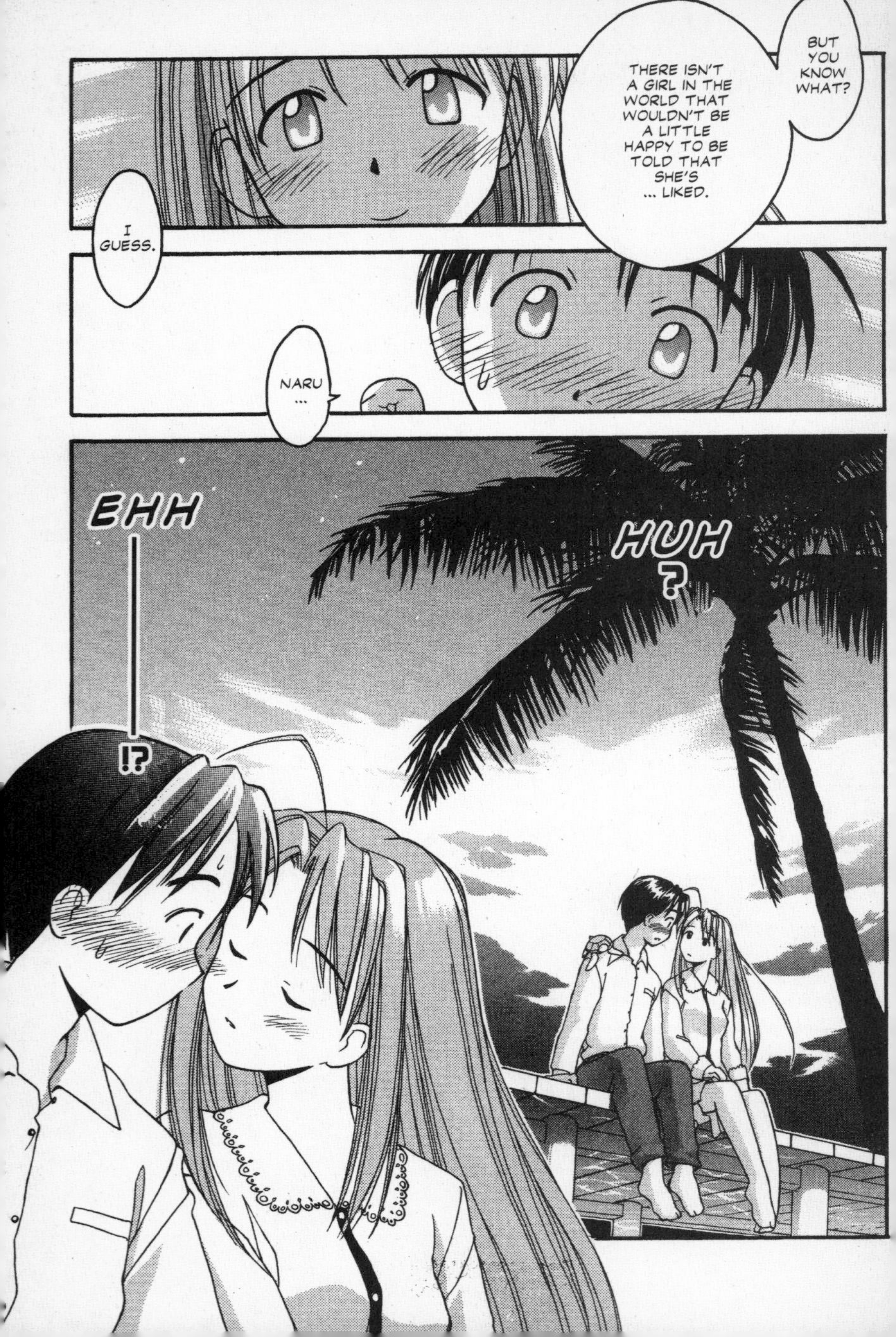
BUT YOU KNOW WHAT?
THERE ISN'T A GIRL IN THE WORLD THAT WOULDN'T BE A LITTLE HAPPY TO BE TOLD THAT SHE'S ... LIKED.
I GUESS.
NARU ...
HUH ?
EHH —!?

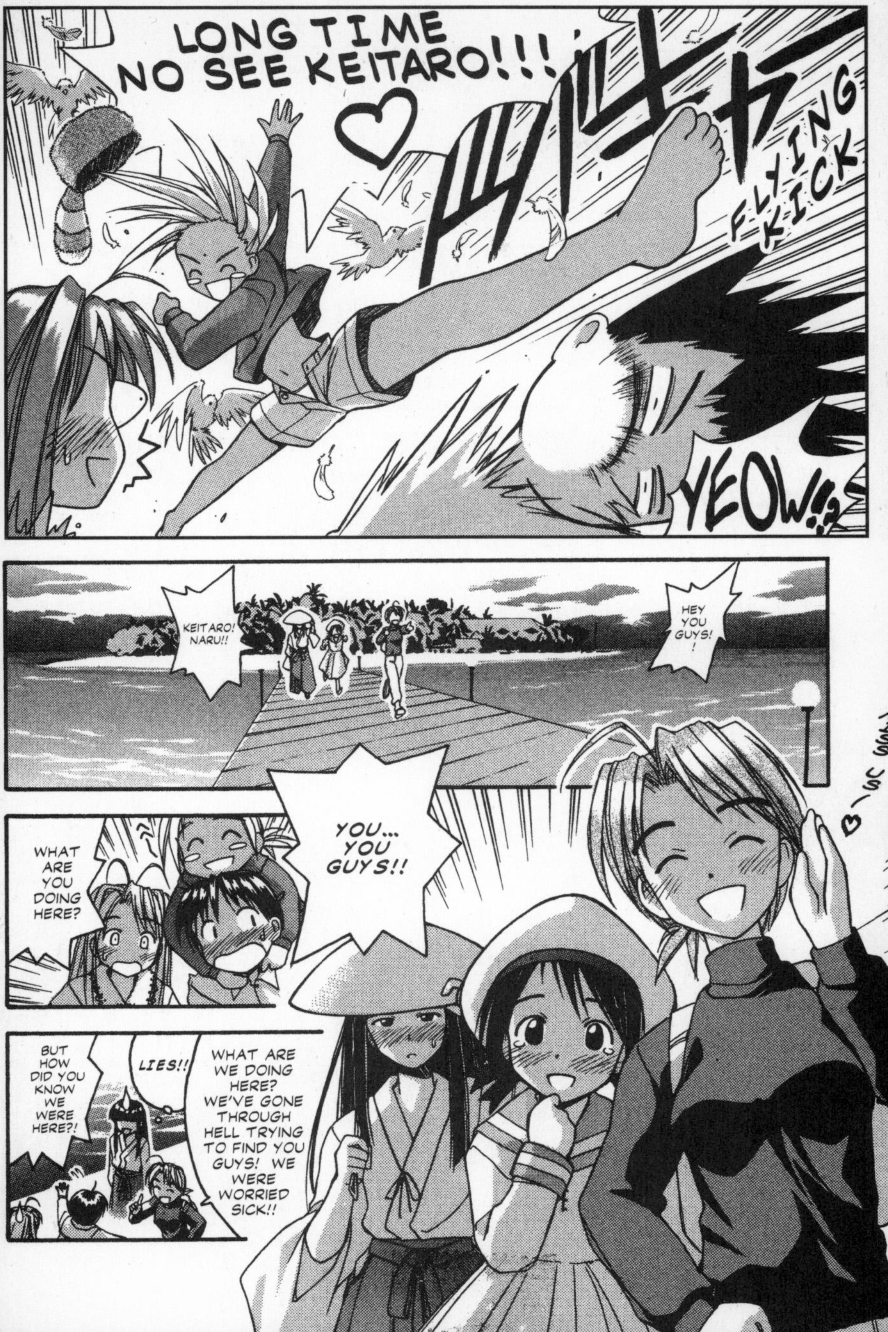
LONG TIME NO SEE KEITARO!!!
FLYING KICK
YEOW!!?
HEY YOU GUYS!!
KEITARO! NARU!!
YOU... YOU GUYS!!
WHAT ARE YOU DOING HERE?
WHAT ARE WE DOING HERE? WE'VE GONE THROUGH HELL TRYING TO FIND YOU GUYS! WE WERE WORRIED SICK!!
LIES!!
BUT HOW DID YOU KNOW WE WERE HERE?!

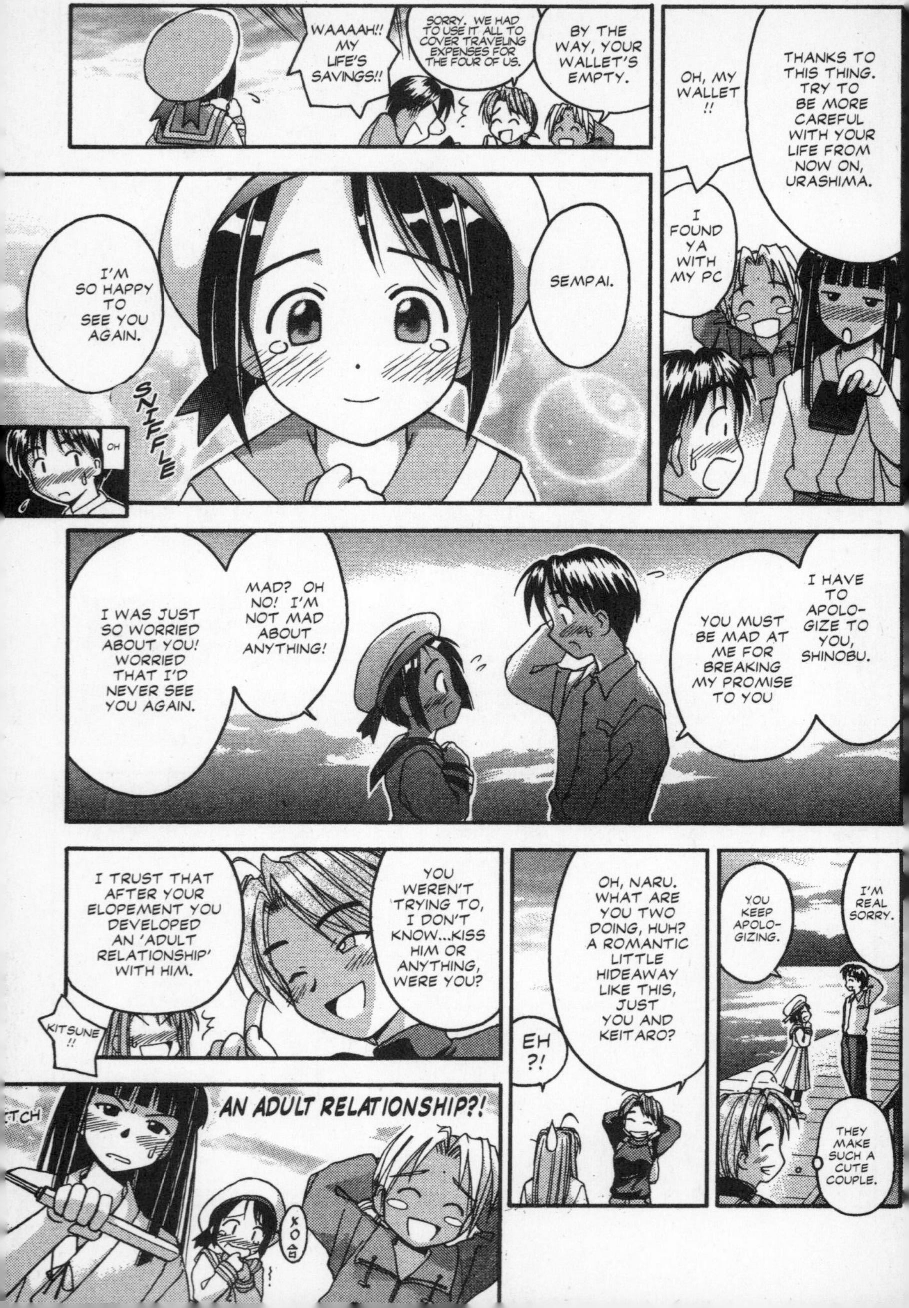
THANKS TO THIS THING. TRY TO BE MORE CAREFUL WITH YOUR LIFE FROM NOW ON, URASHIMA.
OH, MY WALLET !!
I FOUND YA WITH MY PC
BY THE WAY, YOUR WALLET'S EMPTY.
SORRY. WE HAD TO USE IT ALL TO COVER TRAVELING EXPENSES FOR THE FOUR OF US.
WAAAAH!! MY LIFE'S SAVINGS!!
SEMPAI.
I'M SO HAPPY TO SEE YOU AGAIN.
SNIFFLE
OH
I HAVE TO APOLOGIZE TO YOU, SHINOBU.
YOU MUST BE MAD AT ME FOR BREAKING MY PROMISE TO YOU
MAD? OH NO! I'M NOT MAD ABOUT ANYTHING!
I WAS JUST SO WORRIED ABOUT YOU! WORRIED THAT I'D NEVER SEE YOU AGAIN.
I'M REAL SORRY.
YOU KEEP APOLOGIZING.
THEY MAKE SUCH A CUTE COUPLE.
OH, NARU. WHAT ARE YOU TWO DOING, HUH? A ROMANTIC LITTLE HIDEAWAY LIKE THIS, JUST YOU AND KEITARO?
EH ?!
YOU WEREN'T TRYING TO, I DON'T KNOW...KISS HIM OR ANYTHING, WERE YOU?
I TRUST THAT AFTER YOUR ELOPEMENT YOU DEVELOPED AN 'ADULT RELATIONSHIP' WITH HIM.
KITSUNE !!
AN ADULT RELATIONSHIP?!

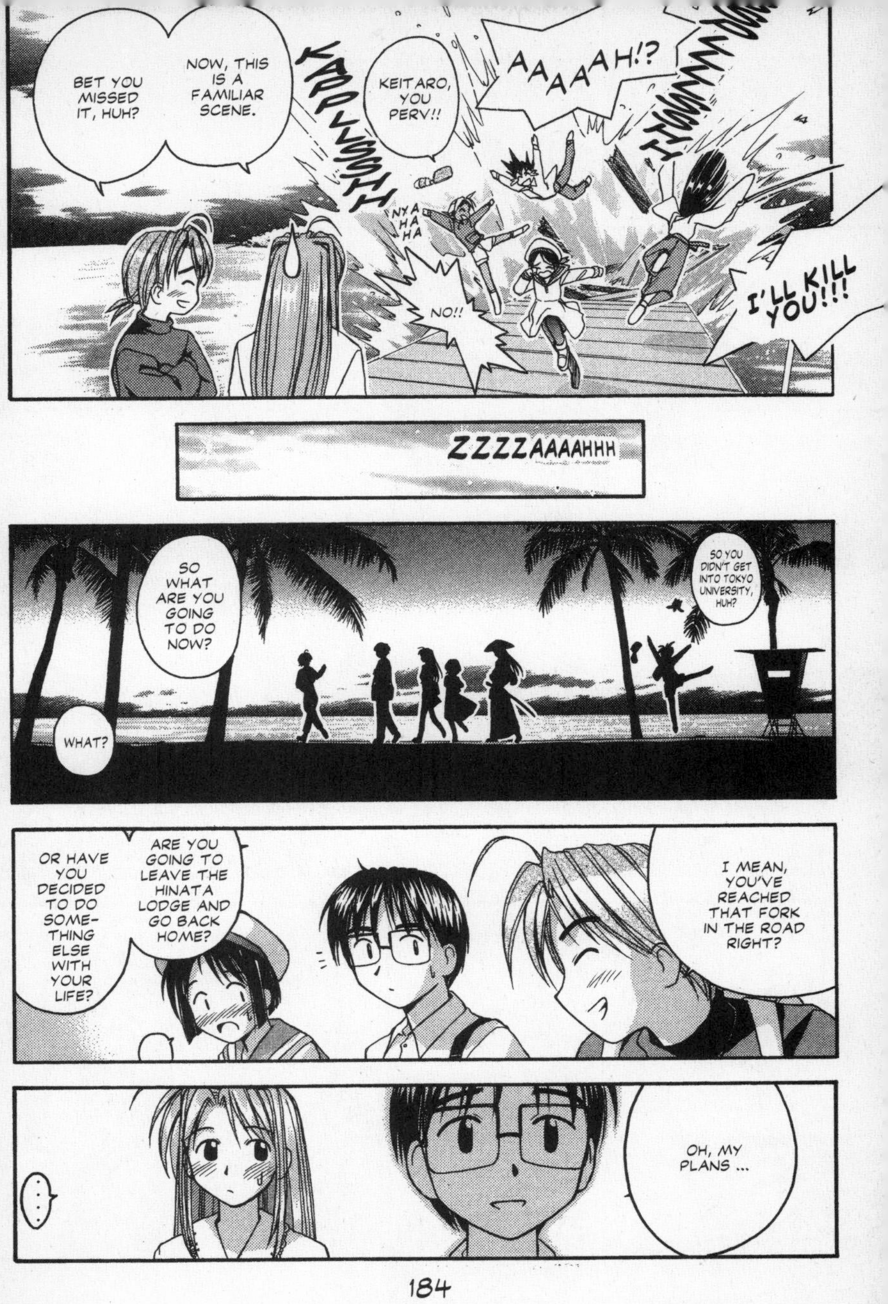
I'LL KILL YOU!!!
AAAAAH!?
KEITARO, YOU PERV!!
KAPPLUSSHH
NYA HA HA HA
NO!!
NOW, THIS IS A FAMILIAR SCENE.
BET YOU MISSED IT, HUH?
ZZZZAAAAHHH
SO YOU DIDN'T GET INTO TOKYO UNIVERSITY, HUH?
SO WHAT ARE YOU GOING TO DO NOW?
WHAT?
I MEAN, YOU'VE REACHED THAT FORK IN THE ROAD RIGHT?
ARE YOU GOING TO LEAVE THE HINATA LODGE AND GO BACK HOME?
OR HAVE YOU DECIDED TO DO SOME-THING ELSE WITH YOUR LIFE?
OH, MY PLANS ...
...

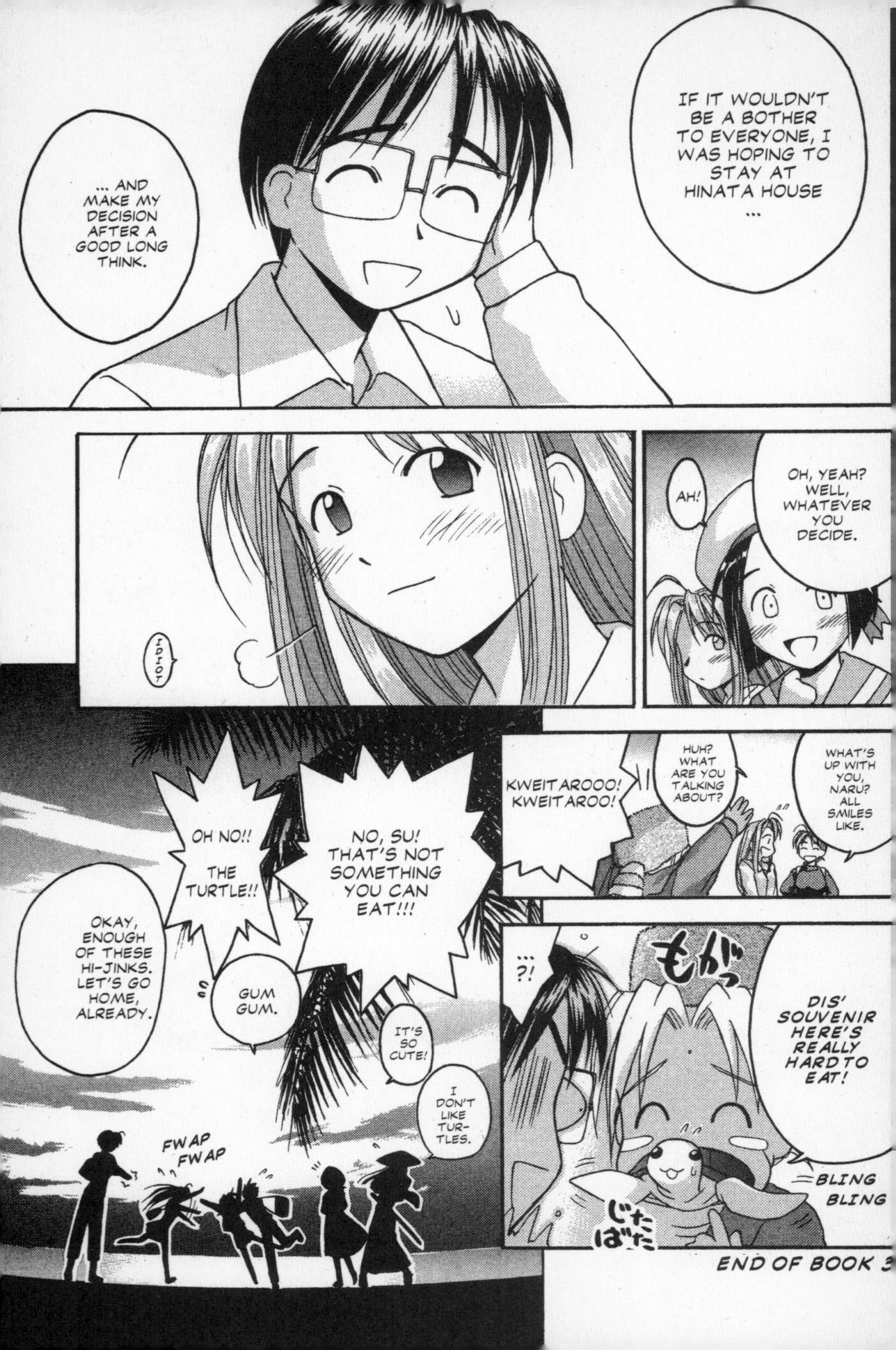
IF IT WOULDN'T BE A BOTHER TO EVERYONE, I WAS HOPING TO STAY AT HINATA HOUSE ...
... AND MAKE MY DECISION AFTER A GOOD LONG THINK.
OH, YEAH? WELL, WHATEVER YOU DECIDE.
AH!
IDIOT
WHAT'S UP WITH YOU, NARU? ALL SMILES LIKE.
HUH? WHAT ARE YOU TALKING ABOUT?
KWEITAROOO! KWEITAROOO!
DIS' SOUVENIR HERE'S REALLY HARD TO EAT!
もがっ
... ?!
BLING BLING
じたばた
NO, SU! THAT'S NOT SOMETHING YOU CAN EAT!!!
OH NO!! THE TURTLE!!
OKAY, ENOUGH OF THESE HI-JINKS. LET'S GO HOME, ALREADY.
GUM GUM.
IT'S SO CUTE!
I DON'T LIKE TUR-TLES.
FWAP FWAP
END OF BOOK 3

STAFF

Ken Akamatsu
Takashi Takemoto
Kenichi Nakamura
Takaaki Miyahara
Tomohiko Saito
Masaki Ohyama

EDITOR

Noboru Ohno
Tomoyuki Shiratsuchi

KC Editor

Mitsuei Ishii

OWBOY BEBOP

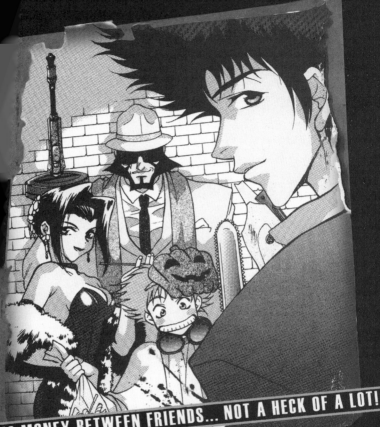

IT'S MONEY BETWEEN FRIENDS... NOT A HECK OF A LOT!

Based on the smash hit anime series seen on CARTOON NETWORK

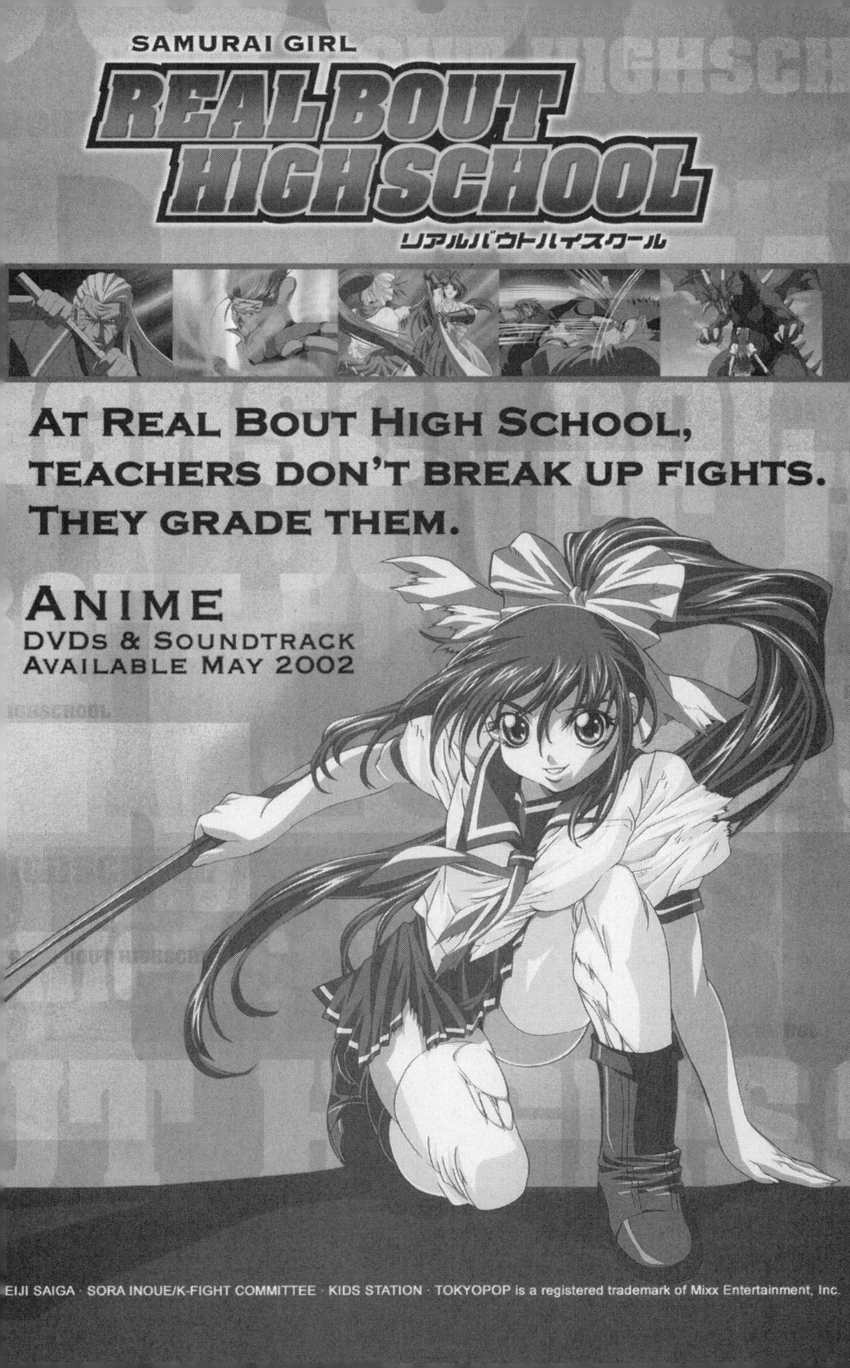
SAMURAI GIRL
REAL BOUT HIGH SCHOOL
リアルバウトハイスクール
At Real Bout High School, teachers don't break up fights. They grade them.
Anime
DVDs & Soundtrack
Available May 2002
EIJI SAIGA · SORA INOUE/K-FIGHT COMMITTEE · KIDS STATION · TOKYOPOP is a registered trademark of Mixx Entertainment, Inc.

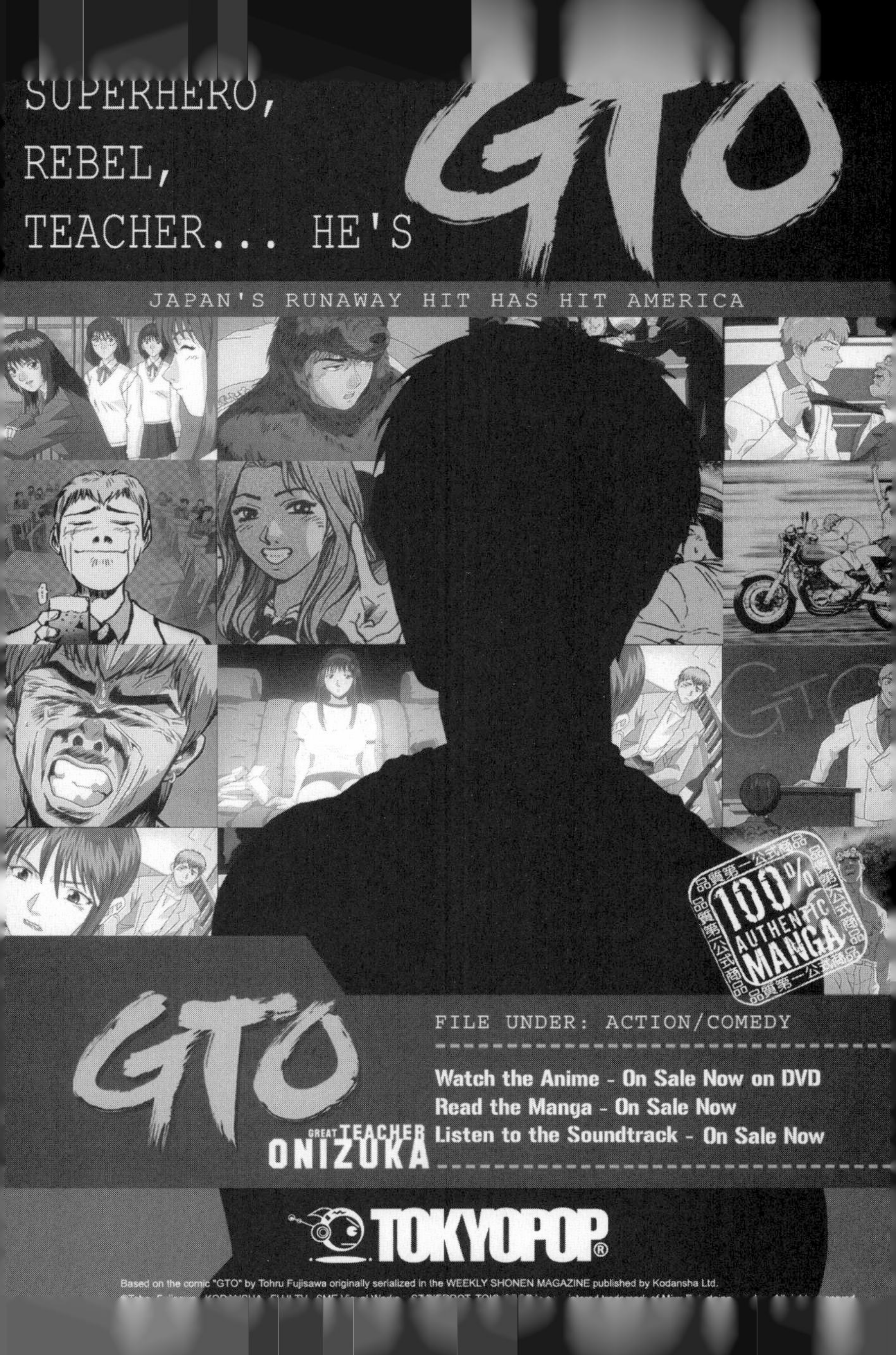
SUPERHERO,
REBEL,
TEACHER... HE'S
GTO
JAPAN'S RUNAWAY HIT HAS HIT AMERICA
100% AUTHENTIC MANGA
GTO
GREAT TEACHER ONIZUKA
FILE UNDER: ACTION/COMEDY
Watch the Anime - On Sale Now on DVD
Read the Manga - On Sale Now
Listen to the Soundtrack - On Sale Now
TOKYOPOP®
Based on the comic "GTO" by Tohru Fujisawa originally serialized in the WEEKLY SHONEN MAGAZINE published by Kodansha Ltd.

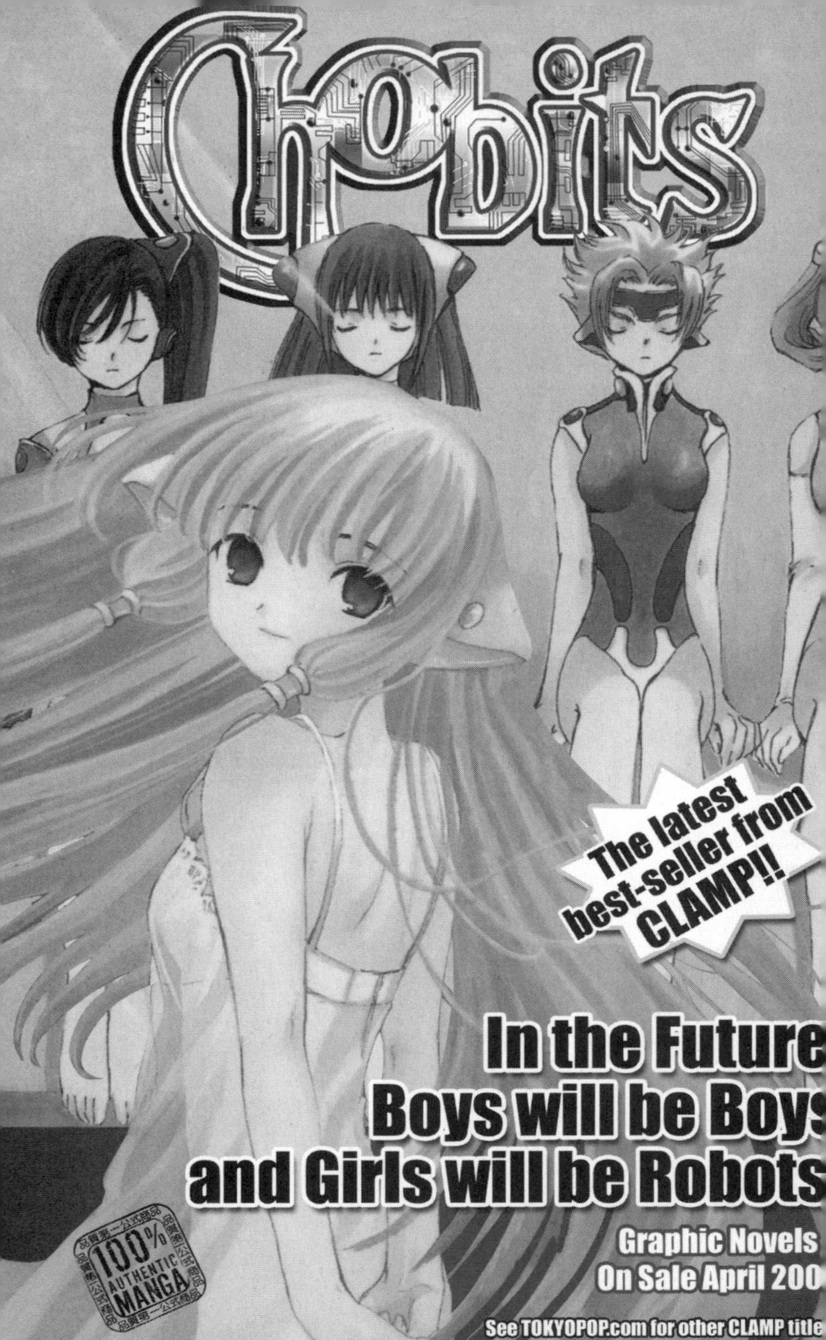
Chobits
The latest best-seller from CLAMP!!
In the Future Boys will be Boys and Girls will be Robots
100% AUTHENTIC MANGA
Graphic Novels On Sale April 200
See TOKYOPOP.com for other CLAMP title

STOP!

This is the back of the book.
You wouldn't want to spoil a great ending!

This book is printed "manga-style," in the authentic Japanese right-to-left format. Since none of the artwork has been flipped or altered, readers get to experience the story just as the creator intended. You've been asking for it, so TOKYOPOP® delivered: authentic, hot-off-the-press, and far more fun!

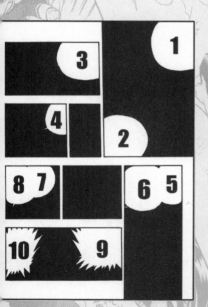

DIRECTIONS

If this is your first time reading manga-style, here's a quick guide to help you understand how it works.

It's easy... just start in the top right panel and follow the numbers. Have fun, and look for more 100% authentic manga from TOKYOPOP®!

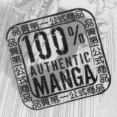